Praise for
For Slavery and Union

"Well-researched, well-argued, and well-written, *For Slavery and Union* is an exemplary study. Benjamin Buckner of Kentucky personifies the dilemma of the Upper South proslavery unionist, both during and after the Civil War. Patrick A. Lewis ably portrays the trials, contradictions, and struggles of those who favored the Union, but also saw it as capable of protecting slavery. Once the conflict became one to end slavery, Buckner zealously joined blue and gray allies in protecting whiteness. By placing Buckner fully in the context of his time, Lewis reveals that the old unionist did not change, but rather the circumstances in the world around him did. To Benjamin Buckner, the best way to protect slavery was to keep the Union together. He joined the Union cause as the Civil War began, but his opposition to emancipation brought about his resignation from the army. Soon he joined his former enemies in trying to shape a postwar world that would replicate the prewar racial one. All of this is well told in Lewis's wonderful case study."—James C. Klotter, state historian of Kentucky and professor of history at Georgetown College

"Patrick A. Lewis's splendid *For Slavery and Union* is a most welcome contribution to Civil War, Kentucky, and border-state historical scholarship. Deeply researched and gracefully crafted, Lewis's book provides the best insights available into the conflicted ideological and social worlds of Benjamin Forsythe Buckner and like-minded proslavery unionists during the Civil War era. Better than any previous scholar, Lewis untangles the conundrum conservative and upwardly mobile white southerners confronted as the nation dissolved. They believed not only that unionism and slavery went hand in hand, but envisioned that secession signaled the death knell not only of the 'peculiar institution' but also of white southerners' much-boasted-about way of life, a weltanschauung predicated on white supremacy. Lewis's mature, richly interpretive study places Buckner's postwar life in the whirligig world of Jim Crow/New South Kentucky, a world he quietly embraced."—John David Smith, author of *Lincoln and the U.S. Colored Troops*

"Benjamin Forsythe Buckner was a conservative proslavery unionist who was for the Union because he thought slavery would be safest in the Union, and who never accepted emancipation as a Union war aim. This insightful book positions Patrick A. Lewis among the cutting-edge scholars who have punctured the mythology about Kentucky's benign slave system, harmonious social order, and enlightened political leadership."—Daniel W. Crofts, author of *Reluctant Confederates: Upper South Unionists in the Secession Crisis*

"Patrick A. Lewis paints a splendid picture of proslavery unionism in the form of Major Benjamin Buckner. His portrayal of the Kentucky planter gives texture, depth, and nuance to an ideological position that has confounded historians for many years.

"This may be the first biography we have seen that captures the cultural and political center of Civil War–era Kentucky, including the state's embrace of a conservative Union in 1861 and its rejection of a transformed Union in 1865."—Aaron Astor, author of *Rebels on the Border: Civil War, Emancipation, and the Reconstruction of Kentucky and Missouri*

"As part of a recent book project, I researched the letters Benjamin Forsythe Buckner wrote to his fiancée. This revealing collection of Civil War documents offers the perspective of a Kentucky Union officer who resigned his military commission in 1863 specifically to protest the Emancipation Proclamation, long before his home state saw its slaves freed by wartime realities. Patrick A. Lewis has turned this small set of letters into a larger, more troubling story—the postwar transformation of the formerly loyal Bluegrass State into an unreconstructed southern state, accomplished by the defiant politics of racial hatred, war allegiance, and fictive memory."—Christopher Phillips, author of *The Civil War in the Border South*

"Patrick A. Lewis has written an engaging and insightful portrait of a man who embodied the struggle many loyal whites in the Upper South endured during the Civil War era. His nuanced examination of Benjamin Buckner's outlook and choices elucidate the phenomenon of proslavery unionism shared by many white southerners. This is a biography that deepens our understanding of an important but understudied wartime faction."—Anne Marshall, Mississippi State University

"Deeply researched and narrated with elegance and verve, *For Slavery and Union* is the story of a fascinating Kentuckian whose life mirrored the larger ordeal of the state in the era of the Civil War and Reconstruction. In Lewis's skillful hands, Benjamin F. Buckner's life becomes an account of loyalties divided but never fully reconciled, and of a proslavery unionism that foundered in the face of emancipation. The result is essential reading for anyone wanting to understand why Kentucky sided with the Union in the Civil War—and then turned south to align with the former Confederate states in the decades beyond. A sobering but thoroughly enjoyable read."—Amy Murrell Taylor, University of Kentucky

"White unionists in Kentucky, argues Lewis, fought with the Union for the *benefit* of slavery, not *despite* slavery. This insight is the basis of a gracefully written, beautifully argued reinterpretation of Kentucky's experience in the Civil War era that also speaks to American political culture more generally. Even as the Civil War divided the nation, support for slavery and racial inequality flourished in both the Union and the Confederacy, suggesting how difficult it would be to resolve the conflicts that led the nation to war."—Laura F. Edwards, author of *A Legal History of the Civil War and Reconstruction: A Nation of Rights*

For Slavery and Union

For Slavery *and* UNION

Benjamin Buckner
and Kentucky Loyalties
in the Civil War

PATRICK A. LEWIS

Copyright © 2015 by The University Press of Kentucky
Paperback edition 2019

Scholarly publisher for the Commonwealth,
serving Bellarmine University, Berea College, Centre College of Kentucky, Eastern Kentucky University, The Filson Historical Society, Georgetown College, Kentucky Historical Society, Kentucky State University, Morehead State University, Murray State University, Northern Kentucky University, Transylvania University, University of Kentucky, University of Louisville, and Western Kentucky University. All rights reserved.

Editorial and Sales Offices: The University Press of Kentucky
663 South Limestone Street, Lexington, Kentucky 40508-4008
www.kentuckypress.com

Library of Congress Cataloging-in-Publication Data

Lewis, Patrick A., 1984–
  For slavery and union : Benjamin Buckner and Kentucky loyalties in the Civil War / Patrick A. Lewis.
     pages cm
  Includes bibliographical references and index.
  ISBN 978-0-8131-6079-5 (hardcover : alk. paper) — ISBN 978-0-8131-6081-8 (pdf) — ISBN 978-0-8131-6080-1 (epub)
  1. Buckner, Benjamin Forsythe, 1836–1901. 2. Unionists (United States Civil War)—Kentucky—Biography. 3. Kentucky—History—Civil War, 1861–1865—Biography. 4. United States—History—Civil War, 1861–1865—Biography. 5. United States. Army. Kentucky Infantry Regiment, 20th (1862–1865) 6. Slavery—Kentucky—History—19th century. I. Title.
  F455.B83L48 2015
  973.7'469092—dc23
  [B]   2014039418

ISBN 978-0-8131-7751-9 (pbk. : alk. paper)

This book is printed on acid-free paper meeting the requirements of the American National Standard for Permanence in Paper for Printed Library Materials.

Manufactured in the United States of America.

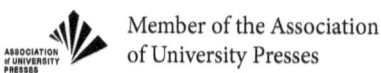

Member of the Association
of University Presses

Contents

Introduction: Relationships, Interests, and Identities   1

1. The World Is a Cruel and Cold Place   15

2. Firstborn of the Union   43

3. Brave Hearts and Stout Hands   67

4. I Feel Impelled to Pause   89

5. Privileges and Elections   119

6. Democratic Partisan Militia   157

Epilogue: Glen Avon   187

Acknowledgments   201

Notes   205

Bibliography   241

Index   259

Introduction

Relationships, Interests, and Identities

For Benjamin Forsythe Buckner, the major of the Union army's Twentieth Kentucky Volunteer Infantry Regiment, a dissonant note of defeat accompanied the repulse of the Confederate invasion of his home state in the fall of 1862. Despite the military victory, Buckner was left gutted by the news of President Lincoln's preliminary Emancipation Proclamation. Halted during the pursuit of the Confederate army back into Tennessee, Buckner vented his conservative proslavery unionist outrage at the president's new war measure in a letter to his secessionist fiancée, Helen Martin.[1] "The Union Kentuckians are not shamefully heated," Buckner wrote, "and by reason of the presidents want of good faith, which is only equaled by his lack of sense, we find ourselves in arms to maintain doctrines which if announced 12 months ago, would have driven us all, notwithstanding our loyalty to the Constitution & the Union into the ranks of the Southern Army."[2] Furious as he was, though, Buckner never seriously considered turning rebel. "The people of the South have brought all this upon us and are not worthy of our support," he continued. "Nor can they give us any guarantee of protection or assistance." Buckner was trapped between the government he loved and the section of the country (and its institution) with which he identified—which, indeed, shaped his identity as a white man. "We joined the people of the North (a people whom we did not love) to fight the South (a people with whom we were connected by ties of relationship, interest, the identity of our hearts and institutions) merely upon principle and to preserve that Constitutional form of government which was the wonder and admiration of the world. But the president has by the shake of the pen taken away all that." Stunned, he could only ask, "But what are we to do[?] Where can we go[?]"[3]

What, then, *was* he to do? The world seemed upside down, uncertain, and hostile. The long-held truths that had shaped the world in which he and Helen had grown up and expected to live their lives suddenly disappeared. If he had been wrong to believe the United States the one true defender of slavery, what else could he have been wrong about? What was he to do? Buckner resigned his commission, went home, married Helen, and set about a lifetime of using his considerable talents to reconstruct his familiar landscape, which the earthquake of emancipation had thrown into disarray. He worked to construct a New South state that reestablished and protected the power and position of white men like himself at the expense of African Americans and, often, lower-class whites through a tangled web of legal, economic, and cultural barriers to equality. But Buckner's postwar life was not an attempt to build what the Confederacy might have been, as similar stories have been told about rebel protagonists. Rather, it was a restoration of the vision he had for Kentucky *and* the United States in 1861.

Buckner sided with the Union *for the benefit of* slavery rather than siding with the Union *despite* slavery. This seems a minor semantic switch, but it has significant implications. Without it, it is difficult to fully appreciate the ways in which slavery operated in Kentucky, the political culture in which the state's Civil War generation was raised, the Commonwealth of Kentucky's process of reconciliation, and its reputation for postwar racial moderation and harmony that was purchased at the price of violence and discriminatory laws. Buckner was not a slave owner who was also a Unionist; he was a proslavery unionist.[4] The two identities were inseparable.

It is important that the label be stated correctly, for misstating the conditions of Buckner's loyalty can lead to some faulty, if not dangerous, destinations. The conclusion I most want to avoid is that if white Kentuckians remained in the Union *despite* the presence of slavery in the state, then slavery must not have been as important to the economic livelihood, politics, social structures, and selves of white Kentuckians as it was to the residents of the Confederate South. I am uncomfortable with what a unionism *despite* slavery says about the experience of slavery for black Kentuckians. Imagining a slavery about which most white Kentuckians were apathetic enough to fight on the "antislavery" side of the conflict opens the door for an understanding of slavery akin to J. Winston Coleman's interpretation of the institution as smaller, milder, more familial, and more beneficial to black Kentuckians than slavery in the cotton states. That is to say, a unionism *despite* slavery fuels a myth of mild slavery within which modern Kentuckians can hide from the messier realities of race relations in the commonwealth from statehood to the present. A unionism *despite* slavery perpetuates what Barbara Jeanne Fields labels the "presumption of benignity that has given border-state slavery a better reputation than it deserves."[5]

If, however, Buckner volunteered to defend both Union and slavery as a set of interconnected and symbiotic institutions, ideas, and ideals—loyalty *because of* and *for the benefit of* slavery—then the picture looks different. If many white Kentuckians fought with the Union *for* slavery and, like Buckner, resigned, deserted, or otherwise stopped supporting the Union war effort after its turn to a war against slavery on January 1, 1863, then we can begin to understand that, for them, slavery must have been a thing worth protecting. Further, black Kentuckians' struggles to claim the benefits of citizenship and equal rights from 1862 onward show that African Americans were not content with the life that antebellum slavery had dealt them, just as Buckner's equally long efforts to deny those rights reveals the degree to which whites were not indulgent paternalists who would gladly welcome an end to the institution.

Buckner's proslavery unionism also challenges the idea that slavery was dying in Kentucky, a corollary to the mild slavery myth. It only makes sense that if Buckner enlisted to defend slavery and the Union, then he must have believed that slavery had a future in Kentucky and in the Union. The economic and social picture of slavery in Buckner's Clark County suggests that he planned for it to change in similar ways to the generally nonplantation, semi-industrialized, and ever-adaptable brand of slavery practiced in Kentucky and the upper South on the eve of the war. Like Virginia's "last generation" of slave owners who were Buckner's upper South contemporaries, many Kentuckians hoped that a renewed and rejuvenated slavery would incorporate more of the industrializing and modernizing market economy across the Mason–Dixon line and the Ohio River, while still retaining its tight controls on the lives and bodies of enslaved people.[6] As a university-educated, town-dwelling professional eyeing a marriage into a family with land, slaves, and an increasing stake in a mixed-labor iron operation in a neighboring county, Buckner was prepared to usher Kentucky into a new era of slave-based profitability. Of course, he never got the chance.

I am also uncomfortable with what a union *despite* slavery line of thought suggests about the causes of the war. If Kentucky was a slave state but decided to side with the Union *despite* the institution, then—in a defense I myself more than once articulated growing up as a western Kentucky Confederate apologist—slavery must not have been the central issue of the war. If slave-owning Kentuckians could fight against fellow slave owners, then they canceled out one another; the issue that divided the country must not have been slavery.

In reality, the logic of Kentucky's proslavery unionism actually undermines a neo-Confederate states' rights fundamentalism that rejects slavery as the cause of the war. Much of Buckner's opposition to secession stemmed not from his apathy toward the institution of slavery and not from his faith in federal power alone but rather from his fears about the protection of the rights of upper South states in a cotton-state Confederacy. Doubtless, the rebels were devoted to the theory of state sovereignty when it benefitted their cherished institution of slavery, but so were Kentucky's loyal masters. Buckner made a calculated decision about which federal system, the United States or the Confederate States, would best accommodate the right of Kentucky to practice the institution of slavery in a manner most beneficial to the state's interests. Perhaps in light of emancipation that decision was poorly taken. Or perhaps it was not. By defending its state rights within the bounds of the Constitution, Kentucky delayed African American enlistment within its borders longer than its neighbors Virginia and Tennessee, Kentucky stood alone at the end of 1865 as the last state in which slavery still (mostly) functioned, and Kentucky kept its government in the hands of conservative Democrats such as Buckner who ensured that no black political enfranchisement and subsequent Republican takeover occurred in the Bluegrass as it did in the states of the former Confederacy. And it was loyal Kentucky, not the failed Confederacy, that showed the postwar South how effective a states' rights–based opposition to social and political change could be.[7]

This relationship between government and slavery is fundamental. As one of Buckner's comrades in arms, Colonel Marcellus Mundy of the Twenty-Third Kentucky Infantry, wrote to President Lincoln, these Kentuckians were "masters for loyalty's sake."[8] Their mastery was dependent on their loyalty to the United States and the Constitution, a document flexible enough to allow for both a federal fugitive slave law and the guarantees of state sovereignty in the Tenth Amendment, both of which were necessary to nurture and protect slavery. Buckner and Mundy were also simultaneously loyal for mastery's sake, bound to love the Union because of their ties to the institution of human bondage. Slavery was the glue that bound white Kentuckians to the United States, its government, and its ideals while that same government allowed them to continue to exercise the prerogatives of mastery in all their forms. The "unionist sentiment of Kentuckians was anything but a lack of commitment to slavery," argues Matthew Salafia in a recent analysis. "On the contrary, their commitment to slavery was a foundational component of their unionist sentiment. The union was what gave slavery its vitality in Kentucky." A Buckner cousin from western Kentucky stated the case most plainly, "If the Union is lost, all is lost. Of what use are my slaves if we have no government?"[9]

To frame this position within his own terms, Ben Buckner's stand by the Union was not a rejection of those relationships, those interests, and that identity that he shared in common with his Confederate foes. Instead, his loyalty was a desperate bid to save his central Kentucky slave society from destruction. To him and his fellow proslavery union Kentuckians in 1861, the principle of constitutional government was far more than a legal technicality; it was the foundation, protector, and guarantor of everything his society held dear. The Constitution—the Union—upheld slave owners' absolute property rights, allowed the pursuit of fugitive slaves anywhere within the country's borders, defended the institution and its basis in white supremacy in the courts, gave slave states electoral benefits from holding African Americans in bondage, had bought or taken new lands into which generations of masters had migrated and flourished, and through its adaptability and amendability had allowed for new defenses of the institution to evolve in the face of every antislavery challenge yet posed. The Union and its Constitution were the spring from which that institution flowed, and from there came slavery's subsequent relationships, interests, and identities that knit Buckner's world together.

Buckner is a subject through whom we can see the intersection of the public and private worlds of upper South conservative unionists, through whom we can piece together a holistic picture of a life and a world not only during the war years but over the course of a generation. His is a perspective that Civil War historians have not yet fully grasped. The assumption that the North was the Union and the South the Confederacy has made Kentucky a difficult interpretative fit in general.[10] Scholars who look for dissent and resistance to the Lincoln administration within the Union tend to look at Copperheads in the states north of the Ohio without paying particular attention to the protests of loyal slaveholding Kentuckians.[11] And similarly, Kentuckians, especially those outside the mountains, often do not show up in studies of wartime Unionism in the South, which have generally looked within the borders of the Confederate state.[12]

Ultimately, proslavery unionists such as Buckner made up a small minority of those young men nationwide who flocked to defend the United States in 1861. They had, however, a far greater impact on the war's outcome than their numbers alone might suggest. What might have been if Kentucky's loyal masters had not placed their faith in the power of the Union to protect slavery and joined the Confederacy? What strategic challenges would a Confederate Kentucky have presented to Lincoln's generals? How might emancipation have proceeded differently if proslavery Kentucky congressmen and senators had not been present in Washington to voice and vote opposition to Republican policies? Could freedom have come to African Americans throughout the South a year earlier if Lincoln had not been afraid of angering loyal masters in the border states?

Even after emancipation, when Kentucky proslavery unionists distanced themselves from the Lincoln administration's changing war goals, Buckner and men like him continued to have a national impact through the power they wielded within the state. Although the state's 1861 Union coalition, like the United States as a whole, included a range of groups with differing levels of commitment or opposition to slavery, men who valued both the Union and slavery kept control of the state government in Frankfort. Proslavery unionists such as Buckner made up the majority of the state's loyal population—somewhere around six in ten or perhaps two-thirds. Seven in ten Kentuckians voted for George McClellan over Abraham Lincoln in 1864. That ratio holds for soldiers who voted in the field, too, demonstrating that there was not the same sort of pro-administration feeling among Kentucky troops as there was in the balance of the Union army, which gave eight of every ten votes to its commander in chief. The 1865 Kentucky House of Representatives initially sat fifty-eight Conservative Party members, of which Buckner was one, to forty-two Union Party men. That Conservative majority, though, would grow by seven seats, as we shall see, through Buckner's agency.[13]

The return of the rebels to the electorate in 1867 makes it difficult to trace how many old boys in blue voted the Democratic ticket, as Buckner proudly did. Kentucky Republicans, however, always hoped to woo all of the Union men to their side—and never could. The state's first Republican governor, William O. Bradley, believed that old conservative unionists represented two-thirds of the Democracy's (i.e., the Democratic Party's) strength in the 1880s.[14] Loyal proslavery men, then, dominated state politics during the war years, and their votes, along with those of their former rebel neighbors, sustained the Democratic Party—and its opposition to meaningful social and political change—for decades to come.

From the first rumors about emancipation in 1861 through the end of the Reconstruction era, Kentucky's state government was a leader in denying civil rights, economic opportunity, and social equality to its black citizens *because* it had remained loyal to the Union. The loyal proslavery men in Frankfort ensured that Kentucky was the last state in which slavery was legal and functional in 1865. Their political resistance to the federal government's Freedmen's Bureau limited access to education, employment assistance, legal justice, and physical protection for Kentucky freedpeople. They stood as spokesmen for dispossessed and politically disabled former rebel masters across the South. Not content to stop there, the state marshaled its militia forces to support the Ku Klux Klan's paramilitary campaign, using state guns against black Kentuckians and the institutions that supported their claims to equality. The state government fought against the enfranchisement of black men until forced to allow them the vote by the Fifteenth Amendment and then provided a testing ground for strategies of disfranchisement that would later become staples of Jim Crow governments across the South. Discouraged, impoverished, and frustrated, black Kentuckians fled the state by the thousands in the decades following the war, whitening the state and beginning yet another great African American diaspora. Buckner joined in all of these efforts to contest the results of the war his army had won.

The political work that Buckner performed in service of white supremacy during the war years and Reconstruction, though, was only the first act of his efforts to construct a postwar society as close as possible to that which he promised to Helen when he proposed to her in 1859. Alongside his good friend and longtime law partner W. C. P. Breckinridge, Buckner worked in the interests of the New South brand of economic growth and racial control, setting up an interlocking system of formal and informal structures to ensure white supremacy in Kentucky. There were many parts of this New South whole: railroads, coal mines, tobacco, and hemp paid for it; unequal access to education and courts plagued with systemic inequality and supported by informal lynchings perpetuated it; and smiling Confederate colonels with juleps in hand sold it as good and right to the nation.[15]

There is no indication that Buckner ever joined a Union veterans' organization such as the Grand Army of the Republic (GAR) or spoke out in print or in person against the Confederate reimagining of Kentucky history. Why would he have done so? The GAR was, with some exceptions, an integrated institution associated with the Republican Party. Moreover, proslavery unionists may not have simply declined to participate in commemorations of the Union cause after the war; what happened to Buckner suggests that they were actively excluded. As a result of an 1867 row, men who were soon to become leaders in the state's Republican Party publicly served notice that Buckner and other prominent officers who had quit the army in protest of emancipation were not to lay claim to the memory of the Union cause in Kentucky to advance their conservative, white supremacist ends.

Little wonder, then, that Buckner found friends among the Confederates. He pined for the return of the old (and, of course, imaginary) antebellum world of happy slaves and benevolent masters as much as any author in the postwar Confederate nostalgia mouthpiece *Southern Bivouac*. The men in the United Confederate Veterans knew his pain, frustration, and regret better than the men in the GAR. Buckner was not silenced by a Confederate memorializing juggernaut. Rather, he stood to the side while it performed the cultural work that he, as a New South man, needed it to do: rehabilitate the national memory of antebellum southern slavery and attract investment to Kentucky railroads, mines, and farms. Why stand in their way? Why unnecessarily clutter a memory landscape in which Buckner's interests were already being served—well—by his Confederate friends? Kentucky took on such a decidedly Confederate flavor in part because conservative wartime Unionists such as Buckner were more pleased with the effects of neo-Confederatism in their present than they were concerned with remembering and commemorating their own wartime service in their past.

This book is both a biography of an individual and an analysis of his mid-nineteenth-century world. Though it will flow mostly chronologically, each chapter is thematic, concerned more with investigating a particular set of questions about Civil War–era Kentucky than with maintaining a day-by-day chronicle of Buckner's life. There are three broad sections of two chapters each. Chapters 1 and 2 take place before the war and often overlap one another in time. The first is, in effect, a short microhistory of slavery in and around Buckner's Clark County, beginning before Buckner's birth and carrying up to the eve of the war. Economic history intersects with social histories of power relationships between and among free and enslaved Kentuckians to show how slavery had adapted to a different environmental and political climate along the border with the free states to develop a diverse yet interconnected economy of slave-produced crops and products and to develop young men such as Buckner, the next generation of the master class who would take the reins when they came of age.

The second chapter is also fundamentally about slavery, but whereas the first examined the institution as a lived reality, the second interprets it as a political issue that shaped Buckner's personal political culture—the interconnecting assumptions about society, race, gender, and power that informed and influenced partisan politics. Chapter 2 follows the Buckner family to Jacksonville, Illinois, where Ben[16] was born, and introduces what Stanley Harrold has recently termed the "border war" along the Ohio River that encouraged upper South masters to value federal protection for their slave property when the question of secession was put to them in 1861.[17] Moving forward, this chapter also places Buckner's politics during the secession crisis in the context of his courtship of Helen, arguing that his conception of the slaveholding Union he defended was grounded on the ideologies of race and gender he hoped to establish in their future household.

The wartime chapters are the heart of the book, where Buckner's voice comes through the strongest. Chapter 3 uses his correspondence with Helen during 1861 and 1862 to uncover the linkages between the home front and battle lines. Like the previous chapters, it continues to situate Buckner within the context of local expectations of a young white slave-owning man, reading his accounts of his wartime experience in light of the social and cultural meanings of military service for white Civil War soldiers. Yet again, Buckner's personal and political goals intermingle. His characterization of himself, his soldiers, and the enemy works to define what he wanted from his military service—confirmation of honor, prestige, respectability, whiteness, masculinity, political advancement, and Helen's hand in marriage. Chapter 4 puts these principles to the test of emancipation. If the previous chapter showed the war going right for Buckner, this one shows his world come crashing down as the war and the Lincoln administration turn against slavery and push Buckner toward resignation from the army. It details Buckner's reaction to both the federal government's and an enslaved people's pushing the process of emancipation forward while loyal Kentucky masters such as himself were caught, for the first time in their lives, powerless to stop either.

In these wartime chapters, Ben's letters home to Helen frame the issues and shape the narrative. For all the riches these letters provide, this approach has its limits. We must remain conscious of Buckner's editorial hand. The war that we see is one that he repackaged for consumption back home, and what he tells and chooses not to tell speaks as loudly as the lines on the page. The extant correspondence is also one-sided; we hear only an echo of Helen's voice in Ben's letters. She could fill out the other half of the discourses on gender, race, loyalty, and society that she and Buckner shared through the mail while he was away in the army. Her voice would raise intriguing questions about the contours of the fundamentally unequal yet constantly negotiated power relationships that characterized nineteenth-century life in Kentucky. Whether Helen's letters were lost amid the baggage on some army wagon or deemed not worthy or interesting enough to warrant preservation, they did not survive, forcing us to reconstruct her voice through Buckner's pen. Of course, the difficulty of understanding Helen and incorporating her opinions, actions, and motivations into this analysis pales in comparison to the difficulty of understanding the often nameless and nearly always voiceless African Americans who populated the Buckner household and the army camps of the Twentieth Kentucky.

The two postwar chapters have a different feel and come from a different base of historical evidence. With Buckner back home, his correspondence with Helen ended. We no longer have access to his inner thoughts, and, more tragically, we lose Helen as a character almost altogether. A biographical sketch of Buckner written late in his life sums up the situation well: "The public career of such a man as Mr. Buckner is often quite well known, while that of his private life is an unread page." After their marriage, Helen falls behind a curtain of domesticity—due to "a degree of what might be termed secrecy attending the sacredness of home relations"—reemerging from archival oblivion only after her husband's death, when her appearances in the society pages of the local newspapers allow at least a glimpse of her final years in Winchester.[18] Fortunately, the public career of Mr. Buckner was, indeed, well known in the decades following the war, and he is not difficult to trace through newspapers and official government documents.

Chapter 5 begins two years after his resignation from the army. This silence is not by choice. Aside from legal casework, Buckner's documentary trail goes cold until he surfaces again in the summer of 1865, when he was elected to the Kentucky General Assembly. This chapter narrates Buckner's time in Frankfort primarily from the House and Senate journals of the critical 1865–1867 legislative sessions. Those years saw the Thirteenth Amendment rejected, the rebels reenfranchised, and proslavery Union firebrand Garrett Davis returned to the U.S. Senate for six more years of outspoken resistance to the Republican majority. Most importantly, this chapter reevaluates the narrative of a Confederate takeover of the Kentucky state government after 1865. Buckner shows that rather than being overtaken by returning rebels, most wartime loyal masters embraced them as allies in the fight against black civil rights and social equality. This chapter concludes with an 1867 battle for custody of the Union regimental flags, showing how Republican-leaning Unionists took rhetorical control of the Union Cause. Their accusations of a "rebel Democracy," which historians have taken at face value, were, instead, partisan labels that did not reflect the complex realities of the postwar Democratic Party.

Chapter 6 finds Buckner and his proslavery Union–Confederate Democratic alliance tested after the passage of the Fifteenth Amendment. In 1870, Buckner raised a battalion of militia in and around Lexington that for the next three years would harass, intimidate, and murder black men at the polls. Enlisting Confederate veterans and with the backing of both Union and Confederate veterans in government office, Buckner's militia provides an excellent example of largely harmonious postwar cooperation between blue and gray in defense of whiteness. The chapter concludes with a critical case stemming from Buckner's militia work. When Republicans challenged the legality of a poll tax passed by Lexington Democrats in 1873, Buckner stepped up to defend the new law. Without any explicit mention of race, the tax effectively disenfranchised black voters unable to pay the tax, and Buckner's victory before the Supreme Court in *United States v. Hiram Reese* (1876) would be one of two landmark decisions that dealt African American suffrage in the South a blow from which it would struggle to recover for a century.

An epilogue sketches Buckner's life and career after *Reese*. It concludes that Buckner and others like him had little desire to revel in their Union service, especially after 1867, when the Republican Party claimed the Union Cause in the state. Living in a Jim Crow/New South present—as close as Buckner could ever get to the slave society he had set out to defend in 1861—was more important than dwelling on the past.

As in Buckner's pre-emancipation lament, then, this book uses him to blur the line between the principle of "that Constitutional form of government"—the political history with which Civil War historiography has long been fascinated—and the "ties of relationship, interest, [and] the identity of our hearts and institutions"—the broader social and cultural world that historians have better explored in recent decades. It is impossible to understand Buckner's politics without understanding his relationship with Helen and what he hoped he could make the world. Politics was the means by which most nineteenth-century Americans sought to bring about their vision of what the world could and should be. This is why Buckner so desperately fought against the secessionists in 1861, why he so eagerly welcomed them back into the state in 1865, and why he so vigorously worked to block African Americans' access to the ballot in the 1870s. Much of this account of Buckner's life has to do with electoral politics, but, of course, he was a politically minded lawyer, and, more importantly, as Glenn Feldman reminds us, "Southern politics is not now—nor has it ever been—predominantly about politics. It's about culture."[19] Nothing Buckner did was solely economically motivated, prompted by the concerns of partisan politics, fueled by the need to prove himself a man, driven by his goal of assuring white power and control, recommended by his religious beliefs, or encouraged by personal and family loyalties. Everything he did was motivated by all of those things.[20]

Buckner is a character whom another Kentuckian, Robert Penn Warren, would have been keen to write. Buckner seems to exemplify what David Blight has termed the "the overarching theme of Warren's literary career," the sticking point of human nature, and the burden of truly understanding our past: *"Evil as the cost of good."*[21] Like many of Warren's characters who are tortured by the necessity of murder, fraud, and betrayal to make the world into what they imagine to be good and just, Buckner embraced the evils of slavery and racism to bring about the domestic happiness that as a young man in 1859 he had promised to his beloved Helen. Everything going according to their plan for themselves, their state, and the nation would have meant generations of slavery for black Kentuckians. The Buckners' happiness was inseparable from slavery, built upon it.

Yet I understand parts of those dreams that drove Ben Buckner. I share his pride in Kentucky and being a Kentuckian. I share Buckner's hope that Kentucky can make itself into something great for all of its citizens, even as I recognize that Buckner and I define greatness and citizenship in ways that separate us as much as the intervening 150 years do. This is why I think Buckner is important not only for understanding the past but for understanding our present as well. He makes us confront the ways in which we interact with the Civil War and its connections to slavery, race, and the meaning of the American republic. It is up to us to use the insight about ourselves and our world that Buckner's life provides. We should not hide from what we learn about the past, like Warren's Jack Burden did. Rather, I hope that we can, echoing Tara McPherson, find "new ways of feeling southern that more fully come to terms with the history of racial oppression and racial connection in the South." I hope that understanding the political, social, and cultural worlds that Buckner and his generation left as their lasting inheritance might allow us in the present to move "toward more flexible modes of southern identity," which refuse to "abandon the South to . . . stasis and fixity."²² I hope that Buckner might illuminate the ways of thinking, feeling, and acting developed by and for his era so that we might combat new, more ostensibly color-blind forms of oppression that would deny rights and opportunities to those falling outside the boundaries of white, fundamentalist, heteronormative orthodoxy and threatens to constrain the potential of Kentucky, the South, and the United States.

Buckner's proslavery unionism is a Civil War story divested of most of its glory to modern eyes. The proslavery war aims of white Kentuckians on both sides made the state a place where, as young Robert Penn Warren grew up in Todd County, "the color of the uniform your grandfather had worn" was never "of burning importance," and most everyone could agree that the "Civil War seemed to have been fought for the right to lynch without legal interference."²³ But in different ways than remembering a proslavery Confederacy, recalling a proslavery unionism reminds white, culturally southern Kentuckians of one last ugly truth from which they have largely been able to hide: they fought a war alongside Yankees for reasons divested of moral legitimacy. They fought on the wrong side for the wrong cause. Buckner's is not a narrative of triumph of our cherished American values and liberties over repression. Instead, he demonstrates how the United States has both succeeded and failed—often at the same time—in its efforts to realize protection of life, liberty, and the pursuit of happiness for all people. Just as much as any of his rebel neighbors who rode with John Hunt Morgan, Buckner shows in action C. Vann Woodward's "burden of southern history," the great regional counternarrative to the grand story of continual American progress toward equality and freedom.²⁴ But because he casts that burden in Union blue, Buckner shows that that burden is not the South's alone; it is not somehow un-American. He did not make war *against* our government to preserve black men and women in bondage; he made war *for* our government to preserve his rights and deny them to others.

1

THE WORLD IS A CRUEL AND COLD PLACE

As soon as Major Benjamin Forsythe Buckner stepped off the steamer onto the shore of Smithland, Kentucky, at dawn on December 15, 1861, he could tell that his war had changed. A glance around the western Kentucky town at the confluence of the Ohio and Cumberland Rivers impressed upon the young lawyer turned soldier "the idea that we are in the midst of a war which is no childs play [more] than any thing I have seen."[1] Though Buckner was still within the borders of his home state, Smithland and the war he found there were a world away from the home he had left in Winchester, a central Kentucky town just east of Lexington on the edge of the fabled Bluegrass region. Smithland contrasted starkly with a summer and autumn of patriotic rhetoric and promises of glory enticing young men from the eastern and southern Bluegrass to defend the Union and the Constitution. Buckner's war had so far been flag presentations and fine speeches, capped by a glorious victory at a small skirmish that had earned him statewide acclaim.

This was not that summer war. Two earthen forts, rising squat and brown from the bleak winter landscape and studded with a pair of sixty-four-pound heavy-artillery pieces, were now the most prominent landmarks in town. Or, rather, in what had been a town. Most of the houses, outbuildings, and trees that had once made up the productive port community of Smithland had been leveled to clear fields of fire. Buckner found the place to be nearly as "deserted" as its town lots and adjoining fields were bare, and one of his fellow Bluegrass officers noted that the "appearance" of the town was "anything but attractive," with civilians "scarce and the whole settlement . . . absorbed in the 'fighting science.'"[2] Along with the dull gray sky that blankets wintertime Kentucky in a damp gloom, the mountainous mud ramparts, acres upon acres of tree stumps, and the debris of a town destroyed by war combined to make an otherworldly scene. In Buckner's eyes, more than just the town had been absorbed by the fighting science; civilization, order, property, and dignity had all been lost to this war as well.

Buckner had come to Smithland with the promise that there were more soldiers eager to help put down the rebellion. The companies that he, his best friend and fellow Winchester lawyer Charley Hanson, and Lexington businessman Sanders D. Bruce had recruited in the Bluegrass had not made up a complete regiment. The three had been ordered to Smithland to fill out the unit, and they found eager recruits. And the town was not as deserted as Buckner had thought on first glance—quite the opposite, in fact. It was swollen with refugees from across western Kentucky. Union people like Buckner, but, unlike him, Union people who had seen the worst that civil war could bring.

"I have almost wished that you could come hear some of the tales that the Union men here tell of the horrid outrages committed by the Secessionists," Buckner wrote to his fiancée, Helen Martin, on his first day in Smithland. "The property of Union men has been indiscriminately seized," and their "lives and liberty have been at the mercy" of their rebel neighbors. Driven off from and burned out of their homes by secessionist neighbors, the loyal men, women, and children of the region huddled in tents, river caves, and what remained of the town. The closest the Confederates had come to engaging the Union army directly was when a western Kentucky recruit, home from Smithland with measles that ravaged the camp, had been dragged from his sickbed by a Confederate patrol and was run through a sleeting winter night from "house to house & exhibited as a '*Lincolnite*,'" an example to discourage other Unionists. "Farmers tell us of having 30 cattle driven off at a time," Buckner told Helen. "Others of having every horse & cow taken from them—others robbed of all their negroes—in short every Union man has been plundered of all his moveable property."[3] Buckner was aghast at the idea of making war on families, women, children, and the elderly, not on legitimate combatants. And he was even more aghast at the war on slavery. "Such," Buckner concluded, "are a few of the events of secession."[4]

Buckner was horrified by these events of secession that he saw in Smithland because they were the realization of his greatest fears come to life. Rebellion was one thing when it was talked of in the safe confines of courthouse squares, in parlors after dinner, or in the states of the cotton South, hundreds of miles away from what would become the theater of war. Rebellion was one thing when it was theoretical. These events of secession had proved otherwise. Whereas the rebels feared what Lincoln and his Republican administration might do to slavery and turned to revolution to create their own republic, Buckner and many thousands of loyal slave masters in the upper South feared revolution and were wary of risking the benefits that the American "slaveholding republic" had bestowed on them for three generations.[5]

Rebellion was fine in theory, but where were law and restraint? Where had the lofty constitutional theories about respect for all species of property—especially property in slaves, "the greatest material interest of the world"—been on those November and December nights in the Jackson Purchase when secessionists had turned on their neighbors?[6] Where was the solidarity among white southerners that held their slave society together in the face of challenges from within—from the slaves themselves—and challenges from without—from abolitionists and antislavery advocates across the Ohio? What Buckner really lamented in Smithland was that rebellion had divided Kentucky and its slave masters, divided the South, at precisely the time when they most needed unity. Tired of fighting the legislative battles over slavery that had gone on since the earliest days of the republic—battles that white southerners had by and large been winning—the rebels had sought a battlefield of a different sort.

Buckner preferred the legislative battlefield to the literal one. That preference was practically born into him, the son of an old Whig family nearly raised in the Clark County Court House, where he watched the legal luminaries of Henry Clay's generation practice. But success in Congress required southern unity. So Buckner and thousands of other Kentuckians of his political stripe reluctantly marched off to war against their fellow white southerners, fellow slave owners. They would crush the rebel dream of independence, return them to the national fold, and get down to the serious business of thwarting the Republican Party's antislavery legislative agenda. For this to work, Buckner and the upper South's proslavery Unionists needed the rebels. They needed a clean war, a quick war, a gentlemanly war. They did not need animosity between Unionist and Confederate; they did not need war to be conducted outside of the conventional battlefield where winners and losers were difficult to determine; and they did not need an internal war on slavery. Buckner had to kill rebels but never hate them, destroy their nation but preserve their trust, crush their armies but preserve their society. He did not need what was happening around Smithland.

It was important, too, that Buckner underscore these horrid events of secession in his letters back to Helen; she and her family were staunch rebels. Both Buckner and the Martins sought to steer slavery—and along with it their livelihoods, their lifestyles, and their status—safely through this sectional crisis, but Buckner could not help but think the path his rebel fiancée and her family chose a dangerously naive one. Rebellion must have seemed so dashing and adventurous to Helen from the safety of her father's Bluegrass farm. But what Buckner saw in Smithland was another side to that coin, proof of the dangers to Kentucky slave society that secession and rebellion brought.

Ben and Helen chose different paths through the wilderness of sectional crisis and civil war because of the very different lives they had led within the same Kentucky slave society. Growing up the sheltered youngest daughter of one of the most successful and respected farmers and slave owners in Clark County, Helen seemed not to grasp the fragility of life in the master class. She had always known security in the old brick house that her grandfather had built on some of the richest pastureland in the Bluegrass. But whereas Helen had only known security, Ben had seen firsthand how fragile wealth and status in Kentucky's slave society could be and feared that secession would affect that delicate balance that kept men like him near the top of society. By coming to Smithland, he risked everything—his life, his family's modest wealth, and his relationship with Helen—to prove the point that slavery could exist safely only within the United States. His memories of the past and his hopes for the future had led him to that conclusion.

Clark County, the stage for the successes and failures of both the Buckners and the Martins, had been formed out of neighboring Fayette and Bourbon Counties in 1792, one of the first acts of the newly created State of Kentucky. The land that would become Clark County, however, had a much longer history. The Shawnee town of Eskippakithiki—renamed "Indian Old Fields" by later white settlers—was one of the earliest places of cultural interaction and trade across the mountains. Daniel Boone's famous fort was located just across the Kentucky River from what would become southern Clark, and as the first Bluegrass families fanned out from the refuge of Boonesborough's walls, they found the clearings around the old Shawnee town an excellent location to plant corn and establish land claims.[7]

The county was positioned on the eastern edge of the inner Bluegrass, which made it a geographically diverse place. Henry Clay described its advantages at length.

> The soil of that region is a rich, deep vegetable loam, free from sand with but little grit. It lies on a bed of clay, interspersed with small fragments of iron ore, and this clay in its turn reposes on a mass of limestone lying many feet in depth in horizontal strata. The general surface of the country is gently undulating. The rich land, (and there is but little that is not rich,) in the whole region, is well adapted to the growth of hemp, where it has not been too much exhausted by injudicious tillage. The lands which produce it best, are those which are fresh, or which have lain sometime in grass or clover.[8]

As Clay noted, the unparalleled pasture land, which made neighboring Lexington and Paris Kentucky's centers of livestock breeding and sales, encouraged the same sorts of land use, particularly in the western and northwestern districts of Clark, which bordered Fayette and Bourbon Counties. In addition to its famous horses, mules, cattle, and hogs, Clark was also one of the largest hemp producers in the state. In the southern and eastern parts of the county, mineral deposits were found in the foothills of the mountains and spurred the building of iron furnaces on the county's eastern and southern borders. A web of roads—either state funded or built by private turnpike companies—connected Winchester to the neighboring county seats in all directions, and the Kentucky River, fed by the Red River along the county's southern border, provided a navigable riverine outlet for the county's products.

In 1804, four sons of Revolutionary War veteran Thomas Buckner Jr. made the journey to the Bluegrass. The Buckners, though late to the postrevolutionary land rush to Kentucky during which so much of the prime land was claimed, managed to secure a foothold in central Kentucky, perhaps employing some of the family's Virginia wealth to that end. The first Buckner had come to the mother colony just before Bacon's Rebellion, and generations of his descendants had done well for themselves in and around Caroline County.[9] Through their father's war claim, the Buckner migrants found land in Bourbon County near Cane Ridge and set about establishing themselves in the typical Kentucky manner—in land and slaves.

Benjamin Hawes Buckner, one of the four migrant brothers, married the next year and was soon off in search of new lands in which to plant his own future. Even by 1804, land in one of the prime Bluegrass counties was becoming both scarce and expensive as wealthy and well-connected sons of leading Virginia families snatched it up, so Benjamin, like so many other Kentuckians, headed west. The 1810 census found Benjamin and his growing family of two young children, his wife, Elizabeth, and seven enslaved people in Henderson, an Ohio River town in western Kentucky along the flatboat routes down the Mississippi to the recently opened port of New Orleans. By 1818, though, Benjamin had made enough money in Henderson to return with his growing family to the central Bluegrass, coming to Clark County, which shared a border with Bourbon, where the majority of the immediate Buckner family still resided.[10]

When Ben's grandfather Benjamin returned to the Bluegrass from Henderson in the late 1810s, he made sure to invest his western Kentucky wealth in ways that would both turn him a profit and connect him with the most important men in the central Bluegrass. He entered into a profitable partnership with Richard Hawes, a Virginia first cousin, Lexington lawyer, and rising star in the state political scene. Finding the bar too crowded in litigious Lexington, Hawes moved to Winchester after inheriting some land in the county in 1823. The plot was a fine hemp producer, and Hawes and Buckner joined in establishing a ropewalk in Winchester to convert the county's bounteous hemp crops into baggage and cording. Lexington had been (and would continue to be) the center of the rope and bagging manufacturing in the state, but the move to establish a factory in Winchester seems to have been a wise one. It attracted the business of local men as well as some from outside the county. Henry Clay, who had played a small role in settling the estate that brought Hawes the hemp land in Clark, sold a portion of his crop to the firm in 1825.[11]

Operated by enslaved labor, the Buckner–Hawes operation was indicative of the unique shape that the institution of slavery was taking in the Bluegrass. Kentucky slavery looked little like the slavery found in the cash-crop-producing plantation monocultures of the coastal South and on the expanding cotton frontier of the Southwest. Slavery in Kentucky was unique in its smaller scale, its economic flexibility and adaptability, and the complex social networks between and among enslaver and enslaved. However, "smaller scale" should not be mistaken for decreased importance of slavery and enslaved labor to life and the economy in Kentucky. Whereas approximately 22 percent of Kentuckians were enslaved in 1820, 51 percent of rice- and cotton-producing South Carolina was in bondage; 45 percent of sugar-producing Louisiana was enslaved; and even frontier Mississippi already enslaved 43 percent of its population. Not only was the overall percentage of slaves lower in Kentucky, but slaveholdings themselves were smaller as well. The number of white Kentuckians who owned a hundred or more slaves at any given time could be counted in single digits. Even the magical number of twenty slaves, which designated a "planter" in the eyes of the law, was an exceptionally large holding in Kentucky.[12]

The fact that slavery was not present in the eye-catching numbers found farther south again should not suggest that it was any less economically, socially, culturally, or politically important to Kentuckians white and black. The numerical differences suggest only that Kentucky's economic needs were different from South Carolina's or Mississippi's. Scale did not pay in Kentucky as richly as it did in the cotton country. The rich soils that Henry Clay described—known scientifically as "alfisols," which are more neutral, loamy, and productive than the thin, acidic soils found farther south—allowed intensive and repeated cultivation. Slavery developed in Clark County according to the products that its weather and geology encouraged; its demographic and labor patterns accordingly looked different from those seen elsewhere in the slave South. Those products—livestock, grain, and hemp—did not require the large work gangs seen in the cotton, rice, or tobacco South. Instead, they called for smaller but higher-skilled workforces whose labor patterns varied seasonally. Ulrich B. Phillips recognized this as early as the 1920s, writing that "food crops and pasturage permitted the handling of large acreage by small personnel; and in tobacco and hemp culture there was little advantage in largeness of scale. Kentucky therefore did not develop great plantations nor import hordes of slaves to till them."[13]

Despite not requiring "largeness of scale," Clark County's hemp and livestock economies nevertheless desperately needed slaves to function. Although the hand per acre ratio may have been low on such farms, the work necessary to profitably convert bluegrass pastures and fields into profit was dirty, backbreaking, and racialized. Many derisively labeled hemp a "nigger crop," one person remarking that the work was "very dirty, and so laborious that scarcely any white man will work at it." Particularly onerous was the process of "breaking" the hemp, shattering the woody outer stalk with a large wooden apparatus to extract the fibrous interior from which cloth and rope can be woven. Though the work was physically demanding and performed by enslaved men, it was far from unskilled. Advertisements touting enslaved men's hemp-related skills—cutting, shocking, braking, and hackling—testify to this fact. Commentators through the end of the nineteenth century generally agreed, too, that hand harvesting far exceeded any mechanical method in both speed and yield.[14] Hemp's role in shaping the slave system in Clark County did not end when the crop was cut in autumn. Even before the harvest, hemp did not require the constant attention that tobacco, rice, or cotton did. The plant was encouraged to grow thick and tall, the best crops so densely packed that the stalks did not have room to branch out. As a consequence, there was no weeding, and because of the sticky resin the stalks exuded, few insects bothered it. Later in the year after it was cut, the hemp had to lie in the fields for a month or six weeks of damp, prewintery weather before the fibers "dew rotted" into a more flexible condition before being broken and hackled just after Christmas.[15]

In practice, then, hemp provided considerable down time when farm hands could be put to other tasks. The farm owner could reapply this surplus labor to other work on his farm, tending other crops, grain in particular, helping raise livestock, or catching up on repair work on the barns, outbuildings, and fences around the premises. The unusually detailed records of one Kentucky hemp plantation reveal a stunning diversity of crops and livestock tended in down times for the season. There, slaves grew corn, wheat, potatoes, cabbages, and cider apples in addition to raising milk, beef, and working cattle; plow, saddle, and carriage horses; hogs, turkeys, ducks, and chickens. All this, of course, was on top of the hemp-processing operations, all done at the on-site ropewalk, and the other small supportive industries, such as cloth weaving and blacksmithing for replacement parts.[16] A hemp farm, then, was far more than just a hemp farm.

If, as was often the case, the planter had more labor than was necessary, he always had the option of hiring out the slaves to neighboring farmers—both slave owners and non-slave owners who needed extra hands in the field—or for wage work in town. During the lulls in the field phases of hemp raising, slaves were often hired for a time to the ropewalks that were processing last year's crop. This certainly seems to have been what Richard Hawes had in mind when he inherited the Clark County hemp farm in 1823. Not only would opening his own ropewalk in partnership with Benjamin Buckner allow him to process his crop, but he could also employ his seasonally idle farm laborers as well as the enslaved women and children, who generally did not work in the hemp fields, in the process. In an economic climate where Kentucky hemp growers and manufacturers were in constant competition with one another, other American mills in Missouri and Massachusetts, as well as imported bagging from Russia and elsewhere, the economic benefit of employing slaves in the ropewalk or hiring them out to another operation would be a welcome relief.

The practice of hiring slave labor also reveals that slavery was far from being in opposition to liberal capitalism; indeed, this diverse, rationalized production proved that slavery was built within capitalism's framework. In areas where slave hiring was common, historians have noted a distinctly different understanding of enslaved people in relation to the market than one expects to find in the slave South. The care taken to maximize every individual's productivity gave "impetus to owners to view their slaves as investments rather than dependents, as parts of an investment 'portfolio' rather than members of a plantation 'family.' Little room was left for a conception of slaves as dependents in a paternalist system once Southern slaveholders began to look to hiring markets for returns on young, old, and superfluous slaves." A study of Baltimore's mixed labor economy, which depended heavily on slave hiring, found that the widespread practice of hiring reconciled "slavery with the most advantageous aspects of a 'free-labor' economy, namely the ability to hire and fire workers at will and to jettison traditional responsibilities of providing laborers with room and board." Such economic advantages in a constantly changing market economy mean that few upper South masters "sought to abolish slavery or convert all labor relations to a wage basis." There was no need to. Completing the circuit of economic benefit seen through Kentucky's flexible slave labor market, hiring slaves to county, state, or private turnpike projects and other infrastructural development work literally helped build the transportation connections that allowed the agricultural market economy to flourish in the inner Bluegrass.[17]

Civic and economic benefits to the slave owner aside, Bluegrass slavery's flexibility provided benefits for non-slave-owning whites as well. The benefits were not entirely economic, either; indeed, hiring was probably more socially profitable. In Bourbon County, for example, remarkably few hirers sought extra labor in the fields. Instead, non- and small-slave-owning white families hired household help most frequently. In an era when the domesticizing ideal was bringing changes to household architecture, women's work, and cultural expectations, hiring a domestic house slave could doubly reinforce the social benefits of slave mastery; not only could the family claim a black person as their own property, but the additional household labor reinforced their gentility by freeing women from the dirtiest and hardest of the household work. Interpretations of Kentucky slavery that discount the importance of the institution because of its small numbers compared to those in the lower South forget the prestige and power provided by mastery that existed outside of profits in the ledger book. As J. Winston Coleman, an accomplished Kentucky antiquarian of the early twentieth century, noted in his study of slavery in the state, "Many a small farmer, mechanic, or country store-keeper, leading away his first hired slave, swelled with pride as he assumed that enviable position in society known as a slave-holder. He was now a member, even though in a small way, of that much respected and influential class who favored the institution." In other words, according to a more recent analysis, "Property in slaves was a touchstone of both patriarchy and whiteness in the South, and as such it was fundamental to constructions of self-worth and personal identity. At the same time that white Southerners were trying to make money with slaves, they were also trying to 'make'—that is, sustain—patriarchy, honor, race, and proslavery solidarity."[18]

Clark County's livestock farms flourished in the same bluegrass-producing alfisols and diverse and adaptable system of slavery that its hemp farms did. The high concentration of phosphorous in the soils of central Kentucky provided wonderful pastureland. The county's leading agricultural theorist, Helen's father, Dr. Samuel Davis Martin, raised what might have been the finest hogs in the nation, in addition to milch cows, working oxen, mules, and horses, on his farm near Pine Grove along the Fayette County line. Labeled Clark County's "renaissance man" by late state historian Thomas D. Clark, Dr. Martin embodied Clark County's second-generation landed gentry. His father, John, was an early migrant from Virginia and the county's first sheriff. John Martin built one of the state's earliest surviving structures at the site of his first home after he ventured out of the walls of Boonesborough but later moved to the site where the doctor would later develop his famous farm and settled in a style reflecting his extraordinary success. Samuel was born before Kentucky became a state, in 1791, and had attended medical lectures at Transylvania University during the height of its academic reputation. Though he kept up a modest medical practice with his neighbors and their slaves, he seems to have applied more of his scientific training to improving the productivity of his acres of pastureland and the enslaved workforce that managed it.[19]

A gentleman farmer in the mold of Thomas Jefferson, Dr. Martin kept up an avid correspondence with agricultural journals throughout the young nation. His Patton-Durham cattle won approval from New York farmers and the editor of the *Western Farmer and Gardener*, but his greatest triumph came from his two prize hogs, Bernice and Bertha, which topped out at more than 1,000 pounds each before they turned three in an era when the median southern hog rated a scrawny 140 pounds at slaughter. As his correspondence with the national agricultural journals indicates, Martin was an avid evangelist of his farming methods. He spearheaded the foundation of the Clark County Agricultural Society in 1838 and was active in the statewide society that formed two decades later.[20]

Doctor Martin's stock farm was far from the only one in Clark County to meet with success, though his seems one of the finest examples. His and the county's success in employing enslaved people to raise cattle, pigs, and horses, though, runs quite contrary to much of the received wisdom from the lower South. Even while noting the astonishing success of Martin and his fellow "lords of the pasture," Thomas D. Clark claimed that the local stock farms demanded "more responsible types of labor than most slaves could render." Martin's success at directing his enslaved workers to raise such prodigiously fine hogs, however, disproves Clark's claim that such work was beyond the capacity of African Americans while confirming his characterization of the doctor as master of his wide domain. It does seem, though, that enslaved people in the Bluegrass raised finer animals than farther south, where, Eugene Genovese notes, slaves were either not taught how to care for animals or found ways to subtly undermine their masters' profits through neglect or abuse. Regardless of their intentions, slaves and by extension African Americans generally were quickly "known" not to be capable of raising quality livestock, an attitude echoed in Clark's dubious analysis of Clark County's enslaved people.[21]

Of course, this inability to raise fit animals did not lie inherently with African Americans, nor with slavery generally, but instead with the type of slavery practiced by planters who saw poor results. In the lower South, Genovese found that as an afterthought among planters primarily seeking not to produce fine animal flesh but to keep idle hands occupied, stock raising was assigned to slaves too young, too old, or too infirm for work in the cotton fields. Even if such planters—who were primarily cotton farmers themselves—could give advice to the stock raisers, the scale of their plantation operations discouraged spending the time necessary to do so. By contrast, Martin and other operators of Clark County farms kept relatively small slaveholdings that encouraged routine interaction with and observation of their slaves, a practice that taught proper husbandry to the slaves while—lest such close interaction be read as too paternal—keeping a constant watch over them for any suspected misbehavior or mistreatment of the animals. Though Martin's slaveholdings peaked at forty-four in 1840—a boom time that was the peak for most slave owners in the county—his operation seems to have hovered around twenty slaves in most years, echoing one contemporary commentator's call for "such attention" on stock farms "as can only be given by those who are farmers and not planters."[22]

As these nonplantation-size, or at least not consistently plantation-size, holdings show, Clark County's geography and economy determined the size of slaveholdings, keeping them smaller than those seen farther south to maximize the return on the products that slaves raised.

Even in the southern and eastern parts of Clark County, where the luscious pastureland gave way to knobby foothills, slavery took root and flourished. Both iron and timber could be harvested from the hills and hillsides and floated down the Kentucky River to market. On the eve of the Civil War, Kentucky led the South in iron production and the states of the upper South in its production of timber. The most successful of these operations around Winchester was the Red River Ironworks, just across the county line in Estill County. Though the furnace and mill were across the border, Clark Countians were intimately involved with it. The first furnace was built along the Red River by Stephen Collins in 1787. His was joined by Thomas Dye Owings's furnace in 1791, and a third was built in 1806. Until Estill County was created in 1808, all of these furnaces were in Clark County, and it was to Winchester that petitioners came seeking funds for an improved turnpike road to bring the nails, castings, cannonballs, and more to Lexington and Paris. Owings outlasted his competition and in 1830 moved the stone from all the neighboring furnaces to a new location closer to his ore supplies and converted the machinery from water power to steam. He named the new forge the Estill Steam Furnace and soon sold out to a group who styled themselves the Red River Iron Works. Two Clark County brothers, Samuel and Josiah Jackson, directed the Red River operation from then on.[23]

At their new furnace, the Jacksons employed a combination of enslaved black and free white labor, as was often the case in iron operations in the upper South. The approximate proportion of one to the other might be suggested in the 1840 census, where Josiah Jackson's household contained five white men who were not family members and thirty-eight enslaved people, nineteen of whom were men of working age. All told, the census taker noted twenty-five persons engaged in manufacturing in addition to five who primarily farmed. These twenty-five or thirty individuals were in all likelihood not the only ones who worked at Red River. Operating both the furnace to produce raw iron and the forge to manufacture it into consumable goods required an immense amount of labor. White men who lived outside the Jackson household doubtless worked there, as did an unknown number of hired slaves. Jackson hired at least eight enslaved men in 1856, the only year for which receipts survive. The inclusion of farmers in the household is a reminder that an iron operation was far from an entirely industrial concern. Extensive land holdings were required from which to mine ore, harvest timber for charcoal, and grow crops to feed the workers.[24] Buckner himself described the tract and the diversity of operations occurring on the Jackson land.

> The Forge tract contains between 4000 and 5000 acres of land, 1200 of which is fine bottom land, 800 thereof being in cultivation, and as productive as any land in the State, and fully sufficient to support the whole works when in full operation: the balance of the tract is heavily timbered. There is also on this tract a saw mill and a grist mill, with three run of stones, and a ready sale for the products of both.
>
> The Estill Steam Furnace tract contains between 24,000 and 25,000 acres, all of which is mineral land, affording an inexhaustible supply of ore and timber of the very best quality in the State. There is also a farm of 200 acres of good bottom land in the Furnace tract, with a good farm house on it. The buildings at the furnace are all that are necessary for the accommodation of all the hands, with shops, &c., for an establishment of this kind.[25]

The integration of agriculture and heavy industry, of white and black labor, and of owned and hired slaves in the Red River and Estill Steam operation says much about the fluid nature of Clark County's slave-based economy. Far from being considered an aberration to Clark's "lords of the pasture," an antisouthern intervention of Yankee industry, iron manufacturing was a natural—having been present since before statehood—and profitable application of the Kentuckians capital, specie and human. No less than Clark's agricultural sage, Dr. Martin, owned a one-fifth stake in Jackson's operation. And, showing the mutually supporting social and economic systems always at play in Kentucky, Josiah Jackson's marriage to Dr. Martin's daughter Elizabeth secured not only the extension of the Martin kin network but also the expansion and diversification of his investment in the economies of slavery operating in Kentucky.[26]

The upper South market agricultural economy of Clark County, then, encouraged different types of slaveries from those seen elsewhere in the South. Hemp, grain, livestock, industry, and town life demanded different compositions of slaveholdings, labor patterns for both whites and blacks, degrees of workplace or domestic freedom for enslaved people, and more. But although the slaveries that could be found across Clark County were different from one another—and from the types of slavery seen in other areas of the plantation South—they worked together as a slave system that one recent analysis has labeled a "capitalist continuum" wherein Kentucky masters unhesitatingly embraced different forms of free and enslaved labor to suit their particular needs. In Clark, these patterns of work generally shared quite a few characteristics, in particular that they tended to require a smaller enslaved workforce that was usually at least semiskilled (and sometimes quite highly skilled, indeed) and whose tasks could and often had to change with the season. A Clark County slaveholding farmer had to be, in another historian's words, "something of an alchemist, blending together workers who were enslaved and free, black and white, skilled and unskilled."[27] Although distinctive, the slaveries that existed in Clark County shared an adaptability that allowed them to work together as both a labor system and, perhaps more importantly, a social system.

Though different from the cotton slavery that comes immediately to mind when imagining the antebellum South, Clark County slavery—the system of systems—was slavery without question. As eminent agricultural historian Gavin Wright has noted, "An extremely wide range of historical conditions were possible under the name 'slavery'"; the word "does not identify a single well-defined labor relationship, no more than 'free labor' usefully describes the full range of nonslave labor relationships in the world." What was consistent, regardless of the time or place within the American slave South, was the concept of mastery. People were owned, and those who commanded this slave labor received both economic and social profits from their (or their family's or their hired) property. Although certain important features distinguished Kentucky slave systems from cotton belt slavery, the meaning of mastery to white Kentuckians was the same as it was to white Carolinians, Mississippians, and Louisianans. Power over enslaved people confirmed the master's whiteness, class, gender identity, and—for men—membership in the political community. As one important recent study has reminded us, we must remember to think of the South "as a collection of disparate places, rather than as a monolithic society." A region that integrated "wage-earning slaves and numerous other permutations on bound labor" reveals "the varieties of slavery operational in the South" that were different from what has become a remembered cotton normativity but were still, critically, southern—that is, built on an economic and social foundation of slavery.[28]

Though Ben Buckner's father, Aylett, had elected to practice law instead of agriculture, his success was firmly rooted in the Clark County soil. A young Aylett Buckner had set off to find his fortune in Jacksonville, Illinois, in the 1830s but setbacks in business and politics led him and his young family—including Ben, born in 1836—back to the familiar environs of Winchester. Perhaps bearing a mark against his character or skill from his failed venture in Jacksonville, Aylett would have been keenly aware that cultivating a professional reputation as well as a personal one would be of the utmost importance as he sought to reestablish himself. He would be helped, though, by his father's long-standing connections as well as by a return to the more familiar Kentucky society in which personal and professional success could be demonstrated through slaves and mastery over them.

Despite the firm boundaries that we might imagine between the public and private sphere, between the small and large slave owners, and between town and county, Aylett Buckner's prospects for success in Winchester were grounded on all sides of these artificial lines. With each farmer who brought his hemp in to be processed into cordage and bagging, each slave hired for the season to work in the ropewalk, and each new shipment of hempen goods sent south, Benjamin Buckner created a network of potential clients for Aylett's legal practice. Although Aylett's professional work as a lawyer made him ostensibly a middle-class, town-dwelling professional, his reliance on his family name and connections—both rooted in the hemp economy of Clark County and the large land- and slaveholdings that underpinned it—revealed his connection to the agricultural gentry of the county. His practice and the town of Winchester were not islands on the Clark County landscape whose structure, labor patterns, and society were abhorrent to a rural slave system but instead were organic, integrated, and integral products of a diverse yet cohesive slave society. "As centers for the collection of agricultural products and the distribution of manufactured goods," writes one scholar of such places, "Southern villages and towns grew out of the countryside that surrounded them. They were as much a part of Southern society as the farm and plantation."[29]

Just as Aylett Buckner's courthouse career could never thrive without its foundation in the hemp fields and ropewalks of Clark County, his precious public reputation among his fellow citizens—white men—rested in significant part on his affairs at home, in the supposedly private sphere occupied and shaped primarily by those excluded from his public world—white women and enslaved people. Either through what Aylett managed to accumulate himself or through a gift from Benjamin, his family settled themselves into a comfortable townhouse in Winchester, served by four enslaved people. The young lawyer's family, now with a daughter, Susan, in addition to young Ben, was the picture of southern domesticity. Aylett's professional career was dependent on maintaining the image of respectability in the eyes of the community in an era when it was assumed that morality and prosperity went hand in hand. As a lawyer and aspiring officeholder in whom, theoretically, both public and private trust were to be invested by his fellow citizens, Buckner considered his household of great importance to his career. The four enslaved domestic servants enabled an image of domestic respectability to be projected from the Buckner household. What his wife, Charlotte, wore, cooked, served, sewed, cleaned, and laundered—and, just as importantly, what she did not—all spoke volumes to interested Winchester residents who peeked behind the curtain of the domestic sphere to gain insight into the authenticity of the role being performed by her husband in public.[30]

The Buckners and their fellow townspeople shared many domestic standards with the emerging middle class across the country, while adapting these standards to suit their slave society's peculiar needs. Northerners hired domestic servants to ease the burden of housekeeping work for middle-class wives, and slavery provided a similar option for Kentuckians and other southerners. "The work of slaveholding women, or rather those tasks never performed by them, was essential in defining what it meant to be a lady in southern society," states a recent history of small slave-owning households like the Buckners'. "Access to the labor of slave women guaranteed white women's elevated social place and freed them to focus their attention on nurturing their children and molding their homes into domestic havens—both fundamental priorities of slaveholding families." Although the Buckners' domestic servants did not afford a life of utter leisure for Charlotte, their work allowed her to avoid the unglamorous yet necessary cooking and cleaning and to devote her attention to tasks such as decorating and embroidering, menu planning and purchasing, and organizing and managing the household staff—all tasks that showcased her accomplishments as a housekeeper, entertainer, and organizer. Enslaved domestic workers themselves, aside from the labor they performed, enabled masters and mistresses to "demonstrate to the world that they had appropriate standards in their home lives." In short, both public and private respectability for Charlotte—and Aylett—Buckner was "purchased at the expense of slave women's toil."[31]

Such an unequal distribution of toil on which the white members of the Buckner family household based their daily lives and public status should belie any claims about the moderate and kindly nature of small-scale slavery. Alongside the flawed belief that slavery's smaller scale in Kentucky made it a less economically and socially important institution than it was in the cotton states, many have long imagined that this smaller scale made it a less cruel institution there, too. In 1940, J. Winston Coleman set the tone for much of the scholarly discussion of slavery in the state until the 1990s, and his interpretation still rings true in popular white memory. "Situated directly below the free states . . . , Kentucky was not far enough south to be one of the cotton or sugar-cane states, where slavery was proverbially harder and the absentee system of ownership prevailed," Coleman opined. "Numerous accounts have been left . . . with an open and unbiased view, that they saw slavery in Kentucky in its mildest form, better than in any other slave state, with the possible exception of Maryland or Virginia." Indeed, the differences between the slaveries seen in Kentucky and those seen farther south do, on the surface, lend themselves to such an interpretation. Coleman suggests the usual litany. Smaller holdings meant that enslaved people often worked, ate, and slept near or with the white family. Masters and mistresses had better opportunity to get to know enslaved people in such close spaces and, perhaps, could better conceive of them as human beings. The belief that higher-heat crops could not grow in Kentucky encouraged whites to believe that the climate was not as harsh as that faced by slaves on cotton, rice, and sugar plantations. Given these conditions, Kentucky masters often imagined themselves the picture of master-class paternalists, kind and indulgent masters of a devoted and orderly household.[32]

However, such paternalistic theory remained devilishly complex in actual practice. The conflict between masters' authority and slaves' determination to control as much as possible of their lives and labor was particularly intimate in the small-scale slaveries seen in Clark County. The knowledge about the lives of both slaves and owners in the household/workplace produced opportunities for enslaved people to win concessions as well as ample need for owners to exert—often violently—the authority they felt being constantly questioned, challenged, and undermined.[33] Unlike larger plantations where supervision of dozens of slaves in the fields and in the quarters was undertaken by only a handful of masters, overseers, and foremen, enslaved people in Kentucky were far more likely to be closely monitored and controlled in their daily lives. Dr. Martin would have been certain to keep close tabs on how his enslaved laborers fed, bedded, and cared for his prized pigs every day of the year. His meticulous farm journals suggest his constant involvement not only with his livestock, but also with the enslaved men who raised them. Josiah Jackson's nationwide reputation as an ironmaster was built on his close supervision of his foundry and forge hands lest the finicky art of coaxing quality iron out of imperfect ores go awry. Likewise, Charlotte Buckner's reputation as a lady—as well as her husband Aylett's reputation as a man—depended in no small part on ensuring that her enslaved house staff performed the domestic chores both meticulously and constantly.[34]

"The spatial implications of slavery in a small-town context," writes one scholar of places like Winchester, "involved critical issues of population control and discipline, privacy and communal intimacy, and opportunities for slave autonomy." The Buckner townhouse in which young Ben grew up in the 1840s was yet another permutation on the slaveries to be found throughout Clark County, but one that still reflected the ambiguities of slavery throughout the rest of the South. To the world, his father, Aylett, projected a vision of domestic harmony in which genders, races, and ages knew their place and worked together on terms of mutual accord and affection. Below the surface of that projection, though, complex networks of both dependence and tension simultaneously connected and divided all who lived under the roof. Although supposedly in command of his household, Aylett was in fact quite dependent on them to sustain the reputation of respectability and competence on which his career at the bar depended. That household "raised a man's children, tended his home, and maintained the artifacts (social activities, gardens, dress, household furnishings) that symbolized his family's gentility." In practice the hard-working mistress of an even harder-working and unwilling domestic labor force, Charlotte could never represent herself as such nor publically equate her managerial trials with those of the "serious" labor of, say, her father-in-law's management of the ropewalk. If she raised her voice at a cook or struck out at a housemaid, she shed the mask of feminine passivity, showing the very people she hoped to control the frailty of such theoretical roles.[35]

If what historians know of enslaved people throughout the South, in particular those performing domestic service, holds true for the four anonymous slaves within this household, ties of genuine affection for the Buckners and their children existed and at the same time conflicted with the slaves' own desires to have—at the very least—the freedom to work and socialize as they chose. Theirs would not be a social life of the slave quarter, but one of isolation and stolen interaction with other black people at night or on public holidays. They, too, shared the fears and uncertainties that lurked in the shadows of Aylett's law practice. Should he fail to keep up a steady and profitable business and the slaves were mortgaged for his debts, no court would take their wishes and preferences or their family and kinship networks into consideration. The auction block in front of the courthouse and the sight of coffles of slaves bound for Lexington and the southern market were constant reminders of that very real possibility for themselves or their loved ones. Sale away from the familiar world of Winchester was also an immediate threat if they decided to challenge the Buckners' authority on any given day. All of these intimate relationships and stark realities were lessons for young Ben Buckner as he grew up. He would need to master them all if he were one day to become master of himself and others.[36]

Not long after the Buckners returned to Winchester from Illinois, the ability of Aylett's law practice to sustain his family's small slaveholding, middle-class standard of living would be put to the test. The strength of the hemp economy in Clark County had ensured that the success of Benjamin Buckner's ropewalk could keep the family afloat if Aylett could not. By 1840, Benjamin had bought out Richard Hawes's interest in the ropewalk. But a sharp downturn in the markets hit Bluegrass hemp farmers very hard in the early years of the decade, and with production dropping in the face of the falling market prices, the ropewalk was starved for materials. It failed, and Benjamin was left to sell off his assets and slaves and move to Missouri, where land was less expensive. The depression also carried off the fortune of his younger brother, Samuel, who soon followed Benjamin westward. It was only through gifts and loans from the Bourbon County Buckners that the two were able to survive. One brother, William, who weathered the collapse better than Benjamin and Samuel, wrote that "notwithstanding the loss of fifteen thousand dollars within the last two years, I have still more than my full share of the goods and chattels of this world." Nevertheless, he recognized that things around him were not sound. "The people of no state in the Union have suffered more severely by what is generally termed hard times than the citizens of Ky.," he wrote. Perhaps as many as "fifty persons in this county, mostly farmers, many of them once considered rich, . . . are now entirely ruined, indeed destitute of everything. The sudden revolution in the price of our produce has ruined all who were in debt to any extent." Pork and corn had become devalued, and hemp, "the staple of our country," would now "not compensate those who raise it." Further complicating matters, because so many Bluegrass farmers were selling land and slaves to pay debts, the prices of both had plummeted as well, "in some instances not one-fiftieth part of the price of 4 years ago has been obtained."[37]

With such object lessons in both the fragility of the slave economy and the simultaneous necessity for slavery to validate and proclaim personal and professional success in mind, Ben reached the age when he outgrew the local schools in Clark County and attended the institution of higher learning in Kentucky best suited to prepare him to defend against the failures that had devastated his family. A decade after the financial collapse that had ruined his grandfather and great uncle, among many others, Ben enrolled in the Kentucky Military Institute (KMI) in Franklin County near the state capital of Frankfort. Unlike the bastions of wealth and tradition that military schools would become in the years of the late nineteenth century, antebellum academies were by and large founded by and for a growing class of small-slave-owning professionals such as Aylett and Ben. James Oakes has dubbed such men "probably the single most influential class in the antebellum South" for their ability to be elected to state and local political office "in staggeringly unrepresentative numbers by presenting themselves to southern voters as living testimony to the validity of the American dream of upward mobility." They saw military schools as the avenues to train their sons in the life skills necessary to maintain and improve the family's economic and social position in the growing republic.[38]

Chartered by state legislatures as an alternative to more expensive private institutions that served the sons of the planter elite, the state-funded military school had the primary advantage of being inexpensive enough that self-made professional men could send a son there for education and not lose the ability to consume as befit their own status. A term at KMI, for example, cost $160—only slightly more than the hire of a prime slave for the year—and included room, board, books, laundry, and medical care. Knowing his audience, the KMI superintendent took care to stress that the cadet uniform consisted of "plain and neat... Kentucky Jeans," which "will greatly reduce the expense of clothing." Such nods to frugality and the promotion of state manufacture complimented the Whiggish outlook of the middle-class men, Aylett Buckner included, who would send their sons to the school. Helping the cause even more was the inclusion of such Kentucky Whig luminaries as Henry Clay, John J. Crittenden, and John LaRue Helm on the Board of Visitors. KMI drew students from across the western states—both south of Kentucky and north of it—and was one of the few such military institutions to grant bachelor's degrees.[39]

As important as the degree, the habits of character demanded of the new men on whom the economic and political future of the United States rested would be developed at a school such as KMI. The cadets' military instruction, the superintendent stressed, "will not be permitted to interfere with the pupil's progress in study, but will rather take the place of his unprofitable, and often, vicious play." What truly mattered in these schools were the self-discipline, study skills, and practical leadership training that the military school environment fostered. According to a recent analysis, institutions such as KMI were perfectly tailored to the needs of the sons of middling farmers, lawyers, merchants, and doctors who attended them. The curriculum introduced the students into a life where they would likely be forced to work diligently at their chosen profession were they to succeed. The cadets' nominal training as junior officers prepared them for the social position and future expectations they would have as men. As officers, they would be expected to be commanders: leading men, making decisions independently, and receiving the deference of those of lower rank. In the social context of the antebellum South, of course, this was a training for mastery. However, military men were also expected to obey the orders of superiors, and as hypothetical lieutenants upon their graduation they would likely have little chance to exercise independent command. Finding the balance between these impulses was critical for their success both as military men and as middle-class men. Therefore, cadets "modified the hierarchy and honor that southern elites expounded to include" the middle-class "values of evangelicalism, self-discipline, [and] submission." They learned to balance "submission with the impulse of independence, claiming to assert autonomy by internalizing deference," and by doing so they "connected them[selves] to both southern and national middle-class trends."[40]

Ben Buckner did not stay at KMI long enough to receive a bachelor's degree. He left in 1852 at age sixteen and returned home to Winchester, his father no doubt hoping that although he had not taken a degree, he had absorbed the lessons in the "formation of regular habits" that the school promised. Ben took a position as a deputy to his father, the well-connected clerk of the Clark County Circuit Court, and, according to one source, "in his leisure hours he began" a yet more intensive "reading of law under the direction of his father" than their workday afforded. Perhaps some of his leisure hours, anyway, were so occupied. County seat towns such as Winchester were hubs of activity of all sorts—political, economic, social—and were particularly attractive to young people. Joining Ben and forming a peer group with him, as in similar towns across the South, were the "[t]eenaged sons of merchants and planters [who] worked as clerks, living in stores around the public square. Other young men boarded with town families as students and apprentices." There they lived semidependent lives, a stage where the young men both resisted their entrance to and were prepared to enter the social, political, and occupational world dominated by their fathers.[41]

The young clerk or student might one night face some trouble from the local police for getting into a bit too much liquor and serenading the young women of town—sometimes unwelcomed by the girls but almost always unwelcomed by their parents—but the next might see him "establishing masculine associations that mirrored the social and professional world of his father, an active Mason and devoted Whig," through participation in debating societies, militia drills, and, paradoxically enough, temperance societies. Under the watchful eye of elder Winchester citizens, Ben and his friends moved—it was hoped—from irresponsible and ungovernable boys into men of politics, of business, of character, and of mastery of both self and other. This cohort of young men, the sons of well-connected Clark Countians and the heirs presumptive to the county's future, were to be the social network on which a future law practice and political career could be built. Although KMI's lessons about navigating southern hierarchies and the study and work habits necessary to succeed were undeniably valuable, Winchester provided a more practical training. The connections Ben was making in the Circuit Court clerk's office during the day and the networks he was constructing as he socialized at night combined to prepare him for success in Clark County's present and future. It was with this peer group that he headed off to local balls at the National Hotel or to barbecues on summer afternoons out in the county, taking the first steps into the world of courtship.[42]

It was at one of those social functions around 1855 that Ben met Helen Bullitt Martin, the youngest daughter of Clark County's agricultural don. There must have been some spark between the two—certainly not yet strong enough that he was generally acknowledged her beau, but enough for him to feel bold—for when Ben left Winchester in 1856 to attend law lectures at the University of Louisville, he took it upon himself to write to the girl whom many acknowledged to be one of the most eligible in the county. Not only was Helen beautiful, but her family's wealth and extensive connections within the county would improve the prospects of any young man who should be so lucky as to marry her, no matter his own name. It is highly likely, too, that Dr. Martin had imparted precisely this perspective to his youngest daughter. Worse for Ben's hopes, his departure for Louisville for the beginning of the fall term in 1856 coincided with the elevation of Helen's standing within Clark County's pool of marriageable young women. The social event of the season saw the reigning queen, Betty Lewis, married and off to live with her new husband in Philadelphia, prompting Ben to inquire of Helen if she had officially "yet Commenced your reign as belle of Clark?"[43]

Ben's time in Louisville was to cap off his legal training before he stood for his bar examination. Outside of the strict regulations of the military academy, which had been his first taste of college life, and beyond his father's watchful eye in the clerk's office, Ben seems to have been more concerned with making Helen jealous of his social life in the city than he was with his Blackstone.[44] "I came to the city on Saturday week last," he wrote her in October, "and have formed a great many acquaintances, a few of them exceeding agreeable ones, and among the latter number, Some of the prettiest ladies I ever saw, and indeed the most brilliant array of beauty I ever beheld was assembled . . . on Friday evening last." He teased her with the latest rumors being spread around Louisville that Helen was soon to be married. Ben told one such gossip that Helen "denied the truth of the report, but she replied that was a matter ladies never told the truth about, and expected it would come off shortly." Perhaps, given this tone, it is little surprise that his request to correspond with Helen was promptly rejected. "I had hoped," he wrote, "to receive great pleasure from reading your letters, was I so fortunate as to receive any; but as I am entirely unacquainted with the reasons that induce your determination"—disingenuous at best—"I must with this expression of my regrets, bow a silent acquiescence." Repentant, he made his intentions and affections plain enough. "I am fearful that all the Clark girls will marry off while I am in Louisville," he wrote with one girl in particular in mind, "and although I would regret such an occurance because it would interfere with some arrangements I might desire to make, still I think that if I should be lucky enough to get an invitation to the wedding, that I will not be wholly inconsolable."[45]

With the courting clock ticking back at home, Buckner returned from Louisville at the close of the academic year. He passed his examination and was admitted to the bar in 1857, allowing him to begin setting up a practice and courting Helen Martin in earnest. It was a tough period for Ben on both counts. Aylett could have told Ben of the difficulties young lawyers faced from his own firsthand experience, and in the interests of establishing a reputation and a clientele, the younger Buckner was often occupied on legal errands to neighboring Powell, Montgomery, and Estill Counties for his clients. They were not the locations he desired, but business was business. Trips to those counties took him across the eastern borders of Clark County, through sections seen by one Winchester resident as "broken and rough" and "a fitting habitat for the natives, a lot of ignorant, unkempt people, living in log cabins and cultivating little pieces of ground." Cases in the opposite direction, toward Lexington and Paris, would have been more lucrative in those wealthier county seats and, importantly, would have taken Buckner out by Dr. Martin's farm on the main turnpike route to Fayette County. But such work had long been in the hands of better-established lawyers in Clark, and so the aspiring Bluegrass lawyer cut his teeth in the courtrooms of mountain foothill counties. Although his practice in the east earned his keep, it likely did not improve his stock with Helen. Undeterred by her rebuff while he was away in Louisville, Buckner continued to ply his affections at barbecues and dances, as he would later remind her, "without return for two or three years." By the summer of 1859, things had become serious between the two again, but as Winchester picked up on the growing affection, questions about the suitability of the match began to circulate. Both Helen's parents, in particular her mother but Dr. Martin as well, and many of her friends—in particular her best friend, Sallie Moore—objected to Ben as a suitable husband.[46]

A rejection of Buckner's affections could hurt far more than his heart, a fact of which he was all too aware. As they entered adulthood, writes historian Lori Glover, "Southern sons understood that marriage and leadership of an independent household were crucial for full affirmation of their manhood." Assuming the head of the household "gave a husband experience with consensual governance and made him politically relevant." Especially at this early, precarious stage of Buckner's career, a single misstep in courtship could ruin his reputation and future prospects in Winchester. The ritualized pattern of courtship into which Ben and Helen's interactions quickly fell only enhanced the dangers Buckner faced in the situation. "Practicality and ritual combined to encourage women to delay marriage as long as men would tolerate," writes Glover. Women such as Helen "understood that their greatest influence in romantic affairs came during courtship: marriage meant subordination to patriarchal demands. And since so much of a wife's identity and status hung on her husband, wise girls made judicious, considered choices." Although a practical period of examination suited the interests of Helen and the Martins, it was agony for Ben. "Required to repeatedly declare their love to circumspect women, [young men] ran the risk of rejection and public humiliation if they misinterpreted a response." During courtship especially, women "exercised significant sway over their suitors' reputations. Young men rightly feared losing their social status as well as the object of their affections." Even after Ben proposed, he feared "that when assailed through your love for your parents, & plied with all the arguments, that a fond & dearly beloved mother can use, you would yield in your love for me," and he was convinced that even after Helen had consented to marry him, her love for him "could not stand against the amount of parental opposition."[47]

Such opposition to and skepticism about Buckner were logical for the Martins. Dr. Martin was well aware that an ambitious young professional would see the value in his family name, lands, slaveholdings, and reputation as an agriculturalist and businessman. Family pride aside, the future prospects of this man to whom the Martins' youngest daughter would be attached for life had to be fully evaluated before any binding step be taken. The Martins eventually consented to the engagement in the summer of 1859 but insisted that it be a lengthy one, prolonging the examination of this young Buckner. In the first letter Ben wrote to Helen after they were officially engaged, he protested "the time fixed by you" for the "Consummation" of their engagement. "Now dont you think that you can reconsider your determination, and bring it down from twelve to six months[?] You know dearest that if I thought you had a good reason I would cheerfully wait five years if necessary," he wrote with something less than candor, but "[t]here is no particular purpose to be accomplished by waiting longer." Somehow he knew Helen and the Martins would respectfully disagree.

Finding Helen and her family the debating equals of any fellow member of the bar, Ben even went on a flattering offensive that praised Helen personally as the domestic paragon he sought in a wife. He was convinced, he said, that he would "behave well if we were married and I was brought under your more immediate influence than I would situated as at present. Indeed the influence that you have already exerted over me (unconsciously perhaps) is wonderful even to myself &... it would be my only aim to make our life a happy one." Perhaps the most revealing confession came in a letter just a few weeks later.

> I have surveyed the whole past connected with my history, I have seen how as a joyous unsophisticated boy, I sent into the world, & soon my

impressible nature, received the stamp of the calousness, the indifference & the selfishness which I had often told you characterized the world.... I soon became indifferent to all the world, selfish to all but my immediate friends (& they woeful few) desirous of rapidly making money that I might as rapidly make it contribute to my pleasures. Happily I met & know you, I soon came to esteem you, & thought you above, infinitely above the balance of your sex—of whom I thought (I'll confess it to you for you wont tell any body) that they were "weary stale flat & unprofitable" I respected none of them & at twenty one I was at heart a cynic of 45 or 50. But now thanks to you sweet girl, I have found the only true Eldorado the fountains in to which I have plunged & rejuvenated my withered heart & healed my decaying affections—love, love of a true, pure & *womanly* woman. I feel young again, I take pleasure again in the delights of society, & towards all the world I feel kindly. And you have done all this for sure.[48]

Ben was in fact doing quite a bit more in these early engagement letters than praising Helen as the epitome of the "*womanly* woman." He began to steer their discourse away from the suitor-sought relationship in which Helen held all the cards toward a domestic husband–wife paradigm that would define their relationship after they were married. Securing an engagement emboldened many young men at this stage in their courtship, according to Glover, helping them transform "from nervous boys into commanding patriarchs." "As boys won girls," she writes, "they cast off the epistolary rhetoric about their powerlessness and devotion, and began to write the reality of their power as white men." A month after they were engaged, Ben finally consented to Helen's demands for a long engagement. Sensing a victory on the horizon, though, he began to stake claim to his eventual power as her husband. "The world speaks of a woman as the creature of man, as his inferior in firmness & in decision, now in the present instance who has yielded? I'll have my revenge when we get married. I'll be as great a tyrant as you ever saw, & then somebody will wish they had not been so hard to coax into the measures," he wrote, concealing a lecture behind his jest. Referencing her friends' disapproval of him later on in the same letter, he drove the point further home. "And you mustn't be ashamed of your sweetheart anymore unless it is for being such a ninny as to let a little bit of woman like you lead him by the nose wherever she wants to. But you needn't think Miss, because I gave up this once, that I am going to do so all the time & let you have your way about every thing: I intend to assert my independence some of these times for I'm not going to submit to tyranny from a woman, & from a woman that says she is afraid of me too."[49]

The engagement went much longer than Buckner ever anticipated when issuing such threats. Two years on from that summer of 1859, his trial before the Martin family and Helen's friends in town continued. He tried to console himself with the thought that as she obeyed her parents' wishes to delay their marriage, she both proved her love for him and demonstrated traits that he particularly sought in a wife. "That a girl raised as you have been should love her parents and feel a deep desire to please them in every respect & especially in the important items of the choice of a Companion for life is most natural," he wrote in the spring of 1861. He could hope that "conforming her conduct in all respects to the wishes of her parents" suggested that she would do the same in the face of his husbandly authority once they were married. Ben was convinced more than ever of Helen's love for him, "& that your heart is so full of the principle of truth & honesty that you could never consent while you still lived to give me up." Nevertheless, it was "unpleasant & somewhat mortifying to me to feel that I do not command the respect of your friends." Mulling over this awkward state of affairs, Buckner reconfirmed his love for her and restated his case for disproving the observers' analysis of his character and business prospects. Noting his embryonic legal practice as a primary objection against him, he confessed that "I have but little to offer you in fact nothing by way of inducement for you," and much as he might try at present, the "devotions of my whole nature & the workings of my whole heart can in no wise *compensate* you for the sacrifice you are about to make." He reiterated that "I do not offer to do any thing to *pay* you for such devotion to me" and felt "satisfied that I must remain your debtor to the last day of my life." He promised her, however, that "while truth & honor maintain their supremacy in my nature so long will I devote my every exertion toward the pleasing task of contributing to your happiness" emotional and material.[50]

Fortunately for Buckner, events well under way by the spring of 1861 would give him an opportunity to prove his commitment to truth and honor while simultaneously winning fame and glory, solidifying his reputation as a man and a citizen, laying a foundation upon which he could build a political career, and silencing Winchester's skeptics about the genuineness of his abandonment of youthful pride. As the nation tore itself apart and war loomed, Buckner saw that he must act quickly and take as conspicuous a role in the coming conflict as possible. Winning his sweetheart in the ballrooms and parlors of Clark County had proved difficult, so he sought the battlefield.

The gulf of experience that stood between Ben's and Helen's families had, rather predictably, stood between them in their courtship. Dr. and Mrs. Martin were all too aware of the history of the Buckner family in Winchester, and although Ben could claim an old name, some useful family connections in the Bluegrass, and a certain respect at the local bar—accumulated in part on his own and in part by his father—that was not much to offer the daughter of one of the best-connected men in the region. Beautiful, wealthy, and sociable, Helen could have her pick of the lordlings of the pasture. Dr. Martin was an agricultural visionary, with local and national connections and a diverse operation that spread risk—and his slaves—across numerous projects. With his willingness to look beyond the field for ways to make slavery profitable—much as Ben's grandfather had tried to do but had never quite succeeded—the old doctor was at the cutting edge of slavery's future in Kentucky. Though Ben would in all likelihood never take over the hog- and cattle-breeding operations, a marriage to Helen could net him the legal casework required by Dr. Martin and his wide network of associates in the more profitable inner-Bluegrass counties west of Clark. Buckner was marrying into the future of slavery—if he could defend it.

2

Firstborn of the Union

In Smithland in the winter of 1861–1862, Buckner's mood matched the gray, rainy weather. With the disturbing realities of war all around him, there was no escaping the misery of that January cold. Buckner and the Twentieth were constantly out on patrol, moving through the countryside, searching for rebel cavalry sent out from Leonidas Polk's Confederate garrison in Columbus or the informal bands of secesh who drove their loyal neighbors out of their homes and sent them fleeing to the safety of Smithland. Tramping out at all hours of the day and night on these ever-fruitless errands through the creeks and lowlands of Livingston and Lyon Counties left Major Buckner and his soldiers exhausted, damp, and sick. One sortie was just like the rest, and the sleepless nights and shivering days all began to blur in a haze. Buckner would move out with three companies after a reported detachment of three or four hundred Confederate cavalry who were out foraging, scavenging, and recruiting. After hours of feeling their way down dark roads and through muddy thickets, they would find nothing save an inevitable, impenetrable swamp, which would delay their return until well after dark. The only result was that one or two of Buckner's men would catch their death from the damp, cold air.

As the month wore on, Buckner was reluctantly drawn into the boiling local conflict that had led many of the loyal Jackson Purchase men—refugees whose homes, farms, and slaves had been burned, ravaged, and pressed into rebel service—into the ranks of the Twentieth. Coming to Smithland with half a regiment, Buckner and the other field officers were promised recruits there. They found enough to fill out the regiment's compliment, but the war these Purchase men had known over the past few months was decidedly different from the glorious autumn of parades and speeches Buckner had known in the Bluegrass.

Leading excursions through the western Kentucky men's home neighborhoods, Buckner was continually pestered by "each officer and a large proportion of the men" to detour the column "to avenge some insult or wrong that their friends have suffered at the hands of the Secesh." With houses burned, livestock slaughtered, and slaves confiscated, the men had good reasons to seek retribution, but Buckner would have none of it. The nature of his loyalty to the Union cause—a loyalty to the rule of law and social propriety—made him balk. Even, or perhaps especially, in the face of Confederate outrages against slaves and other property of loyal men, Buckner would prove the moral and legal power of the Constitution that the rebellion sought to destroy. "We feel that we are responsible to the Country & to a higher power than that which controls the movements of armies for the good behavior of the troops under our Command," Buckner wrote to justify himself. "We," the Bluegrass gentlemen in command of the unit, "are resolved that our regiment shall not degenerate into a band of reckless marauderz."[1]

More than that, though, Buckner was personally resolved that his unit should be the model of the free discourse of the American republic at work, though others misread his intentions. Judge-turned-colonel Thomas E. Bramlette scoffed at Buckner and some other Bluegrass officers, whom he thought nothing more than "kid-gloved gentry, who pretend to be Union men." So it may have appeared to future governor Bramlette, who would later pursue a hard political line against both the rebellion and the Lincoln administration, but Buckner and the other "kid-gloved gentry" were playing a more subtle game. "They all say here that I am too lenient . . . in my dealing's with those who sympathize with the rebels," he confessed, "but I am fortified by the conviction that I have no authority to punish people for their opinions." After all, as a southerner and a slave owner, he shared with his secessionist foes many fears about the power and intentions of the Republican Party even if he disagreed with them about their chosen mode of protest. Admittedly, "[p]erhaps also the fact that my little sweet heart is of that political stripe" made him "more lenient than I would otherwise be," but on another level Buckner hoped to show secessionists that they had nothing to fear from the federal government, that they would be treated fairly by its military, and that they could safely return to the national family.[2]

Buckner hoped to prove to the local secessionists the fundamental belief that underlay his support for the old flag: the Union and the Constitution were better protectors of slave property than the upstart Confederacy. Whereas the rebels outright stole the slaves of loyal men and pressed the slaves of secessionist Kentuckians to build the earthworks at Forts Henry and Donelson, Buckner strove to embody the law, order, and dignity of the slaveholding republic they served. Buckner was particularly proud of one of his recent exploits, which had, he hoped, sent precisely this message. When a rebel-sympathizing citizen came to complain to Major Buckner that a soldier had taken the man's horse, Buckner "at once ordered the soldier to be arrested & tied hand & foot and put in the guard house on bread & water for forty eight hours," disregarding the soldier's pleas of innocence or at least inculpability "on the ground that the man was a 'damned Secesh.'"[3]

Reinforcing his broader political point with one directed to Helen herself, Ben asked why she had felt the need to apologize for "talking 'Secesh' talk to me" when he was at home. "Dont you know," he rhetorically asked, invoking his cherished model of the benevolent paternalistic household head, "that I allow you and would not prevent if I could the fullest latitude of opinion upon every subject?" Though he regretted, of course, "that we cant think alike upon this subject," he assured her that "I have never & will never desire to do your thinking, deeming you entirely competent to do so for yourself & besides, I have not the right to control you upon that subject if I had the desire." The same latitude for dissent protected within the bounds of the constitutional republic, he implicitly claimed, would be afforded Helen in the future Buckner household. Like the American house divided that Buckner sought to restore through his stern yet gracious command in Smithland, so long as Helen ultimately submitted to the authority vested in Ben as the husband, he had no more room to quash her voice than he had to arbitrarily confiscate the property of the "'damned Secesh.'" There would be no doubt, though, of his (or U.S.) authority. That power was the foundation of the nation and the household. "You know you some times jestingly threaten me that you will trade me off for some other sweetheart," he wrote playfully, "& though I dont believe you will do it sure enough, it still is well enough to keep on the good side of you and not exercise the authority in advance that I mean to when we get married. You know my sentiments upon the subject of wife management too well to make it necessary to elaborate."[4]

Buckner was horrified to see what neighbors, fellow southerners, and fellow slave owners had done to one another—not to mention to the law and its sacred protection of property rights—when they believed their beloved institution of slavery was under threat. The incivility of the war he found in Smithland was stunning. Yet although he was appalled at the civil war between slave owners that he saw in the Jackson Purchase and did his futile best to prevent its escalation, he could not have been surprised to see the restraints of law, order, and civility collapse when slavery was at issue. Buckner had been born in the middle of just such a war, a long-simmering border war that preceded this military conflict in which he now found himself. He himself could not remember that far back, of course, but his father, Aylett, did. That experience must have shaped the family's thoughts when the secession crisis confronted them.

A generation before the outbreak of war, a young Aylett Buckner had traveled north to the Illinois frontier, frustrated with his lack of practice at the crowded bar in central Kentucky and hoping to carve out a more promising career for himself in Jacksonville. He unwittingly rode right into the front lines of a decade of divisive conflict over slavery.

In the wake of the Blackhawk War, the early 1830s were a period of rapid growth for the area just southwest of Springfield. A state census of 1825 showed only about four thousand residents in Morgan County, but a decade later the county population was estimated at twenty-five thousand. Such explosive numbers suggest that an unregulated wave of humanity had descended on the plains of central Illinois, but in reality there were patterns to the migration. Aylett went to Jacksonville not as an opportunistic individualist but as part of a group who sought their fortunes together. Bringing known connections from home made decidedly more sense than hoping to form them once he ended up out west. Folks from home provided companionship, obviously, but also a preestablished clientele for his legal services, a potential voting block if he should ever decide to stand for county office, and a pool of daughters, cousins, and sisters from which he might find a wife whose family, religious beliefs, customs, recipes, and domestic expectations would be more likely to match his own. All of this Aylett found with a group including his friend Newton Forsythe, an "active businessman" whose family lived on Stoner Creek, which ran through both Bourbon and Clark Counties. Newton's younger sister, Charlotte, accompanied him to Illinois, and it was not long before she and Aylett married in 1833.[5]

Three years later, on August 19, 1836, the couple had their first son and named him Benjamin Forsythe Buckner, honoring both of his grandfathers, Benjamin Buckner and Benjamin Forsythe. Yet although the young lawyer's family was growing, Aylett's practice did not seem to be keeping pace. He was only one of dozens of young lawyers scrambling for a place in the new county, and he was finding out that success in the West required far more than skill in the courtroom.

Jacksonville was torn by cultural and ideological conflict, which divided the city's population more deeply than the robust partisan politics of the Bluegrass in which Aylett had grown up. Indeed, the fundamental problem with Jacksonville was that not all of the town's new residents had grown up in the same place with the same institutions and values. "Jacksonville early became and long continued" to be "a storm center for the antagonisms" that swirled around the institution of slavery; the town, in the words of one of its historians, "became a veritable melting pot for conflicting social, religious, and political ideas" from across the country. One of Aylett's fellow Kentuckians recorded the divisions he found on his arrival. There were "two classes in society. Those from the North and East were called 'Yankees' and those from the South and West 'White people.'" As suggested, the new residents of Jacksonville came largely from two geographical areas: the Northeast, in particular Connecticut, and the upper South, especially Kentucky and Tennessee. Interestingly, it was the "White people" who established the first antislavery society in Morgan County. The Morgonian Society, established just after a proposed constitutional convention to legalize slavery in the state had been defeated in 1824, sought to promote "political knowledge and the maintenance of the inalienable rights of Man," in a familiar tone of early-republic moderate antislavery speech. The Morgonians registered their opposition to slavery's unequal distribution of wealth and power to elite whites rather than any especial concern for the "rights of Man" as they might pertain to enslaved African Americans. Historian Don Doyle suggests that although the society sought to block the spread of slavery into their new state, the Morgonians "fiercely oppose[d] the movement to abolish slavery in the South, in part because it threatened racial homogeneity in Illinois."[6]

By the time Aylett Buckner arrived from Winchester, however, the leadership and nature of the antislavery movement in Jacksonville had changed remarkably. The "Yankees" in the town were so labeled with good reason; they formed around a core known as the "Yale Band," a group of educational missionaries seeking to bring the enlightenment of their alma mater in New Haven to the West by founding and staffing Jacksonville's Illinois College. Their drive for societal perfection and their religious affiliation with the Congregationalist church—soon to be known about town with good reason as the "Abolition Church"—led them to establish and support Jacksonville branches of the American Tract Society, the American Temperance

Society, the American Educational Society, and the American Colonization Society. Two subscriptions to William Lloyd Garrison's periodical the *Liberator* came to students at Illinois College, whose president's very name, Edward Beecher, conveyed the influence and ideology of his famous father. Together, the Congregationalist meeting house and the college building were immediately "recognized by the proslavery element as enemies and were counted abolitionist engines." Aylett Buckner, not surprisingly, steered well wide of the Yale Band; rejecting New England theology and social practice, he was a founding vestryman in Trinity Episcopal Church.[7]

By the mid-1830s, the "Yankees" were not the only northeastern transplants causing discord in Jacksonville. The Presbyterian reverend Elijah Lovejoy, who lived first in nearby St. Louis and then even closer in Alton, Illinois, became a valuable ally of the Yale Band. In the fall of 1837, with young Ben Buckner just a little more than a year old, Illinois College president Edward Beecher, Connecticut-born Jacksonville lawyer Elihu Wolcott, and others traveled to Alton for the inaugural meeting of the Illinois Anti-Slavery Society. Beecher produced a declaration of sentiments that became the preamble for the society's constitution and offered a series of lectures on the evils of slavery, and Wolcott was elected the society's first president.[8] The convention inflamed a proslavery crowd in Alton, which had already destroyed Lovejoy's printing press. The meeting was broken up at least once, and just a few weeks later Lovejoy lay dead at the hands of a mob consisting largely of the "White people" of Alton. The Lovejoy murder sent the tensions between the northern- and southern-born populations of Jacksonville to boiling over. Beecher, the faculty, and most of the student body of Illinois College were incensed at the murder and held a public protest. One student, Billy Herndon, addressed a meeting with a rousing speech vilifying slavery and the murder of Lovejoy. His Kentucky father disowned him for the act and blamed the college for poisoning the young man with abolitionist ideas. The threats were more than just familial; the younger Herndon recalled that the college meetings were attended "by certain men of ruffianly habits and pro-slavery prejudices who wished to act as self-constituted guardians of the moral and social proprieties of the occasion," certainly a menacing presence in the wake of what had just occurred in Alton.[9]

The proslavery southerners in Jacksonville had far more to guard than "moral and social proprieties" of white supremacy, however. Some had actual slave property with them in Illinois. Before the destruction of Lovejoy's press, his newspaper, the *Alton Observer,* carried a report that several hundred people were being held in slavery in southwestern Illinois. One survey has found at least 746 people enslaved in the state in 1830. The precise number, of course, is impossible to determine accurately, but two certainly lived in Jacksonville and were doubtless well known to the Buckner family. In 1836, Elizabeth Hardin Clay—the mother of Aylett Buckner's close friend and business associate John J. Hardin and the wife of Henry Clay's brother, Porter—brought two enslaved domestic servants, brother and sister Robert and Emily Logan, to work at the Clays' new house on State Street. The two were apparently promised that they would be freed if they would serve the Clays for four years. Two years into the bargain, in 1838, however, the Logans sought the freedom to which their residence in Illinois entitled them and escaped to the home of Lovejoy's colleague, Elihu Wolcott. A search party of "White people" pursued and captured Robert. The men quickly bound him and packed him off via carriage into a steamboat at St. Louis and thence back to slavery in the South. He was never heard from again. The white Kentuckians did not, however, find Emily, who sued for her freedom and eventually won it in 1840—with legal fees paid by collections taken in Wolcott's Congregationalist church. Two of the posse, including John Hardin's brother, were indicted for kidnapping, though neither was convicted.[10]

The conflict over slavery in Morgan County produced disastrous results for Aylett Buckner's career. There had always been competition at the bar in Jacksonville, but the politics of slavery tipped the balance against him. On his arrival, he found himself in competition with many young and aspiring professionals like himself, but none was more successful at the Morgan County bar than a young Stephen A. Douglas. Buckner and Douglas were bitter political enemies as well as competitors in the courtroom. Douglas's meteoric political career was launched when he was sent to the state legislature by the county's enthusiastic voters in 1836. Two years later, when Douglas sought to advance himself through election to the U.S. Congress, Buckner and his friend John Hardin—who at the same time was embroiled in the scandal surrounding the illegal enslavement of Robert and Emily Logan—took over the editorship of a newspaper, the *Illinoisan*, to back the Whig candidate. The Kentuckians were apparently successful. Douglas was defeated in a close race, and the competing Democratic paper, the *Jacksonville Standard*, promptly folded.[11]

Yet as Aylett Buckner took his very public stand in the pages of the *Illinoisan* against Douglas and his emerging Democratic constituency in Morgan County, he may have simultaneously doomed his chances for advancement in Jacksonville. At the outset, he certainly would have thought otherwise, for as a general rule young lawyers were keen "to favorable opportunities for obtaining popular notice" in the local press. But whereas Aylett's Whiggish politics had been born out of the Bluegrass soil of Clark County—the politics of his father and of Henry Clay—the majority of Aylett's fellow southerners who had come to seek their fortunes in Jacksonville gravitated to the party of General Jackson and the "Little Giant." Aylett found a fellow southern Whig in his editorial partner, but the majority of the Whigs in Jacksonville were Yale Band New Englanders. The "Yankee"-dominated Whig Party in Morgan County had little use for the southern Whig Aylett Buckner, particularly after having it so publically demonstrated that slavery was alive and well at the home of Henry Clay's very own brother. Despite the Whig Party's success against Douglas in 1838, its antislavery and free-soil wings held all the cards in the wake of the Logan slave scandal. Just before the Mexican War, even John Hardin publicly pronounced "slavery the greatest curse which has been inflicted on our land," though whether that view indicated Whig free-soilism or moderate, Henry Clay–style opposition to President James K. Polk's expansionist designs is difficult to tell. Regardless, such statements became the bare minimum for maintaining Whig electoral support in Morgan County. But Aylett refused to give an inch of his uncompromising proslavery Whiggery and thereby cut himself out of the Morgan County party entirely. Left with little hope of being advanced for elected office—or hope of the honor, reputation, confirmation of his success, and perhaps an increase in his casework that such advancement would bring—by a county convention of Yale Band Whigs, Aylett Buckner had plenty of reason to move his family back to the familiar social and ideological world of Winchester.[12]

Thus, though young Ben Buckner was born in the nominally free state of Illinois, he lived with slavery as a daily reality. Moving back to the family home in Winchester would not have been a terribly disconcerting experience, at least in that regard. Slavery had existed in Jacksonville not as an abstract concept for discussion in parlors or debate in the societies of Illinois College, but as a real institution among the southern families with whom the Buckners lived, socialized, and conducted business. Slavery was immediate, slavery was personal, slavery was alive. Though Ben could not have remembered the Logans taking hats and gloves or serving at the table when his parents went to call on the Clay family, the fact remains that enslaved black people formed a part of his world from the very beginning. Slavery was as alive among the southern "White people" of Jacksonville as it had been in their upper South homes. Just as alive, too—in the words and actions of both the enslaved Logans and the white Wolcotts—were the threats to slavery that seemed to spring forth, one after the other, during the 1830s.

Although Aylett Buckner's years in Jacksonville might have seemed a disaster at the time, they gave him and his sons some important perspective when war faced them in 1861. The Buckners had learned just how real the threats to slavery were. Whether in Jacksonville itself or even back home in Clark County when they returned, Aylett could look back and draw important lessons from the first decade of his eldest son's life. The enslaved workers at the Buckner family ropewalk in Winchester and an African American preacher owned by Helen's father, Dr. Martin, were at the center of an 1835 panicked crackdown by Clark County masters. With Garrisonian abolitionism arriving in central Kentucky via James Birney's Kentucky Abolition Society, Nat Turner's revolt and the subsequent debate over slavery in the old mother state of Virginia, and a marked uptick in fugitive slave escapes across the Ohio, some of Ben Buckner's earliest lessons about slavery taught him its fragility.[13]

The decade, too, ended with a lesson about the power of politics to defend slavery in Kentucky when escalating violence and saber-rattling rhetoric had only inflamed the tense situation. With a border war surrounding the white Kentuckians and insurrectionary fears in their midst, society seemed on the brink of destruction to them, needing only a spark to explode into a nightmare of civil war and servile insurrection. Ben's uncle and Winchester native James Clark was critical to calming masters' frayed nerves and shoring up what must have seemed to be the eroding foundations of slavery and respectable society in the commonwealth.[14] His 1837 call for more robust penalties against those who assisted runaways was matched in the legislature by a law targeting stagecoach drivers who offered their services to fugitives on their way north. Later, after an Ohio abolitionist minister was arrested by a posse of Mason County men who accused him of assisting escape attempts in the Ohio River town of Maysville, Clark sent a commission of Kentucky lawmakers to Ohio. There, the legislative mission successfully secured a particularly strong fugitive slave law that removed many procedural barriers that delayed slave catchers as they moved northward in search of fugitives and imposed severe penalties on anyone who enticed slaves away from bondage in Kentucky, assisted them on their way north, or interfered with pursuing owners or their agents.

The conciliations lowered the Kentucky masters' rising temperatures and were celebrated as a patriotic triumph. In language that many Kentuckians would have shared, an Ohio paper hailed the move as a triumph for "the *friends of the Union* against the *separatists!*" and the *Maysville Eagle* was relieved that the issue "of heart-burning and discord" had been resolved through calm political action that assured peace "between the two commonwealths." The new law, in fact, gained Kentucky slave owners less than they first anticipated, however, and it was found inherently unconstitutional in 1842 when the U.S. Supreme Court ruled in *Prigg v. Pennsylvania* that states could not create fugitive slave statutes among themselves but must rely on the federal government to do so. The law's failure, though, did not seem to concern white Kentuckians overmuch. The implicit apology to Kentucky masters from the Ohioans seems to have satisfied the disgruntled owners even if any further protections did not materialize.[15]

Just as James Clark's negotiations with Ohio signaled a new hope for the peaceful exercise of slave owners' rights within the Union, a new state constitution seemed to herald a string of proslavery gains ten years later. Energized to defeat an emancipationist minority that had tried—and largely failed—to make a strong showing in the election of delegates to the constitutional convention, Bourbon County's Garrett Davis, related by marriage to Charlotte Buckner's Forsythe clan, was one of the leading spokesmen for strengthening masters' rights within the state. Davis inserted an amendment to the state bill of rights establishing that "the right of property is before and higher than any constitutional sanction; and the right of the owner of a slave to such slave, and its increase, is the same, and as inviolable as the right of the owner, of any property whatever." Proslavery delegates were delighted. On the floor of the debate, one representative argued that slavery had formed "the most enlightened, the richest, and the most cultivated people upon the face of God Almighty's earth." "Slavery," he continued, "is not an evil, and I rather want more of it." They got it. The new constitution, with the rights of slave owners protected above all others, established Kentucky as a securely proslavery state, leading many commentators to give up any remaining hope that slavery would erode within the Bluegrass. Abraham Lincoln, who had been in the state during some of the convention, concluded that the new constitution "extinguishes" any faith in Kentucky emancipation "utterly"; there could be now, he wrote, "no peaceful extinction of slavery in prospect for us." If Garrett Davis could be proud of his new ironclad proslavery constitutional creation, Aylett Buckner was likewise proud of the name he had given to his youngest son, Garrett Davis Buckner.[16]

Soon enough, too, Henry Clay's lasting legacy as the great compromiser was secured when his legislative package to resolve the 1850 crisis included a much stronger fugitive slave law that went even further than the one that Clark's administration had negotiated with Ohio. By the end of that decade, the *Dred Scott* decision would change the rules of the federal game, tilting them in favor of slave owners' rights in much the same way as Garrett Davis's move guaranteed slave property a permanently protected status within Kentucky. Chief Justice Roger Taney's decision in 1857 expanded the national government's theoretical powers to enforce the property rights of its citizens in such a way that it "transformed a state sovereignty protected by the Tenth Amendment into a doctrine of national proslavery power to determine the future course of the western territories," according to historian Don Fehrenbacher. This was the culmination of decades of victories for southern politicians jealous of their rights and fearful of losing an ounce of control over their institution or their bondspeople. "Whatever it might be as a federal union of sovereign states," concludes Fehrenbacher, "the antebellum United States, as a sovereignty itself, was a slaveholding republic. That was the impression given by the national capital. That was the image presented in diplomacy to the rest of the world. And that had become the law of the land by edict of the Supreme Court." "'The right of property in a slave is distinctly and expressly affirmed in the Constitution,' Chief Justice Taney had declared in 1857," echoing Davis's contribution to the Kentucky bill of rights. "The federal government therefore had no power over the institution except 'the power coupled with the duty of guarding and protecting the owner in his rights.'" By the 1860 presidential election, then, "the slaveholding interest, which had long kept a potentially dangerous federal government in check by means of a strict states-rights interpretation of the Constitution, came to rely on a nationalist understanding in its hour of greatest challenge."[17]

The symbiotic relationship between the institution of slavery and the American state was nothing new. "The continuing presence of slavery in the Southern states did not affect the development of only one side of that house," historian David F. Ericson writes. "It affected the development of both sides, as well as of the house itself." Beyond even its official policy dictates, the federal government's proslavery policies had enabled much of the market-based prosperity that had made slavery a profitable and sustainable institution in Kentucky. "The federal government created more secure and stable slave markets by removing Native Americans, deterring slave revolts, and recovering fugitive slaves," states Ericson. "It created more profitable and national slave markets by enacting a ban on slave imports and by not enacting a ban on the interstate slave trade. It even entered the market by renting slave labor."[18]

In 1861, Ben Buckner's belief in the positive capacity of the Congress and the courts to uphold and even extend slavery's hold in the nation was based on a long history of compromises and new evidence—most particularly the 1850 Fugitive Slave Law, "the most unequivocal congressional response to [slaveholders'] demands," and the *Dred Scott* decision, that slavery could—and perhaps must—not only be defended but be expanded through the power of the federal government. Lincoln had famously predicted that the house could not remain divided much longer; looking back now, we do not give enough credit to the belief that slavery might have won that half-slave/half-free struggle.[19]

What so disturbed Buckner about the war he saw in and around Smithland was that rebel masters in the Jackson Purchase and across the South, in focusing so much on what they might lose, had forgotten everything they already possessed. Worse, in their fear they had turned on their neighbors, kin, and fellow masters in a vicious guerilla war. They had sown division when the South needed unity. As the Buckners and hundreds of other border slave-owning families could attest, slavery faced very real dangers from without—in the form of northern abolitionists and antislavery men, now more powerfully unified, organized, and institutionalized in the Republican Party than ever before—and very real dangers from within—from enslaved African Americans, who all masters, though they tried to tell themselves otherwise, knew resisted slavery in myriad ways in every household and every farm every day. In the face of these threats, why would Kentucky masters or the states of the slaveholding South generally turn on one another and turn on the law and power of the federal government, which had set the political context in which slavery had flourished for nearly a century?

Kentuckians such as the Buckners knew the dangers to slavery that lurked across the Ohio; they believed that they knew them more personally than cotton planters secured hundreds of miles away from the free states. Kentucky slaves sought freedom across the river. Kentucky masters worried about abolitionist-engineered mass escapes or revolts. Kentucky families had cousins living among the antislavery radicals in the Northwest. And because of all this, when slavery faced its greatest threat to date with the Republican victory in 1860, they were not about to rid themselves of the Union and the Constitution, which had ever been the shield and sword of Kentucky slave masters since the founding of the republic. The Buckners judged events from just such an upper South perspective. Aylett Buckner knew the new Republican president, Abraham Lincoln, whose election had sent the cotton states petulantly out of the Union; the two had practiced law together in the central Illinois circuit.[20] He knew Lincoln to be a good, honest man and trusted the new president's pledges to uphold the Union and the Constitution by bringing an end to the rebellion without making war against slavery, even as he worried about how long Lincoln could hold out against the more fervent antislavery voices in his party.

The border masters' long perspective on the sectional conflict played out in the pages of the *Winchester National Union*—Clark County's proudly partisan old Whig sheet—on election day in 1860. "We had exceedingly desired that it should have been otherwise," wrote editor and lawyer James M. Ogden; "we had desired that John Bell, a national candidate, should have been preferred to Abraham Lincoln, a sectional one." That desire was consistent with the balloting in Clark. Ben's and Aylett's votes helped Bell take the county with 959 votes, followed distantly by John C. Breckinridge with 391 and Stephen A. Douglas even farther behind with a mere 60. Lincoln had received a solitary vote.

Despite Kentucky's support of the Bell candidacy, Lincoln was undoubtedly elected. Bowing to the electoral process by which the country was governed, laws were upheld, and society was regulated, Ogden advised his Clark County readership, the Buckners doubtless among them, to accept the verdict of "a plurality of the voters of the United States." Besides, old Whigs had "lived during the past four years under an administration which has not been able to entirely deprive of us of life, though it has filled us with unutterable disgust." Given the constitutional limits on presidential power, Lincoln's promises regarding his policy toward slavery, and the strength of the proslavery vote in Congress, why should Clark County Whigs fear another administration under a different species of political heresy?[21]

Never one to concede an inch of partisan ground, Ogden spun quickly to attack not the Republicans, who had garnered a little more than 1,300 votes in the whole of Kentucky, but instead those men within his own county he held truly responsible for Lincoln's victory. "We are as much opposed to the sectional doctrines of the Republican party as any man, but we have not the least hesitation in saying that as a MAN Abraham Lincoln is both more capable and infinitely more honest than his predecessor, the now ruling tyrant and corrupt despot, James Buchanan." Channeling his anger over partisan defeat and the threats a Republican administration posed to Kentucky's slave economy and society, Ogden unleashed rhetorical volley after volley against the folly of the southern Democracy. "We repeat that as much as we wished for the defeat of Mr. Lincoln, we can live under his Administration; can the Yancey–Breckinridge democracy? To them the election of Mr. Lincoln is due. They did the work. They perpetrated the act. It is a mischief; and on their heads lies the responsibility." Piling on the damnations now, he accused, "They have elected a sectional, anti-slavery candidate. They have just proved ... that they are the strongest *practical* abolitionists in the United States."

Unlike the Breckinridge men, Bell supporters had the boldness and judgment—or, in Aylett Buckner's case, the personal knowledge—to admit that "aside from his notions about slavery we think that Abraham Lincoln will make a good President; good, we say, because we believe him to be an honest man." Kentucky's old Whigs, Ogden continued, would be the last to desire "the violation of the laws and the Constitution" and if "Mr. Lincoln attempts this, we say impeach him," for in point of fact "we have said for two or three years" that the loathed Democrat, Buchanan, should have suffered the same. A parting shot countered the secessionist voices from within Kentucky and the growing chorus in the Deep South that labeled any attempt to work out the issues of slavery and union within the framework of the Constitution as *submissionism*. If any of the disgruntled Breckinridge states that had split the Democratic vote and eased Lincoln's election "attempts to revolutionize the Government, we hope that Abraham Lincoln, exerting his legal powers as President, to maintain the laws and Constitution ... *will speedily thrash her into quiet* SUBMISSION."[22]

At a time when we might expect a Bluegrass Whig to turn to the Sage of Ashland's calls for compromise and cooler heads, Ogden instead looked to counter the secessionists with the words of the father of the party that was now advocating disunion in the South, Andrew Jackson. Although in this different context still counseling law, order, and constitution as the remedies for the South's grievances, Jackson's characteristic bellicosity added a new layer to the argument for the continued relationship between slavery and union. Jackson's powerful rhetoric during the Nullification Crisis of 1832 had made the Union seem bold, assertive, and manly. "You have indeed felt the unequal operation of laws which may have been unwisely, not unconstitutionally passed," counseled Jackson now from beyond the grave in words that echoed the contemporary sentiments of Kentucky's loyal slave owners, "but that inequality must necessarily be removed" by due process, not rebellion. "Contemplate the confidence of that country of which you still form an important part" and the benefits that flowed from the constitutional guarantees that structured society "protecting their commerce—securing their literature and their arts—facilitating their inter-communication—defending their frontiers—and making their names respected in the remotest parts of the earth!" These were some of the few words Jackson ever spoke that would resonate with both sides of the political divide. "And then add, if you can, without horror and remorse—this happy Union we will dissolve—this picture of peace and prosperity we will interrupt—these fertile fields we will deluge in blood—the protection of that glorious flag we will renounce—the very name of American we discard" in the name of pride. Jackson concluded his litany of horrors by predicting the ultimate fear that Kentucky's unionist masters shared in 1860. One fundamental question summed up the horror: "Are you united at home? Are you free from the apprehension of civil discord, with all its fearful consequences?" Could a violent revolution to protect slavery survive slavery?[23]

As much as Kentucky's unionist slave masters feared the influence of northern abolitionism on the health of their slave economy and society, they feared as much the disordered chaos that would inevitably result from secession. "Indeed, order—social, economic, racial, and ultimately political order—was the central pillar to antebellum Upper South social thought," writes historian Aaron Astor. "Kentuckians defended slavery precisely because the alternative meant disorder; order and slavery went hand in hand." White southerners, notes William J. Cooper, "did not believe that their society could withstand any fundamental alteration of slavery because such a transformation meant inevitable disorder, even upheaval." In choosing the known and orderly path of constitutional compromise rather than the chaotic and unknown trail of disunion in 1861, Buckner and Kentucky's loyal masters were not placing Union above slavery. They were expressing their dedication to slavery *through* their adherence to the old flag and its constitutional guarantees, which had established, enabled, and protected slavery since the inception of the republic. Choosing Union, Constitution, and order "above all other concerns," Astor writes, "hardly signified that [order] superseded slavery, considering that slavery itself signified order to those in the Upper South."[24]

Order was the "central pillar" of a holistic ideology derived in part from the idealized vision of a paternalistic slaveholding culture and from the faith in an organic, harmonious society enabled, established, and protected by the exceptional American Constitution cherished by the Whig Party, which was now defunct as a national organization but still alive and well in the values of its adherents on both sides of the Ohio. Whigs conceived of themselves as a "'sober, industrious, thriving people'—a self image that included moral as well as economic virtues," writes Daniel Walker Howe, so "Whiggery was as much a cultural or moral posture as an economic or political program." Men such as Buckner were convinced that they possessed a "more coherent, rational, and constructive program" that was better suited to the market-oriented modern America that had dramatically emerged over the course of Kentucky's statehood than Democratic "patronage, passion, and sheer negativism." In the fertile pasturelands, grain fields, and hemp plantations of Bluegrass counties such as Clark, the Whig belief in "qualitative development" of the American state, people, and economy "through *time*" reigned rather than the Democratic interest in "quantitative expansion . . . through *space*"—if for no other reason than the fact that, unlike the cotton and tobacco men of the Deep South and western Kentucky, Bluegrass crops encouraged long-term investment in the land rather than rapid nutrient depletion and abandonment. Southern Whiggish theories of government also meshed smoothly with the social dictates of the benevolent Christian slave master. No less a person than Henry Clay, a master himself (if never quite convinced of the ultimate good of slavery), advocated the "protecting care of a paternal government" in shepherding commerce, society, and enlightenment in the growing nation—the wording of which statement was both informed by and influenced the small-scale slavery practiced in Kentucky.[25] The fallen Whig Party had dominated state politics for two decades, and its ghosts, in the form of the Know-Nothing Party of the 1850s, the Constitutional Union Party of 1860, and even the active government philosophy of some Kentucky Democrats, continued to haunt electoral politics. The Whig Party's largest lingering impact, though, continued in the minds of its former adherents. Whether expressed as the legacy of Henry Clay, the star power of John J. Crittenden, or a conservative proslavery unionism, the Whigs' shadow was present.[26]

Concerned by the dangerously unbalanced actions of ideologues on all sides—and some even in their midst—Kentucky's loyal masters such as Ben Buckner decried extremists of both abolition and secession stripes with "much of the same rhetoric . . . especially epithets like 'fanatic' and 'incendiary.'" Concerned that each set of sectional radicals was capable of violating the sacred rule of law, a concept one historian labels the "lynchpin to the ideology of southern Whigs," Kentucky's loyal masters saw themselves as the ultimate defenders of true American liberty and hopes for any sort of viable political future for the nation.[27] Both sides disrespected the colossal majesty of the Constitution as the foundation for ordered society. To white Kentuckians, William Lloyd Garrison's famous characterization of the document as a "Covenant with Death and an Agreement with Hell" and William Seward's claim that there existed a "higher law" than the Constitution suggested that few in the Republican Party cared for the restraints of law or religion.[28] Secessionists, of course, sought to renounce their allegiance to the nation's foundational compact and remake the rules of the game. Kentucky was forced to choose between two sides gearing for war, and in the eyes of the state's numerous old Whigs, the Buckner family included, each camp presented its own threat to slavery and the social order that the institution simultaneously depended on and provided.

Just as much as Buckner and his fellow loyal masters were convinced that the Union could (and would, even under the Lincoln administration) defend the rights of slave owners as well as any form of government, he also objected to the Confederacy, its leadership, and the results that might come from Kentucky's secession.

Disunion, in the words of the *National Union,* would deal the "death blow" to slavery, first in Kentucky and the border South but then "sweep on until the beautiful fields of the South, that are now rich with abundant harvests, and which can only be tilled by African slave labor, will soon become a dreary waste at the hands of bloody revolution." The economic ramifications of Kentucky's leaving the Union certainly drove much concern in the state. Hemp and its finished products were usually sold to bale Deep South cotton; but, of course, the hemp region was limited to the central Bluegrass. Livestock, grain, and tobacco were sold to markets regardless of region, though more tended to head north across the Ohio than down it to southern markets. Much has been made of the increasing commercial ties that bound the commonwealth to its neighbors across the Ohio River, the implication being that as Kentucky turned northward to sell its crops, livestock, and products, it increasingly drifted away from its southern cultural cousins and slavery in the process.[29]

True, the *National Union* ran ads for the famous St. Nicholas hotel in New York in addition to publishing the latest market prices from Cincinnati. The degree to which Clark County farmers were looking northward to sell their horses, mules, and cattle was further suggested by a notice from the Cleveland, Dayton, and Cincinnati Railroad Line "To SHIPPERS AND DEALERS In Live Stock" of a "New and Direct Route to Eastern Cities!" The Kentucky Central Rail Road likewise advertised its passenger service to a host of "Cities and towns West and North-West" as well as the eastern express that linked Kentuckians to Washington, Philadelphia, New

York, and Boston among eighteen listed destinations; only three southern cities were listed, Wheeling, Baltimore, and Richmond.[30] Although these economic ties bound Kentucky farmers to markets across the Ohio, it is easy to oversectionalize their meaning. Even if a horse from Dr. Samuel Martin's farm were sold at auction in Cincinnati or New York, did that decrease his reliance on slave labor to raise that horse? When Dr. Martin corresponded with agricultural journals based in the Northeast, was he betraying his sectional identity or simply sharing valuable information with other farmers who raised similar stock on similar soils? Have historians questioned the southernness of Deep South cotton planters because they sold their crops to New York factors?

Many Kentuckians were indeed hesitant to secede, fearing the results if they were to break those commercial ties. Why should they not be? They stood to lose access to lucrative and accessible markets. Kentucky was exploiting the new transportation revolution that the railroad had brought, and it was drawing their trade northward. Twelve rail lines ran northward out of the state on the eve of the war; only two headed south. Those connections across the Ohio are best imagined as connections not to the North but to the Union. The rail lines carried livestock not just to Cincinnati and Chicago but beyond them, to an international market, regulated and maintained by the federal government. Kentucky, in E. Merton Coulter's seminal if flawed analysis, "stood for the Union because their economic prosperity, it was believed, depended absolutely upon it."[31] But, critically, that prosperity depended on the nation, the Union, not just the North. Kentuckians looked to the national government to regulate interstate trade, to the national government to maintain the protective tariff that shielded Bluegrass hemp producers from international undercutting, and to the national government to protect their right to the service of their enslaved body servants when they took the Kentucky Central's eastern express and stayed at the St. Nicholas in New York. So simple as to be almost overlooked, too, is that selling slave-produced products—no matter where the market was located—was a fundamentally proslavery action. The more income slavery generated, the more white Kentuckians could and would want to enter the ranks of slave owners. Taking away Kentucky's markets or threatening them with trade sanctions and an international border was threatening the profitability that slavery needed to survive. Threatening those markets, then, threatened not only pocketbooks, but the society, culture, and sense of self that white Kentuckians had constructed around slavery.

In the eyes of the state's loyal men, the denial of national markets was far from the worst economic damage that the Confederate government could mete out to a seceded Kentucky. The Buckners read terrifying stories in the *National Union* that revealed the horrid economic plans kept secret by the Confederate government, which would be far worse than having to pay an import duty to continue shipping goods across the Ohio. Confederate representatives from Louisiana and South Carolina, the paper claimed, had proposed to the convention at Montgomery the reopening of the African slave trade within the Confederacy. If they were voted down, "another and more dangerous revolution will follow on that southern soil" to secure their object. Beyond the widespread conviction that far too many black people resided in the country as it was, few readers had to be reminded that the reopening of the slave trade would drive the price for slaves sharply down, decaying the value that Kentucky owners had invested in their human property and gutting one of Kentucky's leading exports. The commonwealth's small-scale, mixed-product slave economy depended on the capital gained from selling off surplus slaves to continue to fuel its economic diversification and land improvement. "Will the Border States consent to pass under such a yoke?" the *National Union* asked its Bluegrass audience. Would Kentucky and her sister southern states "voluntarily take the curse of opening the African slave trade, and become slaves themselves by putting their necks under the feet of a purely military despotism, utterly destructive of personal liberty?" On the same page, a reprinted North Carolina article on the same subject echoed the warning. "You now see, fellow-citizens . . . the trap set for you by the Cotton State Confederacy."[32]

Predictions of a despotic, liberty-crushing Confederate government struck a number of chords to the old Whig readership of the *National Union* beyond their pecuniary interest. Though secessionists in Kentucky and elsewhere in the South vehemently disagreed with the characterization, Buckner and his fellow Kentucky unionists consistently understood the act of leaving the Union and establishing the Confederacy as an act of tyranny. Long-standing Whig fears of the power of the executive, borne of Andrew Jackson's administration and never subsequently relinquished, led many to predict that Jefferson Davis would soon proclaim himself king. When the rampant southern Democracy overthrew the constraints of constitutional order, it would be free to establish a new aristocracy of political hangers-on in Secessia. If Davis were king, then a host of men seeking political office and power would make the new power class. At the very least, Kentucky faced an uncertain future as a potential member of a "Cotton State Confederacy" that produced practically no cotton.

Even if King Davis did not ascend to the throne, Kentuckians feared becoming a permanent minority whose interests would be ignored by the Democratic Party cotton states of the lower South in a future Confederate government. Disparaging the patriarchal monarchy that was to be established in the Confederacy allowed Union men such as Buckner to feature their own faith in a dignified, deliberative, republican paternalism. Without question, white men of learning and proven capability would lead, but they should never rule with terror or injustice, only with enlightened concern for the whole of the society they headed. The claims that Davis would set up a very literal kingdom of cotton also served to unman secessionists. Rhetoric that proposed an either–or relationship between freedom and slavery was older than the American republic itself, and set within the southern "politics of slavery," William J. Cooper reminds us, assertions that any man had given up his political freedom to corruption, vice, or lust for power were a public questioning of his whiteness, his manhood, and his economic competency. Antisecessionist southerners were convinced that "southern Democrats had neglected their sacred mission—protecting southern liberty" and the institution of slavery that enabled it. "They had not been the faithful stewards of the trust placed in them by southern voters. Instead the southern Democrats grasped for place and reward while the Republican horde crowded around the gates of southern liberty."[33]

But as much as Buckner and his fellow Union men were intent to slander their political opponents, such attacks were just as concerned with loudly proclaiming their own masculinity and independence. "When secession and rebellion became seen as hot-headed and impulsive—the result of unrestrained passion—self-discipline had political implications," notes historian of Union soldiers Reid Mitchell. A composed, dignified, sober, and civilized manhood rather than a beastly impassioned virility was the model for men such as Buckner in both the North and the South. The "emotional, treacherous . . . feminine, childlike" secessionists, who riled themselves up in a fire-eating fit of passion, contrasted with "the rational, loyal . . . masculine, adult" Union men in antisecessionist rhetoric in Kentucky and throughout the nation. The latter's position as loyal republican inheritors of 1776 set them within revered company. No demeaned slave led by deceitful demagogues, the loyal man was instead the strong and independent defender of the American Revolution. He could see through the tricks and silver-tongued oratory that had fooled so many others; he was sharp enough to grasp Davis and company's true design. How could such a country ever hope to establish a workable political system or compete in commerce with the world when it was composed of such power-hungry thieves and ignorant subjects?[34]

For Ben Buckner, in particular, decrying secessionist tyranny had domestic implications as he tried to prove his worthiness before Helen and the Martin family. Keeping in mind that antebellum political parties "articulated cogent, diverse stands on gender roles and family practices, and that many people who assumed a partisan identity did so in part because they understood the party's gender culture and identified themselves with that worldview," we should understand that Buckner's claims to see through the secessionist falsehoods and lies were demonstrations of his domestic aptitude filtered through his politics. His concern for the continued commerce of Kentucky with states across the Ohio River showed his mindfulness of economic and political systems that bound Kentucky to the nation, not just to the South; so did his awareness of what might happen if Canada were brought to the border as fugitive slave protections would be lifted when Kentucky seceded. More to the point, though, secessionist tyranny was no way to run a country, just as monarchical patriarchal authority was no way to run a household.[35]

Instead, Buckner clung to the Constitution's guarantee of representative governance guided by a strong federal state. He articulated a model of the ideal paternalistic household writ large, making what Amy Murrell Taylor has perceptively labeled the "imaginative link between family and nation." Though the shift away from the ideal household ruled by the absolute authority of the father had begun before the Revolution, the rising popularity of companionate marriage and the accompanying cult of republican motherhood that emerged in the early decades of the young republic infused emerging beliefs about household relationships with patriotic meaning. Rather than rule his household with corrupt absolute authority, Buckner joined many American men of the era in hoping to become a "ruler of the heart." Respecting and genuinely loving their wives, Buckner and men like him hoped to govern their households by consent rather than dictation and to cement their authority with bonds of love rather than with bonds of economic or physical power. The balance was difficult to strike, and such households were "full of contradictions and ambiguities" arising from an ideology that gave a man power but hoped he would not use it. All this was readily apparent when Buckner threatened to "be as great a tyrant as you ever saw, & then somebody will wish they had not been so hard to coax into the measures." His future tyranny was mostly just a threat—mostly.[36]

Lest this household be considered too strange, we should keep in mind that the contradictions and ambiguities of the paternal household in which husbands governed with the input and through the consent of their wives were not unlike the ambiguities of the constitutional government of the United States. The federal government, the father, managed a house full of independent dependents, the states, through goodwill and mutual respect rather than through imperial force; the very fact of the rebellion proved how difficult such a household could be to manage. Nevertheless, Buckner, standing for the Union and rejecting the tyrannical model of governance he believed to be the foundation of the Confederate political project, was making important claims about his commitment to the paternalistic ideal. He acknowledged that problems would inevitably arise under such a system, while at the same time stressing that the family or the nation could settle those problems between themselves. Compromise that maintained the mutual ties of affection that bound the household and the country, he asserted, was preferable to severing those ties through violent, uncivilized, and undignified attempts to assert absolute control.

The paternalistic ideal that found expression in Buckner's stand by the Union made yet another important statement about himself and his character. As much as it confirmed him a prudent and enlightened citizen and husband, embracing the ideals embodied in the American republic made claims about him as a master as well. The fierce denunciations of slave owners' character coming from the abolitionist ministers of the North, the voices of African Americans who had escaped slavery and circulated popular accounts of the cruelties they had suffered, white critics of slavery writing from within the South, and, most popular of all, Harriet Beecher Stowe's *Uncle Tom's Cabin* put pressure on masters to carefully consider how they exerted their authority over their slaves. Then again, so did their own consciences. Defending themselves from outside attack, protecting their expensive investments in human flesh, and assuaging their own guilt could all be accomplished by actively touting their credentials as benevolent fathers to their enslaved "children." Working "to negotiate changing ideals and incorporate new values into their own sense of proper domestic relationships and arguments for slavery," a master such as Buckner simultaneously "insisted [that] fathers held property rights in their wives, children, and slaves," while also "claim[ing] 'a prejudice and weakness' for the modern quality of love and stressed the reciprocal nature of relationships between fathers or masters and their dependents."[37]

No wonder Ben decried the fall of Helen's friend Sallie Moore under the spell of "that mania *Secession* which despite her good sense, has taken possession of her mental faculties, perverting them from the nobler purposes for which they were intended and which they want to fulfill."[38] Secessionism was overly emotional, irrational to the point of insanity, ignoble, antisocial, and, ultimately, feminine—entirely unsuited for a man, father, and master. The rejection of law and order implicit in the secessionist tyranny implied disconcerting things about the ways Confederates ruled both their political states and their households. Kentucky's stand by the Union and the paternalistic relations it embodied confirmed Buckner's and his fellow loyal masters' belief that they were kindly and indulgent fathers to an organic family, white and black, tied by bonds of affection and mutual responsibility rather than by bonds of cruelty, dominance, and sheer power.

In Buckner's conservative proslavery unionism, the Constitution still reigned, ensuring the continued protection of property. Secession was illegal and impossible, and, as events were showing, the armies of the Union would defeat the rebellion quickly and return the status quo ante bellum, a slaveholding republic. The status quo was far safer than this rebellion. No one knew where the forces of war, once unleashed, might drag the nation. Slave revolt, race war, or a military coup might follow. Moreover, for all of its states' rights rhetoric, the new Confederacy did not look welcoming to upper South masters. That country—founded illegally, born into the perils of war, bringing Canada to the Ohio River, dominated by Democrats and tariff-killing extremists—was the paradise of cotton plantation monarchs. It held little appeal for Kentucky, firstborn of the Union, firstborn of Washington's slaveholding republic.

3

Brave Hearts and Stout Hands

When war came to Kentucky in 1861, Buckner saw an opportunity to prove his worth to Helen and the Martins on the battlefield—even if he was to fight against the side they supported. With the landslide unionist victories at the polls in August 1861, the sham neutrality under which both Unionists and Confederates had labored for months was essentially dead. Though Buckner's politics did not line up with the Martins', his military service could still prove his character in their eyes. In his study of the antebellum military tradition of Kentucky, Harry Laver shows that young Kentuckians throughout the century leaped to the colors to join the "fraternity" of military service by "prov[ing] themselves the legitimate heirs of their all but mythical forefathers."[1] Membership in that fraternity, Buckner knew, was an irrevocable marker of an individual's manhood and honor. Acquiring the manly respectability that military service conferred was one of his own motives for going to war. Military service, he believed, would leave him qualified to fulfill his paternal responsibilities in both the public and domestic spheres. As an officer in a volunteer unit, Buckner would have to be elected, a ratification of his social acceptability to the community's military-age electorate that could foreshadow a career in politics. Further, his responsibilities for the welfare of the men under his command would be a proving ground for his suitability as a future father and master; surely if he could manage the feeding, clothing, hygiene, and movement of a company or regiment, he could later manage a law office and household.

Buckner began like he would have started a campaign for political office, building constituencies from his professional and social contacts and gradually winning men to his side through handshaking, debating, and logging countless hard miles in the saddle. He first recruited a company of local men, including his younger brother, Daniel Turney, whom everyone knew as "Tucker" after the popular song. Though the younger Buckner was an enlisted man, he showed an amazing aptitude for the soldiering life; by war's end, he would command the company. The elder Buckner brother's eyes were focused on promotions, too, and he eagerly took the opportunity to expand his recruiting efforts into the surrounding counties he frequented on his legal circuit. In the mad rush to recruit soldiers, the more names a prominent man could bring into service, the higher the rank he was generally due to receive in return. Now Buckner was but a captain in command of his Winchester company, but he saw oak leaves or eagles on his shoulders if he could rally enough men to himself and to the cause.

Off to "the Country" he headed, after striking up a deal with his best friend and fellow Winchester attorney Charley Hanson and Lexington businessman Sanders D. Bruce to raise a complete regiment and place themselves at its head. By the end of September, the scheme looked as if it might actually come off. "I have accepted the position of major—that is if we raise the regiment," Buckner wrote in an uncharacteristically short note to Helen on September 25. Indeed, in his zeal to raise as many men as possible, Buckner became lax in his attentions to the belle of Clark. As he continued his frenzy of politicking and enlisting, Helen had begun to see the prospect of his going to war in a more realistic sense than he did. It does not seem that her objections were ideological but instead centered around the fact that he would likely be gone much farther and much longer than his jaunts to neighboring courthouses had taken him recently. Nevertheless, he consoled her with the current wisdom in vogue for thousands of similar young men eager to head off to war that year. "The war cant be a long one and in a few months, I will come back to you to leave you no more," he wrote optimistically. "And in many an hour of loneliness perhaps of privation the recollection of the noble generous & true hearted girl who I leave behind me will prove a panacea for any anguish I might otherwise feel."[2] Helen remained unconvinced.

Military glory, though, would not wait for Buckner to march away from Clark County at the head of his new command. The state now officially loyal to the Union, secessionists intent on joining the Confederate service were headed south in twos, tens, and hundreds at a time. While the railroads, in particular the Louisville and Nashville (L&N), and well-worn overland transportation routes funneled many

Kentucky Confederates into camps in Tennessee near Clarksville, would-be Confederates from northern Kentucky and the eastern Bluegrass headed east to better avoid unionist authorities. During the same stretch of weeks that Buckner rode the recruiting circuit around Winchester, "a regular, systematized management in forwarding the rebel recruits" was using Clark County as a way station on the road to the Confederate commands gathering in Prestonsburg. Whether consciously or not, the Confederates employed many of the same techniques to head south that enslaved Kentuckians had used for decades to flee north toward the Ohio. There were, according to one report, "regular posts for camping, resting in the day and travelling at night," maintained and secured by "persons who are prepared at regular points to furnish provisions; guards all along the entire route, &c." Receiving a tip that a party of thirty or so would-be Confederates from Owen and Grant Counties had camped at the Clark County property of known-secessionist B. F. Van Meter (a "very large farm, [with] large woodland pastures, well suited for the purpose of concealing rebels"),[3] Buckner saw a perfect opportunity to strike the first blow for the Union cause in the county.

Assembling a little less than thirty of his Clark County recruits with their horses on the morning of October 26, Buckner moved his men the six miles from town to the Van Meter farm. Captain J. W. Craddock was now in command of the Winchester company that Ben had initially raised, though the newly minted Major Buckner commanded and led the expedition. About two hundred yards from the rebel camp, Buckner's men threw down a large rail fence and burst, "pretty fast, I tell you," as one member of the expedition recalled, into the clearing. The startled Confederates, still huddled around their fires awaiting the delivery of their breakfast, retreated into a nearby cornfield, with the Union men only yards behind them. Buckner and Craddock established a rough line amid the remnants of the rebel camp as the pursued secessionists rallied, precipitating a brief firefight. Buckner and Craddock pressed their surprise, even though the rebels, armed with "U.S. muskets, revolvers, and bowie knives," and numbering nearly fifty men should have held the upper hand. Most damning for the hard-pressed rebels, their horses remained in camp, eliminating hope for escape save for four or five men who had mounted and bolted away when Buckner and Craddock had initially thrown down the fence. Constantly pressing in on the rebels, Buckner's men drove their enemies through the cornfield, over a fence, and into an open pasture within just two or three minutes of fighting. Caught out in the exposed field, the rebel leader asked Buckner to talk, and soon the entire remaining force, forty-one men, had surrendered to him with all their arms, horses, and baggage. What had been a rousing blow turned into an absolute triumph just minutes later. As Buckner's command was rounding up and securing their prisoners, a local secessionist was caught close by with a train of slaves bringing breakfast and traveling provisions to the men at the camp. A party dispatched to the rebel's nearby home found and arrested yet more of the Owen and Grant County rebels. A triumphant account written by a participant to the *Louisville Journal* summed up the expedition nicely: "I think that we have made a pretty good haul of traitors in our little campaign of a few hours."[4]

A triumph in the *Journal*, the most widely circulated paper in the state, was for Buckner the perfect end to the whole expedition. Having his brave and daring exploits before nearly every man of his political persuasion in the commonwealth was certainly not objectionable, and, of course, official recognition of his competence and skill as a military man would give Helen some ammunition with which to quiet the ever-present secession beaus who hovered around her. There was, though, a rather serious problem. The initial account that ran in the November 5 issue of the *Journal* correctly identified Craddock as the second in command of the expedition but claimed a Mr. Grigsby had led the party in the attack on the rebel camp. Buckner was horrified. He was also suspicious. In a town as small as Winchester, who could not have known that it was he who led the expedition? Could someone have wanted to deny him his glory? Certainly, L. B. Grigsby was a strong Union man, but all of Winchester knew perfectly well that he was not in the county at the time of the raid. Who had deliberately omitted Buckner's name in the anonymous account in the *Journal*?

Winchester jumped to Buckner's defense. Writing under the name "Clark," one letter sought to correct the *Journal*'s oversight, though the author only did the thing halfway. Clark dispatched the Grigsby rumor, presuming "you refer to Col. L. B. Grigsby, who would doubtless have performed good service had he been present, but he was and is absent from the county and knew nothing of the expedition whatsoever," and mentioned that Ben Buckner had accompanied the expedition. But had Buckner only been *with* the expedition? No, he had *commanded* it! Clark nevertheless took great care in his letter to say that Craddock was in command of the expedition and took special pain to bestow "a commendation on our leader, Captain Craddock, who throughout the entire affair displayed the greatest coolness and judgment." Buckner was furious. The fact that a truer friend wrote the

Journal that the "Union men were under command of Major B. F. Buckner of Col. S. D. Bruce's regiment, with Capt. J. W. Craddock, of the same regiment, second in command" did not assuage the insult, nor did the same friend's stress that it was "an act of but simple justice" to repeat publicly that "credit of the capture belongs exclusively to the two gentlemen above named and their gallant associates." George Prentice of the *Journal* gladly printed the corrections, stressing that the paper only wanted to give "[h]onor to whom honor is due." But honor demanded more than an anonymous correction; Buckner's search for "Clark" was on.[5]

If things were not going well in the press in the weeks after the triumph on the Van Meter farm, they were going worse for Buckner's, Hanson's, and Bruce's recruiting efforts. The state Military Board, which was overseeing the organization of Kentucky soldiers, had ordered their partial regiment consolidated with another before they could be mustered into federal service. The three men had set about recruiting that summer with the understanding that they would be rewarded with the three field officer positions in the new organization; now the board had cut short their efforts. If the other partial regiment with whom they were to be consolidated was larger than their own, all three would be voted out of office and see their hard summer of riding, politicking, and enlisting go to naught. "I have worked day & night, traversed the country spent my money & will unless I am greatly deceived be beaten for the position," Buckner fumed. The Military Board, "in order to give a regiment to a friend from Frankfort," had ruined his chance for rank and recognition, added to his immediate losses, "two months time" and five hundred dollars in travel expenses, "and for my pains [I] will be sent home and some one else will reap the fruit of my labor." "I am in a terribly bad humor," he wrote, "and feel desperately savage." The frustrations about the ongoing Clark affair in the *Journal* seeped into his anger at the Military Board and his suspicion of their corruption. "I have seen men in high positions stand up & look me in the face with an assured air of candor and tell me downright & practical false hoods," he fumed. "I have had ... unsolicited the most unqualified promises of success from men whose ... position enabled them to control my fate. How disgusting for a man to lie."[6]

Meanwhile, Buckner's investigations around Winchester revealed the identity of "Clark." His fury exploding from his pen, Buckner addressed the man who sought to deny him credit before the entire state: James M. Ogden, fellow Winchester attorney and former editor of the *National Union*. "Sir," the letter began with cold formality, "[In] [t]he communication published in the Journal of a recent date upon the signature of 'Clark' which purports to give the facts in reference to the capture of Secession troops near Winchester, I recognize the products of your pen." Channeling the ghost of Henry Clay and a host of other Kentuckians with touchy senses of honor, Buckner turned toward a challenge. "As I have reason to believe that the patent injustice done me in that writing was intentional," he spat, "it is my right & duty to demand such a reparation through the same medium, as shall be deemed full & complete by my friends who witnessed the affair." Falling into the long-standing forms of the code duello, he offered a chance for apology to avoid further escalation, "suspend[ing] a further expression of opinion as to the motives that justified your conduct." If Ogden spurned his conciliatory hand, Buckner would "not hesitate to declare in the most explicit manner my opinion of you, and the motives [that] activated that publication, holding myself to the furthest extent possible for such declarations as I may feel called upon to make." "I shall wait a reasonable time for your action," Buckner concluded, "and in the mean while shall hope that a just sense of propriety will dictate to you the necessity of a proper reparation."[7]

Buckner did not have time to receive that proper reparation or, indeed, even to have his second deliver the note. He, Bruce, and Hanson had friends in Frankfort of their own, some of whom had the ear of the Military Board. The board itself had come into being via a virtual coup by old Whig legislators in the General Assembly to disempower Governor Beriah Magoffin, a Democrat who was suspected of secessionism, and the board was particularly responsive to the General Assembly that had created it. Letters from Clark County state representative John B. Huston and other well-placed allies changed the board's plans and secured the commissions for the regiment.[8] Not three days after Buckner despaired for his commission, the Loyal Ladies of Lexington presented a flag to Bruce's regiment as they left for service. "Such a beautiful testimonial could not be more worthily bestowed, for a finer body of men have probably not been brought together to defend the honor of Kentucky," gushed local editor D. C. Wickliffe.[9] The way in which the men of Bruce's regiment were sent off to war stood in great contrast with their Confederate neighbors' leave-taking. Most Confederates had to leave the state in secret, like those Buckner and his men had captured outside of Winchester in October. The Union men, however, could enjoy the traditional rituals that surrounded a military deployment, important occasions that gave meaning to their military service.

The regiment formed itself in the square along Cheapside and flanked by an honor guard of men, soon to become the Twenty-First Kentucky Infantry. Wickliffe noted that the crowd was "great," and "no wonder," either, that "the flashing eye of beauty glistened with a tear upon the sidewalk, and from door and window, and every other available place of seeing and hearing" Lexingtonians gathered by the thousands. "[T]he stern men in rank and file," Wickliffe boasted, "looked like *Kentuckians* determined to do their duty." When Reverend R. G. Brank addressed the gathering on behalf of the Loyal Ladies, he reminded the soldiers that the flag was given "not for ornament but for use—not for holiday display, but to strengthen your hands and nerve your hearts in the day of battle." Brank concluded with warnings about the true weight of that airy silk, given "in the assured confidence that you will never allow it to be dishonored by cowardice or cruelty," and that it might be forever "the emblem alike of courage and kindness." Lt. Frank E. Wolcott stepped proudly up to confirm the dedication of his fellow officers and men. He pledged the "many brave hearts and stout hands" of the regiment to "protect the soil of Kentucky from the hostile tread of the invading foe," which, successfully accomplished, would allow each individual soldier to "win the admiration of the fair daughters of his native city." Each speech echoed the Bluegrass's sacred charge to defend Union, Constitution, home, fireside, and honor. Surely Buckner and the men under his command would not forget this send-off.[10]

If the flag presented to the Twentieth by the Loyal Ladies that day was to be the embodiment of the soul of the regiment, it was the embodiment of their cause as well. It bore the same thirty-four stars as those carried by their northern comrades, promising a restoration of the rebellious states to the national family. But to Buckner and his Kentucky soldiers, men who enlisted to defend their slave society, the starry blue field represented not only the Union as it was but also the Constitution as it is, the full status quo ante bellum. The Constitution embodied the sacred right to own enslaved human property, the Fugitive Slave Law, and the three-fifths ratio. It guaranteed the legislative processes that could keep Republican antislavery legislation from becoming law and the judicial mechanisms that could protect the rights of slave owners from any such legislation if it should pass or even to actively gain more freedom to exercise such rights as *Dred Scott* had done in the previous decade. The rush to the colors in Kentucky during the fall and winter of 1861 was indeed a rush. All was contingent on a speedy end to the rebellion. The threat that the Lincoln administration and the Republican Congress represented, or that many believed they represented, could be successfully countered with a united block of votes in Washington that would prevent any lasting damage to the institution. A quick end to the war, a successful quelling of the rebellion, hoped many Kentuckians, would see the congressmen from the southern states who had joined the Confederate councils at Montgomery and Richmond restored to their seats in Washington before any radical measures could be taken.

Buckner hoped that his regiment's new flag proclaimed to secessionists and neutrals that the Union cause was joined not only for the interests of the Union, but for the interests of the state itself. Their loyalty to the government was implicitly not a blind devotion to the administration, but to what the government could guarantee local citizens and local interests. It advertised that the brand of unionism the regiment intended to fight for was linked not to abolition and antislavery, as secessionists claimed, but instead to the constitutional guarantees of slaveholders' rights, of order, and of secure progress.

In the war's western theater, there was soon a great deal of progress for Buckner's Union cause. Twin Confederate disasters at Mill Springs on January 19, 1862, and the fall of Forts Henry and Donelson on the Tennessee and Cumberland Rivers respectively in mid-February led to a general collapse of the Confederate line, requiring it to fall back toward Nashville. Late February and early March 1862 found Buckner and the Twentieth headed through southern Kentucky into Middle Tennessee in pursuit of the retreating rebels. As they went, they traveled again through land ravaged already by conflict within the communities, and, as he had around Smithland, Buckner read the signs of moral and political failures of secessionism all around him. A few days of examination around Nashville showed the country to be "a beautiful one, much like our own (except that the 'blue grass' does not grow so profusely) and the improvements are superb. I have in the last two days passed many little cottages, that were perfect gems of architectural beauty, and with the surrounding grounds improved to the highest possible degree they have continually reminded me that if we had such an one, what a paradise of love and happiness we could make it." Sadly, though, the blight of secessionism had choked off that pastoral and commercial promise. "This is," Ben wrote to Helen, "one of the most beautiful little cities you ever beheld, but like every other place that has been under secession rule it bears striking evidence of stagnation of business and an entire absence of commercial communication." Worse still was the condition of the farmland between there and Bowling Green, which could only be described as "deplorable."[11]

Buckner was not alone in associating this property damage with the inherent moral failures of secessionism. Kentucky papers published a spate of articles about property damage in Hopkinsville, where "deeds of the greatest vandalism" and "the grossest outrages" had been visited on the "people of that glorious Union town," its lovely fairgrounds, and its women's college. The Confederate provost marshal, the officer in charge of maintaining military law and order, was reported to have dismissed Union citizens' protests, saying "that he hoped all the d—d Union men in the town would die." In Bowling Green, the "beautiful depot of the Louisville & Nashville railroad" had likewise fallen victim to rebel arson.[12] Even slaves, the Kentucky press told loyal masters, could recognize the secessionists' failing. In the Green River counties, "numbers of slaves, who had been taken from that region to Nashville to work on fortifications," had reportedly returned to their owners when the rebels fled the city. Some claimed that the rebels had made efforts "to sell some of the negroes at Nashville," but the slaves had escaped in the confusion of the retreating army. Disregarding the fact that the enslaved men had their own concerns in mind when they returned to Kentucky—namely, returning to their own families and friends—loyal masters were given to understand that these slaves recognized their masters' paternal benevolence when they chose to return home rather than take a chance on freedom after they had escaped from the lawless and reckless Confederates in Nashville. "These people," read one account of the economy-killing, slave-stealing rebels, "are getting their rights now with a vengeance.... Military despotism and anarchy reigns in Secesh in this State."[13]

Seeing the moral superiority of the Union cause finally winning results on the battlefield, Buckner was supremely confident. When Helen wrote him a "quite unhappy and disappointed" letter lamenting their separation, Buckner urged her to not "bother your brain with *blockades* and steam fleets and such like, but just hope it will all turn out for the best, and that your sweet heart will soon be back safe & sound in body and heart except the wounds you have inflicted"—the latter line likely not helping reassure her. Recounting the string of victories in recent weeks, Buckner predicted that the "day is not far distant when the war will be brought to a close ... by the victorious arms of the Army of the Great Republic." "The American army is invincible in strength," he crowed, "and is composed of soldiers and is *now* commanded by Generals." A bit more than a week later, Buckner could pointedly ask, "[W]hat do you think of Secession, Isn't it pretty much played out, and dont you now think that although you were a bit of a rebel, that it was likely that you always claimed to be Union?" Riding the momentum of the hour, he predicted "that in 12 months, there will not be a respectable man in Kentucky who will acknowledge to his secession proclivities. They will all be Union and claim to have been so the whole time." Chiding her for being "a politician," a most unfeminine avocation, and reading the "trash" coming out of the northern legislatures, Buckner rounded out his optimistic vision for a future where his national and domestic goals had been met. "When things all come right and we get married and we are living happily and contentedly without a loss of any of our rights under the stars & stripes," he dreamed aloud, "you will then confess that it was better to go to war to preserve our country than to give it up without a struggle."[14]

Indeed, though he was wary of being one of the "unfortunate" soldiers whose hard luck it was never to see combat and were consequently "despised in the public opinion though they may have been ever so brave and ever so anxious," a successful quick end to the war suited both of Buckner's goals. The quicker he could get home, the less time Helen would have to feel lonely and abandoned and be set upon by her pack of secession beaux; the sooner the rebellious states could be returned to their seats in Congress, the less time the fanatics in the northern legislatures and in Congress would have to implement their "trash," the antislavery platforms on which they had been elected in 1860. Neither horrid outcome seemed especially likely to come to pass, but just in case Ben took care to remind Helen that although he might be "unfortunate" and not see combat, at least he had stood manfully to his cause.

When a boastful Daniel W. Price entertained the Martin drawing room with tales of how "his" army "picks off" officers like Buckner with their sharpshooting skill, Ben quickly asked, "[W]hy dont you persuade him to go & help pick them off too"? "I cant understand," he continued, "why our secession friends who are so noisy and so bitter, dont go & join the army to help bring about the result they so ardently desire[.] A man with no wife or family dependent upon him who feels as ... Price does and who does'nt go is an arrant coward & his absence from the army is more to be desired than his presence." When Helen's best friend Sallie Moore found herself beset by numerous rebel suitors, Buckner quipped, "There is one advantage in having a secesh beau" who strikes quite the figure about town but has yet to leave the state for active service: "you are not separated from him."[15]

Despite the "full battery of all her charms" that might bring any secesh suitor into a state of complete infatuation with Helen—that is, "unless his heart is more hollow & false than his political creed"—Ben was confident that though his was the more rocky path, it was the more virtuous. "I have capitulated, I surrender to you unconditionally I love you & will continue to love you whether you exact it or not," he had written a few months earlier. "You know how hard I fought against it & how many bitter reasons there were to spur me on in my resistance," he claimed, recalling the years of opposition from the Martin patriarch, "but you know also how complete was my surrender—so complete that in military parlance, you have not thought it necessary to take my parole." Ben could count on the fact that Helen would not fall for one of the Confederate "Princes" riding dashingly around Clark making grand boasts, and he only wished her "better luck in persuading people that you dont care anything about me" than he himself had had to date. "The invariable reply to the rigmarole which I have ready on that subject is 'Now dont lie, it aint any use.' Indeed," he continued, "I have arrive[d] [at] that point where my devotion to you seems to be taken for granted so invariably by those persons that I scarcely have an opportunity to deny it." If their long courtship had made Winchester society certain that Ben was devoted to Helen, honorable military service that brought credit to him and to the community that raised him would prove that he deserved her hand, the only "parole" he sought.[16]

If Buckner could teasingly accept Helen and her drawing room politics, moving through Nashville in the winter of 1862 convinced him that the balance of the secessionists he encountered were degenerate and socially inferior. Compared with his previous posting, a brief stop outside Louisville, the white female population of Nashville had been hostile beyond the point of decency. Camping on the Bardstown Pike a few miles out of Louisville, Buckner was pleased to report to Helen that though "the people generally were badly frightened" when the soldiers arrived, "after we staid there a night and neither negroes nor chickens in the neighborhood were missing we became great favorites." The Twentieth had behaved particularly well, he was proud to note; the Second Kentucky, with whom they were now brigaded, consumed five stacks of hay and more than ninety panels of neighborhood fencing for their campfires one particularly frigid night. The Twentieth, though, had suffered in dignified silence, "the rain falling from sun down till sun up," the "contrast between our conduct & theirs" winning Buckner's men "great praise."[17]

The "women of Nashville," by great contrast, "insult habitually all the soldiers who pass through the city and I am proud to say that our men have merely laughed at them," Buckner wrote Helen. "[A] woman who would relying upon her sex wantonly insult a body of armed men," he opined, "deserves the scorn and contempt of all the world and strips herself of the right to rely for protection upon the generosity and forbearance of the strong. No lady would so demean herself and every *woman* who does so deserves to be so insulted that if she has any lingering remnants of decency in her Composition, that it would make her hide her face for very shame," he lectured. Buckner was particularly enraged at Nashville's secessionist citizens after one of the Twentieth's sick soldiers was murdered while passing through the city on his way to catch up to the regiment.[18]

Buckner was finally, perhaps, gaining an insight into the motives that underlay the eagerness of the regiment's Jackson Purchase men to seek retribution from the secessionist neighbors who had scattered and stolen their families, slaves, and livestock. Nevertheless, he prided himself on the loyal troops' restraint. "Suppose these people who look upon the Federal army as [a] congregation of thieves adventurers and the offscourings of the cities of the North, had been by the fortunes of war placed in possession of the City of Cincinnati," he posited. "Do you believe that they would have left one brick on top of another[?] Do you think that the women of that place would have been permitted to stand in their doors and with safety & impunity insult the Southern soldiers, those very peaks of chivalry & nobility (!)? Do you know that a very different sort of treatment would have been resorted to by the Southern troops from that adopted by us?" "I am content that people should call me a *Yankee*, a *Hessian* a *Vandal* a *thief* & all the other long list of expletives which your secession friends shoved indiscriminately upon us," he vented. "I am even not offended to be called a *Lincoln hireling* as I was the other day by a woman in Nashville but when the lives of my friends and associates are taken without cause . . . I am for immediate retaliation."[19] Though he claimed that such insults did not get under his skin, his hardening attitude hinted otherwise.

Buckner's encounter with the ungentlemanly war only increased his longing to be with Helen, who, though still a secessionist, voiced her opposition within the acceptable limits of a society belle. As the soldiers moved south of Nashville, the people continued to treat them "with great saltiness (especially the ladies)," and either the economic failings of secessionism or, perhaps worse, shameless profiteering had priced "[c]ornmeal [at] $2.00 per bushel, butter $1.00 per pound, bacon 25¢ per pound" and driven laundry "prices so high that it is better to *throw the clothes* away when they are soiled, than to have them washed." Buckner, in short, was miserable with his army life, which had not matched up to his lofty and romantic expectations.

He longed for a way out but was bound by his oath and commission. "Helen," he wrote her from Spring Hill, "while I am yours I could not forget that there were other claims upon me besides yours—those of my country, and I know that if you felt as I feel upon the subject of the unhappy differences that have plunged us into this most horrible war, that so far from wishing me to stay at home, you would tell me to 'go where honor calls.'" He just hoped that victory for his cause and personal honor for him would call a bit more quickly.[20] "[W]e have a very fine opportunity for drill—though it seems to me that we will never have a chance to do anything," he wrote one day to beg for the latest gossip from Clark County to relieve the painful boredom of life behind the front lines. "But there is one consolation—that is if we dont have any fighting to do we will probably get home all the sooner."[21] Celebrating word of a string of Union victories, Buckner optimistically prophesied "that before one month . . . the star spangled banner the emblem of Freedom and Liberty both of speech & action will wave in triumph over every fort of Tennessee. And then if I have the good luck to be in one battle and dont disgrace my self, I will come home to my darling—not on a furlough for 30 days but to stay with her until she grows tired of me & maybe longer." Cryptically, he added, "Circumstances have arisen (not of any political character)"—in fact, a personal conflict with his hard-drinking colonel, Sanders Bruce—"which will make me very willing to go home when I have done something worthy of a man."[22]

He would not have long to wait.

On April 10, 1862, Buckner dashed off a letter on a piece of Pennsylvania Volunteers stationary in terribly pale ink. Both had been scavenged from the wreckage of the battlefield of Shiloh, which he and the Twentieth had occupied since the Union victory there three days earlier. He had moved beyond his baggage in the rush to get to the field, so these were the only writing materials he could find, and with steamboats filled with wounded men making for hospitals in the rear, this was his first opportunity to get a letter through. Helen likely had a difficult time picking out words in the pale lines, but enough of the letter was legible to convey the most important fact: "I made several very narrow escapes and came off entirely unhurt."[23] Buckner was alive; he was a veteran.

Details followed. As Ulysses S. Grant's force encamped along the banks of the Tennessee had been surprised on the morning of April 6, Don Carlos Buell's supporting Army of the Ohio—complete with the Twentieth Kentucky, part of the

Twenty-Second Brigade, along with the First and Second Kentucky regiments under the temporary command of the Twentieth's Colonel Bruce, itself a member of Kentuckian William "Bull" Nelson's division—rushed by steamer from Savannah, Tennessee, into the fight. Buckner and his men arrived around six that evening, bivouacked on the ground in "a cold drizzling rain that fell in torrents until about 4 oclock in the morning," and were formed into a defensive line on the left of Grant's force. The earliest Confederate attacks struck Nelson's division, but not the area the Twentieth defended. Nevertheless, holding position in an open field in sight of Confederate artillery, the Twentieth spent an unnerving morning being "played upon by two batteries" without being able to return their long-range fire. "Never has any thing impressed itself upon my mind as more terrible than the conflict that raged at that point," Ben confided to Helen. Frustrated and "under a most galling fire of shot and shell" that had struck down "about 10 or a dozen" men in the Twentieth "in less than two minutes," Buckner was relieved when a friendly battery of artillery came up to duel with the rebel cannoneers. With their own guns operating at the rear of the regiment, though, Buckner's infantrymen were forced "to lie down every time our own cannon were discharged to prevent being cut to pieces." Hanson and Buckner eventually moved their men into the cover of some nearby trees, though as they ran through the open field they occupied, the Confederate artillery took even greater effect. "One shell burst so near my head that the concussion knocked my cap off and I felt the flame of the explosion on my cheek," Buckner recalled. "My horse became very much frightened but I succeeded in controlling him." No sooner had they reached the relative safety of the trees "in good order" given the circumstances, than the Twentieth was thrown forward in open order as skirmishers to deal with some Confederates who had taken up a strong position in a thicket and were causing some concern for the artillerymen supporting Nelson's line. Deploying the regiment forward with a detachment of the First, Buckner and Hanson "fought the enemy for almost 2 hours when we repulsed them with heave loss though not so great as it would have been but for the concealed and protected position they occupied." Again, Buckner's exposed position on horseback made him a prime target, while his men "were allowed to take advantage of the ground trees &c." "The bullets whistled by my head . . . through the air incessantly. I made several very narrow escapes and came off entirely unhurt."[24]

When the Confederate line collapsed under the weight of Union counterattacks, the Twentieth was finally recalled from its pursuit to support an artillery battery as it threw shells at the retreating rebel lines. Buckner and his soldiers "threw ourselves upon the ground hungry & exhausted to await the approach of morning when we expected to renew the battle. It rained all night incessantly." As on the day before, the Twentieth rose "around four oclock to meet the enemy again. We however found none, and we had leisure to contemplate the battle field and all its thousand horrors." The exultant victors, thrilled not only by their possession of the battlefield but by their successful initiation into the martial fraternity, toured the scene. "[T]he carnage was . . . terrible for acres, the ground was covered almost entirely with the bodies of dead men & horses." Tourism, though, was one of the prerogatives of rank, as at "one little space of about two acres our regt gathered up and buried on yesterday some 249 bodies of which 17 were our men." His commission protected him from physically handling the "numberless bloody stained corpses" torn apart by "shells and the clothing and skin . . . burned off of hundreds of the dead rebels" as "they lay blackened ghastly spectacles in the sun."[25]

While his soldiers dug shallow battlefield graves for their own comrades and the rebels, Buckner reflected on his first combat experience. His rides over the field examining the dead scattered throughout the woods both confirmed his worst suspicions about secession and the Confederacy as well as challenged them. In the rainy days following the battle, Buckner's temper was piqued by a salty secesh comment from Helen's friend Sallie Moore. "I am sure that if you had seen as I have the Corpses of Federal soldiers bayoneted in their beds, by the *chivalry of the South,* the *flower of the land* . . . you would not see that they deserved to be treated as heroes & martyrs with fresh won laurels," he retorted. All was apparent if one could only "look at the contrast between their conduct on the battle field and ours." The catalog of rebel horrors included the following: "One poor fellow I saw my self, was brutally murdered by the enemy while combing his head, without the comb having been disengaged from his hair. Another officer shot in the leg & arm (both slight wounds) lay dead with a bayonet stab through his heart. Others (I saw myself) lay still in their beds, bayoneted in their sleep. And yet people will say & others believe that *we* are waging an inhuman and improper warfare for the desolation of the country the destruction of society." "You have doubtless been lead to believe," Buckner wrote, that the rebel forces were composed "almost exclusively of gentlemen inspired by a sense of duty to battle for their 'liberty'—This is absurd a complete mistake. You may rely on my word and know, that the material of our army is better far better than that of the rebels." In Buckner's mind, men displaying such a disregard for the qualities of discipline and rational judgment as to believe that rebellion against the government was in the interests of "liberty" could hardly be gentlemen. And who could expect such men to fight like gentlemen? Most telling of all, they "were nearly all drunk or at least highly excited with liquor during the fight . . . & I know it because in almost all the canteens of those killed, liquor was found." Examining the faces of the rebel dead revealed not gentlemen but "*ruffians and desperado[s], even as plainly written as letters 'graven in brass.'*"[26]

Nevertheless, there was something to be said for the Confederates whom he had faced in honorable, conventional combat. Perhaps it was the realization of his own honor on the battlefield that allowed Buckner to respect the manliness demonstrated by his foes. He expressed admiration for the bearing of George W. Johnson, "the bogus governor of Ky. who when his horse was killed (he was an aid to Genl J C Breckenridge) took a musket . . . into the ranks as a common soldier," where he was killed not long after.[27] The shared danger and concurrent assertion of socially acceptable virility bred a healthy respect for some of the enemy despite political differences or the seeming irrationality of secession.[28] Because both he and his honorable Confederate foes, such as Johnson, were members of the same martial fraternity, though, Buckner redoubled his criticisms of those secessionists who stayed behind in Kentucky. He authorized Helen to tell "all those of secession proclivities who in the bitterness of their narrow contracted souls" wished ill of "*our people* who are imperiling their lives on this battlefield [so] that the lives liberty and property of all may be respected"—an important reminder of the concern he felt for Kentucky's slave society that motivated his stand by the old flag—that he likewise hoped they "may come to harm and that death defeat & disgrace may be the [fate] reserved for them [and] for all such." He could stomach—grudgingly—a manly disagreement, a difference of political opinion to be settled by the rules and order of the conventional battlefield (though he would prefer it settled by the rules and order of the state and national governments), but those working for the Confederate cause at home—out of the ranks—were of a different breed. "They are at hearts traitors, lacking only the courage to make them[selves] our armed foes."[29]

This class aside, though, he was too much like his Confederate foes to vilify them completely. Even when Sallie Moore, free as usual with her opinion, wished that the whole of the Union army might die of yellow fever in the swamps of West Tennessee, Buckner sarcastically laughed it off as a "Christian and charitable commiseration and was such a direct and palpable observance of that Biblical precept which says 'love your enemies, do good to them that hate you, and pray for them which despitefully use you.'" It was not Sallie's fault she should say such things, of course, but the temporary insanity of her political convictions. "I did not attribute it to any thing except that mania *Secession*" and "therefore dont hold her responsible for it, but hope on her account that she may be speedily convinced of the error of her ways." In much the same way as a caring father forgives slights and insults from ungrateful children, Buckner assumed that Sallie would see sense before long and come around to his point of view. Of course, that was the image of himself that he hoped to project to one secessionist in particular, and although he could rage against her cause, his love for Helen persisted even at the height of its danger to him. "Do you know that the day of the battle, I thought of you again and again, that during the terrible scene that I thought not of mother & father or self only you[?] God bless you darling you are so good, true, and noble."[30]

Even before Buckner's letters could reach home, word of his conduct at Shiloh was winning him another important victory. A report originally published in the *Louisville Journal* under the headline "Kentuckians at Shiloh" was picked up for the Lexington audience by the *Lexington Observer & Reporter*. Buckner was the very first man singled out: the article noted the conspicuous bravery and the sort of "hair-breadth escapes, such as that of Major Buckner's of the 20th Kentucky, who had a cannon ball pass between him and his horse without doing any injury to either," which had ensured that "[n]ever before was the chivalry of Kentucky better represented than on this field." "Let other States boast of the patriotism of their sons," proclaimed the article, "yet Kentuckians can point with pride to the field of Shiloh, and say truly that their loyalty and prowess were proven there."[31] Buckner was the lead story out of the battle in two of the state's most influential and widely circulated newspapers. When the first reports of the battle had reached Winchester, Helen's mother had personally written Buckner a letter, he told Helen, "containing an assurance that she did not feel unkindly towards me." This was, needless to say, a significant improvement over his previous standing in the eyes of the elder Martins, who had long opposed the marriage of their youngest daughter to this unproven young lawyer. Though he had responded to the unexpected letter, Buckner also eagerly bid Helen to reinforce his "kindest regards" to Mrs. Martin and stress that the note had "afforded me the greatest pleasure."[32]

With good reason, then, Buckner was well pleased with himself in the wake of Shiloh. But more than fame and glory, the laurels he won helped him secure the outcome he desired most from the conflict: demonstration of his honor, courage, and leadership in the watchful—and judgmental—eyes of Winchester. There was immediate evidence of the battle's effects on this social front.

It was because of this incalculable social value of military service that the domestic victory over the Martins practically eclipsed the military one for Buckner. "I am anxious to exchange war with its loud alarms for peace," he wrote Helen soon after the fight, dreaming of the day he could be "with my darling to share with me what fortunes" may come. "I can with the full certainty of having served my country fearlessly at least," he continued, "return to Civil life, better prepared to enjoy the quiet & comforts of home than before. If all goes as we wish, how happy . . . we will be, and then we can with a quiet smile look back upon these days of trial and troubles, and reflect that if they served no other purpose they at least gave us a taste of stern and real adversity and have fitted us to enjoy the smooth & placid comfort of domestic life all the more." So complete was his success, he imagined the war nearly won and earnestly wished it could be for the sake of both his relationship with Helen and the health of the nation. Buckner seemed to have little concern for his own health or was too earnestly focused on the pleasant future before him, Helen, their future (slave-owning) household, and the United States. "[A]fter the fight on Monday and coming out unhurt I think that there is no need to fear any other," he said. "To be sure escaping unhurt in one battle is no evidence that the like will occur again but since the fight I have felt more & more assured that I would come out of the war unhurt." As for the conclusion of the fighting, "[i]t is a mere question of time. . . . In 60 days New Orleans and the whole Mississippi Valley will be in our possession, and the Starspangled banner will float from the source of the 'father of waters' to its mouth. How would you like to make a trip to New Orleans this winter?"[33]

If Buckner's head was still in the clouds after his glorious introduction to combat, the grinding drive to secure the boggy lands between the Tennessee and the Mississippi Rivers returned him to earth. Buckner passed a miserable few weeks in the "muddy hole" of the Shiloh battlefield before the army pushed toward the Confederate stronghold of Corinth, Mississippi; the only thing making up for the miserable rain and constant patrols for Confederate activity was his proximity to Helen's cousin, George Martin Jackson. The son of Clark County ironmaster Josiah A. Jackson, now an officer in the Fourth Kentucky Infantry, had made pleasant company for Buckner and the Winchester officers of the Twentieth.[34] Things became far more active with the advance on Corinth, however. "General Nelson seems to think that the 22nd Brigade is equal to any emergency," Buckner wrote Helen after an exhausting three weeks in the field, "and whenever any hard or dangerous work is to be done, we are called on." But Buckner reveled in the danger as well as the opportunities for independent command afforded him by the small-scale probing actions in the swamps and forests of north Mississippi. "Our pickets fire at one another constantly," and the situation afforded him numerous opportunities to recount his dangerous scrapes to Helen. In a replay of the near miss he had at Shiloh, he recalled that "[o]ne shell filled with musket balls exploded just above where I was standing and one fragment and about twenty balls struck the ground near my feet."[35]

He promised to bring her home one of the shell fragments to add to her collection of war memorabilia, as well as honeysuckle from the Shiloh battlefield, famous for its ironic harvest of human life in the midst of springtime blooming. When Ben passed his war stories and physical tokens of the battlefield back to Helen as a reminder of his commitment to the cause and the fulfillment of his duty, she reciprocated by sending tokens of her feminine domesticity to maintain his spirits while on hard duty. In imagining her "plain but neat & well fitting calico dress," Ben conjured "some thing suggestive of a pure, gentle and loving heart" that he cherished so in a wife. Expanding on his domestic ideal, he continued, "One never thinks of the woman that he wishes to make his wife, as dressed in silks or satins—but in the pictures which visit his delighted fancy the idol of his heart always appears in the most simple and unostentatious garb as if to typify the idea, that the companion of a mans life should win him rather by the display of love truth constancy and devotion than by bedecking her person with the most costly fabrics of modern manufacture." He was particularly pleased one day late in May to receive swatches of her latest dress fabric and trimming. "I would be delighted to see you with the dress on, and I know you will look very pretty in it. You have no conception how very much I want to see you how I dream about you at night and in the day."[36]

His dreams about Helen's idealized appearance in the new dress brought Ben back to the messy realities of his own appearance at the moment, however. "Your idea of my personal appearance under the existing circumstances is far from correct," he wrote to avoid any confusion. "I wear a black wool hat, and my face is nearly of the same color, my hair short, my mustache trimmed close, my whiskers cut off—beard of about a weeks growth, (I have no time to shave oftener than once a week as you may imagine, when I tell you that we have been in such a state of watchfulness that I have not pulled off my sword for nearly two weeks)[.] My uniform consists of a stiff pair of soldiers' shoes minus the strings, a pair of coarse army pants and a blouse without shoulder straps." It was an appearance fitting for the work Buckner was engaged in, stripped even of the insignia of his rank as a major—the physical embodiment of his rank and status—to avoid being the target of Confederate sharpshooters. Buckner claimed that campaigning in the Mississippi sun, under which it was widely assumed none but black men could work, had made his lawyer's white complexion nearly black. "Actual service in the field dispels all the romance of soldiering," he continued. "It is a laborious drudging life for anyone of lower rank than Colonel, and I would rather be a negro under Harrison Thompson (for the same length of time) than a private soldier."[37]

"Bull" Nelson's confidence in the Kentuckians of the Twenty-Second Brigade was showing in more than just Buckner's increasingly ragged appearance. Buckner fancied that they had gained quite a reputation; there was a rumor about camp that they were to be sent to the Army of the Potomac to boost U.S. fortunes in the eastern theater. "The Yankees cant fight like our Kentucky boys," he boasted. On the heels of another successful action in late May, Buckner was proud to proclaim that "[o]ur regiment has the reputation of being one of the best in the service and I think that their good conduct entitles them to all the praise that has been given them." Indeed they were, and so, it seems, was Buckner. In the midst of a ferocious, if small, fight for a bridge along a main road into the town of Corinth, an amalgamated unit of men from the Twentieth, First, and Second engaged two full-strength Confederate regiments. Seizing the initiative and hoping to drive some Confederates out of a secure position in a heavily timbered swamp, Buckner led Company A of the Twentieth—his original company of Winchester men, with whom he had attacked the secessionists back at the Van Meter farm nine months earlier—off on its own advance. Charging at the double quick and driving into the midst of the larger Confederate force, Buckner's twenty-five men soon found themselves swarmed upon by a Confederate battalion of at least one hundred. Buckner emptied his pistol into the rebels, firing his last shot at one man who was simultaneously leveling his rifle at the major's chest. Both missed, though "his rifle ball cut a twig within two inches of my head." An instant later, Charley Hanson's little brother, Sam, "sent a minie ball through his head—leaving the poor fellows hat on the grounds with a handful of brains in it."[38] The Confederates fell back as belated reinforcements caught up to Buckner's small group. On the far end of the line, opposite Buckner's newly won position, Lieutenant Colonel Hanson led the balance of the Twentieth in an attack that secured both sides of the road and bridge, prompting the Confederates to evacuate the town the next night, leaving it in federal hands on May 30. Hanson's official report of the campaign noted that Buckner "and his men deserve great credit for the manner in which they drove back the enemy and held them in check." Colonel Thomas D. Sedgewick of the Second, temporarily in command of the brigade, noted that Hanson and Buckner "evinced the greatest bravery, gallantly leading and encouraging their men amid the greatest dangers," and General Nelson endorsed the work of Hanson, Buckner, and the Twentieth in opening the path into the city.[39]

Kicking about camp near Iuka, Mississippi, during a predictably humid June, Buckner summed up all that he had achieved in his first campaigning season in sentiments that had been his mantra throughout his active service. "I believe that for us a brighter and happier day is dawning," he wrote, "and that our happiness so fondly dreamed of, and joyously expected is nearer than you suppose. This terrible war cant last long and when I return, the consciousness of having fearlessly discharged a dangerous and unpleasant duty and your smiles, will more than compensate me for all the hardships and privations, that I have undergone." Those smiles had been conditioned on the successful and fearless discharge of that duty, but he had earned them. Buckner had tested himself in the forge of combat, stood for his principles and the rights of all white citizens, and received due adulation from an appreciative Kentucky press—all of which, he hoped, was enough to demonstrate his worthiness for Helen. His mission looked very nearly accomplished by the summer of 1862. He hoped that his pleasant vision of his and Helen's future would be that of the nation as well. "Our union then, though long delayed by adverse circumstances, will be all the more happy, because of the cruel and severe tests to which our affections have been subjected."[40] Seeking refuge from the summer heat, Buckner built "castles in the air" in which he envisioned "a neat little cottage furnished in a plain manner" and "a lovely woman whose heart is filled with all the noblest impulses of womans nature." Such a perfect picture of domesticity seemed close at hand. "How delightful to shut out the stern and horrid realities with which I am surrounded" by imagining the perfect wife, a respectable living, adoring children, and devoted slaves—all of which loomed just months out of reach.[41]

4

I Feel Impelled to Pause

With the rebel army driven dramatically out of Tennessee and into Mississippi in the summer of 1862, Buckner's greatest daily irritation had been not with thousands of cheering rebel soldiers intent on his death, but local secessionists in farms and towns along the army's line of march. Though he claimed in a letter to Helen that he was "content that people should call me a *Yankee,* a *Hessian* a *Vandal* a *thief* & all the other long list of expletives which your secession friends shoved indiscriminately upon us," the misperception of his cause by fellow white southerners was, in fact, quite disturbing to him. Those barbs were particularly irksome because he imagined himself to be the opposite of each of them. He was no Yankee, but a southern member of the master class, like the ladies who routinely insulted him; he resented being called a thief when he had enlisted to defend the property rights of slave owners under the existing laws and the Constitution and had upheld even the claims of secessionists against his own men; far from a Lincoln hireling, Buckner distrusted the president and the president's party but had placed his own partisanship aside to serve the country. But rebels outside of the Bluegrass frustratingly could not seem to see past his blue uniform.

The assumption that his coat and flag made him an agent of abolition was confounding and enraging. Even Buckner, the self-conscious stickler for the rights of citizens in temporary rebellion, had slipped when one slave owner had made that mistake in judgment. When Buckner rode up to ask for a drink of water, the "old fellow . . . replied very gruffly that he had none and immediately drove his three negroes who were standing in the yard when I rode up into the house and locked the door." "I was of course in a very bad humor," he admitted, "& was on the point of making some angry reply when I looked around & saw about 50 of the 2nd Ky going into his cabbage hole and knowing what would be the fate of the cabbage, I felt that my revenge was complete. I quietly turned my back & dont know what befell [the] place but have'nt much idea that there was any cabbage left in five minutes."[1]

Although most white loyal Kentuckians were secure in their faith in a fundamentally proslavery Constitution and Union, fears about the threat to slavery posed by the federal government had been at the back of their minds for the first year of the war. Lincoln had, in fact, been very careful of the rights of loyal slave owners, due in part to fear of losing Kentucky—famously "the whole game" to the president—and in part to a recognition of the constitutional obstacles to antislavery moves. The rescinding of John Frémont's famous emancipation order, which exceeded the bounds of the 1861 Confiscation Act by freeing the slaves of both loyal and disloyal masters in Missouri in September 1861, had assured Kentucky's loyal masters that a conservative stance on slavery could be expected from the Lincoln administration. Such a pronouncement encouraged the state to abandon its neutrality and fully embrace the cause of the government just days later. The assurance that the property rights of loyal owners were to be ensured was the bedrock on which Kentucky's loyalty was built.[2] D. C. Wickliffe of the *Lexington Observer & Reporter* conceded through it all that "[t]he President certainly entitled himself to great credit for his action" in response to Frémont and other crises of army-led antislavery talk and activity, but he also recommended that "it would be better not to invest such men with power at all" because it could "create distrust and apprehension in the minds of those who are for sustaining the Government as it is, and not as the Abolitionists would have it." In the struggle between antislavery Republicans in Lincoln's party and proslavery politicians along the border—including a sizable number in the congressional delegations of western states, Indiana in particular—Wickliffe counseled Lincoln not "to try the dangerous experiment of 'riding two horses at once.'"[3]

The question of what Kentucky's loyal masters might do if the government made any further inroads into the rights of slaveholders absorbed the entire border region's attention. In December 1861, *Cincinnati Gazette* correspondent Whitelaw Reid was in Frankfort covering a particularly fascinating session of the Kentucky legislature when, by chance, a leading member of the House stumbled into Reid's hotel room one evening. Never wasting the opportunity for a good story, Reid invited the representative to sit and have a conversation about Kentuckians' views "on the inevitable negro question," which had consumed no small part of the debate in Frankfort and Washington. Reid thought that the "real views" of this member, "from a neighboring county *east* of Fayette," might be of particular interest to his readers "in the North," who were having difficulty understanding Kentucky's loyal masters. Reid's new friend remained anonymous, but geography and political sentiment point to John B. Huston, the House member from Clark County, an old Buckner family friend whose old Whig, John Bell, and proslavery union politics were in perfect harmony with those of most loyal men throughout the state.[4]

"[W]e surely ought to use the best means to put down the insurrection. Slavery is the weak point of the rebels," Reid proposed to his Kentucky friend, "why not strike them there?" "Because you don't need to," the Kentuckian replied, "and because the evils would be a hundred fold greater than the benefits. Let me tell you: Proclaim the general emancipation of all slaves . . . and destroy any hope of a Union party" in Kentucky or elsewhere in the South, "and unite the whole South as one man in a struggle of desperation for the institution of Slavery—a struggle which would end in the wildest anarchy." Intrigued, Reid pressed his friend. Would Kentucky "rather plunge into that anarchy and despotism than give up Slavery?" "In reason, no," was the frank response, "but there's no reason about this matter. Haven't you learned yet that reason hasn't anything to do with the nigger? A decree of general emancipation would irrevocably and hopelessly plunge Kentucky into the rebellion with the rest. It might be very foolish, very insane, but that doesn't alter the fact." White Kentuckians, the representative mused, "have been educated to regard Slavery as one of their rights." Even Kentuckians who own no slaves themselves would stand and die to defend their perceived rights. "Don't you see there's an infatuation about the nigger? And, besides, you would be violating the Constitution to confiscate and emancipate; and taking away constitutional rights, even in things they haven't much interest in, is the best way to make men desperate."

"'There is no use disguising the matter," said Reid's friend; "theoretically you Northern people may be right in opposing Slavery—we'll not discuss that—but a decree of emancipation would be the opening of a frightful war, and the end of Republican institutions. Liberty would be gone, anarchy would be upon us and *sauve qui peut!*"[5] Every man for himself.

Huston's speculations about the future of slavery in the loyal states would be put to the test in March 1862, when Lincoln made a speech urging the slave states to accept a federally funded, compensated emancipation scheme.[6] Writing to Helen after she had "gone & got mad at poor old Lincolns foolish message," Buckner sought, in good paternal style, to show her the error of her ways and bring her around to his more mature reflections on the topic. "I have enjoyed several hearty laughs at it since the disgust which a first reading inspired has worn off," he wrote.[7] "It will have no effect, and as long as the poor old dotard confines himself to *recommending* the abolition of slavery, I am content." There were limits to Buckner's patience with the president and the federal government, though. "[W]hen ever he goes beyond that and endeavors in violation of the Constitution and laws of the country to take the property of people from them then I am no union man," Buckner threatened, "but in the parlance of your braggadocio secesh friends, I will spill the last drop of blood &c &c to prevent it."[8]

But Buckner could hardly imagine that such a series of events could take place. The passage of the District of Columbia emancipation bill through Congress may well have given him some more pause, but it came at precisely the wrong time for him—or, indeed, for much of the Kentucky press—to be too angry at. Despite a furious attack on the bill led by Kentucky senators Garrett Davis and John J. Crittenden, it cleared both the House and the Senate within a week of the Union triumph at Shiloh. The intoxicating victory on the Tennessee at Shiloh, continuing the string of successes that had driven the Confederates out of Tennessee, promised an end to the rebellion soon and with that a return of a full-strength southern congressional delegation, which could prevent any future moves in the direction of emancipation. Nevertheless, that day needed to come soon because, as Allen Guelzo has noted, the District of Columbia bill was "the first time in the history of the Republic" that Congress had diverted from its role as guardian of the slaveholding republic and "taken a direct step against slavery."[9]

Buckner remained unworried. Helen wrote him asking his opinion on what must have been Lincoln's May 19 message revoking David Hunter's confiscation and emancipation order along the South Carolina and Georgia coast but reemphasizing the government's right to seize contraband slave property. "I am as much opposed to Lincolns proclamation as you are," he responded, "and think he has covered himself with infamy." If anything, though, Buckner took solace in the thought that he was fighting "not for any particular administration" but for the "great government" guaranteed by the Constitution and the Union instead. "Lincoln has as yet not permitted any anti slavery steps to be taken by his Generals," Buckner reminded her, "and that until we are convinced, that there is positively *no* hope, I think it better to fight for that side, which has heretofore given us peace prosperity and happiness, than for that which only promises us lawless violence and commercial ruin." As had been the case since Lincoln's election, Buckner was not pleased with the Republican administration but preferred it and the Constitution to what he considered the political, economic, and moral failings inherent in secessionism and the Confederacy. When Helen raised the issue of Lincoln's well-publicized use of martial law and denial of habeas corpus, Ben applied the same logic. "I admit it all," he wrote about the violations of the Constitution, "and while I condemn it, I know that in all times of war and violence '*the laws are silent*.'" Again, though, he turned the tables on the rebel partisans. Though "Lincoln has violated the Constitution," Buckner countered, "Jeff Davis has made his *own* will the supreme law of the land, and no man dares hold an opinion adverse to that of their president. Look at the Conscription act, the thousands of men who are reluctantly dragged into the army & tell me where Lincoln has done any thing that equals this."[10]

Although Buckner chose not to worry himself overmuch with the Hunter issue, that issue was to have quite the "unusual afterlife," to borrow Eric Foner's term, throughout the summer. The precedent Hunter set by declaring the slaves in the coastal Sea Islands "forever free" and accepting volunteers into the Union service, spurred both pro- and anti-emancipation forces into action, besieging Lincoln throughout the summer. An angry group of border-state congressmen were not satisfied with Lincoln's adherence to his scheme of compensated emancipation for loyal masters and were even more disturbed by antislavery Republicans' push for an all-out proclamation of emancipation regardless of slave owners' loyalty. It was the latter sentiment, though, that held sway in Congress—just as Buckner had always feared it might with the majority of southern representatives now meeting in Richmond rather than in Washington. Early July saw legislative fruits of the antislavery majority; the Second Confiscation Act eased the restrictions on seizing the enslaved property of rebels as a justifiable act of war. Buckner made himself perfectly clear about the ramifications of the new law when Helen asked about what it would mean for his loyalty. "And you dont know whether I would be willing to advocate Emancipation to save the government do you or not. You must believe I have changed most sadly from what I was," he stated quite firmly, "if you believe that I would ever consent to any thing so cowardly & mean[.]" Buckner had always and would always act in ways he considered beneficial to slavery first; that was, of course, why he had sought to defeat the rebellion so earnestly for the past year. Had he known that Lincoln began drafting early copies of the preliminary Emancipation Proclamation within days of the Confiscation Act's passage and distribution to military officers in the field, his convictions would only have strengthened.[11]

The war, though, took Buckner's attention away from regular contact with the events rapidly unfolding in Washington. On the road from northern Mississippi through Alabama, communication had been difficult. "We know nothing about what is going on in the world," he wrote in a quick note on reaching Athens, Alabama, where the regiment "received a few newspapers, though as yet no letters." A few days later he reminded her that "that it is not an easy thing to write on the march, for writing materials are locked up and packed away in our trunks" in the baggage train at the rear of the column.[12] Although he was largely unaware of the increasing threats to slavery brewing at the capital, he did observe some disturbing scenes that evidenced the hardening approach to the war from Union army commanders. Staying in Athens for about a week, he found the "people of the town & neighborhood," though "mostly Secesh," were quite "easy to get along with," a welcome change from the hostile and inhospitable rebels that had enraged him in Middle Tennessee. The white residents of Athens were glad to see fellow southerners, too, even if they were in blue. They made "bitter complaints" about their treatment by the Union troops who had garrisoned the town before the Twentieth, "and," Buckner noted, "if a tithe of what they say is true our army is disgraced by the conduct of these wretches."[13] The Nineteenth Illinois and their brigade commander, Russian transplant John Basil Turchin, frustrated at the official army policy of respecting the civil and property rights of rebel citizens even as the unit was continually harassed by Confederate cavalry and irregulars, had vented all of their pent-up anger at both the Alabamians and General Don Carlos Buell's soft-war policy in one furious explosion of violence. The May 2, 1862, "Sack of Athens" left buildings burned, houses ransacked, townspeople harassed and some allegedly raped with Turchin's tacit consent, which he gave when he said to his men before the chaos began, "I shut my eyes for two hours." A month on, the residents of Athens were still recovering and increasingly bitter. Buckner's welcoming hosts compiled laundry lists of the outrages they had suffered—at which they were well rehearsed, many of them participating in the court-martial proceedings then under way against Turchin.[14]

The Athens incident was a signal moment in the transition from a policy of conciliation toward Confederate-sympathizing white southern civilians to a hard-war policy that attacked not only Confederate armies on the conventional battlefield but also the material and productive base of support for those armies—slavery and slave-produced crops and goods central to it. Buell, who had married a slave-owning Georgian and had owned as many as eight people before the war, was popular with the Kentucky officers under his command because both he and his officers hoped to fight a limited war that did not risk the social and political chaos that would stem from any challenges to slavery in the loyal or disloyal states.[15]

As a consequence of this hope, Buell sought to make an example of Turchin and stacked the court-martial to make a statement about what he believed to be the proper conduct of the war. Brigadier General James A. Garfield presided over a court-martial board that included three Kentuckians, whose sympathies with their fellow southerners in Athens were in little doubt, and a former Indiana Know-Nothing.[16] They did precisely as expected, returning a guilty verdict that recommended that Turchin be cashiered from the service, a sentence that Buell fully endorsed. The nation, the president, and Garfield, however, did not. The stalling of the Union advance in the East and the violent and nonviolent hostility faced by advancing Union armies in the West had convinced many commanders in the field and observers back at home that a stricter policy toward rebel property and activity was necessary. Perhaps Turchin had gone too far, Garfield argued by the end of the trial, but Buell's extreme hands-off policy was even less effective, a "dancing-master policy" that offered the rebels war on their own terms, not on those terms that would speedily bring the war to a close. Pulling rank on Buell, Lincoln's War Department kept Turchin in the service, found him a new brigade to command by September, and raised him to the rank of brigadier general. "Short of actually removing Buell, it is hard to imagine what more devastating insult the administration could have offered him," writes Mark Grimsley. "Soldiers, public opinion, and government had all had a bellyful of conciliation."[17]

Loyal Kentuckians such as Buckner had not. Despite their objections, no longer would white rebel southerners be treated as a loyal population temporarily occupied by the Confederate government and military but instead would be treated as a hostile foreign foe. It was the same thinking that was at that moment driving the Second Confiscation Act through Congress. If the government could end slavery for one class of citizens—as Buckner always continued to classify rebels, still clinging to the hope of a peaceful reunion and a reunited southern proslavery congressional delegation—could it eventually find ways to apply the same logic to loyal masters? If secessionists confused him for an abolitionist because of his blue uniform, was it eventually conceivable that the northerners who now controlled the government would confuse him for a rebel because of his proslavery convictions? Turchin's men certainly had not stopped in their rampage to ascertain the loyalty of some of the citizens of Athens. Some of the worst damage that Buckner saw in the town "was done to" the house and property of "a Union man. What punishment," he asked Helen rhetorically, could be "too severe for officers who permit such conduct?" As the U.S. government looked toward a hard war against slavery, Buckner wanted to assure Helen and all at home that he hardly reflected his superiors' sentiments. Finally catching up with his mail in August at McMinnville, Tennessee, he scolded his fiancée for ever "believing me to have turned Abolitionist."[18]

The hard war followed the armies to Kentucky in the fall of 1862. Buckner and the Twentieth marched furiously through a late-summer drought to catch Braxton Bragg's Confederate army, which had slipped out of northern Mississippi and was driving, virtually unopposed, toward Louisville. Kentucky was in crisis. The rebel-sympathizing governor, Beriah Magoffin, had been deposed by what amounted to a legislative coup; the government had fled Frankfort; Lexington and Winchester were under rebel occupation; and outriders from gray columns were within sight of Cincinnati. During a brief halt in Bowling Green, Buckner pulled his writing chest out of the regimental baggage train. There, he dashed off the only note Helen was to receive from him for the next two months as he pursued the rebels through Kentucky. Its urgency spoke to the pressing issues on his mind.

> We have just arrived here—and I write you a line before I have time to wash off the dust because I dont know at what moment we may be ordered to move and I hope that this may reach you. We are going to whip Bragg and Capture Kirby Smith and you know we will fight hard when our sweethearts are beyond the enemy and we know we have to whip them before we get to our darlings.
> —Good bye, Yours Ever B.[19]

After a glorious spring and summer of successful combat, Buckner must have expected a grand confrontation in the Bluegrass, a heroic final battle that would simultaneously win him glory on the soil of his home state, cut off a major Confederate army, and doom the rebellion to destruction. The Kentucky campaign produced none of that. The long-expected battle that would decide the fate of the campaign, at Perryville in western Boyle County on October 8, was a small, hard-fought affair that was in many ways a Confederate tactical victory. Buckner and the Twentieth were frustratingly near the battlefield but never did engage the Confederates. That was, in fact, the fate of the majority of the Union army, which because of acoustic tricks played by the knobby hills in the area was largely unaware that the battle for control of Kentucky was being fought just miles away. Rather than in crushing Union victory, the campaign ended much as the battle had, with the Confederates allowed to slink back south, hauling away tons of food, materiel including thousands of yards of the famous Kentucky jeans, and the state's equally famous livestock.[20]

During the Perryville campaign, both the face of the Union army in Kentucky and the institution of slavery there were forever changed. Before the Confederates struck north to "liberate" Kentucky, the state had been garrisoned largely by local troops under a Kentuckian, General Jeremiah Boyle, an army and a commander sympathetic to the property rights of loyal men. But the Confederate offensive had drastically changed the balance of power in the state. The old northwestern states, fearing a rebel assault north of the Ohio River, had sent thousands of new recruits southward to stop the Confederate advance. Meanwhile, Buell's veteran corps of men hailing primarily from north of the Ohio, "whose months in Tennessee and Alabama had taught them the usefulness of slaves to the Union cause and made them reluctant to defer to slaveholders or proslavery military commanders," entered the state from the south, bringing the army's new confiscation and hard-war doctrines with them. The "invasion boomeranged against Kentucky slaveholders," write a team of prominent historians, "by increasing the number of troublesome Union soldiers in their midst," and though the state's loyal masters were glad to have the rebels driven back into Tennessee, they were "not thereby relieved" of any threat to their slave property and slave-based prosperity. "Scattered amid the state's largest slave population, the camps of the midwestern regiments proved to be irresistible magnets for fugitives. With the state rid of Confederate soldiers, Kentucky slaveholders and midwestern soldiers turned upon each other, forced into confrontation by the slaves' determination to be free."[21]

There were few outright abolitionists among the young men in Union blue, though many of them were free-soilers who desired a white republic cleansed of the evils of slavery and of African Americans' moral and social failings, in which the racist climate of the nineteenth century had encouraged them to believe. There were exceptions; Albion W. Tourgée, a lieutenant in the newly formed 105th Ohio Infantry, for example, would begin a lifetime's work of fighting for an end to racial injustice during his regiment's first deployment to Kentucky. "All [of the midwestern Union soldiers]," though, "had cause to regard with suspicion the very Kentucky slaveholders whose vacillation had seemed to place their own home states in jeopardy," and their first views of slavery in practice in Kentucky did nothing to improve their estimation of Kentucky's cherished institution or those who defended it—in either blue or gray. "Whether from high motives or low, Midwestern soldiers defied orders and welcomed runaway slaves into their camps," and when "the masters followed in pursuit, the soldiers jeered, threatened them with bodily harm, and helped the slaves elude recapture."[22] Historian Victor Howard has found evidence of at least ninety-one military units from other states participating in slavery's collapse in Kentucky during that fall, with just seven other out-of-state units upholding the state's laws governing the institution.[23]

Flashes of conflict between slave owners—loyal and disloyal—and western Union troops erupted across the Bluegrass. The Twenty-Second Wisconsin, nicknamed the "abolition regiment," made national headlines when it was assaulted by a mob of enraged white Kentuckians in Georgetown "with revolvers, stones, and whatever missiles they could lay their hands to, demanding the negroes" the regiment concealed within its ranks. Fed up with the harassment, regimental commander Colonel William Utley marched his men out of the town the next day with loaded guns and fixed bayonets, "then advised the citizens that if they intended any hostile demonstrations upon him . . . to clear the city of women and children, for, as sure as there was a God above, he would shoot down every man who interfered with him, and lay their town in ashes."[24]

Winchester itself saw one such conflict erupt during that tense fall. Colonel Smith D. Atkins and his Ninety-Second Illinois Infantry had enraged the white citizens of Mt. Sterling with a terse order reminding "[l]oyal citizens who are the owners of slaves" to "keep them at home, as no part of my command will in any way be used for the purpose of returning fugitive slaves" in early November. "It is not necessary," Atkins continued, "for Illinois soldiers to become slave-hounds to demonstrate their loyalty—their loyalty has been proven upon too many bloody battle fields to require new proof."[25] Whether he found proof of loyalty in such actions, Atkins failed to grasp that much of loyal Kentucky did indeed put stock in a slaveholding Union's strict adherence to the law and Constitution as an important demonstration of loyalty. General Boyle moved quickly to defuse the volatile situation. He appealed to Atkins's commanders to remove him from Montgomery

County, which was soon done. Of course, Buckner's long-circuit rides into the eastern counties could attest to the fact that the road back into the Bluegrass from Mt. Sterling brought the Ninety-Second right through downtown Winchester.[26]

Clark County slave owners were glad to be garrisoned by Kentucky troops, who shared their concern about the new antislavery policy taking shape in the state. Some of the officers of the garrison unit, the Fourteenth Kentucky Infantry, got early notice of the Ninety-Second's movement and decided to give them a fitting reception. A number of prominent Clark County men collaborated with the officers to gather a mob like that which had confronted the Twenty-Second Wisconsin in Georgetown. Together, "the citizens threatened, with the aid of the 14th Kentucky to 'clean out,' the Illinois boys" when they neared the town. As the Illinoisans approached, they found the Fourteenth drawn up in ranks, and though the regiment was never ordered to fire, Atkins later noted that the Kentucky officers had their revolvers drawn, ready for conflict. "Col. Atkins," read a letter to a Cleveland newspaper, "accordingly marched through the town with fixed bayonets and loaded guns, and an excellent stomach for the fight." A violent confrontation did not occur, but army officials were infuriated with the Fourteenth for encouraging "a military offense second only to mutiny." One of the conspiring officers was arrested, though nothing ever came of the charges against him.[27]

Winchester having been left in relative peace, a Lexington crowd did actually force itself into Atkins's regiment, trying to forcibly remove Henry, a Fayette County resident's slave, from the ranks. Atkins rode to the scene of the disturbance from his place at the head of the line and dispersed the crowd quickly when he ordered one of his companies to prepare a volley for the mob. If Kentucky mobs could not stop Atkins, Kentucky lawyers could. Just outside of town, Atkins was met with a civil suit for having "stolen" Henry and other slaves. But the courts would take time to work; Charles S. Rogers, an officer in the Tenth Kentucky Cavalry, appealed to his and Atkins's commanders for a more immediate solution using the chain of command. He claimed that a number of specifically named slaves of loyal masters "and about 30 more are now harbored in said regiment" and noted that "it will be appreciated" if some action were taken so that "we soldiers of Kentucky, can have some assurance, that our property is being protected at home, while we are away battling for our loved country." For his part, Atkins had long run out of patience with Kentucky slave owners, even—maybe especially—the loyal ones. He vented in a letter to his division commander that "Kentucky soldiers are no more willing to fight for our beloved Country, than the sons of Illinois," asking, by implication, why Kentuckians were treated with such kid-glove care. "Illinois is loyal without conditions," Atkins shot back. "She imposes no 'ifs' in her devotion to the Union."[28]

"Ifs" were beginning to creep into Buckner's thoughts. Not only was the campaign into the Bluegrass disappointingly inglorious for him personally, but it finished on a note that changed the course of his war. Pursuing the Confederates out of the state, the Twenty-Second Brigade was ordered to Clay County to sweep out rebel strongholds along the approaches to the Cumberland Gap. In addition to the roadway, Buell was eager to regain control of the salt works in and around Manchester, which had been occupied by the rebel army since the Confederate advance in the summer. Throughout the summer and fall, secession forces had confiscated an estimated 3,500 to 4,000 bushels of salt from salt works along Goose Creek, owned primarily by the White and Garrard families, including Colonel T. T. Garrard of the Seventh Kentucky Infantry. The brigade easily brushed aside two thousand or so Confederate cavalry in the vicinity on their way into the county, but it was quickly decided that there was no practical way to defend the valuable works from future rebel raids. Buckner and the loyal Kentuckians were needed in the army's main body as it pursued Bragg into Middle Tennessee. "[E]very circumstance," read the report of brigade commander Charles Craft, "led to the belief that the quantity [of salt] on hand would have been shortly taken" by the Confederates as soon as his forces left the area and that "as a matter of economy, the destruction of the works seemed to be a wise movement."[29] The brigade detailed five hundred men to work for thirty-six hours straight, "doing in that time a vast deal of work," reported the three regimental colonels. "The wells and pumps upon which the works depended for supplies of water to manufacture the salt" were "taken out of the wells, broken to pieces, and the pieces forced back into the wells, into and upon the pipes," and into a few "we forced . . . cannon balls" to complete the destruction. Conferring among themselves, the commanders of the expedition "permitted the loyal citizens around and in the neighborhood . . . to remove enough salt to supply" themselves "in order to prevent great suffering" during the coming winter, and "binding them by oath not to permit any of it to go to the benefit of the southern confederacy." The rest they dumped into the local streams.[30]

Rather than fighting the romantic and climactic battle for his home and facing the final test of his mettle as a man in October 1862, Buckner found himself bringing the hard war to Kentucky's slave society. Aside from being a valuable military target, the salt industry had been the cornerstone of the slave economy of Clay County, linking both agriculture and industry together through economic exchange and a flexible market for enslaved labor in ways very similar to Buckner's Clark County. The Whites and Garrards, who dominated the local political and social scene in addition to the economy, led lives "predicated on slave labor" in much the same way as did Dr. Martin and his fellow "lords of the pasture" back home. For the Garrards, the salt operations were the "final link" in their "vast agricultural and commercial empire," which included the family's extensive landholdings in Bourbon County.[31]

Just as in Clark, the Clay County salt economy provided an adaptable platform for slavery to thrive outside of plantation staple-crop production. The Garrards and Whites shifted labor between their salt wells and their farms depending on seasonal need, in addition to hiring some slave labor to and from local small slave owners and non-slave-owning farmers. Even the poorest farmers in Clay County were tied into the slave economy ordered by salt; they were able to purchase the product at prices well below market value in other locations, facilitating their family subsistence agricultural operations, and in years where they found themselves with a surplus of grain, meat, or other products, they had a ready market in the slave-owning salt operations. Even when the transportation revolutions of the 1850s and the shifting of the meat-packing industry away from the Ohio Valley led to the decline of the much larger salt industry in western Virginia, the Clay County slave system, which had heavier investments in land and slaves compared to the Kanawha Valley salines, was able to shift more hands into agricultural work. Clay County effectively rode out the market changes because it could decrease its salt production in accordance with the lowered demand while still keeping slavery a viable economic and social institution in the county.[32]

But what would the destruction of these salt wells mean for the future of that slave economy and society now? If the salt works of Clay County were valuable enough targets to destroy in the name of denying the Confederates access to their products, then what of Clark County's wealth in livestock, its hempen cloth, and its iron foundries? Would Dr. Martin's own "agricultural and commercial empire," which was heavily invested in two of those three industries, survive? Could Buckner sustain a legal practice when there were no longer wealthy farmers and hemp factors to do business in Winchester? These were only the economic questions at stake. What would happen if there were no more demand for slave labor? Who would buy the surplus slaves if the cotton states were a hostile, foreign country or, worse, had been declared free states as a war measure? The republican disinterestedness of Mrs. Garrard, who "expressed her entire willingness that not only that valuable property, but all else that she and her husband . . . owned, might be destroyed, if such destruction would help to restore the Union," was of little comfort. It was no comfort to her husband, Colonel Garrard, who would later reflect "that he would not have heeded Lincoln's call to arms had he known it would mean the abolition of slavery in Kentucky."[33]

Ben Buckner and Charley Hanson were of much the same mind as they sat on their horses watching their Kentucky soldiers deal slavery in a Kentucky county a mortal blow.

Halting on the march away from Clay County on the road into Middle Tennessee, Ben sent Helen the first lengthy letter he had had time to write in months. Things had changed during the months the armies had been in Kentucky. The Union forces had driven back the Confederate invasion of the state, but at what cost? All the fears that had grown since the spring about the administration's policy toward slavery had come true. The preliminary Emancipation Proclamation had been issued. "It is a most abominable & infamous document, and falsifies all" of Lincoln's "pledges both public and private," Buckner thundered in the opening volley of a furious rant. The country was forever dishonored, he believed, and even if it did survive, the antislavery moves "will remain upon the history of [the] country as a black blot, a mark of our national degradation and our Presidents weakness & infamy." "The Union Kentuckians," he continued, "are not shamefully heated, and by reason of the presidents want of good faith, which is only equaled by his lack of sense, we find ourselves in arms to maintain doctrines which if announced 12 months ago, would have driven us all, notwithstanding our loyalty to the Constitution & the Union into the ranks of the Southern Army." Though indulgence of passion and emotion could be dangerous to honorable character, Buckner asserted that this anger over the attempt to unman, enslave, and degrade white citizens was not one to be ashamed of. As he came to embrace this anger against the federal government, he recalled his common interests as an aggrieved white southerner with his Confederate foes. "[N]o Kentuckians can have any heart for this contest. We joined the people of the North (a people whom we did not love) to fight the South (a people with whom we were connected by ties of relationship, interest, the identity of our hearts and institutions) merely upon principle and to preserve that

Constitutional form of government which was the wonder and admiration of the world. But the president has by the shake of the pen taken away all that." The tyrant's pen ruled in Washington, said Buckner, and would topple both sound government and the very foundations of society. The young lawyer, whose family and county's "interest" and "identity" were tied up in the institution of slavery, had, in seeking to prove himself a worthy, dutiful, and honorable citizen, enlisted in an army that was now the agent of attacks on the very social order in which he hoped to secure a prominent place. Lawless tyranny, he believed, had invaded his ordered world and turned it upside down.

> But what are we to do[?] Where can we go[?] The people of the South have brought all this upon us and are not worthy of our support. Nor can they give us any guarantee of protection or assistance. Suppose Kentucky were to secede now. The ruin devastation & slaughter would be visited on our own state and our rivers would soon be red with blood and our plains would be the final resting place of thousands upon thousands of our Citizens, and as for slavery not a vestige of it would remain. We can only hope (if even that is left us) for the return of reason and common sense. As for my self I have no hope that my resignation will be accepted, but I intend to tender it whenever we receive orders to leave the state.[34]

As beneficial and even necessary a decision as serving the Union cause had seemed to be in the summer of 1861, less than a year later that decision would prove to have unimaginably threatening consequences for Buckner's dreams of social, professional, and domestic success and stability. Buckner's letters to Helen show that the Lincoln administration's changing war goals, moving beyond a war to save the Union to a war against slavery, brought about this change. The language of law, order, and rational governance—of society, household, and self—that he had employed to justify his unionism was conditioned upon the U.S. government's continued constitutional protection of the rights of slaveholders. The federal government's attacks on slavery that began in late 1862 increasingly raised questions of honor, respectability, and masculinity that were inextricably intertwined—as were the identities of many white southern men—with the assurance of white supremacy and black inferiority provided by the institution of slavery. Buckner's decision to leave the army was not as clear-cut as the choice to join it, though. To resign, he would have to make the case—to Helen, to Winchester, and to himself—that the social dictates of manhood were better fulfilled by a stand on principle than by military service.

There were alternatives to resignation. The invasion had demonstrated the need for stronger garrisons in Kentucky towns, railroads, and river ports. And the conflicts between free-state military men and local slave owners in the fall had shown that the former clearly were not who loyal Kentucky officers wanted defending the lives and property of loyal white Kentuckians. Surely, Buckner and his fellow officers reasoned, the tension between military authorities and loyal masters would be eased if Kentucky troops were pulled off of the front lines to garrison the state—protecting its territory from invasion by rebels and its institution of slavery from interference by antislavery northerners. Talks about recalling the Kentucky regiments home went on throughout November 1862 as the army moved over the increasingly difficult muddy roads to Nashville. The early winter rains reflected Buckner and his fellow officers' mood. Although most Kentucky officers, Buckner reported, seemed to be "enlisted in the scheme" to have the regiments return to the state, and some were even "sanguine of success," he had lost faith in the Union army entirely. His denunciation of the preliminary Emancipation Proclamation earlier in the month had convinced Helen that he would be home by Christmas. That might not be possible, he warned her, but she could "rest assured that I will come whenever I can. This is my private intention and I will permit no opportunity to affect my purpose to pass me without seizing it." With emancipation now on the table and an uncertain future ahead of the state, Clark County, and his future family with Helen, Buckner had now become "determined that my first duty is to you and to myself."[35] *Sauve qui peut.*

A transfer to a Kentucky garrison was better than remaining in the field, of course, but it still would require that he be subject to the orders of Lincoln's War Department and, worse still, might leave him stationed on the other side of the state from home and Helen when yet another "collision between the people & troops" might occur, Buckner prognosticated, flaring up into "a series of bloody tragedies [that] will signalize the beginning of one of those revolutions which will sweep over the Country leaving like those in France a trail of blood behind it." It was a telling prediction, which had particular meaning for the young Kentuckian raised on a diet of horror stories from slave insurrections past. All white southerners knew that the trail of blood that began on the guillotine in Paris had spread across the Atlantic into the slave insurrection on Saint Domingue; according to the U.S. senator from

Bourbon County, Garrett Davis—friend to the Buckner family and namesake of Ben's youngest brother—both the thought of armed slave uprising and black claims to freedom and political voice "make human nature shudder." The "living, glowing, horrid colors" of stories from white refugees from Haiti "haunt[ed]" Davis's "memory to this day." "When the slaves come as invaders," he predicted in a speech on the Senate floor, "with arms placed in their hands, it will be like letting the young tiger taste of blood. When he gets a taste, his savage fury will know no bounds, but will rave and rage as a demon from the infernal regions."[36]

D. C. Wickliffe used his platform in the *Lexington Observer & Reporter* to prepare for such raves and rages. On November 26, he issued a call for the citizens of Fayette County to mount vigorous slave patrols until and past the January 1 enactment date of the Emancipation Proclamation. Despite the fact that the proclamation exempted the loyal slave-owning states and other areas under Union control and thus held no water in Kentucky, Wickliffe argued, the "wide spread, if not universal belief amongst our slaves that they are to be free" with the new year had demanded action. "Humanity, personal and public interests of the highest kind, and private and public safety make it the absolute duty of the community to forestal the terrible consequences that are actually the product of this belief of the slaves." He proposed patrols of twenty men in each of the county's eight voting precincts, ten on duty at all times in shifts running around the clock. "If they do their duty, even tolerably well, the fatal delusion of the slaves of the county can be corrected in ten days, and every evil effect of it prevented," the editor argued. In the familiar pattern of slave-revolt scares in years past, Wickliffe called for a "small executive committee, *with full powers*" to be elected and collect subscriptions from slave owners to pay the patrollers. "The men of Fayette know their danger, their strength, and their duty," he proclaimed in this new call to arms. "*They may rest assured that the Federal officers in military command in Kentucky, are not responsible for the evils pressing on us, and that they will do nothing to aggravate them,*" he wrote, trying to reassure those same officers that he was not raising a battalion of rebel troops. "But, it is our part to provide the remedy, for the impending explosion. Let the law be what it may, this is a case which is best met, by our being, for the emergency, a law unto ourselves."[37]

Back in camp, Buckner worried about what white Kentuckians would do in such a volatile situation. What would happen if they became a law unto themselves? If he expected black people to lash out with savage violence, the proud martial reputation of white Kentuckians—which he himself had upheld—inclined him to worry about what they might do in the face of such a threat to their rights. "We have much to fear, and much reason to exercise prudence and caution," he wrote to Helen, hoping that peace and deliberation would rule the day. "[B]ut a people like our Kentuckians can never permit such tyranny as has been attempted in the last few months. It were better far better for all to be killed in the resistance of such usurpation than to quietly acquiesce. The people can not & will not permit them to continue." With such horrid predictions a very real possibility in the minds of white Kentuckians, Buckner was convinced that the only place for him was by Helen's side. He had gone to war to defend Clark County's property, honor, and institutions; now that all three were threatened by both Union and Confederate armies and by the very slaves within their midst, there was no question about where his proper post was. In light of these predictions, perhaps home—perhaps Helen—would be better defended with Buckner out of the army rather than in it.[38] The only difficulty now was getting there.

Although many Kentucky soldiers hoped to be posted closer to home, for Buckner *"consolidation"* was the likeliest "mode of getting out of the army." With the Kentucky regiments—like most units that had seen active field duty—reduced in numbers due to combat casualties, disease, and disability from hard marching, Ben and his fellow officers sought to convince military authorities that paying "a number of officers sufficient to manage 1000 men for controlling a little over one tenth the proper number" was fiscally irresponsible. If regiments were consolidated, a number of supernumerary officers could be allowed to go home without—importantly—the potential disgrace of resigning their commission. "Most Lt. Cols. & Majors favor consolidation and a few Colonels," Buckner reported, though he foresaw some problems where "ambition overrides all other considerations," which might lead some not to "favor it because they might loose their places." Individual ambition was not the only obstacle the consolidation scheme had; the army's new commander, William S. Rosecrans, was a disciple of the War Department's new hard-war stance, quite the departure from Buell, whose reputation for inactivity and sluggishness was due in part to his reluctance to wage the new kind of war in favor in Washington.[39] Despite his Democratic politics, Rosecrans had little patience for walking on eggshells to protect the rights of slave owners, loyal or disloyal. "I think Kentucky troops stand in bad order with Genl Rosecranz," Buckner wisely surmised after only a couple of weeks' observation of his new commander. "I think he is too radical & they too Conservative to suit each other well."[40]

Such suspicions about army officials were rampant in the Kentucky troops' camps. James C. Morris, the *Observer & Reporter*'s camp correspondent, wrote a pair of letters to the paper questioning Rosecrans's and other army officials' motives in resisting the consolidation plan. After recounting the Twentieth's long suffering in combat, disease, and hard marches, he made the case plainly. "After the ordeal she has not more than one hundred and seventy-five men for duty. On parade she had not two good companies," he said of the regiment, which had numbered 850 in January. "To these few men we have 38 commissioned officers with an average salary of $130 per month," Morris argued, making a "business transaction of it." Consolidation, he maintained, was both prudent and patriotic if men "who love their county so well as to give their time and services to support it" could be persuaded "to give up their positions to promote its interests."[41] In his next missive, however, Morris found a larger conspiracy afoot than reluctant Kentucky officers. "The Kentucky regiments," he wrote, "are decimated and reduced," yet the new northwestern units that had caused so much trouble with loyal slave owners that fall—or in Morris's words, those units that had been "quartered upon our people"—"number from 800 to 1,000 men." Why should these new antislavery units, "who by their acts are infamous and despicable," garrison the state while Kentucky troops, "who are acquainted with every foot of our State and appreciate every feeling and interest of its people," be "pressed to the van, away from our homes, which are constantly threatened[?]"[42]

Morris believed he knew precisely why. "There must be some ulterior end in view in sending Kentuckians from their homes—there must be some pet scheme of the war which cannot be worked out if we remain at home—and thus we are sent off." Lincoln, Rosecrans, and the Republican congressional delegation, he alleged, schemed to send Kentucky troops into the crucible of battle against their fellow slave owners, the rebels, and to destroy slavery once the state's loyal sons were too weak to resist. Kentucky, Morris insinuated, had been betrayed. "Look well lest the vestal fires of Kentucky be permitted to go down and her few people be disgraced," he warned his fellow citizens. His next warning was for the antislavery men in Washington and in their midst: "Our state despises alike the enemies of her dearest interests North and South. She respects the enemy who meets her in the field upon an issue fully made up . . . infinitely more than one who, under the guise of protection gives a fatal stab to her best interests." Nevertheless, his duty as a soldier and his honorable reputation as a Kentuckian demanded that he keep "pressing on with our army, performing ... to the best of my ability." Appealing to his friends at home, Morris concluded, "Our rights and interests are confided to you—they are sacred to us—and if in the course of this unhappy contest they are to be sacrificed, we hope that other than treacherous hands will tear them from us."[43]

"Treacherous hands," though, seemed firmly in control of the situation. Rosecrans resisted when the Kentucky officers put forth a plan to consolidate the Third Kentucky Infantry with the Twentieth, a plan that carried the endorsement even of Kentucky governor James F. Robinson, to whom the officers had appealed "by a special messenger," not trusting their mail to arrive in Frankfort unmolested by government authorities. Rosecrans had good reason, however, to doubt the Kentucky officers' sincerity and patriotic motives. A large majority of them had placed their resignations on his desk just days before putting the consolidation scheme before him. Rosecrans had been flooded by Kentucky resignations since the middle of November, when Buckner noted that "the Kentucky troops are in a Considerable Difficulty. Many officers are resigning. Many others desire to resign and some dont know what to do."[44] By early December, though, they had decided. On December 2, Buckner tendered his resignation, albeit with "but a faint hope that it will be accepted." He took heart, however, knowing that he was not alone. "All of the officers except Col Hanson will immediately tender their resignations just as soon as the Presidents message is received—that is if he adheres to his Emancipation proclamation." He felt his case was just, being "based on the ground of business & the dissatisfied condition of the officers of the regiment—16 already having resigned because they are required to remain in the South when their property & that of their friends is being stolen by our supposed friends."[45]

Sixteen officers—now seventeen with Buckner—resigning from the Twentieth was a critical mass. In such numbers, Buckner was relatively sure that little negative stigma would attach itself to him for resigning. The ambitious but yet financially and socially insecure young man was about to take a radical step to preserve his good name—the one thing yet fully in his possession. "I want to get out honorably" he wrote, "& while prudence dictates one course, principle dictates another."[46] Prudence and the long American tradition of young men making their names—and winning their sweethearts—on the battlefield told him to see out his term. But principle, the uniquely southern principle of white male identity built on the foundations of slavery and domination, demanded his resignation. Buckner explicitly listed his reasons for resigning to Helen because, as he saw it, she would determine their validity.

Her protest to his decision, her questioning of the honorability of his actions and therefore his character, would have negated them immediately.

Resignations needed to be justifiable. Just as a man could expect community denigration for running away from battle, an officer could expect the same for abandoning his men—a number of whom, it must be remembered, were from the same county as he—to return to the safety of home. Cowardice or even the perception of it had the opposite effect of honorable military service: it was a good way to lose reputation. Buckner himself had criticized those who would leave the service without sufficient cause in months past. On one occasion, responding to one of Helen's many requests that he resign and return home to her after the battle of Shiloh, Ben wrote, "I feel that I would give everything in this world to see you and to be assured that we would part no more but I know that if I were to resign now, my resignation would be accepted, and I could only return in dishonor. You don't want to see me come in that way do you[?]"[47] It was all but a rhetorical question.

If, however, Buckner was part of a massive protest of loyal proslavery officers, standing up for the health of the institution that defined themselves, their communities, and their loyalty to the Union cause, the stigma of resignation was not so threatening. Perhaps. On the one hand, he had a strong case for resignation. "I cant fight against my principles and those of my friends in order to satisfy the absurd desire of a faction at the north," he wrote. No one could accuse him of disloyalty, either, just because he was "utterly indisposed to fight for Lincoln-abolitionism"; he was "further from joining the Confederates. They brought all this upon the country and upon them the blame of all this ought to rest." On the other hand, "We don't want to be driven to the wall," and he hoped to "prevent so unpleasant a step as a dismissal from the service, but we are determined to *quit*." Revealing his insecurity over taking the plunge into potential disgrace, he cautiously scouted Helen's opinion on the subject. "[M]y heart as well as my judgment tells me that we are right," he boldly claimed, just before timidly probing, "I am sure that my Sweetheart will never think less of me for it, will she?"[48]

If Rosecrans seemed to be the very personification of misguided and disingenuous government policies on slavery, Buckner and the other Kentucky officers could take comfort in the fact that they had some allies in the new Army of the Cumberland. William Lovy Smith, their division commander, had treated Buckner and the other officers "with great kindness," talking them down from resigning as their outrage flared early in December. In "order to settle the matter as amicably as possible," Smith offered to broker a deal with Rosecrans by which the Twentieth would be posted to Lexington if the officers would pull their resignation letters. The plan pleased Buckner and the other Bluegrass officers well enough to enlist their support (though Buckner did not say how the Purchase men took the news), but it was not to be. When all the parties sat down to negotiate, Rosecrans explained that he could not make it work. "[H]e would gladly defer" to the Kentuckians, Buckner reported, "were it in his power," but "circumstances would not permit him to gratify our wish just at this moment . . . without injury to the public service." The general called on the Kentucky men to put aside their personal interest and to act now for the good of the country, "to do their duty, &c &c." Rosecrans had a point, of course. Having pursued the Confederate army south of Nashville, he was attempting to maneuver into one final battle for control of Middle Tennessee before winter set fully in. He needed all the veteran troops he could muster to take on the regrouped rebel army under Braxton Bragg. The old Twenty-Second Brigade would deny Rosecrans three veteran Kentucky regiments if their officers kept up their protest and stood fast to their demands for transfer, not to mention the potentially harmful effect on morale their departure could have army-wide. He needed them to stay, on one hand, and genuinely thought they should, on the other. His pleas to the Kentuckians' patriotism fell flat. "This is not satisfactory to any of us," Buckner bluntly retorted. "We feel that we are duped."[49]

That feeling was quickly reinforced when Charley Hanson personally took his concerns to Rosecrans. According to Buckner, Hanson had previously vowed that he would "not fight to free his own negroes."[50] Now, in his closed-door meeting with Rosecrans, Hanson candidly made his case that as he "owned several thousand dollar[s'] worth of slave property," he "did not feel satisfied to fight in a cause so detrimental to his own interest." The general told Hanson that if he were so concerned about his financial interest, he should turn his slaves over to the army for use as laborers and "that he would after a while get pay for them" from the government. "This is a sweet proposition for the General commanding now 100 000 men nominally engaged or supposed to be engaged in a war for the maintenance of the Constitution & the law," Buckner commented. He scoffed at Rosecrans's assertion, sarcastically remarking that trusting "to Lincolns slavish abolition congress to remunerate him" was "Truly a delightful prospect."[51]

Such prospects led Buckner to believe that the federal government had abandoned its founding principles and commitment to preservation of personal liberty, particularly for slaveholders. The government's disrespect for property rights, he was convinced, had spilled over into violations of other constitutionally protected rights. Not only had Kentucky officers been persecuted by "tyrannical military authorities" such as Rosecrans, but now, Buckner feared, the conspiracy extended even into the post office—controlled by Republican postmasters appointed by the president. By December, he was writing guardedly unless his letter was being carried by private hand to Helen, a situation increasingly made possible by the stream of dissatisfied Kentucky officers resigning and returning to the Bluegrass. He encouraged her likewise to "[w]rite cautiously upon political topics."[52]

"A union man engaged in the service is given to understand by the General Commanding the army," Buckner summarized, "that his rights of opinion and of property are held as naught, and that he and his friends are to be sacrificed in this Crusade against slavery notwithstanding his undoubted loyalty." "It is absolutely disheartening," he concluded, "[t]o men who not only have no sympathy with the rebellion, but who have perilled their lives for the preservation of the government and the Constitution, to hear from the lips of the Commanding General such a sentiment." After all this, Buckner had "no heart to write" and certainly less to command troops in the field. "To be handed over to the tender mercies of the abolition soldiery who look upon this war as the means of plunder is almost as distressing as to have John Morgan make a series of raids. One is just about as bad as another." Both were insults to the very manhood he had enlisted to defend, flaunting his inability to protect his home and property from the enemies that seemed to surround him on all sides. As he wrapped up his December 7 letter to Helen recounting the week of wrangling with Rosecrans, Buckner took his only hope in a meeting called by corps commander, Major General Thomas L. Crittenden, the loyal son of Kentucky's stalwart senator, to plan for the Kentucky troops' future. Buckner wished for only one outcome: "I hope soon to be at home."[53]

The meeting with Crittenden was everything Buckner hoped for. *"I am coming home,"* he opened in his letter to Helen. "This is as certain as any thing which is uncertain," he said, with a bit of his playful wit having returned after a month of despairing gloom. Crittenden had agreed to ease Buckner's resignation through the chain of command "as soon as matters quiet down a little in our regiment," which, Ben allowed, might be a while, but no later than January. Switching into a domestic tone, he proposed that he and Helen marry "as soon after my return as we can make our arrangements—our long engagement rendering any further *'probation'* unnecessary." In his ecstasy, Ben reminded Helen that she was his true cause, particularly now that the government had seemed to abandon him and all white Kentuckians. "Your beautiful dark eyes still haunt me," he wrote at the end of a litany of praise for her beauty and charm, "and the recollection of your devotions makes me anxious to devote my life to *your* service, believing that the reward will be greater and the recipient more grateful than if I suffered myself to be killed in the supposed service of my country."[54]

The agreement, though, did not stand. The day after Buckner spoke with Crittenden and forwarded along his resignation letter, the Twentieth unexpectedly received orders to return to Kentucky. Rosecrans, it seems, had not waited for matters to quiet down with the Twentieth, which had proved itself more problematic than the other Kentucky regiments the general had under his command. Instead, seeing an opportunity to remove a headache unit from his army and strengthen his supply line along the L&N against a threatened Confederate cavalry raid, he dispatched the Twentieth to Bowling Green. Federal commanders in Kentucky had become apprehensive as Rosecrans had pushed south of Nashville. With Confederate cavalry reported in force around Lebanon, Tennessee, they asked Rosecrans if he could spare a regiment. Rosecrans knew just the unit to send; as disgruntled as the Twentieth's officers were, they would be of doubtful fighting capacity with him south of Nashville, but during his long conversations with them over the past weeks, he had no doubt heard the Twentieth's repeated denunciations of the rebels and of John Hunt Morgan in particular. In the letter ordering the regiment home, Rosecrans's chief of staff hoped that "if the rebels dare enter" Kentucky, the Twentieth would be sufficiently stirred by defending their own state to "fit up [an] expedition to cut them to pieces."[55]

Far from rekindling the embers of Buckner's martial pride, though, the move to Bowling Green sealed his disgust with the Union army. At the same time as the Twentieth was given the orders to move north, he received his resignation letter, "returned disapproved." Whether Rosecrans had intended it or not, by moving the Twentieth, he had mapped a new chain of command through which all requests, resignations included, would have to proceed. Now, Buckner's "resignation would have to pass through different intermediate hands than Genl Smith & Genl Crittenden's," his formerly safe route, making the "prospect of resignation . . . far from brilliant just now." Despite being temporarily reversed, however, he was daily growing more sure about his decision to leave the army. Thus, when he "received two letters, one from my father imploring me not to leave the service, and one from my mother urging me to come home at once," he was better prepared to put aside his father's concerns for public reputation. The decision was nevertheless an agonizing one. "It is needless for me to tell you," he commented to Helen, "how distressing this difference of opinions is." His father, unsurprisingly, made a strong case. "I dont believe that my father would survive my dismissal from the service, and although nothing on earth would be so pleasant as to quit the service, yet when my friends at home or a patron of theirs and especially my father feel so decidedly opposed to any violent steps and feel that such an one would compromise both my own honor & theirs, that I feel impelled to pause a moment before I take any step which would procure my dismissal from the service."[56]

On the other hand, his mother's letter provided the justification he needed to overcome any lingering uncertainty. "She says that my duty to myself, to *you* and to her all demand that I should at once leave the army and come home."[57] Buckner had felt it his duty to go to war and prove himself a man in the eyes of Winchester, Helen, and the Martins. Now that he had done so at Shiloh and Corinth, his mother argued that another duty—that of an adult man, the head of a household—was to return home and secure a future for himself and Helen.

By the time he had finished reading his mother's letter, he had mentally resigned from the army. He was still keen to move the wedding up as soon as possible, "just as soon as the regiment is located for the winter." His longing for Helen, of course, was only increased when he was met in Bowling Green with a backdated letter from Helen and a photograph of her. Rather than teasing his fiancée about all the pretty girls about town as he had been doing since the very beginning of their courtship, he observed "that the women here all look horrid & ugly," particularly compared with her image, which was radiant, "though you are ten thousand times prettier" in person. But it was not only pretty girls who failed to stir Buckner. "I am inattentive or rather utterly indifferent as to all military duties," he wrote, "and although every one is excited because of prevailing rumor in regard to John Morgan['s] movements, I am perfectly unmoved." So much for Rosecrans's plan to reignite the hearts of the Kentuckians. "What effect the booming of the Cannon or the rattle of musketry will have I cannot tell," Buckner said, "but I fancy in my present mood I will not make a very dashing soldier."[58]

Christmas improved that mood a bit, so much so that Buckner, ever the temperance man, was not even disturbed by the "twenty fellows whose potations have been 'strong & deep'—egg nog" or by the less-refined beverages that had sparked "quite a row in camp" among the enlisted men. Nor was he particularly put off by the fact that his body servant, Jim, had gone "off on the train to take his Christmas holiday," likely heading south in the L&N cars toward Nashville. Jim had taken the initiative and expanded upon the liberties that enslaved people had grabbed around Christmas in years past now that the balance of power seeming to shift more in his direction. The Emancipation Proclamation loomed just a week away. Rather than be angry, Buckner was reflective on this new spin on the master–slave relationship. "How much more *free* the servants than the master." He was so uncharacteristically unmoved because it appeared that a new avenue to his own "freedom" from the army had opened; a change in commanders placed the Twentieth under Indiana general Mahlon Manson, a conservative Democrat whose command Garrett Davis had praised earlier in the year as "not fighting for the emancipation of slavery but for the restoration of law and order." Buckner now expected "but little difficulty in getting any reasonable request through."[59]

By the time Davis made his comment, in February 1863, it was only a matter of time until Buckner could "have a private talk with Genl Manson," who was "so busy" organizing his new command and dealing with the frustrating Confederate cavalry raids buzzing around the state's southern border "that it is almost impossible to have a word in private with him."[60] Buckner's greatest annoyance in the meantime was, in fact, due to those Confederate raiders under Morgan, who, Buckner remarked a month earlier, had cut telegraph lines, "destroy[ed] the trestle work at Muldraughs hill" along the L&N, so that it "would be fully a month before it could be rebuilt & perhaps longer," leaving only the low river to connect him to Helen. The most reliable way to pass letters along was through his fellow disgruntled Kentuckians, who were either resigning or taking furloughs home to survey the changed landscape in the Bluegrass before deciding on their course of action. Charley Hanson and James Morris were specifically mentioned as taking furloughs to mull over their future, and Buckner reported sending at least one more letter by an unnamed officer who was returning home.[61]

Though Buckner was glad for his good friend Hanson to get the opportunity to go home, in January it put Buckner in command of the regiment and kept him in Bowling Green for the foreseeable future. He used his time to plan his exit from the army. His latest "project on foot" was to secure an appointment as "assistant

Inspector Genl with rank & pay of Colonel in the Kentucky State Guard, which is to be organized and armed for the state protection," through the assistance of "several friends of influence & position." Buckner was excited about the plan, which would allow him to stay in nominal military service but under the command of the governor, not the increasingly mistrusted federal War Department. "This will enable us to be together a great deal—in fact we will never be separated except for a few days at a time," he happily reported.[62] It was, however, not to be. Federal military authorities were not thrilled with the idea of raising state troops independent of their command and hostile to many of the regiments still garrisoning the state. Buckner's commission died with the plan. One way or the other, however, Buckner wanted out. In between trips to Evansville, Indiana, escorting rebel prisoners on their way variously to be exchanged or to be imprisoned at Camp Chase, Buckner mostly counted down the days until Charley Hanson returned from his furlough. A number of the married officers in the regiment had brought their wives to Bowling Green, only amplifying Ben's longing for Helen and his frustration with Charley. "Cant you hurry him back[?]" he asked Helen while Hanson was in Winchester. "Tell him he has got a wife that he can bring with him but that I have to go to see my darling as she Cant Come to see me." As soon as his friend returned and the paymaster visited Bowling Green—"He owes me about $700 dollars and I dont feel like losing that amount these hard times if it can be avoided"—Buckner would be on his way home.[63]

While Buckner was waiting to disentangle the bureaucratic red tape that kept him in the service, he became even more firmly convinced that he had no business in the Union army any longer. The official sanction for recruiting African American soldiers into the Union army contained in the Emancipation Proclamation made any continued association with the federal military abhorrent to him. Because political equality was not yet a reality, the army was now the first place a white man would potentially be forced to stand side by side in line of battle with freed slaves. Would the rifle and military service, the crucible of civic character for budding citizens, now lead black men to the ballot as it had done for generations of young white men? Having observed from the periphery the social implications of antebellum political rituals, African Americans certainly believed—and hoped—that it would. Buckner was indignant. "[W]e are very much *edified* by reading the proceedings of the Congress upon the Negro Soldier bill," he wrote Helen on February 1, a month after the Emancipation Proclamation had gone into effect. "All men of decency ought to quit the army if that bill becomes a law."[64]

His syntax is revealing. Implicitly, those without decency, without honor, willing to submit to the orders of an integrated army, could remain in the service. But Buckner was far more concerned with the orders of the slave society back home in Clark County. Now the military, that institution that had minted white men and Kentucky citizens since statehood, would be tainted by black recruits. His carefully chosen and underscored word, *edified*, speaks to his resolve. No longer did he speak of resignation with immature timidity, but with the rock-solid authority of a matured patriarch. In resolving to leave the army, Buckner had matured into the decisive, principled (according to his standards), and fearless man he had hoped the army would make him in 1861.

Within the week, he had secured a furlough to come home for "20 or 30 days," during which time he and Helen could "consult as to what we will do in future." There was but little planning left to do, of course. "I have no doubt," Buckner wrote, "but that we can agree to what we want to do—First to quit the army marry & settle down to a quiet life."[65] After having to wait for another officer to relieve him as provost marshal of Bowling Green (so the position would not fall to "a mean Michigan Abolitionist utterly despised by all present"), Buckner finally left for home on February 20. Persevering despite the numerous obstacles the war continued to throw between him and Helen, he managed to make it to Winchester but could not stay long. "Bob Stone and about forty rebels had returned to Mt Sterling," he heard, "and thinking it possible that a dash might be made on Winchester . . . I came back to Lexington and will go home this morning if I can." All was eventually well, and he even used his time in Lexington profitably. The court clerk in Winchester was away on business, so Buckner secured a marriage license in Fayette County.[66] Rebel cavalry and absent county officials aside, Ben and Helen were married on March 5, 1863.

Buckner returned to Bowling Green from his furlough only long enough to submit his resignation letter on April 13. Learning his lesson from his previous attempts, it contained no mention of slavery, emancipation, or the looming race war he feared. "My business owing to the disturbed condition of the Country, and the repeated occupation by rebels & guerrillas of the town in which I reside," he wrote, "is in the greatest confusion and requires my immediate personal attention to avoid great pecuniary loss." The greatest pecuniary loss he feared, of course, was his and Clark County's investment in human property. That loss would be more than monetary, of course; it threatened to destroy Buckner's society, his sense of self, and his future with Helen.[67]

Buckner's agonizing over whether to leave the army was more than a question of political principle. His tortured decision-making process was in reality a frantic scramble to understand himself, his community, and his future in a world suddenly absent the one thing that had defined all three all his life: slavery. Slavery, in this context, was not only a political issue or an economic system—though it was undoubtedly those things—but also the framework of a social world being shaken to its core. Buckner's resignation letter concluded with a particularly candid declaration. "Neither my duty nor the exigency of the Service requires me to make so great a sacrifice as a longer continuance in the army will require."[68]

5

Privileges and Elections

So much was uncertain on the morning of Monday, August 7, 1865. In the predawn hours, small detachments of soldiers from the Second Wisconsin Heavy Artillery fanned out from Winchester while people across Clark County saddled their horses or set off walking to their local voting precincts. Election day was tense and uncertain for the Kentuckians who would elect a new state legislature, for the Kentuckians whose future would be shaped by that legislature but had no say in its election, and for the occupiers of a loyal state that too often felt as if it were not.

A deeply divided white electorate included people who claimed to be loyal to the federal government but who could muster few kind words for any of its representatives and some staunch supporters of the government who were glad to be through with the war but not sure about how much more they were willing to give to see the nation restored. All of them brought their conflicts over the conduct of the war, over the fate of slavery, and over the power of the federal government with them as they came to town to vote. Like the two previous elections in 1863 and 1864, armed men in blue uniforms would oversee their exercise of the electoral franchise. To some Clark Countians, this military presence was a comforting protection from the lawlessness and violence—some of it motivated by ideology but increasingly more of it simply murder and robbery—that had plagued Kentucky communities during the last year of the war. To others, though, it was yet more proof of the federal government's despotism.

The conservative reaction to emancipation and black recruitment after 1863 was driving an ever-growing wedge into the Unionist coalition that had banded together in 1861 to put down the rebellion. Officers such as Buckner resigned their commissions rather than serve an integrated, emancipationist war effort; soldiers refused to reenlist in 1864 when their terms expired; and conservative politicians made scathing anti-Lincoln speeches in nearly every county of the state. Unconditional Union men—for whom defeating the rebellion was of utmost importance, regardless of the ultimate fate of slavery—gradually warmed to the harsh repression of rebels and suspected rebels and gravitated toward a practical emancipationism that believed that the death of the Confederate slaveholders' rebellion could be accomplished only by the death of slavery itself.

The Union coalition of 1861 was turning on itself. Men who had waged antebellum political campaigns on the same side and men who had more recently fought actual battles in the ranks together started to see treason in the words and deeds of their fellow Kentucky Unionists. The nature of that treason differed for each group. For conservatives such as Buckner on one side of the coin, the federal government—the White House, Congress, and the federal military—was the agent of that treason: subverting free elections, arresting political dissenters, ignoring loyal men's property rights in slaves, and generally abusing constitutional process in the name of military necessity. Unconditional Unionists, on the other side of the coin, rallied round the flag and the government in its peril from within and without. They found the fierce and constant denunciations of the president, the Congress, and the generals as well as the pledges of "no-men-or-money" to support the war signed by Kentucky conservatives but a hair's breadth away from outright rebellion.

All of the disconcertingly familiar trappings of recent Kentucky elections would be present this Monday in August 1865. Troops would be at the polls, potential voters would have to swear loyalty oaths, some would be denied, and a handful of men with enough whiskey or zeal—or both—would be arrested. Yet 1865 added to the mix two new populations whose future status in Kentucky would be in large part decided today: rebels and African Americans.

The rebels could not vote, of course; they were disenfranchised by both state and federal law. They had, however, returned to the state, and because elections were both political and social events, they would definitely be gathered around the polls. To prevent both rebel veterans and stay-at-home rebel sympathizers from voting, local Union men—usually unconditionalists—had compiled lists of citizens whose votes were not to be taken and had distributed them to election judges and garrison soldiers, who might not be able to tell who the rebels were now that they had returned to civil life. Men who had been in rebel armies seemed straightforward choices for exclusion, but determining rebel supporters among the old men at home was a dangerous game bound to cause trouble.

Clark County was also home to thousands of African Americans whose relationship to the crumbling institution of slavery and whose relationship to their (current? former?) masters was as unclear and contradictory as anything else. The Thirteenth Amendment, not yet officially ratified but looking likely, doomed slavery eventually, but until that time the institution existed as a legal fact by the laws of this loyal slave-owning state. Yet if it existed in law, the final years of the war—which saw widespread enlistment of black men in the Union army, a massive population movement of their wives, children, and extended families to cities and military posts across the state, and a massive influx of African American refugees into Kentucky from across the South—raised serious questions about whether slavery still existed in fact. For every master who had accepted the obvious and let his enslaved people seek their own lives and fortunes wherever they might be, there was another who desperately cracked down and demanded the same laborious work from an ever-dwindling number of slaves who stayed to perform it. For every enslaved person who had sought freedom, education, and, they hoped, citizenship in the army, another stayed in Clark hoping to ride the transition to waged work in the same houses, farms, and ropewalks in which they had been enslaved.

If one were to judge by the newspapers alone, the amendment was the only issue in the campaign, yet there was a deep subtext to positions for or against ratification. What a voter or candidate thought about the amendment spoke volumes about how he imagined the postwar, postemancipation world. Conservatives such as Buckner intended to fight over the corpse, urging rejection of and resistance to the amendment. They planned a full-on states' rights obstructionist agenda that would throw up barriers to every policy the Congress or the U.S. Army might devise. They would demand control over African Americans within the borders of the state, pass restrictive and discriminatory criminal codes, allow exploitative labor practices to continue, and hold out for compensated emancipation from the federal government. This was not entirely dissimilar from the society Union Party men imagined. With a few exceptions, they did not believe African Americans capable of self-government or worthy of social equality with whites. In contrast, the Union Party, led by governor Thomas E. Bramlette, hoped that Kentucky could ratify the amendment—even if they did not like it—look beyond slavery, and elect a legislature that would address the economic devastation and social chaos that the war had brought, incorporating African Americans into a free labor system that would attract investment in the stagnant state economy while still relegating black Kentuckians to a second-class citizenship that would certainly not include the vote.

Clark County would elect both a representative and a senator to send to Frankfort for the upcoming session. These men would set the tone of postemancipation, postwar Kentucky. It would fall to them to shape the legal relationship between freed African Americans and the state government. Criminal codes, hiring and labor practices, civil rights at the polling place and in the courtroom, educational opportunities, and more were on the table. This session would also determine many of the same questions for Kentucky's large population of former rebels, who had lived in a sort of legal limbo since the spring. They all were theoretically felons against the state and traitors to the national government—hence the lists—but by and large they had also been welcomed back into the state by their loyal neighbors, cousins, and siblings.

More than just an interested observer in this election and the issues at stake in the upcoming session, Buckner was standing as the Conservative Party candidate for Clark's seat in the House. Buckner's party stood for just what its name implied, the same conservative unionism that had sent him to war in 1861 and compelled him to resign in 1863. When he took his first step onto the public political stage in the summer of 1865, still committed to established, constitutional remedies for the ills that he believed faced his dying slave society, he opened up another front in his evolving war to defend the power and position of Kentucky's slave owners even amid the collapse of the world they had so carefully maintained for generations. For Buckner, the goals still remained largely the same as they had all along; he intended to defend the social, political, and economic benefits of mastery for white people even if—perhaps *especially* if—their actual status as masters would soon be no more. Buckner hoped to be elected to a state legislature that would ensure that Kentucky's postwar society would be as close as possible to that which he and thousands of other loyal masters had fought to defend.

Buckner's opposition for the seat in the House told the tale of the shifting post–Emancipation Proclamation political landscape as well as anything else. Helen's cousin George Martin Jackson, the son of Estill County ironmaster Josiah Jackson, ran against Buckner. During the war, when their units were often camped near one another, Ben and George had seen each other often and developed a strong friendship. Now they stood on opposite sides of the important questions that would shape Kentucky's postslavery future. A staunch Unconditional Unionist, Jackson represented those white Kentuckians who were willing to accept the verdict of the war and of emancipation, willing to move on into an increasingly industrialized, free-laborer future for Kentucky, and willing to work with the moderate elements of the national Republican Party to achieve those ends. Like that national Republican Party, Jackson and Kentucky's Union Party men were unsure about the place of African Americans in this postemancipation future, how or even if black people should integrate themselves into the economy, society, and body politic, but they were certainly more open to accepting a more expansive slate of rights and protections than were Buckner's Conservatives and their allies in the national Democratic Party, who largely remained convinced of African Americans' fundamental racial unsuitability for freedom and citizenship.

The political divide that had grown between the two friends was not a recent development, though it had recently come to the surface as the war drew to a close. Rather, Buckner and Jackson represented two fundamentally different understandings of the Union cause. Whereas Buckner had fought for slavery and understood the Union as the best means by which to uphold the institution, Jackson—whose father had employed and benefitted from slave labor for decades—had gone to war to maintain Kentucky's place in the Union. If slavery was the price that had to be paid, it was a steep one, but so be it. These tensions had been papered over in the heady days of 1861, but the gradual yet dramatic collapse of slavery during the war had revealed the cracks in the foundation of Kentucky's Union coalition. Now the two factions squared off for control of the state, and the two friends met one another at the polls.

Buckner's path to the Conservative candidacy in 1865 began as soon as he left the army. He came home to a Kentucky still recovering from rebel invasion, infested by guerillas, increasingly incapable of controlling enslaved African Americans, and faced with a fundamental choice about where to go next. How far did the state's loyalty extend? Were white Kentuckians willing to pay the ultimate price for union? As one Kentuckian put it in a private letter in 1862, "Now the question is, I think, will Ky stand by the realization of this conviction which was given in her pledge when she gave herself to the Union cause[?] Will she make the sacrifice in reality? or continue to occupy an anomalous position, suspicioned by her own government & subjected to the constant annoyances of brigands & conspiracies from the other quarters[?] The question is as important as was ever submitted to a free people. Kentuckians must answer."[1]

"What is to become of Kentucky it is impossible to tell," Buckner moaned in the misery of the emancipation winter of 1862–1863 in Bowling Green. "All is dark in her future. I am sick at heart with the prospect before us."[2] Buckner's bleak forecast included strong chances of race war and an intensified civil war—perhaps a three-way one—if Kentucky revolted against the government, the collapse of constitutional liberty and protection of all species of property, the establishment of a Republican oligarchy if not a Lincoln tyrannical monarchy, and the destruction of the fields, stores, mills, foundries, railroads, and homes that had thrived over the decades and provided wealthy Bluegrass residents a marvelous standard of living built on the exploitation of enslaved black labor. All this just when he had finally won Helen's hand in marriage.

All, though, was not as dark as Buckner imagined on that miserable evening in his Bowling Green boardinghouse. When he returned to Winchester in April 1863, newly married and freed from his connection to the Union army by which he felt so betrayed, he could finally see a way forward, illuminated by a family friend and political mentor, Clark County's representative in the State House, John B. Huston. The 1860 John Bell elector and former Speaker of the Kentucky House preached salvation to Kentucky's loyal masters, reeling from the blows to slavery landed in the preceding months. "*Here is hope,*" Huston proclaimed. "The dark clouds are lifted, and the light of hope is streaming in upon us." It was a call to conservative revival. "Let us by all constitutional means, *(I counsel no revolutionary action)* earnestly strive to correct the errors, and remove the bad, faithless trustees from their places of power," Huston preached. "'Let the people but be right, and no President can long be wrong. Nor can he effect any fatal mischief should he be,'" he counseled. Loyal Kentuckians, he proudly claimed, could "distinguish clearly between the *Government* itself and the *administration* of that Government. The men in authority are but temporary trustees of the powers of government," he reminded the loyal white men of the state, hearkening back to their antisecessionist rhetoric from 1861. The remedy to the evils that threatened Kentuckians—that threatened not only them and their beloved institution but, they were firmly convinced, the country, the Constitution, and the hope for republican government throughout the world—could, Huston advised, be found in "the ballot-box, and more immediately through the mighty power of active, outspoken public opinion."[3] Huston was among the first to call for the formation of the Conservative ticket on which Buckner ran in 1865. This fusion party of old Whigs and Democrats would be based wholly around resistance to any form of antislavery legislation from Washington. "[A]lthough always an old Whig," Huston proclaimed, "I am prepared to unite with the Democracy of the North and Northwest in the contest for our Government against Abolitionists and Rebels. I do not object to the name.... I will unite with a just conservative sentiment everywhere, under any name, for the salvation of our country."[4]

When Buckner returned home from the army, the absolute life or death of slavery in Kentucky was not yet on the table. The Emancipation Proclamation—whatever it portended—had no legal standing in the loyal commonwealth. The immediate issue was the possible recruitment of enslaved Kentuckians into the army, theoretically possible under the Enrollment Act of March 3, 1863. Protests poured in to Washington from white Kentuckians, and federal military commanders Jeremiah T. Boyle—little surprise—and Ambrose Burnside—more telling—reported that recruiting African Americans in Kentucky would prove an ultimate net loss when white recruitment dried up in response. To deal with this problem, first unofficially and later officially by act of Congress black recruitment was outlawed in Kentucky.[5]

Of course, Kentucky's loyal masters had played this game before, so they no longer trusted that their exemption would last forever. Both candidates standing for governor in August 1863 were strictly opposed to black recruitment, each trying to outdo the other in their opposition to the policy. Peace Democrat and former governor Charles A. Wickliffe ultimately proved the more vehement in his denunciations of the Lincoln administration, though a fair few judged his pledges to end the war and restore the Union upon the status quo antebellum as flirting dangerously with rebellion. The voters instead chose Bramlette, a Union Democrat, after a contentious election in which federal soldiers appeared at the polls for the first time and some of Wickliffe's supporters were jailed. In his inaugural address, Bramlette summed up the arguments that Buckner had articulated just before leaving the army: that enlisting black troops "humiliates the just pride of loyal men" and fired up the supposedly bestial nature of black men to the point that they could "never remain and live amongst those whom they have been set in battle array"—white southerners in Confederate gray. "It was," remarks E. Merton Coulter, "past the comprehension of Kentuckians that anyone could advocate the elevation of an inferior being, a slave, into a soldier, a rank of distinction held particularly high in the traditions of the state."[6]

Black Kentuckians and white enrolling officers on the periphery of the state—stationed just across the border in Tennessee or across the Ohio from major port cities in much the same way that white recruitment had been conducted by both sides during Kentucky's neutrality in 1861—eroded the ban on African American recruitment in Kentucky over the course of the winter. A blistering letter from Bramlette to Lincoln in February brought a cold, legalistic reply from Secretary of War Edwin M. Stanton. His justification was followed by a War Department circular at the end of the month that laid out the procedure for the enrollment of black soldiers within Kentucky. The state nearly exploded.

All eyes turned to Bramlette to see how the state would react to the reality of black recruitment, but it was not he who made the first public move. The governor attended a ceremony in Lexington on March 10, 1864, to honor Frank Lane Wolford, celebrated colonel of the First Kentucky Cavalry. The "Loyal Citizens of Garrard Co. Ky." presented Wolford with a jeweled sword for his service, including notable victories over John Hunt Morgan. With Bramlette seated on the stage behind the colonel, Wolford launched into an anti-administration harangue whose words echoed all the way to Washington. No transcript of the Lexington speech survives, but some witnesses sketched its rough outline. It was, said Wolford, Kentuckians' "duty to resist" the "enrolment and drafting of negroes with all the power of their noble state." "[H]e had confidence that his excellency," Governor Bramlette, "would sustain them in such resistance." This claim gave Republicans within the state and in the capital serious pause. Bramlette had ordered the raising of ten thousand troops (white, of course) for six-month service within the state and had promised Wolford command of the organization. Were the governor and the colonel raising a Kentucky army to resist federal recruitment efforts? The question was legitimate, particularly after that afternoon in Lexington when Wolford offered "that it was as much their duty to protect themselves against the traitor at Washington as the traitor at Richmond." Closing, the colonel "addressed himself to reporters of his speech . . . and said 'Tell the tyrant at Washington'" all of what Wolford had encouraged his fellow white Kentuckians to do. They did, and for it Wolford was arrested, taken to Tennessee, brought before General Grant, and cashiered from the army within two weeks.[7]

As Wolford traveled south in handcuffs, Bramlette was on the verge of taking a very drastic and dangerous step. The governor had remained silent during Wolford's speech, though it was quite plain that he agreed with the tough old cavalryman. He had written a draft proclamation to the people of Kentucky that urged the people of the state to forcibly resist the enlistment of slaves. It was a declaration of war against federal authority, a very real potential prelude to Kentucky's secession in 1864. Knowing he should solicit outside opinion, though, Bramlette called a conference in Frankfort between himself, proslavery minister and Union stalwart Robert J. Breckinridge, the new military commander of the state and native Kentuckian General Stephen G. Burbridge, and some others. Over a long night in Frankfort's Capital Hotel, the advisers talked the governor down from the precipice. His proclamation went into the fireplace, and a new one was drafted that denounced the fact of African American recruitment but advised no resistance to the policy from white Kentuckians.[8]

As black recruitment picked up steam throughout the summer of 1864, so did Union Democratic resistance, just in time for the presidential election. Huston, Wolford, and Lieutenant Governor Richard T. Jacob were outspoken in their denunciation of the administration and made plain their belief that any election with military interference was a usurpation of the rights of a free and loyal people. They raised the ire of General Burbridge, who had quickly earned a terrible reputation by his hard line against rebels, rebel sympathizers, and suspected rebels among the population at home. Democratic presidential candidate George McClellan cleared an overwhelming majority in the state, 64,301 votes to Lincoln's 27,786, but Burbridge found the overwhelming rejection of the current administration suspect.

Huston was arrested on election day. His "influence & speeches have been of a treasonable character," Burbridge reported to Washington, and "he persisted in making the latter after several warnings of what the consequences would be." Bramlette countered with a telegram to Lincoln. The governor demanded to know why "a loyal man and prominent citizen" had been jailed and marked for exile to the Confederacy "for no other offense than opposition to your reelection. You are doubtless reelected," Bramlette said provocatively, "but surely it cannot sanction this ostracising of loyal men who honestly opposed you." Lincoln characteristically met the governor's fury with wit, noting that "if that had been deemed sufficient cause of arrest, I should have heard of more than one arrest in Kentucky on election day." Burbridge reluctantly released the Winchester politician "under oath & bond not again to oppose his Govt." but remained firm in his belief that a "vigorous policy against rebel sympathizers in this State must be pursued & if I have erred I fear I have made too few arrests instead of too many."[9]

Though Burbridge was replaced by the 1865 election, his successor, John Palmer, would have no more luck navigating the hazy lines between political dissent and treason and between free, fair elections and military interference with them.

As the election approached in 1865, Clark County Conservatives needed a candidate to challenge George Jackson and the county's Unconditional Unionist minority—a group now labeled the "radical" faction by most anti-Republican papers in the state. Huston was free, but his run-ins with federal military authorities did not give him much room for political maneuver. He had also moved to Lexington, leaving the Clark seat open.[10] Buckner saw an opportunity. Despite the crumbling of the institution of slavery around his and Helen's new household, things had gone as well as possible since his return from the army. The death, displacement, and destruction of public and private property that he had so dreaded and believed foretold the doom to Kentucky's slave-based prosperity at the outset of the war had, in an ironic twist, cultivated a rich pasture of legal entanglements, inheritance disputes, and bankruptcy settlements on which his practice could feed and grow. At the same time that Buckner ran against George Jackson, in fact, he was engaged in settling the estate of his opponent's father, Josiah, who had died fleeing from Confederate troops in 1862. He would soon take up the case of a Lexington slave-trading house ruined even before the Emancipation Proclamation by its inability to collect on debts owed by cotton masters in the months after secession.[11] Expanding Ben's family at the same time he expanded his clientele, Helen had given birth to a son, Maurice, in late April 1864. With his personal and professional life falling into as much order as the circumstances allowed, Buckner decided to stand for Huston's old seat, a move he undoubtedly hoped to be the gateway into a long career in public service.

A term in the legislature would allow Buckner to take positive action in defense of his new family and growing practice. It would allow him to address the fears he harbored for the future—rampaging freed slaves instigating a race war, state and federal military tyranny, and well-armed and experienced bands of marauding white outlaws of no particular ideological affiliation that still prowled the state stealing their living from the population. Serving a term in Frankfort would afford Buckner the opportunity to shape the future of his legal work, to have a hand in addressing practical problems of restructuring state law and society in what increasingly looked to be a postemancipation world—civil and criminal law as it applied to black people who were no longer slaves, the question of compensation to dispossessed slave owners, and tough decisions about the labor supply for Kentucky households, fields, and foundries. There was no end to the work he could do to protect and improve the life he and Helen were attempting to build for themselves in the wreckage of everything they had known, believed, and assumed. The prestige of office and the chance to forge personal and professional networks with men of similar public stature across the state were bonuses, as was the fact that the short winter sessions would keep him away from Helen, Maurice, and his clients at most only six weeks or two months a year.

The 1865 electoral process began in May with a convention of the "Democratic and conservative Union citizens of Kentucky," which included many names that had been quite prominent in denouncing the administration's antislavery policies over the past year. Both U.S. senators for Kentucky, the fiery Garrett Davis and former governor Lazarus Powell, were in attendance. Bourbon County farmer-turned-congressman Brutus J. Clay was present, as well as former congressmen Richard A. Buckner, Joseph R. Underwood, and Henry D. McHenry. The latter's son, John Hardin McHenry, had been removed from command of the Seventeenth Kentucky Infantry for refusing to follow the War Department policy toward fugitive slaves and lost in a bitter, military-influenced congressional election to George H. Yeaman in 1863.[12] General T. T. Garrard, whose Clay County salt works had been destroyed by Buckner and the Twenty-Second Brigade in the fall of 1862—sealing both Buckner's and Garrard's contempt for the army's hard-war policy—was on the convention's Committee on Resolutions, and while Garrard and his fellow committee members worked in a separate room, the irrepressible John B. Huston addressed the crowd.

The slate of issues was a laundry list of opposition to the extremes of federal policy to which the convention attendees had believed themselves subjected for the past three years. In "order to maintain and preserve the lives, liberties and properties of the people," the convention asserted in one sweeping resolution, "the military should be kept in strict subordination to the civil power." Getting more specific, they protested the suppression of a number of presses in the state—the *Lexington Observer & Reporter* among them—and the abuse of habeas corpus and other civil protections, declaring "free speech, a free press, [and] free elections" to be "the vital principles of civil and constitutional liberty," which these loyal, if angry, Kentuckians demanded be upheld. A further short resolution called for a reduction of the national war debt and an end to the "oppressive and exhaustive taxes upon the people." All of these resolutions, of course, obliquely referenced race in one way or another, most pointing directly to the previous year of violent and rhetorical resistance to the recruitment of black troops. Without the federal government's unconstitutional and unholy war against slavery, they maintained, there would have been no speeches from Huston, Wolford, and Jacob that needed to be suppressed, their trials need not have been handled in military rather than civil courts, and the papers would not have been ruled to be preaching treason when they defended their fellow aggrieved masters. Had the government pursued a conciliatory policy toward the slave owners in rebellion, as most loyal Kentuckians desired, they could even imagine that the rebellion itself would have collapsed under the weight of federal benevolence rather than dragging on, spurred by the Emancipation Proclamation into a righteous frenzy, to a bitter end, costly in both blood and treasure.[13]

Then came the resolutions directly aimed at slavery and black recruitment. They resolved "[t]hat no power has been delegated by the constitution to the government of the United States to emancipate the slaves of any State" and "that such power is, therefore, reserved to the states respectively, or the people." Further, they declared Kentucky "unwilling to delegate any such power . . . or in any manner to place it in the power" of the federal government "to prescribe the terms upon which the slaves of Kentucky shall be emancipated and determine the social and political rights they shall enjoy." They were "therefore decidedly opposed to the adoption and ratification of the amendment recently proposed by Congress to the Constitution . . . granting powers to the national government on the subject of slaves and slavery in the United States." For men who had stood loyally by the old flag in 1861 and defended the slaveholding republic as the once and future guarantor of slavery, the states' rights rhetoric here seems a wildly changed stance. Then again, as one historian reminds us, "Southern slaveholders, like most other Americans, supported federal action when federal action served their interests and federal inaction when federal inaction served their interests. . . . [T]heir commitment to states rights was pragmatic." When a fugitive slave law and the protection of federal courts had made slavery seem far more secure in the Union than in Jeff Davis's Cotton Kingdom, these same men had stood proudly to be counted among the loyal sons of Clay and Washington. Now, still loyal to the Constitution but as jealous of their rights as any prewar southern ultra, they found new ground on which they could defend their cherished institution.[14]

The Conservatives were searching for new allies to shore up their defense, too. In "view of the fact that the war is now virtually ended," the convention proposed, "we are in favor of the exercise of a liberal, kind and conciliatory policy toward those who have been in arms against the Government," so that, they argued, "the Union may be harmoniously and fraternally preserved, and that good feeling and confidence may once more prevail throughout the length and breadth of the land" that would "restore speedily the peace and harmony of the Union: to preserve the just authority of the Federal Government, the republicanism of the States," and be "in strict accordance with the true theory of the Constitution." If the rebels could be speedily returned to power in their respective state houses, the Conservatives hoped that the old proslavery veto could be reestablished before the Thirteenth Amendment could be ratified. That done, they envisioned a wave of state-generated challenges to the wartime antislavery policies mounted in both Congress and in the courts, bogging down the emancipation process while buying yet more precious time for the best southern legal minds—who had worn both blue and gray—to dream up new strategies, justifications, and theories to resurrect slavery.[15]

This reunified southern legal and legislative defense of slavery would come later than these Kentucky Conservatives hoped, but it had always been their plan to put it in motion when the rebellion finally collapsed. Buckner and the men at this convention went to war believing that this day would come in late 1862, before the Republican congressional majority and the Lincoln administration could do serious damage to their institution, but just because the timing was off did not mean the plan had changed in any significant way. Delay and prepare were the order of the day; the Kentucky Conservatives' twofold mission was, first, to hold off Republican encroachments on the institution and, second, to ease as many of the restrictions on the rights of former Confederates as possible at both the state and the national level with an eye to bringing those reinforcements to the fight in years to come.

The Conservative cause was dear to the majority of white men in Clark County and throughout the state. Although Republican-leaning Union Party men such as George Jackson were present nearly everywhere, their only majorities were found in the Ohio River cities and along the mountains. A Louisville observer summed up the challenge that faced the Union Party in his characterization of the heart of the state's voters. "The love of the State for slavery" was similar to "that other 'true love' of the poet, whose course 'never did run smooth'" yet "seems all the stronger on account of the very obstructions to its genial and agreeable exercise." For white Kentuckians to "cling frantically still to the beloved but defunct object" was, by now, "the lover's insane act, in clinging to a corpse, stubbornly refusing to have it buried out of sight." The Union Party tried hard indeed to wake white Kentuckians up to their position as the last defenders of slavery. Lovell Rousseau, the Union Party congressman from Louisville, tried to shame his fellow Kentuckians into stepping in line by pointing out that "in the whole Christian world, there remain but three slave States—Cuba, Brazil and Kentucky."[16] The Conservatives, though, were well aware of the company in which they stood, and they were not ashamed of it. In defending the corpse of slavery until and even after the ghost had fled, Buckner and his compatriots understood themselves to be defending the whole of their rights and guarantees in the Constitution of the United States and defending the government of the republic as an institution and republican government as a philosophy. They had melded the causes of government and slavery together, believing in the symbiotic relationship that had enabled the growth of both institutions, and they held that their honored place as the last defenders of slavery was not the mark of their moral degradation, as Rousseau intended to cast it, but instead proof of their commitment to the American political project. Although Kentuckians such as Buckner may have been in despotic company with Brazil and Cuba, they would counter that, unlike the rebel states, which had subverted the political process and lost slavery as punishment for their impetuosity, and unlike the northern states, whose Republican majority had unconstitutionally made war on the institution of slavery within the commonwealth and throughout the South, their last gallant stand by the corpse of slavery in 1865 made them the only heirs of Washington still to be found in the nation.

As Huston set off on a speaking tour of Clark's neighboring counties to gain support for the cause, the Clark County Conservatives chose Buckner as the man best suited to "the purpose of uniting and harmonizing all the Conservative elements in opposition to the radical party." Harrison Thompson, whose prosperous Clark County livestock farm Buckner had joked about being easier on its slaves than the army was on its soldiers during the miserable Mississippi summer of 1862, was advanced to run for the state Senate seat representing a two-county district, Clark and Madison. Thompson's promised to be a closer race than Buckner's; whereas Clark was almost assured to give Buckner a resounding Conservative majority, Madison was another world entirely. The northern part of that county was home to the feisty antislavery advocate Cassius Marcellus Clay, and its southern reaches included the town of Berea, home to the abolitionist congregation and school of John G. Fee. Elections in which slavery and race were prominent issues were normally fierce and violent in Madison. Clay, everyone remembered, had killed an attacker in self-defense during the 1848 constitutional referendum, and things would be no less tense in this upcoming canvass. Amid its coverage of the election speeches, the *Observer & Reporter* printed a letter from a correspondent in Mississippi who warned that "[e]very negro that has ever lived in Kentucky will soon be upon you," no small number considering the commonwealth's booming trade in human property with the cotton South as that trade exploded across the southwestern frontier over the course of a generation. "The desire to return to old Kentucky is universal among them," wrote the Mississippian, who accurately interpreted the mass migration of former slaves who sought long-lost relatives scattered across the region. "Such is the feeling of many others," the correspondent continued, "who fear that they will not be as safe in the thinly-settled South," referencing the informal acts of terroristic violence that were already being directed toward rural freedpeople. If Thompson was going to face a strong fight in Madison County, it was a fight that he had to win so as to deny the seat to Dr. A. S. Allan, a Winchester resident whose politics polled better across the county line than at home.[17]

The polls opened across Clark County on election day, the Wisconsin soldiers posted nearby with what they were told was a list of Confederate veterans and sympathizers to be barred from voting by state law. Some reports said the list included more than 400 names, though a more precise number of blacklisted voters that gained favor in the press was 124. Regardless of the numbers, the Clark County list, like so many others across the state that day, was assembled by what one Conservative correspondent labeled a "small and insignificant set of men" on Sunday morning, "when all the quiet and peaceable citizens could have been winding their way to their different places of worship." In Winchester, David S. Goodloe, the U.S. district assessor and relative of a prominent pro-administration judge, oversaw the group drawing up the initial list, assisted among others by the man Buckner had threatened with a duel in 1861, the former editor of the *National Union,* James M. Ogden "(better known as 'Dirty Jim')." Later, a number of Union Party men from across the county, including Buckner's opponent, George Jackson, checked and amended the list.[18]

"Under the ruthless and sweeping proscription but few conservatives were allowed to vote," wrote one of Buckner's local supporters in the days following the election. "Gray haired old men, of most undoubted personal integrity, were rudely ordered away from the polls, and some were driven from the ground." This, the correspondent argued, was the worst of horrors. The state law had sought to keep rebels from voting, but it was being manipulated, they claimed, to disenfranchise all opponents of the election. The rebels numbered only "30 or 40" men "cunningly placed" on the lists "to give some show of plausibility to the outrage." For themselves, the Confederates "wished to abide by the decision of the law in regard to their several cases," knowing that "if they attempted to exercise the right of a freeman, that the judges would of course refuse them." In Clark, as elsewhere, the rebels seem to have genuinely wanted nothing to do with the vote; they were well aware of the political stakes at risk and eager to have a sympathetic Conservative slate elected. Loyal men such as Buckner could express their outrage as dispossessed masters just as effectively as the rebels themselves could. The trickier points of discerning loyalty or disloyalty, though, came with those gray-haired old men who had fully supported the rebellion but due to their age had never left home to serve it actively. One of them, Helen's father, Dr. Martin, was barred from casting his ballot at the Germantown precinct near the family farm. After the doctor and several other "respectable citizens of this precinct" had been barred and "cursed and threatened" by the soldiers, both county election officials—largely in sympathy with the Conservatives—and the gathered citizens protested so violently about the course of their "free election" that some polls were shut down entirely, and others were closed intermittently.[19]

Given the highly partisan nature of accounts on both sides, it is difficult to put together just what happened, who was responsible, who was actually barred from voting, and whether this was, in fact, a radical plot to steal the election as the Conservatives claimed. Any election where U.S. troops were stationed at the polls was automatically suspect in the minds of the state's Conservative white citizens, and the lists and poll closings only justified further Conservative outrage, particularly after A. S. Allan won the Senate race over Harrison Thompson. The *Observer & Reporter* claimed that Thompson would have carried the district by 800 or 1,000 votes "had not the freedom of the ballot box been so grossly outraged." Further, reports coming in from northern Kentucky of similar election tactics had thrown the entire vote into question. Thompson wasted little time in formally challenging the result and days later had set about collecting depositions from witnesses to the "infamous proceedings enacted on the 7th of August." Thompson promised to prove that "but little more than one half of the usual vote of this Senatorial district was polled at the late so-called election," which was indeed the case, and he hoped that "a fair and free trial of strength between Dr. Allan's friends and my own" would prove that the Conservatives justly represented the will of the electorate. "When I entered upon this contest I hoped to be permitted to treat my opponent as one gentleman does another," Thompson flung in at the end of his message. "His course from the beginning, however, has shown that he was not entitled to the courtesies which rob a political canvass of so many disagreeable features" and only highlighted his "cowardly disregard of whatever is honest and true." Resolution of the contest would have to wait, like the rest of the contested election cases across the commonwealth, until the General Assembly met.[20]

The General Assembly session opened on December 4, 1865, with Union Party men, Governor Bramlette, and outside observers across the country desperately hoping that the legislators would put the ghost of slavery behind them and bring stability to the chaotic semi-postslavery labor market. Bramlette begged the lawmakers to address the "entire breaking up of our labor system, and the necessity of adopting a new system upon the free basis," to farm Kentucky's "fertile lands and genial climate," develop the "vast extent of our mineral wealth," and attract "capital to our State for investment." "What is to become of the negro?" Bramlette bluntly asked, and "What shall become of us?" "He will be free—what more"? "It rests not in human power to reinstate or longer preserve slavery," Bramlette lectured. "Shall we fold our hands and refuse to act, and content ourselves with sullen submission to unavoidable results; or shall we manifest our just appreciation of existing facts by timely and appropriate action?"[21]

Bramlette received his answer immediately. The Conservative majority would neither sullenly fold its hands *nor* gracefully accept the advent of black freedom. They took the offensive. Hoping to enlarge the slim Conservative majority before an important session and what promised to be a close series of ballots for the election of a U.S. senator, Conservative claimants challenged three Union Party seats almost as soon as the clerk finished reading the governor's message.

When the House returned to session the next day, it divided up committee assignments. Given the contested elections pending, the Committee on Privileges and Elections, which would gather and weigh the evidence concerning the seat challenges, was of the highest importance. Buckner was chosen as one of its Conservative members, a vote of confidence in the freshman representative's abilities. He was in excellent company. Among the other Conservative members of Privileges and Elections were the old firebrand Frank Wolford, elected to the House from his southern Kentucky district, and James M. Harlan from Frankfort, the brother of John Marshall Harlan and one of the state's most stalwart proslavery old Whigs from the beginning of the war through its bitter end. Along with the chair, Henry County's Isaac Webb, they made a Conservative majority of four to three. Once Conservatives in the Assembly knew the makeup of Privileges and Elections, even more seat challenges arose. Before long, Conservative aspirants had laid claim to seats in Bath, Bracken, Hopkins, Garrard, Madison, Pendleton, and two each in Kenton and Campbell. All told, ten House seats were up for grabs along with four in the Senate, including the Clark–Madison district challenged by Harrison Thompson.[22]

The House and Senate Privileges and Elections Committees set furiously to work. They were appointed their own secretary to take depositions and were granted the use of the House chamber when it was not in session. They had help from outside the legislature, too; partisan lawyers had already begun collecting depositions for some cases in the months before the session started. The committees' Conservative majorities gladly compiled all of these depositions, new and old, into a series of reports, which, for all their variations in specific names and places, largely followed one narrative trajectory. "The testimony shows that these arrests, and the threats made by the officers and soldiers to arrest certain citizens if they attempted to vote, and the presence of armed soldiers at the polls," read one majority report in language found nearly verbatim in the other cases, "for the evident purpose of carrying these threats into execution, had the natural result of intimidating large numbers of the legal voters of the precinct, and of preventing many from attempting to exercise the right of suffrage." Commanding the House in ways they could not command the polling places in August, the Conservatives flatly rejected any discrimination against those considered to be "*Southern sympathizers*' and '*Southern rights men*'" or those "*considered* by those entertaining similar political sentiments with the sitting member,"—that is, the Union Party men—to be "*disloyal*,"' a charge leveled during the canvass at nearly every Conservative candidate then sitting.[23]

Buckner and the other Conservative members had no patience for any attempts to discriminate against those rebels who agreed with them on matters of race and rights. When one sitting Union Party member countered that some of the deponents on whose testimony the Conservative case rested had been Confederate soldiers, the majority shot back that they "know of no law disqualifying any of the various classes above named"—rebels included—"from testifying in the courts of this State.

... Many citizens of the State, of the highest character for personal integrity, joined the Confederates," and although "we disapprove of their conduct, we cannot say that they are not worthy of credit on oath." Not coincidentally, as the report on these cases were being prepared, Buckner submitted resolutions calling for a denial of the right to testimony for another class of citizens whose character he was not prepared to credit. *"Be it resolved,"* Buckner proposed, "that the people of Kentucky are unalterably opposed to the passage of all laws permitting negroes to testify as witnesses and to sit as jurors in the courts of justice in this Commonwealth." Once the General Assembly had finished decimating the Union Party minority, it would look to making Buckner's resolution a legal reality.[24]

The Privileges and Elections purges did not go perfectly, but they still removed enough Union Party members from their seats to leave a cherished legacy in the legal annals of the state. One chronicler referred to the House Privileges and Elections as the "celebrated Committee" that had paved the way for the string of Conservative legislative victories that followed this fortification of the Conservative position.[25] Nine of the Union Party members whose seats were challenged were dismissed from the House or resigned before that nearly inevitable verdict could be reached. Only two cases were dropped for lack of evidence; both of Kenton County's seats were initially challenged, and one representative quickly resigned. His replacement, another Union Party man, was predictably challenged, but that case was dropped, along with the challenge to the other Kenton seat. Harrison Thompson won an overturned seat in the Senate, and the Conservatives successfully vacated the Kenton County seat in that chamber. Firing back, Kenton's northern Kentucky neighbors in Campbell County managed to give a symbolic black eye to the Conservatives. The voters of Campbell returned both of their deposed representatives and their senator in a special election. Despite these reverses, though, the Privileges and Elections Committees had, by the opening of the January 1867 session, gained six Conservative seats in the House and two in the Senate.

The Privileges and Elections business consumed much of Buckner's first session, and the House committee's work also buried much of the House's significant business under a stream of reports and votes on contested seats. It was time-consuming work for the Conservatives, but a necessary precursor to the session's other important business, the election of a U.S. senator, which would be done by a combined vote of the General Assembly, both the House and Senate. The original deadline set by the previous House to begin the process of electing a senator was

January 25, 1866, but as Buckner and his fellow Conservative committee members worked, they realized the opportunity they had within their grasp. The legislature's Conservative majority, it seems, did not feel sufficiently strong to take on a senatorial election—which because of personal loyalties, regional squabbles, and a host of other inter-Conservative divisions was in danger of a shock Union Party victory in the event of a split Conservative ticket. With so many contestable elections across the state, delaying the vote for senator would allow more time to investigate and call new elections. Privileges and Elections could stack the deck. On January 23, then, just two days before the vote was scheduled to begin, Buckner introduced a successful resolution that moved the date to sometime in December 1866, giving Conservatives almost a year to eject Union Party members and elect their own.[26] Winning the delay virtually ensured Kentucky an anti-administration, anti–African American conservative senator in Washington for six more years; it was Buckner's most significant legislative achievement.

Buckner and his allies sought to expand their majority outside of the House, too. Conservatives rushed to remove all legal and political disabilities leveled against former Confederates in order to flood the electorate with yet more voters committed to fighting any federal encroachment on white Kentuckians' traditional power over the state and its black population. Leaving no doubt as to where he stood on the question, Buckner introduced another set of resolutions that plainly staked out his position on former rebels in Kentucky and elsewhere. "[I]n legal contemplation," he argued, "they were never out of the Union, but . . . they are still component parts thereof, entitled under the Constitution to equal rights and privileges" enjoyed by those who had not rebelled. Because secession was always illegal and "inasmuch as they have ceased to oppose the execution of the laws of the United States, and have declared their intention to return to their allegiance in good faith," their votes should be counted in Kentucky. Likewise, throughout the rest of the South, "their Representatives in Congress should at once be admitted." The House almost immediately passed pardons for those convicted of treason by the state during the war. The zealous legislature of 1861 had declared all Kentucky Confederates traitors to the commonwealth as well as to the federal government. Their October 1861 Anti-Rebellion Act, which made the rebels felons and barred them from voting, was repealed two weeks into the 1865–1867 session. Rounding out the early triumph was the repeal of an act requiring ministers of the gospel to take a loyalty oath before they could perform marriages. The latter repeal received the most attention of the three actions, oddly enough, but ultimately it was decided that an oath to the Constitution of Kentucky rather than to that of the United States be required.[27]

Not content with attacking only the "Radical" Union Party members of the legislature, toward the end of the session Buckner set his sights on two of the most important white advocates of black civil and political rights in the state. Buckner found his first target while taking depositions in Privileges and Elections. He introduced resolutions calling for the impeachment of Circuit Court judge William Clinton Goodloe, recently moved to Lexington from Richmond and one of the most consistent Unconditional Union men in the state. Like the election against George Jackson, Buckner's targeting of Goodloe showed just how fundamentally the end of slavery had changed Buckner's political world. Goodloe was the judge of the Circuit Court district for the counties surrounding Lexington; Buckner's father, Aylett, had been the Circuit Court clerk for Clark, making him Goodloe's right-hand man in the county. During his legal training, Buckner had been his father's deputy clerk, and after he passed the bar, he had argued countless cases before Goodloe. The judge was, then, one of Buckner's most influential professional mentors and a powerful family ally. When the Buckners had hoped to get Ben's younger brother, Tucker, promoted in 1862, Aylett had solicited a letter of recommendation from Judge Goodloe, which went to Frankfort in a dossier alongside those from John B. Huston, state senator and soon-to-be governor James F. Robinson, and Speaker of the state House Richard A. Buckner, among others. The unity and friendship that had existed among those union men three years earlier was nowhere to be found in this desperate, postslavery political world.[28]

Seizing on an incident where Goodloe had dismissed a grand jury indictment against some Union Party men (including one of the judge's family members) for violating election laws via the usual litany of military interference in the August 1865 election, Buckner alleged that Judge Goodloe was guilty of a high misdemeanor that warranted trial in the Senate. With a plan to follow the same procedure that had brought them so much success in removing Union Party members of the House, a committee was formed to take depositions against Goodloe that could be edited into an irresistible evidentiary force when the trial came. Becoming sloppy in their overconfidence, however, Buckner and his Conservative House allies were outmaneuvered by the learned Judge Goodloe. The old judge still had some things to teach Buckner, though now his lessons would not be so pleasant as they once had been. In a blistering letter to the House, Goodloe dressed them down for beginning a politically motivated impeachment and declared the whole proceeding illegal because any testimony given in an impeachment trial must be given in person in the Senate chamber. Depositions would not do, and the House had little choice but to drop the charges against Goodloe.[29]

Even before Goodloe had time to respond to Buckner's call for his impeachment, the Conservatives put a bigger prize in their sights, Major General Clinton B. Fisk, the head of the Freedmen's Bureau in Tennessee and Kentucky. Because slavery had remained legal in the commonwealth until the ratification of the Thirteenth Amendment, the state initially had no bureau presence at all, depending instead on private educational, sanitary, and other philanthropies to assist black Kentuckians in their liminal state between slavery and freedom in 1864 and 1865. But with slavery finally at an official end in Kentucky, Fisk was authorized to expand his operations in Tennessee across the state line into Kentucky in late December 1865. Not surprisingly, Kentucky's loyal masters argued there was little reason for the introduction of what they termed one of the most "clumsy and corrupt pieces of machinery invented since this war" began, spearheaded, they claimed, by "the Northern philanthropist—backed by his Kentucky ally, who has perhaps sold his negroes since the war begun and put the money safely in his pocket." Both sorts of men, the characterization implied, possessed characters unfit to benevolently protect and care for childlike black people. Those who were deemed so fit, the state's former masters, both loyal and disloyal, hoped to have as little oversight as possible so their supposed benevolence could continue to ensure unequal labor contracts, poor or nonexistent education, laughable police and judicial protection, and political disfranchisement for black Kentuckians outside of slavery. The *Observer & Reporter* praised the "ease with which the negroes have passed from a state of slavery to that of freedom," there having been "no riots or disturbances" and "very little, if any drunkenness." This ease, naturally, was due to "their old masters," who had sustained "the kindliest feelings" between themselves and their former slaves, and "the yoke of slavery bore very lightly on a large number of them before the war." But let the bureau be established, abolitionist-philanthropists and traitorous white Kentuckians would sew "discord, confusion and hostility" in "place of peace, order and kindness."[30]

Fisk knew that there was not then nor had there ever been the sort of harmonious peace and kindness spoken of by those who upheld the old order. In a speech given in Cincinnati on January 18, the new bureau commander claimed that "thirteen discharged colored soldiers stood in the streets" of Lexington "in full sight of Henry Clay's monument, with their backs bleeding from the cruel lash, their heads cut to the scalp, and one or two of them with their eyes put out" for "going to their former masters and asking for their wives and children" to be freed from now-illegal bondage. Such scenes, everyone knew, occurred in counties across the state. Returning black soldiers, men and women who attempted to negotiate new labor contracts for their farm or domestic work, individuals or families who attempted to find lost family members, and any number of other black Kentuckians faced violence at the hands of masked groups in the night, local sheriffs and policemen, and their former masters. Given the indignation with which white Kentuckians had responded to the recruitment of black soldiers in 1864 and 1865, though, these black soldiers in particular made tempting symbolic targets for violence in Kentucky and throughout the South. Because they had claimed for themselves the mantle of manhood that had previously been the preserve of white men such as Buckner, retaliation to reassert control over black men, the laurels of manhood, and claims to citizenship was particularly common.[31] Despite knowing full well that such attacks were taking place across the state, the House was furious that such incidents should be brought to light to discredit the mask of paternal benevolence that white Kentuckians presented to themselves and the world. They voted to form a special investigative committee to disprove Fisk's claims and secure his removal, hoping by so doing to discredit the bureau's mission and administration and to restore the state's honor and self-image. Who else would the House turn to for such a job but Buckner?[32]

Buckner, Union Party representative J. M. Armstrong from Louisville, and Lexington senator W. A. Dudley, who had spent the early days of the session as the Conservative head of the Senate Privileges and Elections Committee, took the train to Lexington, where they published calls in the *Observer & Reporter,* a paper taken by few white Union Party men because of its Conservative politics and certainly taken by even fewer African Americans, for witnesses to any violence against freedpeople to come forward and testify. Even if one or more black people heard of Buckner's call, decided to brave any potential reprisal, and came forward, there was no guarantee that any evidence they gave would be determined admissible. African Americans were still not allowed to testify against whites in state courts; although the committee investigation was not, strictly speaking, a court of law, even Judge Goodloe, who was gaining a reputation for disregarding the ban on black testimony in his courtroom, said as much when Buckner and the committee interviewed him.[33]

Not surprisingly, no testimony from African Americans was recorded, and only three white men came forward with any details. They told of at least seven instances they knew of where black men in uniform and in civilian clothes had been beaten, shot at, kicked, mobbed, or verbally abused in and around Lexington, but because none of the actual victims came forward—wisely so, given the dangerous climate and the lack of protection available to them if their names were known—there was little on which to follow up. These seven cases—an undocumented seven—were summarily dismissed because they did not equal the thirteen that Fisk had claimed. Buckner had a field day with both the absence of witnesses and the small number of reported instances; with such meager evidence at hand, he could claim that there were in fact no confirmed instances of racial violence in Fayette County and that Fisk, the Union Party men within the state, and the Republicans outside of it had conjured these stories out of thin air. When Armstrong refused to be party to such a gross manipulation of evidentiary gathering and twisting of fact, Buckner and Dudley simply ignored him and sent their report back to the legislature. Because "not one instance is reported where a negro soldier was cut with the lash; not one where the eye of a negro soldier was put out; not one where a negro soldier was in any way maltreated for asking for his wife and children," the whole of Fisk's speech was declared false. Quite the contrary, Buckner and Dudley argued, the evidence "clearly establishes the kind and indulgent treatment of the negro, whether slave or free," in Lexington.[34]

The two-man majority concluded "that the charges made by General Fisk, in reference to the maltreatment of negro soldiers . . . and the conduct of the civil authorities of the State . . . are false and slanderous." Rather than representing but the smallest fraction of the violence freedpeople faced across the state, Fisk's and the witnesses' incidents "are but a continuation of the system of misrepresentation to which the people of this State have been exposed for several years—a system introduced and persevered in," Buckner maintained, throwing back to the language of corrupt political usurpers, "by office-holders of the General Government, in order to extend and continue their own profits and powers" and recommend "themselves thereby to the patronage of the party in power at Washington."[35]

Fisk recognized that Buckner and Dudley's intentionally shallow investigation and partisan report were precisely why the bureau needed to have a presence in Kentucky. In a letter to Armstrong, Fisk detailed how he himself had met and talked with the thirteen men who hailed from across the Bluegrass—namely, Garrard, Bourbon, Woodford, Madison, and Montgomery Counties. Fisk begged the committee to stay in session long enough for him to come to Lexington or Frankfort to testify, but Buckner and Dudley declined to wait for him. Sick of the bureaucratic pretense, Fisk let the committee know precisely what he would show were he ever given the chance. "Let us go down to the 'hard pan' and ascertain the *exact condition* of the freedmen of Kentucky, and the disposition of your people toward them," he suggested. "Reports of outrages upon returned colored soldiers especially are continually reaching me from the 'blue-grass' and tobacco-producing sections of your State." "I also stated," he continued, turning the focus from himself to those investigating him, "that the Kentucky law-makers would be reluctant to enact laws that would secure impartial justice to her freedmen, and I certainly reached that conclusion when I was at Frankfort."[36]

The "hard pan" was one thing Buckner and Dudley were certainly keen to avoid; they preferred their narrative be the one presented to the world. Furious at the inaction, Fisk remarked that he should have expected as much from Buckner and the others, as "a more select number of vindicative, pro-slavery, rebellious legislators cannot be found than a majority of the Kentucky legislature."[37] His contempt for the lot of them evident, Fisk never heeded the legislature's summons to Frankfort and continued his operations from his headquarters in Louisville and Nashville. The Freedmen's Bureau lived. Proslavery and vindictive Buckner certainly was, but Fisk's charge that he was a rebel is certainly untrue. The charge does, though, highlight the difficulty that many northerners had—and had had since 1862—in distinguishing enraged loyal masters from enraged disloyal ones. When both spoke of federal military tyranny, a corrupt Congress, and the usurpation of their state and personal rights, what, really, was the difference between them now that the shooting had stopped?

Privileges and Elections business and the Fisk investigation consumed much of Buckner's first House session, but the whole of Kentucky needed to be rebuilt; while devoting the majority of his time to ensuring the political power of conservative white men who had worn both blue and gray, he did not neglect the health of the commonwealth's economy. Buckner's Whiggish political upbringing shone through as he, rather unsurprisingly, became a leading defender of developing the state's transportation infrastructure (introducing a bill in support of the Paris and

Winchester turnpike road company), encouraging and protecting its native industries (introducing resolutions opposing the federal taxation of cigar manufactures, chartering the Red River Iron Works, and chartering the Continental Petroleum and Mining Company), and securing future economic success through state-funded education for young white men (voting to authorize twenty thousand dollars to put the state Agricultural and Mechanical College—now the University of Kentucky—into immediate operation).[38]

Each of these bills reflected his commitment to rebuilding the state in the image of the preemancipation Kentucky he and Helen had dreamed about. When the second session opened in January 1867, Buckner came loaded with more bills to shore up the economic future of Clark County: one authorizing the county court to take stock in internal improvements, three chartering road companies (one between Winchester, Colbyville, and Lexington; another between Clark and Bourbon Counties; and the third the Kentucky River turnpike road company), and another—no doubt championed by his father-in-law and the other Clark County "lords of the pasture"—to prohibit the importation of cattle from Texas into the state. His commitment to improving the state's transportation routes even earned him a place on the committee on the Kentucky River navigation and on a later one "in relation to giving State aid to railroads."[39] There was, though, no bill to establish regularity in labor contracts for African Americans or to secure their testimony against white men in courts so that they might bring suits when they were refused wages for work done or driven violently off of land they had farmed and whose crops they had harvested. Kentucky African Americans would have to shift for themselves in the new world of postslavery work.

But with the special elections having taken place and six new members of the House sitting, there was more pressing business than road bills to attend to. After the initial flood of private bills subsided and a brief interlude where the House casually rejected the Fourteenth Amendment, the senators crossed the rotunda into the House chamber for a joint session to elect a U.S. senator on January 15. The first ballot confirmed the fears that had spurred Privileges and Elections to clean out as many Union Party members as they could before the voting commenced. The Union Party candidate, W. H. Randall from Laurel County, received thirty votes, but the once-unified Conservatives scattered their ballots among four men—Lazarus Powell, Aaron Harding, Garrett Davis, and Elijah Hise. The consensus of the previous year had crumbled.

The intersession months of 1866 had seen former Confederates reinsert themselves into statewide politics following the removal of their political disabilities. Although that insertion had helped anti-Republican candidates easily win the seats that Privileges and Elections had vacated, it had split the Conservative Party in two. Long-standing resentment toward the antebellum Democratic Party and wartime animosities were still too much to overcome for many Conservative politicians. It was the rebels, they could remember, who had begun the war that ended slavery, even if it had been the slaves themselves and the Republicans who finished off the institution. Not so comfortable with this new inclusive Democracy, a group of men led by Governor Bramlette clung fiercely to the Conservative name. The senate balloting in the General Assembly began a year of rhetorical posturing on all sides; the next year, 1867, would see a three-way political race between the Democrats (often pejoratively labeled the Rebel Democracy), the Union Party (or the Radicals to their opponents), and the Conservatives (termed the Third Party by the Democratic press).[40]

The Senate vote and the important state elections on the horizon in August were about more than control of offices. As the three parties sparred, they fought one of the earliest and most decisive battles in the war over the meaning of the war, in particular who would control the legacy of the Union cause in the state. Each of the three groups envisioned the Union cause during the war as having been about something different, and the ways in which they conceived of Kentucky Unionism gave them three different visions of what postwar Kentucky should look like. As the groups struggled between themselves for political power, they simultaneously worked to enshrine the legacy they favored as *the* Union cause in Kentucky. What they strategically forgot in the process, of course, was that the Union coalition in the state or in the nation had never agreed about what their cause had meant when it came to slavery and race, particularly after January 1, 1863. The terms by which white Kentuckians would remember the Civil War were largely hashed out in the newspapers, on the electoral stump, and in the ballot box in 1867.

As the days went on and the number of ballots grew, it became clear that the Union Party could claim forty votes if all their adherents were in attendance, but the Conservatives and Democrats could muster double that number, up to ninety, if they could come together. They could not. As the fifteen days of ballots passed, individual names came and went. Randall was replaced as the Union Party candidate by James Speed at first and then by Benjamin Helm Bristow later. The Powell, Harding, and

Davis factions continued to compete among the Conservatives and Democrats, occasionally producing slightly different combinations but no real progress.

The Democrats pushed for all anti-Republican votes to combine behind Powell, but the Conservative caucus refused and stubbornly backed the incumbent, Garrett Davis. The stalemate continued until January 30, when Powell removed his name from consideration to unite the vote. His note to the General Assembly was a perfect statement of old Whig statesmanship combined with political necessity. "Most earnestly desiring that harmony should prevail in the ranks of those who intend to act in good faith with the National Democracy, and sustain the President and the Supreme Court against the illegal and revolutionary policy of the Radicals," he wrote in language that both Conservatives and Democrats could agree with, "and believing that all who desire to see the Union restored, the Southern States speedily represented in Congress with perfect equality of rights under the Constitution, the reserved rights of the States preserved, the constitutional and civil liberties of the people maintained, and the fundamental laws faithfully executed," Powell encouraged like-minded gentlemen to "unite, in solid phalanx, in opposition to the wicked and destructive policy of the Radicals." Fulfilling his "patriotic duty," Powell bowed out of "this protracted contest" to ensure that some anti-Republican voice be sent to Washington. His wish was granted the next day when the Conservatives and Democrats united around Davis, who had been Buckner's candidate since the opening ballot two weeks earlier.[41] The "celebrated" work of Privileges and Elections the previous year had ensured that the two wings of the old Conservative Party could burn through ballot after ballot to choose their spokesman without feeling any real threat from men more sympathetic to the Republican Congress, the Freedmen's Bureau, and the freedpeople themselves.

At a meeting during the senatorial voting, the Democracy of Clark County met to cheer the legislature, which had fought "to defeat the schemes of those who would turn our now free and prosperous State into a Fletcher-ridden Missouri, or Brownlowized Tennessee" and promised, further, to help their "friends in Frankfort who have so nobly striven to unite discordant elements" during the Senate vote by pushing to elect a yet greater majority, who would "let by-gones be by-gones and vote on the true merits of the case." Curiously, they did not mention their representative, Mr. Buckner, among those Democratic friends in Frankfort.[42]

It is difficult to know precisely where Buckner stood in the tripartite political division of the state. He attended neither the Democratic nor the Conservative state conventions that preceded the 1867 session. Indeed, Winchester as a whole is difficult to read. Clark County was represented at each of these conventions by only one man; in the Conservative convention made up entirely of old Union men, that Clark County representative was none other than Buckner's younger brother, Tucker. True, Buckner voted for Garrett Davis, the Conservatives' candidate, consistently throughout the balloting, making it appear that he favored their cause. The long-standing friendship between Davis and the Buckner family may have had more influence over Buckner's votes than over his politics, however. Analyzing his voting record in the House is problematic because the Conservative and Democratic factions agreed on nearly every issue of policy. More frustratingly, that voting record is incomplete because Buckner was also absent from the House quite often, eventually being granted a leave of absence. His father had become quite ill, and Buckner spent a great deal of his time in Winchester sorting out Aylett's personal practice and at times taking over his court clerk's duties—ironically under Judge Goodloe.[43]

It is not inconceivable that Buckner was intentionally trying to remain hard to pin down in the early months of 1867. It was by no means clear which party would come to dominate the state. Just as much as secession had done in 1861, this political split left Buckner with friends, sympathies, and interests on both sides. His politics leaned Democratic; bringing the rebels back into the body politic locally and nationally had always been his goal. Yet the leadership of the Conservative Party was drawn from the same set of old conservative Whigs who had led the state through the secession crisis and been the backbone of the loyal resistance to the federal government after 1863. In addition to a desk full of unpaid notes, Aylett Buckner bequeathed his eldest son a wealth of personal connections to the leadership of the Conservative Party. Just as in 1861, there was something to lose—up to and including his budding political career—if Buckner alienated either camp and events turned against him. And just as he had during the war, he tried to take sides while constantly making overtures to his opponents. As a gesture of filial piety or at least respect to his Whig antecedents, then, Buckner supported Davis for senate but then cast his lot with the Democracy.

Buckner left the House in good standing with the Democratic leadership statewide. So ably had he served the cause of dispossessed masters of all wartime loyalties that there was a rumor floating about the state that either Buckner or Wolford, both "gallant soldiers and conservative Democrats, men whom the State respect[s] and can trust," might be advanced for the position of lieutenant governor on the ticket to be formed later in the year.[44]

Buckner fit the profile of the new Democratic coalition perfectly. "It is indubitably true that the Democratic party of Kentucky is composed of various elements—which in the past were hostile," wrote the *Observer & Reporter*. "There are in its ranks men who fought in either army—who were earnestly Union men from the beginning to the end—men who prayed for the triumph of the 'Bonnie Blue Flag'"; the party included "old Whigs, honest Know-Nothings, Breckinridge and Douglas Democrats—men representing every possible shade of past political distinctions" who had now "formed themselves into one great party to accomplish one great result—the restoration of true peace to the whole country, founded upon the proper rights of the states and the sacred liberties of the citizen." In language especially resonant for the Buckners, the paper proclaimed that "[i]ntermarriages have united families bitterly opposed during the war. Union parents have welcomed with true parental love the gallant son who won laurels in the gray. Southern sisters have thanked God for preserving brave brothers over whose breasts the blue was buttoned. In the parlor, at the festive board, in the ball-room, upon the street, meet and mingle in happy forgetfulness of the past persons of all shades of past opinions." Not only in families but in "business a similar amnesty has been proclaimed," evidenced particularly when Buckner and his fellow legislators had repealed the rules barring Confederates from practicing law and welcomed their brothers back to the bar. "In this new crusade" to roll back the changes brought by the revolution from below and above, when black Kentuckians demanded through their actions that the Johnson administration enact the same emancipation policies in Kentucky that had been done throughout the Confederate South, it was proclaimed that "Kentucky will stand upon the same level with the South," taking its place in the ranks of the dispossessed slave states and, perhaps, being "more hated, because more powerful" than her sister southern states restrained by what white southerners, Kentuckians included, termed a military tyranny. "Kentuckians can do a great and noble work if united; if torn by factions, she will fail ingloriously, despised, condemned and hated by every section of a country to whose highest interests she was untrue."[45]

Although the opposition press liked to paint Buckner and men like him as having "turned" rebel, they had not become anything they were not in 1861. Like the Confederates' war, theirs had been a war for slavery and white supremacy, and although Buckner himself certainly wished that his hotheaded rebel neighbors had not provoked the war in the first place, he and his proslavery unionist comrades had always planned to reunite with their wayward Confederate kinsmen after having defeated them. If the war had ended, as Buckner once hoped in a long-ago letter to Helen, with a triumphant Union victory in the summer of 1862, slavery may yet have been saved. But that had not happened. So they and the rebels had come back together, putting aside the governments for which they fought and focusing on the cause each of them shared.

Buckner would have cheered the sentiments of his old comrade Frank Wolford, who gave a "Grand Effort" of a speech before the state Democratic Convention in March. "I have been glad to see to-day at this Convention," Wolford opened, "men with whom I have fought, and men against whom I have fought." Now, he was proud to "hail" his former foes "as countrymen and as friends" and to proclaim them, in words that echoed some Buckner had written to Helen during the war, to have been "actuated by the purest motives in the course they pursued in the war, though I believed them mistaken." It did not matter in the least now, of course; both rebel master and loyal master were reunited in their lost mastery. For, indeed, "at the head of my brave cavalrymen I marched, while a flag, bearing its full complement of stars, floated over our column," and Wolford proclaimed it beneath his birth "in this proud old Commonwealth" to ever consent to striking "dark and dead eleven stars in the blue field" and "degrading them to political servitude to illiterate and brutish negroes." He beamed with pride in the convention, where he had seen for the first time "many soldiers of the Union army . . . voting side by side with those who have struggled on the other side." "It was," Wolford proclaimed, "a miniature spectacle of what I would like to see the entire nation present." Only when former Confederate states were finally restored to full equality—an unspoken precondition of which included legitimate white congressional delegations who would vote alongside the outnumbered Kentucky defenders of the old racial order—could Wolford "look at my old battered sword with renewed pride, and feel that the mission for which it was drawn is complete. I should then regard it no longer as an instrument of tyranny, but as a symbol of national mercy." But if that end were never accomplished, and the "subjugation of the Southern States, for the purpose of elevating the negro to political power, at the expense of white men, born freemen, descendants of our revolutionary sires, then I shall turn from that sword with sorrow, if not with shame."[46]

Buckner, too, hoped that the triumph of the Democracy in Kentucky could lead a charge that would overcome what he characterized as the Republican tyranny visited on the South. Like Wolford, he too intended to validate his military service and his long-held faith in the constitutional procedures of the U.S. government by seeing white supremacy maintained in the Bluegrass and restored in the former Confederacy. Though he did not stand for reelection to his seat in the House, he made known his support for the Democratic gubernatorial slate of former governor John L. Helm and John W. Stevenson. Doubtless, Buckner had long been an admirer of Helm, who had been one of the state's many Whig governors before the war, and he had had a chance to get to know the man better during his time in the General Assembly in Frankfort because Helm had also served on the Senate Privileges and Elections Committee. With his old Whig credentials, Helm made an attractive candidate for wartime proslavery unionists such as Buckner. Further, Helm's son, Confederate brigadier general Benjamin Hardin Helm, who had married the youngest sister of Mary Todd Lincoln before being killed in command of the First Kentucky "Orphan" Brigade at Chickamauga in 1863, won Helm a place in the hearts of the state's Confederates.[47]

Whereas Buckner and Wolford were fully ready to forge ahead under the banner of the Democracy, Buckner's old friend and wartime comrade Charley Hanson was among those who joined Bramlette in trying to uphold the Conservative Party and keep the anti-Republican movement in the state free from rebels. But even as Hanson announced his candidacy for Brutus J. Clay's congressional seat in April, his defeat was already a fact accomplished to most onlookers. The Democrats recognized that the Third Party, the Conservatives, would collapse after the August elections and spent a good deal of ink flattering the few Third Party voters in the state. The *Observer & Reporter* believed the Democrats could win over the Thirds because their policy positions were virtually identical. As a consequence, the editors pronounced themselves "sorry for Hanson" for being "shoved into a hopeless fight." "Col. Hanson was a gallant soldier, and as he will be badly beaten," they continued, "we don't intend to say one word, except in praise or good humored opposition—He will be with us in a few months—next year any how." The Union Party's *Kentucky Statesman*, the newly established Lexington mouthpiece of the Goodloe family, was more tepid on the Thirds. The paper encouraged the Conservative Thirds' anti-Confederate stance, yet the editors were nevertheless stung by the Thirds' "usual fling[s] at what they are pleased to term the Radical party."[48]

If the Thirds wanted to understand the real positions of the Union Party, whose members were less influenced by its vocal minority of outright advocates of full racial equality, such as John G. Fee, than the Democratic press would have everyone believe, and if they wanted to do productive work to rebuild the state and the nation with or without the rebels and the Democracy, then they were welcome in the Union Party camp.[49] The Union Party knew the direction it wanted the state to take, but it could see little difference between its two opponents' platforms. "You all claim to belong to the Democratic party of the Nation," the Goodloes said to both Thirds and Democrats, "you both denounce, with all bitterness and hate, the Union party, and oppose with rancor all its policy. If there is a single iota of difference between you . . . we cannot discover it."[50]

Differences between union men who had become Democrats and those who had become Thirds were real, however, if slight. They split on how Kentucky should best resist the U.S. Congress and its Republican majority for the benefit of white people in the state and across the South. In place of Democratic resistance and ferocity toward the congressional Republican program of Reconstruction, the Conservatives promised cooperation and compromise to rebuild Kentucky and the South. Both they and the Democrats agreed that the "South lies bleeding and powerless," but the Conservatives were convinced that "Kentucky, acting alone" as the spokesman for the crippled master class in Washington, "can afford them [the southern states] no aid. We ask, how does the exhibition of defiance on the part of Kentucky against the Government advance the interests of the Southern States?" Governor Bramlette and Lieutenant Governor Jacob, men who had felt Washington's political muscle during the war, were ready to face the new realities of state and federal power relations and wanted to broker the best deal for Kentucky and the former Confederacy that they could. "All the power is in the hands of the North. From them relief must come, if it comes at all." Antagonistic resistance to the Republican majority in Washington would only spell further ruin, "arous[ing] the North . . . and consolidat[ing] the Republican party and force the denial of all favor to the South."[51]

Buckner must have sympathized with them a little, having once declared that the Confederates "have brought all this" havoc upon Kentucky's slave society "and are not worthy of our support." Indeed, the Thirds' logic had remained unchanged from the proslavery union orthodoxy in 1861. The Third Party stubbornly wanted to make the point that they had been right. Kentucky had been right. The rebellion had been disastrous for the South and for slavery. "You, people of Kentucky," the Conservatives pleaded, "think from what an abyss of ruin these same conservative

'Union Democrats' saved you" in 1861. "Look to Virginia, look to Missouri, look to Tennessee and learn thence what would have been your fate and your present condition had the counsels of these revolutionists"—of both the secessionist and abolitionist stripe—"controlled your action."[52]

Bramlette and his allies believed that votes for the Democratic Party in 1867 were the same as votes for secession in 1861. Such votes were ultimately harmful because "they give strength to the Republican party, just as the Southern leaders carried out the wishes of the Abolitionists in the opening of the rebellion. Extremists thus strengthen and aid each other."[53] But 1861 conservatism no longer suited Buckner and the majority of Kentucky's union men. Caution and cooperation had been the order of the day when they still believed in Lincoln and a limited war. Now, on the other side of the end of the world, Kentuckians were in no mood to cooperate with the men who had betrayed the state's loyalty and killed the institution that knit its society together. The end of slavery, congressional Reconstruction, and the battles with the Johnson administration gave them no hope that their good faith would be rewarded. Buckner and the majority of union Kentuckians felt betrayed and angry; they intended to pay back Republicans—black and white, national and local—with full-throated denouncement on the floors of Congress and full-fledged resistance in the legislative halls, in courtrooms, and on the ground in Kentucky.

The Third Party was utterly destroyed in the 1867 elections, as nearly everyone predicted. "The Conservatives are only a party of Generals," the *Statesman* perceptively observed, "without rank or file, and totally incapable . . . of polling ten thousand votes in the State." The majority of the 1861 Union coalition had left them behind, with their old appeals to constitutional conservatism; more Kentuckians wanted to satisfy their feelings of anger, disappointment, and betrayal by lashing out, not to broker legislative compromise. Charley Hanson's campaign followed statewide trends. He took his loss with relatively good humor, and the Democrats were there to welcome him into the fold as they did with most Conservatives. The *Observer & Reporter* had some fun comparing his electoral defeat to the two military defeats he had suffered during the war—one in the summer of 1863, after Buckner had resigned, when the Twentieth Kentucky stood bravely against John Hunt Morgan's entire cavalry force at Lebanon until compelled to surrender due to exhausted ammunition, and the other when Hanson had been wounded in 1864 at the battle of Saltville and nursed back to health in a Confederate hospital. "Well! Colonel, your luck is not very flattering," remarked the paper. "You are again met, captured and released. You have a knack of making foolish fights when certain, inevitable result is hopeless defeat. We admire your pluck, but we would dislike to bet on your judgment." In this election battle, just like that at Lebanon, Buckner had already removed himself from Hanson's side and did not share his fate.[54]

The gubernatorial election further confirmed the result; the Democratic Helm and Stevenson ticket won the governor's mansion. Helm easily carried Clark County with more than 800 votes, and John Conkright, who had ceded the nomination to Buckner in 1865, was sent to Frankfort without Buckner's opposition. Strangely, Buckner did draw 183 votes from the county's Third Party men, who did not have a candidate of their own. There was no evidence that Buckner had ever wanted their support. A similar situation occurred in Woodford County, when James P. Ford, "the staunchest of Democrats, and the most popular of men, was without his knowledge or consent" put on the Third Party ticket in order to take votes from Democrats. When he found out, Ford furiously rode to the county seat of Versailles to repudiate "the whole proceeding, denouncing it as unwarranted, unauthorized and outrageous" and promising not to accept the office if he won. Buckner's votes seem to have come from a similar scheme.[55]

Buckner's support for John Helm's Democratic candidacy was no secret in Clark County during the election, and it would soon be statewide news. In the days after the Democratic landslide, Union Party men throughout the state met in conventions to call for the removal of their wartime battle flags from state custody. The *Statesman* gladly published resolutions from meetings in Bowling Green and Louisville and even hosted the Lexington meeting in its office. When the war had finished, the flags had been returned to the state government in Frankfort, where they had been kept on display at the arsenal and in the state House. The Lexington meeting, chaired by Brigadier General Samuel Woodson Price and former captain William Cassius Goodloe, was attended by sixty-three former Union soldiers, who signed their names to the drafted resolutions. The meeting included no shortage of notable names in the Union service. Seven colonels, five majors, nineteen captains, eleven lieutenants, four surgeons, and sixteen enlisted men had come to protest the election results. The resolutions called for a statewide meeting in Louisville to consider whether the "persons elected, to the State offices of Kentucky, some of whom fought us under another flag, and most of whom would have been glad to have seen ours trailed in the dust," were the "proper persons to have the custody of these glorious emblems."[56]

Of course, the Democrats who had just carried the state were not exclusively rebels; with at most only one in three Kentuckians being Confederate sympathizers during the war, it was impossible for Helm and his party to have carried the state so decisively without support from Democratic Union veterans. But to the convention's Union Party men, the issue was plain. If a man stood alongside the former Confederates now, he was no better than the rebels. If "there are any of our former companions in arms who desire to commit our colors to the enemy," the convention resolutions read, "we will act independently of them, just as we would have done in battle, had they deserted."[57]

It was a strong claim, particularly in the wake of an election that had seen Wolford's very public declaration that if the Union cause was to be associated with racial equality and Confederate disfranchisement, then he would turn from it in shame. The Union Party was more than willing to call Wolford on his bluff. If he wanted to turn from those results, then let him—and Buckner, too, for that matter. The *Observer & Reporter* challenged the Union Party claim to represent the whole of the Union cause in Kentucky. "What say Wolford, Garrard, Winfrey, Cochran, Owsley, Buckner, Dowden, Dawson, Towles, and the thousands of such, who voted for Helm[?]" the paper asked.[58] Those Democrats believed themselves the only heirs of the Union; it was they who stood by the prewar understanding of the Union and Constitution that had protected and promoted slavery since 1789. In their minds, they had not betrayed the Constitution and the republic by allowing—like the Thirds—or, worse, by aiding—like the Republicans—the unconstitutional war on slavery. Surely their say mattered when thinking about what Kentucky's wartime loyalty meant now and in the future.

"We imagine what they say will be matters of perfect indifference to the men engaged in this matter," retorted Goodloe's *Statesman*. The paper then turned on the "military record of these gentlemen." Two of them, Wolford and T. T. Garrard, Goodloe pointed out, "have openly said that they were ashamed of the uniform they wore"; the others were little better. Both Wolford and Garrard had been dismissed from the service for their anti-Lincoln outspokenness, and the balance had resigned their commissions in 1862 and 1863, with Buckner's resignation in April 1863 falling right in the middle of the pack. The *Statesman* published the date that each man had left the army, by their own will or by legal force.[59] The meaning was clear. Because these men had quit serving in the Union army when that army no longer served *their* unionism, they had no right to call themselves Union men.

To the Goodloes and the Unconditional Unionists of Kentucky, Buckner and his conservative proslavery unionist allies—who had made up the majority of Union men at the outset of the war—were no different than rebels. If Ben Buckner and Frank Wolford wanted to go weep over the corpse of slavery with John Helm and the Confederate comrades of his late son, then they were more than welcome to do so together. But rebels they all would be.

For their part, Buckner and Wolford seemed perfectly willing to leave the legacy of the Union cause to the Union Party and their allies. To their minds, the Goodloes and the Fees tainted the memory of the Union as it was and the Constitution as it had been with their advocacy for the rights of freedpeople. Just as Buckner had washed his hands of the abolition army in 1863 when he resigned his commission and left such a disgraceful project as the destruction of slavery to those who were indecent enough to participate in it, he likewise left control of the meaning of the Union cause in the state to those who were, in his mind, dishonorable enough to use that memory to seek independence, dignity, and equality for black Kentuckians.

Even though the Union Party had lost the election in 1867, the flag controversy had won them the power to define what the Union cause had meant. The very name "Union Party" associated its members' moderately emancipationist memory of the war and their comparatively liberal racial politics with all of the state's wartime Union men. A Union Party that represented all Kentuckians who had worn the blue uniform during the war, though, is as erroneous a notion as a Rebel Democracy.[60] At the time, it seems that Buckner was not especially concerned with how later generations would remember or understand the previous seven years of his life. He was dedicated to eliminating the changes those years had brought, to reclaiming the republic as the sole possession and birthright of white men, and to resisting the tyranny perpetrated by the Republicans in Washington. What did it matter if the men Buckner associated with, spoke in support of, and voted for had been Confederates? At least they were honorable men, dedicated, like him, to seeing the white man's republic restored. If the new Kentucky Democracy that emerged in 1867 appeared on the surface to be a "rebel Democracy," as the *Statesman* and its proto-Republican allies claimed, it was a conservative proslavery unionist Democracy in its philosophy, methods, and constituency.

6

Democratic Partisan Militia

In late July 1870, Frederick Douglass's periodical the *Washington New Era* foretold a great revolution in the Bluegrass State. "The Democrats in Kentucky are in sore tribulation lest they should loose [*sic*] the Ashland Congressional district, through the colored vote, which will be cast for the first time at the coming election." As Buckner and many white Bluegrass Democrats—now embracing the former rebels, wartime unionist supporters of John L. Helm such as Buckner, and the majority of the Conservative "Third" Party, which had folded into the Democratic Party after 1867—saw it, the elections in August 1870 would either stem the tide of sweeping social changes that began with the Emancipation Proclamation, saw the abolition of slavery and the collapse of the wartime Union coalition, and now had seen the ratification of the Fifteenth Amendment earlier in the year or realize their greatest fears. Douglass quoted from the *Louisville Courier-Journal*—a new entity edited by former Confederate officer Henry Watterson, recently spawned from the merger of George Prentice's redoubtable *Louisville Journal* with the Confederate-sympathizing Democratic *Louisville Courier*, reflecting the tack of post-1867 state politics—which had asserted that "no event could happen in Kentucky which would spread a more general feeling of humiliation than the transfer of the renowned Ashland district to the control of the former slaves of the voters who elected a Clay, a Crittenden . . . and a Breckinridge." But such a reality, Douglass warned, faced the Kentucky Democracy.[1]

That same summer Douglass observed that the Kentucky Democrats had "built their shanty on the bank of slavery, but the rising tide of freedom and equality has flooded back into the wretched hovel. . . . That tide is resistless." Kentucky whites, too, sensed the rising tide. W. C. P. Breckinridge recalled that 1870 was a year of the "Black Peril." With the loss of Democratic political control a potential reality after the amendment, whites convinced themselves that a subsequent domino effect would end in Republican control and "negro domination" of the state. "The fate of New Orleans and other Southern cities under negro rule," said Breckinridge, "were terrible object lessons."² As Breckinridge's allusion to New Orleans and the rest of the Reconstruction South suggests, the "humiliation" of falling to "negro rule" was something that Kentucky's Democrats had watched happen to other southern whites after congressional Reconstruction realized black suffrage in the former Confederacy. However, because Kentucky had not seceded and was not being formally reconstructed, the Democratic state government was able to deny the ballot to African Americans until the passage of the Fifteenth Amendment.³

It had succeeded not for lack of trying on the part of Kentucky Union Party Republicans. Following the Democratic victory in 1867, Buckner's Winchester nemesis James M. Ogden wrote to Joseph Holt encouraging him to use his influence with the "Committee on Republican form of Govt." in Congress to apply the same congressional Reconstruction to Kentucky as it had to the states formerly in rebellion. Ogden, Judge William Clinton Goodloe in Lexington, and other prominent Republican leaders, he said, "hardly know what to do." Recognizing the weakness of his party in the state, Ogden candidly admitted that there was "great personal danger to those who advocate the measure" and that if "Congress will not back us up, we shall be in a very bad condition." He remained convinced that it was "only by Reconstructing us here"—which would virtually guarantee the advent of African American suffrage in the commonwealth—"that we can be politically saved."⁴ Yet Ogden's hopes were not to be realized. Undoubtedly, the uproar that would result from overthrowing the government of a state that had never seceded was more than either Holt or the Republican Congress wanted to incite. With no action in 1867, then, the elections of 1870 would be the first in which the solvency of the post-1867 Kentucky Democracy would be challenged by a Republican Party consisting of both whites and blacks.

The challenge would be a formidable one. Although Kentucky's freedmen had not been allowed to participate in elections for the five years since their freedom from slavery, black leaders throughout the state had used the time to prepare the state's African American population to have an immediate impact upon their enfranchisement. A "Convention of Colored Men of Kentucky" with delegates elected locally from across the state was held in early 1866; the twenty thousand black Kentuckians who had served in the Union army during the war became apostles of freedom and citizenship as they returned home; and although the hostile state government had followed up on Buckner's initial harassment of General Clinton B. Fisk and limited much of what the Freedmen's Bureau could accomplish, it could not prevent the establishment of one of the bureau's most successful school systems. By the time the bureau pulled out of Kentucky in 1870, schools for African Americans were spread throughout the state, received the majority of their funding from local black communities, and employed an 80 percent black teaching staff.[5]

White Kentucky Democrats hated more than the education for freedom that black Kentuckians gained at the bureau schools under black teachers. They hated the schools as an institution, too; every class meeting that took place was a condemnation of white paternalistic ideology. Around the same time that Fisk received authorization to bring the bureau into the state, Buckner and the General Assembly had passed bills directing any tax revenue raised from black people to go into a combined state fund for "support of their paupers and the education of their children." Of course, because black Kentuckians were forced into the lowest-paying jobs in the fields and in the cities nearly the entire population were paupers to begin with, there was no appreciable money to be raised. Although it appeared on the surface that Buckner and the legislature had passed a magnanimous bill to provide a state-administered education for blacks, the reality of the legislation showed how hollow the measures—and white paternalism—truly were. There would never be enough money in any place outside of Louisville, Lexington, or perhaps Danville to establish schools for blacks; pauper relief would come before any of the revenue could be spent on education; only half of the fund could ever be spent on schools; and the bill provided only for the education of black children, not adults, guaranteeing a generation of illiteracy and economic exploitation at the hands of white farmers, domestic household managers, and factory operators who could continue to manipulate work contracts. Further, the state administration of the schools would ensure Frankfort's control over both teachers and curriculum. The *Lexington Observer & Reporter*, always keen to paint itself as benevolent protector of black Kentuckians, advocated for "negro schools," while insisting that their ideology be shaped by "persons who are not strangers to our habits, customs and civilization, and inimical to any part of our population." But at least the editors were in favor of the scheme. A letter to the paper penned by "Better than a Negro" predicted racial amalgamation and a degradation of poor white labor if blacks were allowed any education at all.[6]

Late in the 1867 session, Buckner and the General Assembly passed the bill authorizing the black state schools—a year after granting twenty thousand dollars for the establishment of the Agricultural and Mechanical College, which would educate the next generation of Kentucky farmers, lawyers, and doctors—but, unsurprisingly, the better-funded, less-supervised, and more inclusive Freedmen's Bureau schools proved more attractive to the overwhelming majority of black Kentuckians. They learned important lessons. Increasingly literate, mobile, and connected through social networks, bureau agents, and an emerging Republican press, Kentucky's freedpeople made themselves well aware of how the power of the vote had established and maintained the Republican governments farther south. The "rising tide of freedom" that had swept over the former Confederacy in 1867 and 1868 with black electoral participation would finally reach Kentucky in 1870. Nurtured for five years in rundown schoolhouses and nocturnal meetings, Kentucky's African Americans had learned to be free, to be literate. Now they were eager to be citizens.[7]

For those five years, though, white Kentuckians had been resisting these schools of personhood and citizenship—as well as any assertion of black independence and self-determination in the legislature and in the countryside. Kentucky was the only nonseceding state that had any significant Ku Klux Klan presence, and the violence in the state lasted longer than it did in some others farther south.[8] "Regulator" groups throughout rural Kentucky rode under any one of many different local names, their white and black opponents knowing them variously as the "party styled and known as Kuklux, Regulators, or *Judge Lynch*." Before long, Kentuckians generally grouped them all under the heading "Ku Klux Klan," regardless of whether they operated under the guises, ritual, and hoods of that particular order.[9]

Klan violence was so prevalent as to spawn a host of new names in Kentucky and the South. "Kuklux" or "Kukluxers" were the most common names used for participants, and the new verb *to kuklux* came to be interchangeable with *to lynch, beat,* or *harass* in the southern vocabulary. The goals of the Ku Klux Klan and the other night-riding white supremacist groups were the same: combating African Americans' attempts to establish equality in the social and economic realms by driving freedpeople off of the land, burning bureau schoolhouses, and beating and murdering local leaders—white and black—engaged in organizing in the state's black communities.[10] The Klan was, according to Eric Foner, "a military force serving the interests of the Democratic party, the planter class, and all those"—wartime Unionists and Confederates alike in Kentucky—"who desired the restoration of white supremacy."[11]

Kentucky's Klan members, in great contrast to their fellows in Republican-governed states elsewhere in the South, rode secure in the knowledge that their Democratic state government was hardly concerned with punishing them for their crimes. Furthermore, because Kentucky was not undergoing the Reconstruction process, there were but a handful of federal troops in the state to counter their activities. They were free to harass the freedpeople and ensure that white conservative social and economic agendas were carried out. Unlike the former Confederate states where the Klan had often intervened on the side of the Democratic and Conservative Parties in elections, though, Kentucky's "Regulators" had not concerned themselves with the partisan political sphere before 1870. The threat black Kentuckians presented to the old order before then was, in Foner's words, "political, but political in the broadest sense, for it sought to affect power relations" in the workplace and in the community.[12] By 1870, that had changed. If many whites had been disturbed to see the emergence of literacy, agency, and leadership in the state's African American population after the war, the new "Black Peril" of political participation was the greatest horror yet.

Unsurprisingly, Democrats vehemently claimed that the state's violence and lawlessness sprang not from a desire to "regulate" the freedmen, but from leftover hostility born of wartime guerrilla fighting. Governor John W. Stevenson, who had assumed the office after Helm's death just five days into his term, linked the current Kuklux violence directly to wartime animosities. "It cannot be disguised," Stevenson claimed, "that since the war, and as kind of outgrowth of it, lawlessness has, to a greater degree than ever before, displayed itself" throughout the commonwealth.[13] But the Klan and other such groups, regardless of where Stevenson and other politicians claimed they originated, benefited directly from the Democratic legislature's refusal to act against them. The Republican press repeatedly charged that the Democratic government did little to halt the violence rampant throughout the state. Their charge was not without merit. Democratic politicians often simply denied or ignored the problem, distancing themselves from the violence that was working in their interest. Stevenson claimed that Kentucky had seen but a handful of incidents of violence during his term as governor. Republicans begged to differ.

The *Frankfort Commonwealth* listed no less than 115 reported episodes of Kuklux or Regulator violence in the state, many of them having multiple victims.[14]

More recently, George Wright has confirmed at least seventy-one lynching deaths from the end of the war to August 1870, though precise figures can never be known. The end of that violent year would see the number rise to at least ninety-two. Such levels of violence are in every way comparable with those in the Deep South. These figures are made more startling by the fact that they count only deaths, not the serious and permanent injuries or destruction of property that were just as common.[15] "We had thought that Kentucky with her 70,000 *Democratic* majority would give us that long coveted peace," wrote a dismayed Republican on one occasion, "but there is hardly a week passes but that we hear of some startling outrages committed . . . for the purpose of aiding Democratic Kentucky."[16]

Although the Kuklux and other Regulator organizations had been active against freedpeople since 1865, since the war had ended, the state militia force had only taken the field once in a halfhearted attempt to end the violence. In 1868, the state mounted a brief expedition to look into the violence in the southern Bluegrass counties of Marion, Boyle, Mercer, and Lincoln. States elsewhere in the South with Republican governments had used their militias—often integrated forces—to great effect in countering violent terrorism within their borders, and on the surface it appears that the 1868 Kentucky expedition was the same sort of enterprise. On the surface of the thing, it appeared that this anti-Klan activity and denunciations of the violence from Democratic politicians—especially Governor Stevenson—showed the Kentucky's Democratic government employing its militia in a genuine effort to curb the violence and protect black residents, just as Tennessee, North Carolina, Arkansas, and other states with Republican governments had done.[17]

From beginning to end, though, this expedition of the Kentucky National Legion, as the state militia was known at the time, was an entirely different proposition. Governor Stevenson's intentions for the three cavalry companies' ideological and political bent were made perfectly clear when he selected the old conservative warhorse Frank Wolford—Buckner's ally on the Privileges and Elections Committee—to command the troops. Wolford dutifully led his column south, and, sure enough, the masked bands dispersed, but many in the Republican press charged that the Kuklux had only left the area because Wolford had tipped them off to his arrival and wanted no conflict. "The coming of the militia was known and heralded," wrote one observer, "and the individuals sought to be captured had opportunity to get away and keep away, so long as their would-be captors were at hand." The force, in Republican eyes, "either from the lack of previous arrangement or from the management which it received, did virtually nothing."[18] There is no evidence, of course, that Wolford or other State Guard officers secretly cooperated with members of the Ku Klux Klan to force failure on the expedition in the interest of white supremacy. That having been said, Wolford's efforts were at best a token response to a widespread problem. The force sent was far too small to combat Regulators in four counties. Standing in great contrast to the Kentucky effort, Tennessee's Republican-led anti-Klan efforts the same year employed twenty-one companies of (often integrated) militiamen. Wolford's force, one-seventh the size, could hardly have hoped for success at the outset. But, then again, as one Republican concluded, "so goes Democratic law in a Democratic State."[19]

Practicing Democratic law in a Democratic state had its rewards for those on the inside. Buckner's legal career had grown bigger than Winchester by 1870. The notoriety he had gained among influential Democrats across the state for his service during the 1865–1867 session of the General Assembly had paid off. After being sent as a delegate to the 1868 Democratic National Convention, his political star seemed to rise even further still. It was a wise move, then, to relocate across the county line into Lexington, where he could have much more contact with his important friends across the state in that hub of the Bluegrass. Buckner formed a law partnership with former Confederate colonel W. C. P. Breckinridge. Breckinridge had defied the wishes of his father, staunch Unionist and moderate antislavery advocate Reverend Dr. Robert J. Breckinridge, when he had raised a regiment of cavalry to follow John Hunt Morgan in the summer of 1862, but the brand of unionism that Buckner had espoused during the war and his support of reconciliation in the name of economic growth and racial control meant that the two new partners got along very nicely indeed.[20]

Like Buckner, Breckinridge presented himself as a racial moderate; the former Confederate colonel had recently lost a race for district commonwealth attorney because of his support for black testimony rights in courts. It seemed that more of his father had rubbed off on the colonel than his Confederatism would suggest. During the race, though, Breckinridge's opponents portrayed his support for testimony as support for black suffrage, and though he repeatedly denied the latter—revealing the limits of his paternalistic conception of black men's role in the postemancipation

Kentucky—the damage was done.²¹ Breckinridge lost the race, but it was apparent to all that his was a rising star; Buckner could not do poorly by connecting with him. So Helen and Ben moved to Lexington, bringing with them two young daughters, Elizabeth and Sarah, who would, if all went well, grow up in the city along with their father's prominence and reputation. (The Buckners' son, Maurice, had died of whooping cough in August 1865, a little more than a year after he was born.)²²

However, black freedom and black Kentuckians' claims to the rights of free citizens continued to threaten Ben and Helen's plans for professional success and domestic bliss, as they had since 1862. In the wake of the Fifteenth Amendment, put into law the same year that the Buckners moved to Lexington, the white community began to sense their greatest fears being realized. Black enfranchisement had always been a specter in the back of white Kentuckians' minds and in the newspaper dispatches from other southern states, but it had never been real. Now, when blacks, riding Douglass's "rising tide of freedom," would attempt to claim their equal share as voting citizens, whites began to believe they would try to claim their share of another traditional reserve of white manhood: the right to bear arms. Just as Buckner and many other white Kentuckians in both blue and gray had balked at the enlistment of black troops during the Civil War, the idea of armed and organized blacks claiming and defending their freedoms was abhorrent to many whites. The formation of a "Negro Kuklux" was rumored during the summer of 1870.

Little evidence exists outside of Democratic newspapers that company-size organizations of black men gathered or drilled together, and similar fears and wild rumors had attended the realization of African American suffrage throughout the South. More often than not, what whites took to be paramilitary training musters were Freedmen's Bureau school meetings, religious gatherings, or Republican political rallies. All such gatherings were threatening to white supremacy, of course, though not in the violent, confrontational way whites imagined; instead, they were intended to educate, empower, and prepare freedpeople for citizenship.²³ Little surprise, then, that after speaking at a black political meeting in Lexington, Buckner's Republican foe, Judge William Clinton Goodloe, was accused of calculating "to frenzy and embitter the natural brutal passions of the negro toward the Democratic portion of the white race" and incite "the baser passions of this brutal race to deeds of blood and violence against the whites." That Goodloe was joined by infamous Madison County abolitionist John G. Fee, former General John T. Croxton in Bourbon, Sam McKee in Fleming and other northeastern Kentucky counties, and freedmen Reverend G. W. Dupree and Elijah and Henry Marrs in western Kentucky and Frankfort, respectively, only enhanced the belief among whites that they had literally been laid siege to by advocates of racial equality.[24] Barely ten years removed from the persecution of Fee and his followers after John Brown's raid, less than a decade after white Kentuckians had debated not whether slavery should be preserved but whether the Union or the Confederacy could best defend the institution, and only five years after the institution had formally ended, such scenes were nearly unimaginable. Who knew what could happen next?

Rumors of armed black men terrified white Kentuckians, as had the tales of Saint-Domingue, Nat Turner, the 1856 western Kentucky ironworkers, and John Brown in the years preceding the war. Whites quickly turned the reports into a justification for violence in "defense" of the white community, just as they had in the wake of those antebellum insurrection rumors.[25] They understood these African American organizational efforts not as intending to claim legally bestowed rights or of protecting property and family but as an assault on the purviews of white society and white masculinity: political participation and arms bearing.[26] Democrats had no difficulty believing what they were told by their leaders that tense summer, and they rallied to the leaders' calls to arms. "It is time that measures be taken effectually to stop these systemic outrages," read one Lexington article, "and to let these scoundrels know that they are not masters of the land. They have commenced as did the Indians, and their fate will be similar."[27] Buckner was loathe to let those outrages be visited on his family or his practice, and if his legislative efforts three years earlier had not been sufficient to reclaim his position as the master of the land, violence would.

A changing geography of race in Kentucky enhanced Buckner's fears about Lexington's future even further. In the years following their emancipation, many African Americans had moved off of the farms where they had been enslaved and into Kentucky's towns and cities, seeking employment, education, and protection from the Ku Klux Klan. The farming counties of the southern Bluegrass—an area that had seen the heaviest Kuklux activity in the state—lost on average 17 percent of their black populations, which drastically reduced the counties' agricultural production. Bourbon, Clark, Garrard, Jessamine, Madison, and Mercer Counties saw their tobacco production decrease from 1860 to 1870. Counties in the upper Bluegrass with larger towns that attracted black refugees, such as Woodford, Scott, and Harrison, saw equally dramatic increases in their output. With the available migrant labor, for example, Fayette increased its hemp production more than 50 percent from its 1860 numbers.[28] As the rural counties whitened, towns and cities saw the reverse. From 1860 to 1870, Lexington's black population increased by 300 percent, but the white population grew just 10 percent; the 1870 census shows that 7,215 of Lexington's 14,845 residents were black.[29]

The dramatic expansion of urban black population in Kentucky was linked to the state's refusal to protect, employ, and educate black people in the rural counties in which they had been born. Most southern freedpeople moved only a few miles from the plantations where they had worked in bondage, with only a few moving into the cities to seek refuge from continued harsh treatment and violence at the hands of rural former masters as well as the better opportunities for educational and social organizations found off the farm. The Freedmen's Bureau and Republican state governments could provide protection, education, and employment assistance to rural black people in the states of the former Confederacy, but in Democratic-controlled Kentucky freedpeople were left largely to fend for themselves. They had little choice but to seek security and opportunity in the crowded shantytowns on the outskirts of Lexington and other Bluegrass cities and towns. While the black population of the South's largest cities doubled on average in the five years after the Civil War, the black population in Lexington grew nearly three times and brought the ratio of blacks to whites to just shy of one to one.[30] Politically speaking, this African American urban migration meant that the elections of 1870 were going to be closely contested. African Americans were expected to vote overwhelmingly Republican, and thus it was more than conceivable that Democrats could lose control of city offices.[31] Paris, Versailles, and other neighboring towns had also seen the same patterns of migration from rural areas. Settling in cities with better access to education and political organization, and present in numbers to constitute a sizable voting bloc, African Americans were in strong position to secure rights for themselves in the upcoming elections.[32] Buckner and his fellow Democrats, though, understood the arrival of these new black residents as the first waves in Douglass's rising tide that would sweep away the old order, setting in motion the "negro domination" that they had heard of elsewhere in the South.

Buckner, Breckinridge, and James F. Robinson Jr., head of the county Democratic Party and son of one of the state's wartime governors, led Lexington's preemptive strike against voting by African Americans. The two former Union officers—the younger Robinson had served as state quartermaster under his father—and the rebel

Breckinridge made a fitting combination that exhibited the postwar cooperation between dispossessed masters in the Bluegrass. They would raise and command a unit of state militia as a political paramilitary force within the city of Lexington to violently harass black voters in the days leading up to the election. The plan seemed inelegant but was in fact ingenious. Kuklux they were not. The men would be militia legally commissioned by the governor, armed with state guns, and protected in their partisan violence by state and local law, which authorized local officials to call out such a force in times of civil unrest. With Lexington city officers and the government in Frankfort behind them, the militiamen were legally untouchable. Buckner was commissioned by the state to stop the de facto enfranchisement of Kentucky African Americans, which the state's Democratic government could no longer prevent de jure after the Fifteenth Amendment. Breckinridge and Robinson cosigned his requisition for arms from the state arsenal.[33]

Buckner organized his first company of militia, styled the "Citizens' Guards," on July 1. The guards were young men—the average age of the rank and file was a little older than twenty—many from the best families in Lexington along fashionable Second Street.[34] One of the few men in the company who had any military experience aside from Buckner was Frank Morgan, who had enlisted in his older brother John's Confederate Second Kentucky Cavalry at only thirteen. After Buckner organized the Citizens' Guards, other young Lexingtonians rushed to raise their own units. July 12 saw the formation of two units. The Ashland Rifles were recruited from the dormitories of Kentucky University, occupying the campus of old Transylvania, and presented much the same picture as the first unit. The Cleburne Guards were a rough-hewn company of Irish laborers. The Cleburnes' occupations further distinguished them from the clerks and students of the other militia companies: blacksmith, laborer, and barkeeper tied for the most common occupations among the men in the unit. The dramatic increase of Lexington's black population in the five years since the end of the war seemed to have sparked conflict between immigrants and blacks struggling for jobs at the bottom of the economic scale.[35] In contrast with the fear and hostility with which whites reacted to rumors of black military organization during and after the war, the native white community welcomed the support from the Irish and accepted them into service beside their own sons.

With the addition of the Ashland Rifles and the Cleburne Guards, Lexington's three infantry companies were grouped into a battalion. The new state adjutant general, J. Stoddard Johnston, promoted Buckner, who had held the highest wartime rank among the commanders, to major.[36] Cornelius "Neal" Hendricks, a city policeman and former lieutenant in the Confederate Second Kentucky Infantry, took his place as captain of the Citizens' Guards. A mounted contingent joined the battalion later in the month. John H. Carter's Forest Rangers cavalry was organized from the residents of farms throughout eastern Fayette. The Rangers were nearly all farmers and, as the sons of some of the wealthiest families of the area, unusually prosperous ones. Nineteen of the twenty-one men whose families could be found in the 1860 census had owned slaves or lived with a family member who did. Captain Carter had held the same rank in Morgan's Second Kentucky Cavalry, and eleven others can be placed in various Kentucky cavalry regiments during the war. Five others had relatives who also wore Confederate gray.

This new coalition of whites drew on the militia's prewar tradition of helping establish and reinforce the community's social order. Service in the militia afforded men the opportunity to display "their unity as Americans and their membership in the exclusive fraternity of white males." Uniforms, the bearing of arms, and military formations all served to separate white male citizens from females, adolescents, and African Americans.[37] Now in command of his young militiamen, Buckner extended the fatherly role he was trying to perfect as the paternal head of his household at home. At the same time as he, in his mind, went out in defense of Helen and his two daughters from the dangers of "negro rule," he could be the proud initiator of a new generation of young men into the military fraternity. He, the battle-tested veteran and respected community leader, was invested by the parents of Lexington's young gentlemen with the responsibility—and honor—of ushering these sons of the state into manhood. For these men—both Buckner and his young soldiers—this violent reassertion of racial control was not only an end unto itself but also a means by which to secure their own status within the white community. The actual threat of black violence that the militia was nominally organized to counter was low, but the potential benefits—social as well as political—to the whites who constructed and acted against that peril made the threat worth conjuring.

Only months after the guarantee of the African American franchise in Kentucky, a sizable force of pro-Democratic militiamen had sprung up to prevent any possible efforts to contest the racial hierarchy or Democratic control of Lexington. The response had been similar in the towns around Lexington. In late July, two companies mustered in Jessamine to the south, one in Woodford to the west, and another in Scott County to the north.³⁸ Like Lexington, these county towns had seen increases in their black populations as lack of employment and Klan activity drove many away from the countryside. Fayette had the highest African American population, nearly 47 percent; Woodford—Kentucky's only antebellum black-majority county—ranked a close second at 46 percent. Jessamine ranked fifth in the state, standing at just less than 40 percent black. As in Fayette, the Democrats in these counties stood a chance of losing the upcoming elections, particularly in the county seats. Blacks outnumbered whites in Nicholasville, Jessamine's county seat, 622 to 461. Midway, a Woodford County district, had 707 black residents and only 680 whites.³⁹ Just as the passage of the Fifteenth Amendment had led to the great newspaper propaganda campaign that warned of "negro domination" and race wars, the fears of losing political and racial control of their towns prompted the whites' escalation of force.

The formation of militia companies only increased the tensions between the parties and the races. "Indeed in those days the unarmed white man who took part in politics was the exception," claimed W. C. P. Breckinridge years later. "There was no doubt about men being armed during this canvass of 1870 in Fayette county and the negroes were not one whit behind the white men in this particular."⁴⁰ "The Democrats," said Judge Goodloe while addressing a black political meeting in town, "have resorted to the political trick of forming military companies in the hopes of scaring you and keeping you from the polls. . . . You have the right to vote, and this right is worth risking something for."⁴¹ Despite the Fifteenth Amendment, the right to vote was, in a sense, one of the issues on the ballot in August. Important city offices and the county attorney election would prove crucial to shaping city policy towards African Americans in years to come. Republicans black and white could use their positions to push for greater economic opportunity for blacks, enforce the federal laws against widespread racial discrimination, and provide a stable home to continue the work begun by the Freedmen's Bureau and other aid institutions. Of course, if the Democrats managed to hold on, they would move to legislate the freedmen out of their new freedoms. For Democrats, the August election was to decide whether a white-only government was still possible in the state even if a white-only electorate had been lost. "The contest was not so much as to persons," Colonel Breckinridge claimed, "but to determine where Kentucky should stand in the politics of the country."⁴²

Taking Judge Goodloe's and the other Republican leaders' words to heart, the black citizens of Lexington and other towns in the region went to the streets in the days before the election. On the night of Saturday, July 31, a meeting of four or five hundred black and white Republicans at the First African Baptist Church in Lexington closed with the rumor that black men would not be allowed to parade in certain parts of the city until the election. In defiance, the crowd began marching down Main Street toward Broadway, singing "John Brown's Body" and other Republican campaign songs.[43] As the group neared the Phoenix Hotel, shots were allegedly fired into the air—though they could well have been manufactured as a pretense for whites to take action—and local police were called to attempt to stop the procession. At the same time, Buckner assembled his militia battalion on the College Lawn, adjacent to the Second Street homes of many in the Citizens' Guards and the Kentucky University dormitories of the Ashland Rifles.[44] Participants on both sides presented an unclear and differing picture of the events of the evening, where Buckner and his militiamen were joined in a short but chaotic scuffle initiated by the police, the sheriff, Breckinridge, and Robinson. In the brief confrontation between the combined police and militia and some of the crowd, one policeman was killed, and at least one or two members of the Republican procession were seriously wounded. The crowd soon dispersed after the deadly scuffle, and Buckner and the city authorities had the militiamen remain on guard all night, patrolling to quell any further disturbances. Tensions were at their highest. Said one commentator in the days after, "If a single gun had been fired after the assembling of the militia the dead bodies of scores of innocent . . . negroes . . . would have covered the streets of Lexington that night."[45]

As dawn broke, the attack proved not as useful in and of itself as was the excuse that legitimized it. Claiming to be fearful of what the supposedly "riotous negroes" might do on election day, city officials made Republican leaders promise not to hold any public gatherings on election day. Worse—and with echoes of antebellum slave codes—all black men were to return home and stay inside before and after voting, and no black men were to gather or congregate in groups anywhere in town. Black men therefore arrived at the polls in trickles. Republican Party communication and coordination were devastated, and the standard Democratic bag of vote-suppression tricks was especially effective. Obsessive questioning about and demanding witnesses to prove black men's identity under false suspicion of fraud was reportedly widespread. The delays were amplified when polls in black neighborhoods closed just after midday, with hundreds of voters still yet to cast ballots. The tactics were crude but effective. Democrats carried the city offices. Breckinridge himself was elected to the city council.[46]

Republicans were outraged at the open intimidation of their constituents. Blame for the violence was laid solely at the feet of the militia for attacking the procession. One Republican account spoke mockingly of the young militiamen's zeal in defending the old order, "full of military arder [sic], ready and anxious to 'strike (somebody) for their altars and their fires.'" Douglass's *New Era* knew the pretense was a shallow one that "gave these valorous sons of a defunct pro-slavery empire the occasion to alarm the whole city."[47] The *Cincinnati Gazette* called the election "a fraud upon the rights of free people." The *Louisville Commercial* charged, "We have, then, a militia for the State of Kentucky composed of members of one political party, and designed solely to operate against members of another political party. These militia are armed with State guns, are equipped from the State arsenal, and to a man are the enemies of the national government."[48] Republicans throughout the state called for federal troops to come oversee the elections later in the year. "Suppose," wrote one concerned citizen of the new militia companies, "as no Republican voter is allowed in their ranks, they should propose another little rebellion. What then?" Practically every Republican editor in the state was convinced that the best way to secure free elections in November was to have the "Democratic partisan militia ... disarmed and disbanded."[49]

In the victorious Democratic press, however, the mood was jubilant. Not only had the Democrats carried the election, but they had thwarted the greatly feared "revolution" of black suffrage.[50] For them, August 1870 was a victory both at and away from the polls. Lexington's Democratic newspapers celebrated the use of the militia to stop the "disorderly" and "insolent" blacks from exercising their civil rights. Messages of praise for the actions of the Kentucky National Legion companies filled the *Observer & Reporter*, coming not only from citizens, but from the mayor himself. One article called the militiamen "our protectors" and lauded their service "during the long nights while [residents] enjoyed a quiet and refreshing sleep, our citizen soldiery, awake and watchful and untiring, guarded the little children, the women and the property of our city from all the lawless outbreakings of that vindictive exasperation incited in negro beasts by base men."[51]

The "riot" they had suppressed was, of course, far from physically threatening to the white community. The stray shots that Democrats heard fired could have been later conjured as an excuse for breaking up the Republican procession. With white fears of race war (and the reality of black political participation for which the war fears were a front) as high as they were that summer, white Democrats needed little excuse to assemble the police and militia. The facts of that night are not necessarily the greatest issue; what remains clear is that whites were looking for a confrontation and used the occasion to create one. In the days following the "riot," whites convinced themselves that the militia had saved them from certain calamity. For whites, the militia actions were a comforting reassertion of the old order's stability, and, for the militiamen, the praise and support they received afterward cemented their reputations as defenders of both community and household. The grateful Forest Rangers made an appearance en masse at the *Observer & Reporter* office to cheer the paper for its validating comments.[52]

Of course, the election had shown something else as well. Lexington's African Americans had demonstrated that they were still willing to go to the polls despite the harassment directed toward them. They had taken Judge Goodloe's words to heart: the right to vote was indeed "worth risking something for." Importantly, too, African Americans had proved that they would vote as peaceable citizens and had not fulfilled the racist predictions of their ignorance, childishness, and brutality. In great contrast to the white militiamen, black Kentuckians had proved to be the citizens who had respected law, order, and the sanctity of free elections. The election of 1870 was not the great confrontation, the war of the races, that the Democratic press had predicted throughout the summer. Instead, the African Americans had showed themselves determined to claim their rights despite the violence, and white Democrats understood that this was only the beginning of an unforeseeable period of conflict in which the fate of the Bluegrass was uncertain. Though they had not effectively prevented black political participation, the city's Democratic leaders and its concerned white citizens came to see the militia as at least one important means of maintaining white control. In five short years, Kentucky's white Democrats had lost their chattel labor and their exclusively white citizenship and were faced with an unpredictable political battle of unforeseeable length. If whites could not control these changes in blacks' status in society, they hoped they could nevertheless still control blacks' bodies. The Kuklux and armed militia could still employ the same physical threat that had enforced antebellum slavery with the whip. The Bluegrass's white community clung to that final refuge of prewar power.

Interest in the militia grew in the region after the unrest surrounding the elections, and before the summer was over, new units were being raised, often around the nuclei of old Confederate commands. Athens, Bardstown, and Harrodsburg all raised companies in August.[53] The Harrodsburg Guards were formed in a community that had thought itself defenseless when the feared war of the races nearly erupted. On the evening of election day in the Mercer County seat, a personal dispute between a young white man and a young black man erupted into open hostilities between the races after the two killed each other. One report claimed that more than five hundred shots were fired in the course of half an hour. The blacks were eventually driven out of town after suffering three dead and an estimated twenty wounded. White casualties were significantly fewer: one more man was killed in addition to the original death, and a handful were wounded.[54]

In neighboring Woodford, two consecutive nights saw Versailles brought to the brink of widespread violence as groups of black men, some of them reportedly armed, gathered in town to protest the beating of a local black man by a policeman the previous Thursday. A mob of whites formed as well, and the likelihood of bloodshed remained high. It was even rumored that armed blacks were picketing the roads into the town to prevent any whites from aiding those in the city. The reports remained unclear on exactly how many of the blacks were armed. This ambiguity may suggest the degree to which the "threat" that blacks posed during this time was inflated by white fears and exaggeration. Regardless of its dubious nature, the idea of armed blacks controlling access to the city prompted reaction. "Just about the time they [the blacks] were putting on their most extensive airs," read one report, Captain Sam Leavey's cavalry arrived from Midway to break up the gathering, "and the nigs concluded very wisely to simmer down." Stephen Sharpe's Ashland Rifles, who had no doubt been on heightened alert after the riot a few days earlier, eventually joined Leavey's militiamen. Sharpe and Leavey's companies patrolled the city throughout the following three days to ensure that quiet was restored.[55] The reports of the incident in Versailles reveal the extent to which Bluegrass whites were convinced of the coming great racial conflict. Again, mere rumors of armed African Americans had brought out the militia from two counties. The *Observer & Reporter* looked back on the violence surrounding the election and drew the same paternalistic conclusions as it had all summer: blacks "must stop acting. . . . upon their own evil instincts, or the teachings of bad white men. They cannot stop such work too soon for their own good, and the good of the communities in which they live."[56]

Those words had venom for black and white Republicans alike. The men who had stuck unconditionally by Lincoln's abolition war and became the backbone of the Union and Republican Parties had after 1867 declared themselves the only legitimate heirs of the Union cause and had unceremoniously labeled Buckner a common rebel for allying with his fellow dispossessed masters in the new Democratic Party. If those "bad white men" could call him a traitor to the Union cause, Buckner could take comfort in imagining them outside the bounds of respectable, white manhood. They were not the "men of decency," compelled, like himself, to resign rather than serve in an integrated army. They were not the "men of decency" who dressed in militia uniforms and Kuklux hoods to defend the old racial hierarchies upon which Kentucky had been built.

Throughout the rest of the summer of 1870 and well into autumn, Buckner led Lexington's battalion as it took up the functions of the political militia companies of Jackson and Clay's heyday. At a barbecue and rally in mid-August for James B. Beck, the Democratic candidate for the Ashland District seat in Congress, the Lexington companies "formed in battalion" and "made a grand and imposing spectacle as they marched to the grounds."[57] Republicans could not help but notice the Kentucky National Legion's endorsement of Beck's candidacy. After one of the summer rallies, the *Frankfort Commonwealth* asked, "Have these Militia fully entered upon the Democratic campaign?"[58] Though they were not called out to deal with "riotous" or "insolent" African Americans as they had been in August, the militia was still a prominent issue during the November canvass. The same Republican convention that nominated Beck's opponent passed resolutions condemning the use of both the Ku Klux Klan and the militia as tools to influence the earlier vote. The convention directed its appeals to the deaf ears of Governor Stevenson "to disband their armed partisans, put an end to their roaming at pleasure, in pairs, by squads, and companies through the counties."[59]

Demonstrations, drills, and other gatherings of the militia through the last weeks of October were more than enough to remind black voters that Democrats were still vigilant, organized, and well armed. Nevertheless, the Republican Party dominated the polls in the city districts, taking every ward and winning a 574-vote majority. In the rural districts of Fayette, however, the opposite proved true, Beck cleared 641 votes there, granting him a slim 67-vote majority in the county. The race was decided in the agricultural counties of Ashland District, where the rural Bluegrass gave the Democrat a 3,841 vote majority. Overjoyed, Democratic editor George Ranck taunted, "How are you, Africa?" as the "glorious result" came in.[60]

That result made it clear that the militia's direct intimidatory intervention was unnecessary in elections where Lexington's black voting population could be balanced by white voters in the rural counties, which had been whitened by Klan harassment or economic pressure since slavery's fall.

As the summer elections of 1871 rolled around, none of the issues at the intersection of race, labor, and politics had come to any resolution. Both Democrats and Republicans were uneasy about the prospects for peace and order surrounding the election for Fayette's state representative—an election unlike the one for Beck the previous November—where Lexington's Democrats could not rely on whitened rural counties to defeat the challenge from the city's formidable Republican Party. Republicans ran Colonel William Cassius Goodloe, another member of the family that had done so much for black civil rights in the city, against Democrat Douglas L. Price. The Republican papers were filled with reminders of Democratic abuses of power and attempts to deny African Americans their rights. Responding to Democrats' continued assertions that they had the political interests of blacks in mind, the *Lexington Kentucky Statesman* warned voters to "look on the ACTS of these men when judging their loud professions."[61]

Republicans were convinced not only that the Democracy's new rhetoric was insincere but that the same scenes of violent intimidation were likely to repeat themselves during the close-run contest. Though Buckner had passed off his command of and active role in the militia to a subordinate after Beck's election the previous year, the organization still stood ready to defend the interests of the Democratic Party and the conservative white community in the streets of Lexington. They were better prepared than ever to do it, too. As the dust settled after the 1870 elections, Stephen Sharpe wrote to Frankfort requesting improved weapons for his company. Originally, most of the Ashland Rifles were not equipped with rifles at all, but with sixty antiquated smoothbore muskets that had been altered from flintlock to percussion during the Civil War. In light of the recent conflict and the potential for more yet to come, Sharpe was quite "anxious to get the 'needle' gun," a new breech-loading rifle that would provide the company with superior, rapid firepower. He was not the only "anxious" Lexington resident either. As early as August 10, the *Observer & Reporter* was arguing for such an upgrade to continue "the good work which they have begun." State quartermaster General Fayette Hewitt, formerly the adjutant of the Kentucky "Orphan Brigade," was quick to oblige; Governor Stevenson personally signed off on the requisition. By the end of September, the new Springfield rifles were delivered to Lexington.[62]

The militiamen faced more opposition, too. In addition to a better-prepared and better-organized Republican Party in the city, the federal government finally heeded Republican calls for U.S. troops to protect voters from militia and Kuklux harassment and to maintain peace during the election. Resurrecting a line from the 1864 and 1865 elections and their contemporary allies throughout the South, Democrats charged that the troops would interfere with the election and obstruct the polls. Republicans, of course, could easily counter by accusing the Democrats of having done no different with the state militia the previous year.[63] Even with the federal presence, Republicans warned their black constituents to be cautious: "Our opponents are wide awake, and will spare no efforts fair or unfair, to defeat the will of the majority," one wrote.[64]

Moreover, the Republicans were not alone in questioning the militia's legitimacy. The year had seen a bitter split among Kentucky's Democrats regarding, among other issues, the continued violence and lawlessness that plagued the state. Henry Watterson of the *Louisville Courier-Journal* was the leading figure in Kentucky's New Departure movement, which had criticized the legislature's inaction on the "Kuklux bill" as enthusiastically as had many Republicans. Representing a powerful business and railroad investment faction in the Democracy—interests favored by both Buckner and W. C. P. Breckinridge—Watterson began to worry about the continued violence discouraging the economic development of the state.[65] Despite this rhetoric, the Republicans claimed, even the New Departure men would be no better than the Democrats of years past. The "'New Departure' has brought itself to acknowledge the popularity of the Republican principles," read one warning. However, "[i]t hopes to win by clothing the wolf in the lambs skin." Another concluded, "If then any colored person votes for a Kentucky Democrat he votes to make and keep himself a slave."[66]

By all accounts, the election on August 6, 1871, proceeded smoothly until its final act. As the polls closed around dusk, the election seemed too close to call. At first, the Democrats believed Price had won, but soon it was revealed that Goodloe had carried the election, barely. Republicans black and white began to celebrate. Their merriment was most animated around a poll that had been opened exclusively for African American voters in the courthouse square. Fearing Democratic retaliation in the wake of their defeat, both black and white Republican leaders attempted to usher the crowd out of the square and toward their homes. But they were too late. Like the previous year's riot, exactly who fired the first shot was a question roundly debated in the papers for weeks to come. Breckinridge and most Democrats claimed that the celebrating blacks had fired the first shots in the air. The *Cincinnati Commercial*'s correspondent was convinced that a man in a white coat had fired first. Rumors abounded that the courthouse bell had been rung three times as a signal to begin the shooting. Others claimed that a policeman had run into the crowd yelling, "Stop this damned yelling, now!" and pulled the first trigger. Perhaps the most candid report of the incident came from the *Statesman* the day after the incident: "There was a pistol shot off by some one, which was followed by numerous others. . . . How the shooting commenced we cannot say."[67]

As had been the case the year before, though, the militia did not wait to determine who had fired first before pitching in. The Ashland Rifles, believing that this was the beginning of another "riot," if not the long-predicted race war, began to assemble. "This time the colored men suffered," Breckinridge recalled. The militiamen descended onto the scene firing their weapons, some at street level and others down from the upper windows of the Democratic *Lexington Press* office, where the battalion armory was located. All of the casualties from the fray were black. Two men, Green Bird and Joseph Walker, were killed outright, and at least ten more were wounded, two listed as seriously. Some reports put the number of wounded as high as seventeen or twenty-one, though those reports failed to provide names.[68]

Continuing from the previous year's script, the militia troops began to patrol the city streets while blacks wisely shut themselves indoors. By this time, two companies of the Kentucky National Legion had assembled, commanded by Captain Neal Hendricks. As the shooting started, the alert deputy U.S. marshal John Wyatt sent word of the disturbance to Major Alexander Chambers of the Fourth U.S. Infantry on the outskirts of town. Anticipating trouble, Chambers had already prepared one company to respond and immediately sent it forward under the command of Lieutenant A. W. Vodges.[69] As the troops headed toward the courthouse, they were first met by Sheriff Robert S. Bullock, who inquired about their intentions. Pointing to Hendricks's militia, formed in the courthouse square along Cheapside with their line extended across Main Street, Vodges replied that he was ordered "to put down those rioters." Indeed, it must have been difficult for him to determine who were the true rioters in the square. According to Kentucky's perverse racial and legal logic, the "riot" was not caused by the men holding guns, but by those who now lay bleeding on the ground. It was, in the end, easy enough to sort out; by the time the troops arrived, only a handful of people remained in the square besides the militia.[70] As the two bodies of troops stood nervously eyeing one another, Sheriff Bullock, Captain Hendricks, Marshal Wyatt, and Lieutenant Vodges met between the two lines and conferred.

In a heated discussion, Hendricks and Bullock argued that the U.S. troops could not force the militia to disperse. Ordered again to remove his troops, Hendricks was reported to have replied that he was there by "order of the Mayor, and he would be damned if he would disperse them." "The situation was menacing," remembered Breckinridge. "The street was lined with armed men and if a single shot had been fired . . . there would have been terrible slaughter on that day."[71] Hendricks, though, was correct, and with Sheriff Bullock supporting him, he could not be moved. The militia had been called out according to state law by the constituted local authorities. They had successfully dealt with what the mayor had deemed a riot and had the situation well in hand. That was all the authority they needed. Vodges led the U.S. troops from the square; besides, they were needed elsewhere. Telegrams had come in from Paris telling of yet another shooting that had occurred at the polls that day. The incident had sparked an armed standoff between blacks and whites in the town, and a detachment of the Fourth had to be sent to calm the situation there as well.[72]

In the days following the election, Republican elation over Goodloe's victory was tempered by disgust with the militia's tactics. Lexington's *Kentucky Statesman* brooded over the true causes of the bloodshed: "What are the prominent facts? Did the Republicans bring on the trouble in reckless devilry . . . or was it the sudden ebullition of pent up passion on the part of armed men in the mortification and disappointment of defeat?" The paper showed a lucid grasp of the situation: "There was no fight—no conflict between the two parties—no 'war of races,' but a sudden onslaught of [a] . . . well-armed mob upon defenseless and fleeing negroes, who had dared to exercise the right of voting their sentiments, and to give a shout of triumph over the success of a chosen candidate."[73] Just as had occurred a year earlier, Lexington militiamen attacked African Americans as they exercised their political rights. The timing of such attacks was not unintentional; it was precisely at those times that the danger to white supremacy was the greatest. The long-predicted race war, though, was a sham. The "attacks" that white Democrats used to justify the violence were not on persons or property, but on a social structure that had ceased to exist in 1865. Lexington's black citizens, however, could sorrowfully attest that the reprisals the Kentucky National Legion meted out, just as those perpetrated by the Ku Klux Klan, were far more than theoretical.

The presidential elections in 1872 were free of militia interference. A Republican meeting was harassed by some of the Lexington militiamen: four or five "of the State militia in uniform, a portion of whom had guns," made a nuisance of themselves, "inciting and encouraging" the verbal harassment of speakers. The meeting dispersed after several Republican politicians were pelted with eggs thrown from the crowd. Of course, no arrests were made. Watterson's influential New Departure and the Horace Greeley candidacy, though, divided the local Democrats.[74] Republicans might have had an opportunity to make significant gains in Kentucky if they too were not split. After 1871, a minority of black voters were fed up with their low representation in Republican offices and bolted to the Democracy.[75] Despite both parties struggling to retain old constituents and woo new ones in Lexington and other divided towns and counties, the statewide result was in little doubt. The militia was unnecessary when the state's electoral votes were securely in Greeley's camp.

In January 1873, just months after the presidential campaign ended, however, Lexington's city council elections saw perhaps the greatest controversy yet. After winning the city elections in 1870, the Democratic city council members appealed to the state legislature to extend their terms of office. This request was granted, giving them three-year terms and blocking the city's Republicans from participating in the council.[76] During these extended terms, the Democratic-dominated council voted into place a $1.50 poll tax to prevent more blacks from voting. W. C. P. Breckinridge, one of the councilmen, recalled that "the burden was light to the Democrats but, as was expected, it was oppressive to the negroes." The tax was as morally dubious as militia attacks upon African Americans had been in 1870 and 1871 and every bit as legal. Again, Breckinridge and other local Democrats justified their actions "as an act of necessity—a last resort for the protection of the community from negro rule."[77]

Though the militia was on hand, nothing materialized because U.S. troops and marshals were still posted in the city to ensure peace during the election.[78] That the militia was formed before any disturbances occurred suggests that they had more in mind than simply keeping the peace. Democrats no doubt knew that African Americans would be angered over the tax, and they likely expected resistance. More important, the militia was a check to the continued presence of the federal troops. The adjutant general came with orders from Governor Preston Leslie that "if the [federal] soldiers interfered with the election in any way," he was to shut it down and appeal to the legislature for a new vote.[79] In short, had federal authority overruled the Democrats' poll-tax gambit, the militia was to be on hand to ensure—violently resisting U.S. troops if necessary—that no result that included the disfranchised blacks would be recorded.

As it was, the federal troops were content to allow the election to proceed without any disturbance of the peace. That decision, of course, meant that the voting concluded without two-thirds of Lexington's African American population being allowed to participate.[80] Removing most of Lexington's blacks from the electorate, the poll tax proved more effective than the militia's intimidation had been. Although the election of 1873 marked the transition from violent control to legal regulation of African American political activity, the militia was nevertheless present, mustered, and ready to intervene if this transition did not go as planned. If the Democrats' trick had not worked, had the federal troops and officials intervened, white Democrats were more than willing to fall back on their militia enforcers to ensure that their political and social will was carried out.

The threat of conflict between the federal soldiers and the militia may have prevented Republicans from countering the tax on election day, but once the militia had gone home, they began to try to reverse the unjust outcome in the following days. Incensed Republicans immediately sought a federal indictment against two Democratic election judges, Hiram Reese and Matthew Foushee, who had refused to allow the vote of William Garner, an African American man whose ballot had been denied on election day. A grand jury hearing was held in Louisville, where emerging Republican leader and future Supreme Court justice John Marshall Harlan was lead prosecutor. Breckinridge defended the Democratic officials who had carried out the questionable statute he had helped pass.[81] No indictment was secured on the strength of the defense's cunning argument about the constitutionality of the Fifteenth Amendment and the Enforcement Act, which Congress had passed to support the amendment. The case was referred to the Supreme Court.

As the case moved forward in February that year, the General Assembly found the commonwealth "interested to defeat the said actions . . . and thereby to establish the validity of the State laws regulating elections" and so authorized a fund to defend the law. Kentucky was keen to see Lexington's poll tax sustained by the courts so that the discriminatory policy might be enacted elsewhere if needed. Governor Leslie assembled a legal team that would not only defend the two election judges who had been charged with refusing the votes on election day but also try to undermine the federal government's guarantee of African American suffrage. Leslie chose three men for the job: Henry Stanbery, a New York native now living in northern Kentucky; W. C. P. Breckinridge, who had defended the election judges at the federal circuit court in Louisville; and his law partner, Ben Buckner.[82]

Buckner and Breckinridge were obvious choices. Both had been intimately involved with the case from the beginning, and both were deeply invested in the political ramifications of its outcome. Stanbery was the more interesting choice. He had come to Cincinnati with his father as a young man and had established a thriving legal practice there. Before the war, he had been Ohio's first attorney general. But it was as the fighting drew to a close that Stanbery had risen to national prominence. In 1865, President Andrew Johnson called Stanbery to Washington to argue the famous *Ex parte Milligan* case.[83]

Johnson's team of conservative constitutionalists defended Lambdin P. Milligan, a northern citizen who had conspired to liberate rebel prisoners and lead them in a coup against the government of Indiana and several other states. The case hinged on the question of civilian trials in military courts. Stanbery and the other defense lawyers maintained that the military tribunal, which had sentenced Milligan to hang, had no jurisdiction over civilian conspirators. The fundamental issues at stake were not so much about the particulars of the case, but about the climate surrounding the arguments. The case was but one battle in Johnson's war with Congress over the future of the South and Reconstruction. Johnson's plan of limited reconstruction would leave former Confederates and former masters at the head of the states formerly in rebellion, whereas the Republican Congress recognized that no justice could ever be done to African Americans in those states if such a plan persisted. Repressive "black codes" and other legislation passed in 1865 and 1866 proved the validity of their reading of the southern political situation. To subvert these rebel-led governments in some states and to support the fragile Republican administrations in others, military tribunals prosecuted acts of racial violence and unfair labor practices that went unpunished in civilian courts. Stanbery and Milligan's defense team won precisely the victory that Johnson hoped: the decision found that citizens could be tried in military courts only if civilian courts were not being held.

Johnson was so pleased with Stanbery that he appointed him attorney general of the United States at the conclusion of the *Milligan* case. Ever a staunch ally of the embattled president, Stanbery resigned his position in 1868 to help defend Johnson during his impeachment trial before the Republican Congress. After Stanbery successfully but barely navigated the administration through that politically damaging scrape, Johnson attempted to reappoint his friend and counselor first to the cabinet and then to the Supreme Court. Congress would approve neither appointment.[84] To the local familiarity and deep investment in the Kentucky case that Buckner and Breckinridge brought, then, Stanbery added valuable experience. Having tangled with both the Supreme Court and Congress, he knew his way around the political world of Washington and had compiled a useful tactical playbook with which he had previously successfully outmaneuvered leading Republican legal theorists.

When the case *United States v. Hiram Reese, et al.* was argued in January 1875, Buckner was the public face of conservative Kentucky's defense. Although Stanbery and Breckinridge did significant preparation behind the scenes, Buckner authored the two principal briefs submitted to the Court. Stanbery was the mentor and guide; his taking second chair was not unexpected. Breckinridge's absence from the case is more curious; he did not even appear before the Court. Did he bow out due to a conflict of interest as a councilman who had helped pass the poll tax law? That had certainly not stopped him from defending the election judges in Louisville. Was it because he had been a Confederate officer, and a loyal defense team might seem less biased in arguing against an amendment directed primarily at the states so recently in rebellion?

In any event, Buckner's arguments expertly exploited a chink in the Fifteenth Amendment's armor, the 1870 Enforcement Act. Buckner freely conceded that the two election judges, Foushee and Reese, had refused Garner's vote but stressed that there was no allegation in the indictment "that the rejection of this vote was on account of his race or color."[85] Reese and Foushee had simply refused to accept Garner's vote because he had not paid the tax.

Of course, the circumstances under which Garner had not paid his taxes were suspicious. The government's legal team argued that racial discrimination had been at play when city collector and local Democratic Party chairman James F. Robinson Jr. refused to accept Garner's tax. Following the procedures laid out in the Enforcement Act, Garner came to the polls armed with an affidavit to that effect, but Reese and Foushee still refused, overruling a third election judge who argued to allow Garner's vote.[86] Whether Robinson denied Garner's request to pay the tax on account of his race that day was immaterial; the law stated that the tax was to have been paid fifteen days before the election. Some evidence indicates that Robinson predictably made little effort to make himself available for African Americans to pay the tax before the deadline, but that was another issue. Buckner pointed the Court's attention away from context and toward the barest facts. Garner had not paid before the deadline; Robinson was correct to refuse his offer of payment on election day; and Reese and Foushee were correct in refusing his vote.

The Fifteenth Amendment did not give William Garner the right to vote. "Strictly speaking," Buckner argued, "it did not do so directly, although the effect of its adoption was indirect to give him that right, by virtue of its operation on State laws." The amendment restricted Kentucky from making a law that disenfranchised Garner on account of "race, color, or previous condition of servitude." Foushee and Reese had disallowed Garner's vote because he had not paid the required taxes. Regardless of the fact that those taxes were designed to keep poor black men from voting, the tax was theoretically not racially discriminatory. "If it had been intended to make an absolute and direct grant of the right of suffrage," Buckner charged, "the appropriate language would have been 'All citizens of the United States and of the States, of African descent, possessing the other qualifications required by law, shall be entitled to vote.'"[87]

Very simply, "these clauses confer directly no rights upon the citizen." "The negro had no right of suffrage to be maintained," Buckner bluntly stated, and "[a]ny attempt to give" the amendment "any other construction seems forced and unnatural."[88]

Chief Justice Morrison Waite agreed with Buckner's logic. In his majority opinion, he forthrightly declared that the "Fifteenth Amendment does not confer the right of suffrage upon any one. It prevents the States, or the United States, however, from giving preference, in this particular, to one citizen of the United States over another on account of race, color, or previous condition of servitude." The right guaranteed by the amendment is "exemption from discrimination in the exercise of the elective franchise," not the elective franchise itself.[89] The key to the Lexington law, Buckner argued, was that there was no explicit mention of race in it. Black voters had not been excluded from the polls because they were black; they had been excluded because they were poor. Their poverty, of course, was unquestionably due to their race and "previous condition of servitude," but such underlying causes were beyond the scope of the legislation. Because of this, the Lexington poll tax and those who had rigidly enforced it had done nothing in violation of the letter of the Fifteenth Amendment or its affiliated Enforcement Act even if they had trampled all over the intended spirit.[90]

Buckner openly mocked that spirit in his brief. "Not being a party to the social compact, not being invested with citizenship or other political rights, a large number of the statesmen of the Union believed that an additional change in our organic law was necessary to relieve" African Americans "from a condition which they deemed unjust and oppressive." The majority of Kentucky's congressional delegation did not number among that large number of statesmen, and the Kentucky state government, which Buckner represented as both a paramilitary commander and legal counsel, did not deem the condition of the state's freedpeople especially unjust or oppressive. "But while a free man," after the end of slavery "incapable of ever being again enslaved," William Garner "was left in a most anomalous condition."[91] It was a condition of half-freedom that most former masters who had worn both blue and gray in Kentucky and across the South had a vested interest in making permanent. Buckner's legal work had ensured that it would be for the foreseeable future after the Democratic Party regained control of state houses across the South.

Justice Ward Hunt of New York saw precisely what the result of Buckner's argument would be, and his dissenting opinion was a spirited defense of the right to vote as the foundation of security, liberty, and prosperity for all citizens, blacks in particular. "The citizen of this country, where nearly every thing is submitted to the popular test and where office is eagerly sought, who possesses the right to vote, holds a powerful instrument for his own advantage," he wrote. "State rights and municipal rights touch the numerous and the every-day affairs of life," Hunt reasoned, while "those of the Federal government are less numerous, and, to most men, less important. That Congress, possessing, in making a constitutional amendment, unlimited power in what it should propose, intended to confine this great guaranty to a single class of elections,—to wit, elections for United States officers,—is scarcely to be credited."[92] Indeed it was. But that was precisely how Buckner had convinced the majority of the Court to read the law. The right to vote in a local election was a matter that fell to state jurisdiction, not that of Congress.

The *Reese* decision combined with the *U.S. v. Cruikshank* case, which emerged from Louisiana's infamous Colfax Massacre, to give Democratic "Redeemer" governments of former rebels throughout the South a blueprint with which to achieve de facto disfranchisement of African Americans once they regained control of their states. While *Reese* established state, not federal, control over who could vote, *Cruikshank* similarly established state, not federal, responsibility for prosecuting individual violations of constitutional rights. Klansmen, white mobs, white militiamen, city councils, and state legislatures were subsequently immune from federal prosecution or overruling whether they decided to keep black men from exercising their full political rights by means of preemptive laws or by means of intimidatory violence or both.[93] The rest of the South, like Buckner and the inner circle of Lexington Democrats, began with violence and eventually came to embrace legal disfranchisement as the more permanent solution to the "Black Peril." This solution was not, though, a move away from violence, a positive step in race relations in Kentucky or elsewhere in the South. It was nothing more than a change in tactics. The outcry from Republicans and New Departure Democrats finally convinced enough Kentuckians that the clumsy attempts to control politics through violence were a stain on the state's (and the party's) honor. Watterson, who had spoken out against the militia and Klan violence, noted that he believed the city officials had "acted within the pale of the law" and should not be punished. The formal legality of the 1873 poll tax and the *Reese* decision made for far less politically damaging press than murders and "riots."[94]

Legal statute was certainly more politically palatable, and it may have been more effective, too. Consistently high black turnout at the polls showed white Lexingtonians that, despite their best efforts, black men were not easily intimidated. Many of them had enlisted in the army in 1864 and 1865, and some had seen combat in Kentucky, West Virginia, and Virginia or had served lengthy deployments in Texas; they had, in short, been shot at to earn their rights, and, as Judge Goodloe reminded them, those rights were "worth risking" life and limb for again. Black men were more than brave; they were defiant, too. They armed themselves in response to the white hostility and, shot for shot, gave as good as they got in Lexington, Harrodsburg, and Versailles in 1870 and Paris in 1871. Black men, with as many veterans among them as their white Democratic opponents and with just as much to fight for, could fight violence with violence in the cities and towns where they made up nearly half of the population. They could not resist Democratic legal maneuvering as easily, however.

As a consequence, although the 1870 militia organizations continued to exist until their enlistments expired in 1875, their important role as protector of the supposedly threatened white community declined sharply after August 1871 and seemed to cease entirely after 1873. It is important to keep in mind, however, that during the transition from violent coercion to legislative disfranchisement in 1873, the power of the "Democratic Partisan Militia" was on standby. Kentucky's first experiments in disfranchisement, what James Michael Rhyne has labeled the "rehearsal for Redemption" in the lower South,[95] were presided over and supported by Kentucky state troops.

Beneath the Kentucky militia's facade, its claims to protect peace and public order, lay a more sinister intent. Unlike the Republican-led militias throughout the Reconstruction South that sincerely tried to end Democratic Party terrorism, the Kentucky National Legion was a part of that terrorism. The Kentucky militia, along with elected officials resisting through legislation and bands of Ku Klux Klansmen roaming the countryside, was part of the concerted effort among white supremacist Kentucky Democrats to blunt the changes brought about by the end of slavery. It was a legitimate paramilitary organization that complimented Kentucky's illegitimate paramilitary Kuklux.[96] The militia struck a happy medium between the legal authority necessary to save political face and the force needed to drive African Americans back into their antebellum social, economic, and now political positions. Because the militia companies were a state-sanctioned, funded, and armed body, they had a claim to legal and social legitimacy that no band of night riders could have. Any violence they dealt to blacks could be excused as a response to riotous or unruly behavior, of which most whites believed blacks more than capable. The Kentucky National Legion never replaced the Klan, though; the latter's masked bands continued to scour the state during and after the militia's activity. The legion, however, supplemented Kentucky's Kuklux, directly interfering with elections in ways that Kentucky's Klansmen rarely did but that were common to paramilitary white supremacist organizations in the former Confederacy.[97]

This same veneer of civility blanketed the poll tax and the *Reese* decision that followed it. Besides lasting repercussions on Jim Crow voting laws across the South, it also had a significant local legacy. The poll tax set the tone for the future of unequal race relations in the commonwealth. For white Kentuckians, it maintained the veneer of impartiality, allowed them to hide behind a border-state myth of mild slavery, and nurtured the state's postwar culture of what one historian has called "polite racism."[98]

Epilogue

Glen Avon

Though the Kentucky legislature and governor had paid for Buckner, Breckinridge, and Stanbery to deal the Kentucky Democratic Party the poll tax card, they never played it against any future assertions of black civil rights. Delegates considered the measure during the constitutional convention of 1890, in a moment when a rash of voter-elimination measures such as poll taxes and literacy tests were written into revised constitutions of the states of the old Confederacy. The rush to implement Jim Crow disfranchisement amendments in other southern states, according to historian Michael Perman, marked a new phase in southern politics and race relations. "In the first phase," which spanned roughly a decade of Buckner's life and work from his election to the General Assembly until his victory in the *Reese* case, "the vote was manipulated by election laws of various levels of ingenuity and Democratic election officials of varying degrees of criminality." Though the constitutional logic for discriminatory poll taxes and other practices came out of Kentucky, the state never joined its fellow southerners in the next evolution of the idea, in which "the vote was eliminated by constitutional means rather than being manipulated and controlled as before." The fact that Kentucky African Americans were not disfranchised wholesale near the turn of the century, though, does not mean that race relations in the Bluegrass were any better than elsewhere or that white Kentuckians were any less concerned with ensuring "the subordination of African Americans and the dominance of the political and economic elite of the Democratic party," an elite within which Buckner lived out a comfortable and successful postwar life. In the same way as during the secession crisis of 1861, specific political, economic, social, and cultural circumstances in Kentucky dictated a different political *form* from the rest of the South, which should not be mistaken for any defection among white Kentuckians from "the enduring *substance* of the South's system of racial domination."[1]

African Americans' struggle for equality in Kentucky took a unique shape that reflected Kentucky's long history as a border South state. In Kentucky, the years between the end of the war and the Thirteenth Amendment had forged a strong white Republican Party, emerging from the Unconditional Unionists and based in the mountains and the river cities. With some outstanding exceptions such as the Goodloes, the Fees, and eventually John Marshall Harlan, white Kentucky Republicans proved themselves more hostile to slavery, concentrated Bluegrass wealth and power, and former rebels in the Democratic Party than they were committed racial egalitarians. As the 1870s waned, African Americans often became disaffected with the party, frustrated by their lack of support when they sought office. The problem within the party was the same as that statewide. African Americans made up too small a percentage of the party to win nominations and elections as black men did in the states farther south, where African Americans were a larger percentage of the population.[2]

As black Kentuckians had done since before the war ended, they fled the violence and lack of economic opportunity they found at home. Many moved out of the state entirely to the states and cities north of the Ohio River or exodusted to the west. Others sought work where they could, leaving small pockets of farm hands in most rural counties and building larger communities in cities and larger market towns. The small, rural African American population was never a political factor in the vast majority of Kentucky counties. Larger black populations in the cities, in particular Louisville, could band together and win local representation, but the white-majority Republican state convention proved a frustration to Kentucky African Americans, who never saw nominations to state offices in the same numbers as black men did farther south. Frustrated, some tried bolting to the Democratic Party, but things there were worse. When politics proved unresponsive, Kentucky African Americans changed tactics. Where they could, they carved out modest economic opportunities for themselves in de facto segregated neighborhoods, which had grown up from freedpeople's shantytowns on the edge of Kentucky communities, and through skillful balance of assertiveness and accommodation gained some measure of relief from Kentucky's legal and extralegal culture of racism, though these actions were generally the exception rather than the rule.[3]

In the decades after Reconstruction, Kentucky Democrats successfully curbed any major political threat from African Americans and Republicans generally. They tended to employ economic, legal, and cultural means over statutory or constitutional methods. Hence, there was no statewide poll tax in Kentucky because there was no need for one. "This does not mean that Kentucky had no race problem," cautions historian of southern poll taxes Frank B. Williams.[4] White community leaders retained rural black men as an agricultural labor force, relegated African Americans into the worst jobs in the growing industries in the mountains, and cultivated a culture of repression through soft, subjective exertions of Bourbon Democratic power. But, as with secession in 1861, the specifics of politics, economics, and race relations meant that Kentucky never took the step into outright voter elimination. Men such as Buckner shared the cultural convictions and faith in white supremacy with their cousins farther south, but the legal and political forms that culture took differed in the Bluegrass.

Buckner made a fine career for himself wielding these methods of social control in the interests of himself, Helen, and the Democratic Party. Even before he traveled to Washington to argue the *Reese* case before the Supreme Court in 1875, his efforts to restore order—as he conceived it—to Kentucky's political, economic, and judicial systems since the end of the war were already being rewarded. As he was preparing the legal arguments that he would use to dismantle the Fifteenth Amendment, the Bluegrass Democracy elected him to the bench. He would oversee a new Court of Common Pleas, specially created to sift through a backlog of civil cases that had arisen from the chaos and destructiveness of the war years—the legal wreckage of the slave economy. Buckner would sort out the state's past and shape its economic future.

In 1880, Buckner was elected to the bench of the Tenth Circuit Court—Judge Goodloe's old seat—where he would hear nearly every important case in Lexington and the surrounding counties. This made him one of the most important jurists in the state. His colleagues thought as much, too; not long after that, Buckner was named the first president of the State Bar Association. As such, he devoted his inaugural address to the theme of what justice should look like in New South Kentucky. Buckner made a case for a legal system that mirrored the hierarchical society he had long cherished, "harmonious in all its parts and . . . beneficent in its operation."[5] Harmony, order, stability, and benevolence—the values he had absorbed as a young man in Winchester, for which he had fought as a defender of the Constitution and of slavery and which he had sought to restore since the collapse of

Judge Buckner, from William Armstrong Crozier, ed., *The Buckners of Virginia and the Allied Families of Strother and Ashby* (New York: Genealogical Association, 1907). Courtesy of the Kentucky Historical Society.

that institution—were also his guiding principles as a judge. Buckner dismissed the idea of increased "regularity in the infliction of punishment for crime" upon white and black, rich and poor, connected and friendless. He argued for more judicial control over juries. He urged that "the jury should be restricted to the question of guilt or innocence, and the quantum of punishment be left to the court." Such restrictions on jury power would, Buckner argued, leave "the chance of the jury's being led astray by irrelevant or inconclusive matter . . . reduced to a minimum." That is, rather than having their passions stirred by a fiery orator's persuasive arguments, the jury should allow themselves to be guided by the hand of the learned and disinterested judiciary.[6]

Judge Buckner's was not a call for greater equality for all before the bench, but an argument for increased control of community justice by the Bluegrass elite, within which he now found his place secure. Tempering vindictive white juries' passionate decisions—which was Buckner's primary concern in his inaugural address—was not a victory for black civil rights, but rather a victory for the status quo. He proposed a malleable hegemony over black and lower-class white Kentuckians, not mechanistic repression. His proposed paternal guidance of juries through the legal process would steer a middle course that would doubtless see Kentucky courts continue to convict African American men when they were brought to trial yet do so with an air of impeccable legality and fairness that would not stir up undue unrest in the state's black communities. Buckner desired not to purge his society of racism but to make his courtroom a space nominally free of racial discrimination to which white Kentuckians could point as an example of their racial good faith. He wanted only to rid his courtroom of vestiges of the extralegal violence of the lynch mob, not to eliminate the lynch mob as a constant threat to black men and women who challenged community mores. It was justice with the same color-blind veneer as his *Reese* argument.

Buckner imagined his courtroom as a realm of what George C. Wright has labeled "polite racism," an unwritten legal and social code that governed late-nineteenth-century Kentucky race relations. White Kentuckians, according to Wright's study, "often seemed genuinely concerned about Afro-Americans and generously supported a number of black causes," but their support was "very selective," and "in return they demanded that blacks be passive and remain in the place assigned them in . . . society." In this way, white civic leaders such as Buckner could simultaneously feel as if they worked to support black uplift and participation in the community's political and social life while also ensuring that any real change in the hierarchical status quo was never on the cards.[7] Yet as psychologically reassuring as the subtle "polite racism" was for white Kentuckians, it was constantly underscored by the threat of formal and informal, state and community power that had manifested itself most clearly during the violent years following the war and the advent of black citizenship. Even during a period when most observers of race relations in Kentucky judged things to be moderate or even good, "lull[ing] both Afro-Americans and whites into believing that conditions . . . were not as bad as they were elsewhere," both state-sanctioned "legal lynchings" and extralegal violence lived side by side with the mythology of paternalism, and the prevalence of that violence was shocking.[8]

In their house on the fashionable Mulberry Street (now Limestone) in Lexington and later in the heart of old Louisville, where Buckner practiced law for a few years after retiring from the bench, the Buckners were at the social, political, and economic heart of the Democratic Bluegrass. Buckner served on the board of the Agricultural and Mechanical College (now the University of Kentucky) that would make Lexington a hive of new ideas on farming techniques and mining technologies. For his impassioned work in lobbying the legislature for funds to build the modern campus, including the building that still houses the university administration today, Buckner was awarded the first honorary doctorate bestowed by the school. After retiring from the bench, Buckner became an important railroad lawyer. At a time when political favors were handed out by the L&N in the form of vouchers for free rail travel, Judge Buckner was afforded no less than the use of the president's private car to rush him to Louisville for medical treatment during a health scare.[9] Over the last decades of the nineteenth century, the men beside whom Buckner lived, worked, and socialized brought industrialized, extractive industry and agriculture to the state on rails, fueled by northern capital.

With equal zeal, they imagined themselves the protagonists in the sentimental stories of Bluegrass gentlemen, kindly old lords of the pasture, being published in northern magazines. They made up, in the words of one of their own, James Lane Allen, "the flowers of the new social order—sprung from the very soil of fraternal battle-fields, but blooming together as the emblems of oblivious peace." Ignoring the cavernous economic disparities in the state, ignoring the unequal justice that Judge Buckner's courtroom dispensed, they wrote their preferred eulogies in the terms of the past that had been lost when "the war naturally fell as a killing frost" upon their beautiful old Kentucky. They "had spent the most nearly idyllic life, on account of the beauty of the climate, the richness of the land, the spacious comfort of their homes, the efficiency of their negroes, and the characteristic contentedness of their dispositions. Thus nature and history combined," they told themselves of their slaveholding fathers then and of themselves now, "to make them a peculiar class, a cross between the aristocratic and the bucolic, being as simple as shepherds and as proud as kings." They forgot both the careful balancing of crop rotations, slave sales and hires, and nonagricultural business ventures they and their fathers had overseen in the past and those they now brought to the horse farms of the Bluegrass and the coal camps of the mountains. Returning from their day's work in boardrooms and courthouses, they declared the Kentucky gentleman to have "no business habits, no political ambition, no wish to grow richer. . . . His mind could not come down to the low level of such ignoble barter."[10]

To his "carelessness of riches," the Kentucky gentleman "added a certain profuseness of expenditure; and indulgent towards his own pleasures, towards others, his equals or dependents, he bore himself with a spirit of kindness and magnanimity." Just as Buckner had promised himself to be toward Helen and their future household of slaves and children during the domestic crisis that civil war had brought to their relationship and the country as a whole, he could imagine himself to be still as a judge and president of the state bar. "Intolerant of tyranny, he was no tyrant."[11]

"But the war!" asked Allen, "what is to be said of the part the negro took in that?" As little as possible, save how "picturesque" and "patriotic" was "the figure of the African slave, as he followed his master"—who might have worn either uniform—"to the battle-field, marched and hungered and thirsted with him, served and cheered and nursed him—that master who was fighting to keep him in slavery."[12] How his slave Jim had flaunted Buckner's distress in the days before the Emancipation Proclamation and took the rail cars away from Bowling Green on a Christmas spree; how men like Jim who had been servants to Kentucky officers in blue and gray surely did follow their masters to the battlefield, though by 1864 they were doing so with rifles on their shoulders and eagles on their buttons—these things were not to be said. And still less was to be said of the "part the negro took"—and that Buckner took—in the decade of violent conflict that had followed the war and the end of slavery, when Judge Goodloe had reminded Lexington's African Americans of the fact that they had the rights of citizens, had fought to earn them, and urged them to risk their lives yet again for the right to vote in Lexington against the guns of Buckner's militiamen.

Such reminders of the state's very real and very violent recent history fit neither the preferred image of the Kentucky past nor the image of the present. "The kind, affectionate relations of the races under the old regime have continued with so little interruption that the blacks remain content with their inferiority," Allen opined. The midnight kukluxings, the election-day street battles, the legislative and judicial maneuvering were but a "little interruption," hardly to be noticed or remembered. Those things had marked the end of slavery elsewhere, not in Kentucky, where masters were kinder, less driven by profit, and more personally invested in the lives of the people they owned. Allen ventured "that wherever in the United States" African Americans "have attempted most to enforce their new-born rights, they have either, on the one hand, been encouraged to do so, or have, on the other, been driven to self-assertion by harsh treatment." Certainly nothing of the sort had occurred in the picturesque Bluegrass. "But treated always kindly, always as hopelessly inferior beings, they will do least for themselves. This, it is believed, is the key-note to the situation in Kentucky at present."[13]

Just as the pages of Allen's plantation fiction alternated between imagining black people as helpless dependents and imaging them as heartless savages, he and other writers conjured images of rural mountain whites that extolled their lost Elizabethan purity, condemned their feuding barbarity, and reimagined them as the sole defenders of the Union cause in Kentucky. As dissent against the economic, racial, and regional disparities in the state grew in the 1880s and 1890s, a flood of literature from the Bluegrass disseminated useable images of both blacks and mountain whites as shiftless, backward, ignorant. Mountain whites became a "race" whose failings were not those of unfair and unequal American political, social, and economic systems in which they had ended up on the bottom, but of their genetic inferiority to those who now exploited their labor, ruled them politically, and sent missionaries into their midst to bring them the light of civilization.[14] As James Klotter writes of the new logic created in local color lore, "These highlanders had been, after all, only black people in white skins."[15]

When writers cultivated a rose-colored memory of Bluegrass life that came to stand for all of nonmountain Kentucky, they populated their tales with heroes in Confederate gray, in no small part to satisfy the national literary market's desire for "romances of reunion" that extolled and sentimentalized the political and economic reconciliations taking place in the Gilded Age.[16] Where were the Kentucky Unionists in these stories? Usually in the mountains, staunchly loyal and slightly backward yeomen farmers. Buckner's brand of proslavery unionism was quickly forgotten in a new, simplistic formulation of the war where the slaveless loyal mountains were shown in stark relief to the slave-owning rebel lowlands.

John Fox Jr.'s national best seller *The Little Shepherd of Kingdom Come* was the highest expression of the idea. Fox made, according to Anne Marshall, "little provision for the patchwork of loyalties" that had defined the state during the war and portrayed Kentucky "as a state with essentially two ways of life, mountain and Bluegrass, and two corresponding sectional sentiments. Slaveholding almost always correspond[ed] with the Confederacy and antagonism toward or ignorance of slavery with the Union." Though Fox wrote his Unionist protagonist Chad Buford as furious at the advent of black military service—feeling "like tearing off with his own hands the straps which he won with so much bravery"—the instinctive unionism in his mountain genes kept him from quitting the Union cause as Buckner and so many other Kentucky officers had indeed done.[17] With Bluegrass authors as well as mountain reformers such as Berea College's Robert G. Frost echoing these ideas of the slaveless, loyal mountain South, the connection between slavery and the Union cause in Kentucky was eroded away. A complex understanding of what "Union" had meant to Kentuckians in 1861 was lost to popular memory, a casualty to the cultural campaign to legitimize Bluegrass control over the mineral wealth of eastern Kentucky.

Where was Buckner in all of this postwar memory making? He stayed away from these public rhetorical and literary battles over how the war would be remembered not because he did not care, but because his silence worked. Not participating served his interests, just as it had when he resigned his commission in 1863. Republican Union veterans, the heirs of the Unconditional Union Party, the men who wanted to take control of the battle flags in 1867, were free with their opinions on the war. Thomas Speed, Robert M. Kelly, Thomas J. Wright, Samuel W. Price, and John Marshall Harlan, among others, wrote eloquent memoirs and gave speeches to national veterans groups in praise of the Union cause in the state. GAR posts, black and white, thrived in the Ohio River cities, in the mountains, and in the core of the Bluegrass (black posts especially). But Buckner took no part in any of this, and men like him who found a home in the postwar Democratic Party by and large remained quiet about what the war meant to them.[18]

Buckner's Civil War memory was not published; it was lived. The Union and Confederate veterans who came together to run the Democratic Party after the war smoothed over the fissures of war between themselves as business partners and political allies who worked, socialized, and profited together. They were, as Allen put it, the "fathers who had fought madly on opposite sides talking quietly in corners as they watched their children dancing" and those men "toasting their old generals and their campaigns over their champagne in the supper-room."[19] The passions of war were put aside—as Buckner always hoped they would be—and white, elite Kentucky got on with the life it had wanted to live in 1861.

The old colonels of James Lane Allen's stories were rebels, yes, but they were also kindly masters, deferred to by women, African Americans, and poor whites alike. If such stories helped redeem the legacy of the old regime and helped re-create it anew in postwar Kentucky, if they reinforced racial and class hierarchies that were daily being challenged, if they presented Kentucky as a world of harmonious agrarian gentility rather than divisive industrialized capitalism, then why should Buckner object? If Kentucky rebel writers constructed an imaginary world of kindly Old South masters and happy darkies, Buckner was more than happy to join them in it. He had also been more than happy to work alongside them in the less saccharine realities of Reconstruction paramilitary violence and New South economic and political exploitation that those plantation tales covered up.

Of course, the situation in Kentucky during the last decades of the nineteenth century was never as placid as Judge Buckner or James Lane Allen hoped, though they never stopped pretending it was. The imagined Kentucky created by Allen, rebel raider turned railroad lobbyist Basil Duke, and historians such as former Union officer Nathaniel S. Shaler was a haven from the political and social chaos in which the state found itself in the 1890s.[20] The postwar Democratic Party that Buckner had helped shape in the late 1860s and early 1870s collapsed under the weight of the old guard's unresponsiveness to the concerns of most Kentuckians. Unregulated expansion of extractive industry and cash-crop agriculture siphoned profits out of the state through the railroad hubs of Louisville and Lexington, while undermining the livelihoods and pride of lower-class white and black Kentuckians alike. This New South came with the complicity of Democratic governors and legislators, who passed the private bills that chartered the railroads, mining companies, and resort hotels and that blessed these new ventures with an almost nonexistent corporate tax rate.[21] Falling crop prices, particularly after the Duke-dominated American Tobacco Company virtually monopolized the Kentucky tobacco market after 1889, sent small Kentucky farmers into a devastating cycle of debt and loss of land as the national hunger for cheap, industrially processed tobacco soared. In a similar tale, as Bluegrass investors—and the railroads they controlled—expanded into the mountains of eastern Kentucky to harvest and market the timber, coal, and other mineral deposits that would fuel the nation's industrial boom, the rural patterns of life for mountain residents were abruptly and permanently lost to the demands of extractive industry.[22]

The suffering among Kentucky farmers, miners, and mill hands provided a fertile breeding ground for conflict and eventually alternative political organization. As the strength of the Farmers' Alliance and mountain labor organization grew, the new attacks on the vast inequalities within Kentucky society reminded men such as Buckner that their lofty perches of privilege were by no means natural or secure. Agrarian dissatisfaction among small farmers in western Kentucky had begun to override party regularity in the 1890s when Farmers' Alliance and Grange men raised their own politics from their tobacco patches, split Democratic tickets with their candidates, who demanded the coinage of silver to drive down farm debt, or even defected to charismatic home-grown Republicans as they reached the breaking point when relief from economic hardship finally outweighed racial orthodoxy. The state's first Republican governor, William O. Bradley, was sent to Frankfort in 1895 with the votes of men at whose expense Buckner and his close Bluegrass circle of capitalists, lawyers, and politicians had kept themselves in political and economic power for decades.

By the time the next gubernatorial election came around, Buckner had left politics and the practice of law. He played no part in the titanic contest featuring demagogic, antirailroad boss William Goebel and his populist-sounding free-silver campaign, which featured none other than William Jennings Bryan leading the boss's statewide speaking tour. Showing just how much had changed in this volatile political landscape, Buckner's old friend W. C. P. Breckinridge threw his considerable political weight behind the Republican ticket, whose nominee promised a new, "lily-white" Republican Party that would no longer welcome African Americans to hold even the most minor offices, came out strong for sound money and capital interests, and made himself very comfortable with the L&N. The Republican candidate looked as much like a Bourbon Democrat—minus the chivalrous bearing and Bluegrass pedigree, of course—as anyone in the field.[23]

Retiring to Winchester, the Buckners retreated away from the world where the harvest of hardship and inequality they had helped create was being reaped. They went home, physically and mentally, into the old Bluegrass they remembered and loved. Their life of rural ease and recreation stood in stark contrast with the frantic struggles for survival, independence, and respectability that went on all around them. While miners struggled to organize themselves in the coal camps east of Winchester, while railroad workers grumbled at their working conditions in Louisville, while farmers were ground into failure by falling prices and rising debt, and while African Americans in Kentucky and elsewhere faced a hardening of segregation laws and a rash of racial violence not seen since the height of Reconstruction, Ben and Helen contented themselves with happy memories and the company of old friends.

Helen resumed her place at the center of the Winchester social scene alongside her daughter Elizabeth. For his part, Buckner hunted and fished with his old comrades from Winchester's best families. Although he may not have been well enough to ride in former Confederate cavalryman Leland Hathaway's fox hunts, he did his best to control the rabbit and fish populations of Clark County's woods and creeks.[24] Old Judge Buckner's shooting and fishing trips were accompanied by porters and servants to haul guns, tackle, and the day's kill, just as Hathaway's fox hunts were made possible only by year-round management of his hounds, horses, and grounds by a staff of black and poor white workers. These rituals of elite white recreation and black and poor white labor were important reminders of how Kentucky had once been and, for Buckner, how it should be.[25]

One excursion, hosted by Confederate veteran C. B. Ecton at his "beautiful country home, Glen Avon," was recalled as one of "the most delightful and enjoyable social events" in the county during the spring of 1900. After the party of veterans of both sides spent the day reeling in more than a hundred fish, a "sumptuous and elegant dinner was served in the most hospitable style" to a "happy combination" of guests from whom "mirth and wit flowed freely and throughout the day."[26] Here, Buckner could nostalgically inhabit the world of his youth, the world that he had gone to war to defend in 1861, and the world he had struggled to re-create ever since.

Ben and Helen spent their final years insulating themselves from the disturbing other sides of Gilded Age, New South society that were evident across Kentucky. Buckner rejected this new world where the gentle veneer of paternalistic benevolence had been overthrown by fiery populists from the tobacco counties and cold machine politicians from the cities. He could go back to Clark County, live the life he had always dreamed of giving himself and Helen, hunt and fish, and have fine dinners with old friends. Like his fellows across the South, Buckner retreated into an imagined past that, in Peter Carmichael's words, "cast a shadow of Victorian purity that obscured the deep problems of the New South—intense poverty, racial violence, segregation, and demagogic politics—by creating an artificial history of the Old South, where content slaves, women in hoop skirts, and courtly squires lived in a rural utopia."[27]

Only the blinders of retirement from public life and sentimental memory could make such a life seem real—James Lane Allen's "oblivious peace." Buckner could sit by his fire in Winchester, a world away from rival factions of the state militia and gangs of armed men who entrenched themselves around the public buildings in Frankfort after Goebel contested his loss in the election of 1899. He could read with detachment the breathless accounts of Goebel being shot in the yard of the capitol building, of rival legislatures claiming to be the legitimate deliberative body of the people, and of the dramatic swearing in of Governor Goebel on his deathbed. And he could plan his spring outings to fish in Lulbegrud Creek as the *Goebel v. Taylor* case made its way through the courts and the state hung on the perilous edge of civil war for months.

Certainly, the Kentucky in which Buckner died on May 6, 1901, was a different place from the antebellum world he had grown up in—torn by partisan politics, class struggle, and racial oppression. But, then again, had those things not always been there? The long-simmering border war, the constant resistance from enslaved black Kentuckians, and their rush to claim the rights of citizens in the military and in politics showed that the antebellum world in which the Buckners had grown up was never as stable, cordial, and deferential as white Kentuckians before the war or after it preferred to believe.

But while Buckner socialized in comfort at Glen Avon with friends who had fought on both sides of the war, contented and full of the day's catch and surrounded by cooks, grooms, and servants, it was not a stretch to squint hard and make believe the war had never come. Slavery had never fallen. The masks of paternalistic politeness had never come off. White men who had worn blue and gray were reunited in their mastery. Here was the life that Buckner had always wanted for himself and Helen. This was the dream that had sustained him during the darkest hours of the war, when he "shut out the stern and horrid realities with which I am surrounded and in 'fancys glass' [see] you dear Helen."[28] Turning away from the world he knew and loved collapsing around him, Buckner promised himself and promised Helen that a scene very much like Glen Avon was in their future.

This was the Civil War memory that Buckner wanted, not the one celebrated in courthouse monuments and reunion speeches, but a living, domestic memory of the world he had fought—and failed—to save. Together, he and Helen retired into the very "castles in the air" that he had built in 1862. "I will always love you and you will never cease to love me," he promised, "and our lives despite all the obstacles which an envious fate may interpose, will glide away together, as smoothly as the current of a placid stream."[29] Had he not fulfilled his promise? Had Helen not been right to bet on the ambitious young lawyer even when her parents were wary? Here they were now, lords and ladies of the Bluegrass. Even if that life and that world in this New South were only illusions created by ignoring the conflicts and contradictions that supported them, so, in truth, had been the Old.

Acknowledgments

My first thanks must go to my graduate school mentors. Dwight Billings was kind enough to welcome a history student into his sociology seminars. Tracy Campbell taught this Civil War historian nearly everything I know about late-nineteenth-century Kentucky. Ron Eller is truly one of the most supportive and insightful persons I have ever known. Mark Summers's exhaustive knowledge of Civil War–era politics and society has benefitted this work immeasurably. Joanne Melish has pushed me to become a more critical thinker, a wider reader, and a more precise writer. She immediately recognized the importance of this project—even before I myself fully grasped it—and constantly pushed me to make the most of it. She tirelessly worked to create opportunities to test my ideas in front of new audiences with exciting new questions. Her sharp stylistic eye helped curb my tendency toward overwrought, half-page sentences and long strings of intricate clauses. Mostly.

Shearer Davis Bowman was involved with this project from its beginning. His enthusiasm helped it get off the ground. His open office door and willingness to chat at length about scholarship, teaching, and things entirely unrelated to either were a model for what graduate education in history can and should be. I hope that he would be proud of how this book turned out.

This book would never have been possible without the wonderful scholars, interpreters, and friends I was lucky to get to know during my time associated with Chickamauga & Chattanooga National Military Park and the National Park Service in general. In particular, I thank Jim Ogden, Keith Bohannon, and Lindsey Brown, who were consistently excellent sounding boards for new ideas and sources of support. Thanks also to Emmanuel Dabney and Marvin-Alonzo Greer. I rarely get to work with either of them, but I always look forward to talking about the great work they do in public history and, more frequently, venting about politics. Lee White and Christopher Young have been great friends and the best research trip companions—whether we were headed to an archive, walking a battlefield, or cruising North Georgia in search of back-roads southern history. I certainly would never have guessed that Daryl Black's offhand comment to me about those Kentucky Unionists who quit the army before the Chickamauga Campaign would come to anything. I'm rather glad it did, though. I count myself lucky that he stuck by an Orphan Brigade–obsessed public-history neophyte and is a friend and mentor about whom I can't say enough.

The Kentucky Historical Society has been the perfect place to research, write, and work, and its influence on this project is everywhere. Brandon Sloane helped me explore the mysterious world of military records. The library staff—Jen DuPlaga most of all—put up with my too frequent requests for their help. Darrell Meadows, Beth Van Allen, Nelson Dawson, and Russell Harris were, first, a wonderful team of editors who moved my article on Buckner through publication in the *Register of the Kentucky Historical Society* and, later, amazing colleagues. Stuart Sanders, Tony Curtis, Tim Talbott, and Trevor Jones were extremely helpful as I tested out new ideas on them. I cannot thank each of them enough for helping bring Buckner to classrooms across the commonwealth, reaching far more Kentuckians, I suspect, than this book ever will.

I work in a wonderful scholarly community. I have to single out Aaron Astor, Jim Klotter, Anne Marshall, Chris Phillips, John David Smith, Matt Stanley, and Amy Taylor for their particular imprint on the way I have read and interpreted Buckner. Thanks, too, are due to Pete Carmichael, who encouraged me to submit my first article manuscript for publication. I could never have made it this far without the University of Kentucky grad student community, in particular Andy Adler, Mandy Higgins, Amy Murray, Bobby Murray, Stephen Pickering, and, though he deserted us for Athens, Sam McGuire. Thanks also to all of my friends and fraternity brothers in Lexington, who ensured that my bourbon intake remained more than sufficient during grad school. Some of them deserve mention for their contributions to this book, in particular Jeff Gurnee and Patrick Marsh for lending their historians' eyes to parts of the manuscript for this book and Jon Gray for talking me through the finer points of nineteenth-century law.

My family raised a child who could only have become a historian. I thank them for their support in so many ways. My mother, Linda, and grandmother, Sara, must be relieved and, I bet, a bit proud to finally read this book. I am fairly certain my late father would disagree with most of the conclusions I draw here, but I am equally convinced that he would also be very happy that I get to write history for a living.

No words of thanks can be sufficient to express my gratitude to my wife, Jenny. She afforded me a new understanding of the Buckner letters, making me appreciate just how important those sappy love lines were when I wanted to skip over them to get to the juicy bits about war, race, and politics. She has listened to me drone on about researching, planning, and writing this book since we first met (on Derby Day—when else?). She has been patient with me when I have gotten frustrated, forgiving when I have been too wrapped up in the nineteenth century, and indulgent when I blow off steam by riding horses we can't afford. For these reasons, among many others, I love her. And I dedicate this work to her because she has heard me recycle all of Buckner's lines from his love letters but keeps me in check if I accidentally stray too close to his theories "upon the subject of wife management."

Portions of chapter 6 first appeared as "The Democratic Partisan Militia and the Black Peril: The Kentucky Militia, Racial Violence, and the Fifteenth Amendment, 1870–73," *Civil War History* 56, no. 2 (2010): 145–74. Copyright © 2010 The Kent State University Press. Reprinted with permission.

Portions of chapters 3 and 4 first appeared as "'All Men of Decency Ought to Quit the Army': Benjamin F. Buckner, Manhood, and Pro-slavery Unionism in Kentucky," *Register of the Kentucky Historical Society* 107, no. 4 (2009): 513–49. Copyright © 2010 Kentucky Historical Society. Reprinted with permission.

Notes

Introduction

1. Aaron Astor provides the best definition of this border-state "conservative proslavery unionism" in *Rebels on the Border: Civil War, Emancipation, and the Reconstruction of Kentucky & Missouri* (Baton Rouge: Louisiana State University Press, 2012), 4–5. A fine short survey of state politics during the war is found in Stephen Rockenbach, "'The Weeds and the Flowers Are Closely Mixed': Allegiance, Law, and White Supremacy in Kentucky's Bluegrass Region, 1861–1865," *Register of the Kentucky Historical Society* (hereafter *Register*) 111, no. 4 (2013): 563–89.

2. B. F. Buckner (hereafter BFB) to Helen Martin (hereafter HBM), Nov. 5, 1862, Benjamin Forsythe Buckner Papers, Special Collections & Digital Programs, Margaret I. King Library, University of Kentucky, Lexington (hereafter Buckner Papers). Buckner makes appearances in previous studies of Civil War Kentucky, usually because of such lines, but he has never been the subject of a stand-alone study. See John David Smith, "The Recruitment of Negro Soldiers in Kentucky, 1863–1865," *Register* 72, no. 4 (1974): 369–70; Anne E. Marshall, *Creating a Confederate Kentucky: The Lost Cause and Civil War Memory in a Border State* (Chapel Hill: University of North Carolina Press, 2010), 24–25. Amy Murrell Taylor has undertaken the deepest and most insightful analysis to date of Ben and Helen's relationship in the context of the war; see *The Divided Family in Civil War America* (Chapel Hill: University of North Carolina Press, 2005), 42–44.

3. BFB to HBM, Nov. 5, 1862, Buckner Papers.

4. A note about the capitalization scheme for the word *union*. It is capitalized, *Union*, when I use it in place of the U.S. government or its armies, particularly during the war, when it is opposed to the Confederate state or armies. A *Unionist*, therefore, is someone who actively supported, worked, or fought for the federal government during the war effort, as opposed to a Confederate. When I speak of *unionism* or a *unionist*—in particular proslavery unionism or a proslavery unionist—I want to denote an adherent to a political philosophy that included loyalty to the federal government. In these instances, *unionism* and *unionists* remain lowercase, as does the term *democrats*, which is not necessarily the same as *Democrats*, denoting those who belong to the Democratic Party. This scheme is admittedly not perfect. But the distinction between unionists and Unionists is not arbitrary. There were many ideologies of union, many unionisms, which

came together to defend the Union, with Buckner's proslavery unionism being one of them. This terminology becomes even more chaotic—yet all the more important—after the war, when the label, rhetoric, and memory of Unionism in Kentucky was taken over by men adhering to the Union Party, a forerunner of the Republican Party. The Union Party in Kentucky *did not* represent all Unionists and unionists in Kentucky; Buckner shows us that very explicitly. However, the Union Party desired *to appear to speak for* all of the state's Unionists and mobilize the memory of the Union cause for more liberal, often emancipationist political and cultural ends to which many wartime Unionists such as Buckner were opposed. Therefore, when I refer to the members of that party, I explicitly say "Union Party members" to underscore the point that party members neither represented nor spoke for Buckner and other proslavery unionists.

5. J. Winston Coleman Jr., *Slavery Times in Kentucky* (Chapel Hill: University of North Carolina Press, 1940); Barbara Jeanne Fields, *Slavery and Freedom on the Middle Ground: Maryland during the Nineteenth Century* (New Haven, Conn.: Yale University Press, 1985), 90.

6. Peter S. Carmichael, *The Last Generation: Young Virginians in Peace, War, and Reunion* (Chapel Hill: University of North Carolina Press, 2005). The faith in modernizing slavery manifested by Carmichael's subjects is also explored in John D. Majewski, *Modernizing a Slave Economy: The Economic Vision of the Confederate Nation* (Chapel Hill: University of North Carolina Press, 2009).

7. James Michael Rhyne has aptly termed Kentucky a "rehearsal for redemption" ("Rehearsal for Redemption: The Politics of Post-emancipation Violence in Kentucky's Bluegrass Region," Ph.D. diss., University of Cincinnati, 2006). Excellent studies that detail this balancing act between state and federal power include William J. Cooper Jr., *Liberty and Slavery: Southern Politics to 1860*, 2nd ed. (Columbia: University of South Carolina Press, 2000); Don E. Fehrenbacher, *The Slaveholding Republic: An Account of the United States Government's Relations to Slavery* (New York: Oxford University Press, 2001); Lacy K. Ford, *Deliver Us from Evil: The Slavery Question in the Old South, 1787–1840* (New York: Oxford University Press, 2009); David F. Ericson, *Slavery in the American Republic: Developing the Federal Government, 1791–1861* (Lawrence: University Press of Kansas, 2011).

8. In Ira Berlin, Barbara J. Fields, Thavolia Glymph, Joseph P. Reidy, and Leslie S. Rowland, eds., *The Destruction of Slavery*, vol. 1 of *Freedom: A Documentary History of Emancipation, 1861–1867*, ser. 1 (New York: Cambridge University Press, 1985), 546–47.

9. Matthew Salafia, *Slavery's Borderland: Freedom and Bondage along the Ohio River* (Philadelphia: University of Pennsylvania Press, 2013), 310 n. 21; James F. Buckner quoted in Thomas Speed, *The Union Cause in Kentucky, 1860–1865* (New York: Putnam's, 1907), 295.

10. Kentucky, for example, is absent in any meaningful way from Gary Gallagher's pair of studies of the Confederate and Union nations: *The Confederate War* (Cambridge, Mass.: Harvard University Press, 1997) focuses on the states that seceded from the

Union, but *The Union War* (Cambridge, Mass.: Harvard University Press, 2011) also does not fit Kentucky, whose Unionists—white and black—put race and slavery at the center of their war experience.

11. Adam I. P. Smith, *No Party Now: Politics in the Civil War North* (New York: Oxford University Press, 2006); Jennifer L. Weber, *Copperheads: The Rise and Fall of Lincoln's Opponents in the North* (New York: Oxford University Press, 2006); Mark A. Lause, *A Secret Society History of the Civil War* (Urbana: University of Illinois Press, 2011); Michael Thomas Smith, *The Enemy Within: Fears of Corruption in the Civil War North* (Charlottesville: University of Virginia Press, 2011). As their titles suggest, these volumes study the North, not the Union.

12. There are many excellent works on southern disloyalty and dissent. Again, like the literature on the North, most have not examined nonmountain Kentucky or recognized significant proslavery unionism in the South. They include: Shearer Davis Bowman, "Conditional Unionism and Slavery in Virginia, 1860–1861: The Case of Dr. Richard Eppes," *Virginia Magazine of History and Biography* 96, no. 1 (1988): 31–54; Daniel E. Sutherland, ed., *Guerrillas, Unionists, and Violence on the Confederate Home Front* (Fayetteville: University of Arkansas Press, 1999), save for parts of B. F. Cooling's essay "A People's War: Partisan Conflict in Tennessee and Kentucky," 113–32; John C. Inscoe and Robert C. Kenzer, eds., *Enemies of the Country: New Perspectives on Unionists in the Civil War South* (Athens: University of Georgia Press, 2001); James Alex Baggett, *The Scalawags: Southern Dissenters in the Civil War and Reconstruction* (Baton Rouge: Louisiana State University Press, 2003); Margaret M. Storey, *Loyalty and Loss: Alabama's Unionists in the Civil War and Reconstruction* (Baton Rouge: Louisiana State University Press, 2004); John C. Inscoe, *Race, War, and Remembrance in the Appalachian South* (Lexington: University Press of Kentucky, 2008), which does discuss mountain Kentucky; Victoria E. Bynum, *The Long Shadow of the Civil War: Southern Dissent and Its Legacies* (Chapel Hill: University of North Carolina Press, 2010). Some notable exceptions that include Kentucky within the South are William W. Freehling, *The South vs. the South: How Anti-Confederate Southerners Shaped the Course of the Civil War* (New York: Oxford University Press, 2001), though Freehling argues that Kentucky's loyalty came through "slacker commitments to slavery" over the course of the 1850s (32); Armstead L. Robinson, *Bitter Fruits of Bondage: The Demise of Slavery and the Collapse of the Confederacy, 1861–1865* (Charlottesville: University of Virginia Press, 2005), which includes Kentucky and black southerners in a study of the crumbling of Confederate nationalism; and Daniel W. Crofts, *Reluctant Confederates: Upper South Unionists in the Secession Crisis* (Chapel Hill: University of North Carolina Press, 1989), which highlights the Whig-based proslavery Unionism that Buckner and many other white Kentucky loyalists articulated but studies it in states that eventually seceded.

13. The portions of the vote came to 64,301 Kentuckians for McClellan, 27,787 for Lincoln. The Kentucky soldier vote, counted separately, stood at 2,766 for McClellan to 1,194 for Lincoln, according to the returns filed with the secretary of state, though

Horace Greely seems to have slightly misreported the military number in the source cited by most subsequent historians (Horace Greeley, *The American Conflict: A History of the Great Rebellion in the United States of America, 1860–'65*, 2 vols. [Hartford, Conn.: O. D. Case, 1866], 2:672). For 1864 statewide totals, see *Election Returns, 1855–1872*, 343–50, Kentucky, Secretary of State, Election Returns Registers, 1851–1894, Kentucky Department for Libraries and Archives, Frankfort. Military returns are found in Box 42, Kentucky, Secretary of State, Election Records, 1796–1941, also at Kentucky Department for Libraries and Archives.

14. Hambleton Tapp and James C. Klotter, *Kentucky: Decades of Discord, 1865–1900* (Frankfort: Kentucky Historical Society, 1977), 168.

15. Anne Marshall has best illustrated this Confederate-faced New South Kentucky in *Creating a Confederate Kentucky*. Less frequently cited is Thomas Connelly's 1966 argument about the importance of New South economic development to the creation and commodification of this Confederate memory ("Neo-Confederatism or Power Vacuum: Post-war Kentucky Politics Reappraised," *Register* 64, no. 3 [1966]: 257–69). Other Kentucky memory studies that have proved very useful include: Christopher Phillips, "'The Chrysalis State': Slavery, Confederate Identity, and the Creation of a Border South," in Lesley J. Gordon and John C. Inscoe, eds., *Inside the Confederate Nation: Essays in Honor of Emory M. Thomas* (Baton Rouge: Louisiana State University Press, 2005), 147–64; and Maryjean Wall, *How Kentucky Became Southern: A Tale of Outlaws, Horse Thieves, Gamblers, and Breeders* (Lexington: University Press of Kentucky, 2010).

16. The use of the diminutive "Ben" may be jarring within the convention of the academic monograph, where last names are standard. I have tried to be intentional in my use of Buckner's first name, restricting it to two specific contexts peculiar to this sort of study of a small and interconnected cast of characters. First, I use it whenever multiple Buckners are in play at the same time. This most often applies to Ben and his father, Aylett. Second, I find it useful to intersperse "Ben" when discussing his relationship with Helen. In light of their frequent disagreements on politics, "Buckner" and "Martin" seemed to create artificial distance between the two; first names help make that relationship seem more intimate and less antagonistic—as, indeed, it was. This choice was also made out of simplicity; Helen moves from being a Martin to being a Buckner during the course of the book, so first names seemed more consistent. Buckner was "Ben" in both of these contexts. In contexts where he was Mr. Buckner, Major Buckner, or Judge Buckner, I refer to him as "Buckner."

17. Stanley Harrold, *Border War: Fighting over Slavery before the Civil War* (Chapel Hill: University of North Carolina Press, 2010).

18. H. Levin, ed., *The Lawyers and Lawmakers of Kentucky* (Chicago: Lewis, 1897), 653. For examples of Helen's appearances in local news items, see Minnie C. Fox, ed., *The Blue Grass Cook Book* (New York: Fox, Duffield, 1904), 67, 125, 300; *Louisville Courier-Journal*, Apr. 28, May 12, 1907, and Nov. 7 and 9, 1909.

19. Glenn Feldman, "Conclusion: America's Appointment with Destiny—a Cautionary Tale," in Glenn Feldman, ed., *Painting Dixie Red: When, Where, Why, and How the South Became Republican* (Gainesville: University Press of Florida, 2011), 340.

20. I draw inspiration here from Edward L. Ayers, *The Promise of the New South: Life after Reconstruction* (New York: Oxford University Press, 1992) and *In the Presence of Mine Enemies: The Civil War in the Heart of America, 1859–1863* (New York: Norton, 2003).

21. David W. Blight, *American Oracle: The Civil War in the Civil Rights Era* (Cambridge, Mass.: Belknap Press of Harvard University Press, 2011), 56, emphasis in original.

22. Tara McPherson, *Reconstructing Dixie: Race, Gender, and Nostalgia in the Imagined South* (Durham, N.C.: Duke University Press, 2003), 8.

23. Robert Penn Warren, *Jefferson Davis Gets His Citizenship Back* (Lexington: University Press of Kentucky, 1980), 20–21; for Blight's reading of this passage, see *American Oracle*, 35.

24. C. Vann Woodward, *The Burden of Southern History* (Baton Rouge: Louisiana State University Press, 1960).

1. The World Is a Cruel and Cold Place

1. BFB to HBM, Dec. 15, 1861, Buckner Papers.

2. From a letter printed in the *Lexington Observer & Reporter*, Dec. 25, 1861. The letter was signed only with the initial "M," but two later letters published on December 10, 1862, are signed by James C. Morris, a Lexington lieutenant of Company D.

3. BFB to HBM, Dec. 15, 1861, Buckner Papers. On the state of Union refugees in Smithland, see U. S. Grant to J. C. Kelton, Dec. 29, 1861, in *The War of the Rebellion: A Compilation of the Official Records of the Union and Confederate Armies* (hereafter OR), 128 vols., ser. 1, 7:523; General Orders no. 26, District of Cairo, Dec. 28, 1861, in OR, ser. 1, 7:518–19.

4. BFB to HBM, Dec. 15, 1861, Buckner Papers.

5. Fehrenbacher, *The Slaveholding Republic*.

6. "A Declaration of the Immediate Causes Which Induce and Justify the Secession of the State of Mississippi from the Federal Union," in J. L. Power, ed., *Proceedings of the Mississippi State Convention, Held January 7th to 26th, A.D. 1861* (Jackson: Power & Cadwallader, 1861), 47.

7. Thomas D. Clark, *Clark County, Kentucky: A History* (Winchester, Ky.: Clark County–Winchester Heritage Commission and Clark County Historical Society, 1995), 1–10.

8. Henry Clay, from an article in *Western Agriculturalist*, quoted in James F. Hopkins, *A History of the Hemp Industry in Kentucky* (Lexington: University Press of Kentucky, 1951), 14–15.

9. William Armstrong Crozier, ed., *The Buckners of Virginia and the Allied Families*

of Strother and Ashby (New York: Genealogical Association, 1907), 1–3, 20–22; T. E. Campbell, *Colonial Caroline: A History of Caroline County, Virginia* (Richmond, Va.: Dietz Press, 1953), 369, 373; William Armstrong Crozier, ed., *Virginia County Records*, vol. 6 (Baltimore: Genealogical Publications, 1905), 241.

    10. Crozier, *Buckners of Virginia*, 172–73; U.S. Census Bureau, *Third Census of the United States, 1810*, Population Schedule, Kentucky, Henderson Co., Henderson, and *Fourth Census of the United States, 1820*, Population Schedule, Kentucky, Clark County, Winchester (unless otherwise noted, all cited censuses are online databases accessed at http://www.ancestry.com); Edmund Lyne Starling, *History of Henderson County, Kentucky* (Henderson, Ky.: n.p., 1887), 130; "An Act Supplemental to the Act Establishing Independent Banks in this Commonwealth," in Kentucky General Assembly, *Acts Passed at the First Session of the Twenty-Sixth Kentucky General Assembly for the Commonwealth of Kentucky, Begun and Held in the Town of Frankfort, on Monday, the First Day of December 1817, and of the Commonwealth the Twenty-Sixth* (Frankfort: Kendall and Russell, 1818), 491–93.

    11. Henry Clay, *The Papers of Henry Clay*, vol. 3: *Presidential Candidate, 1821–1824*, ed. James F. Hopkins (Lexington: University Press of Kentucky, 1963), 735 n., and vol. 5: *Secretary of State, 1826*, ed. James F. Hopkins, Mary W. M. Hargreaves, Wayne Cutler, and Burton Milward (Lexington: University Press of Kentucky, 1973), 613–16, 616 n.

    12. Only seven Kentucky planters owned more than one hundred enslaved people in 1860. See Keith C. Barton, "'Good Cooks and Washers': Slave Hiring, Domestic Labor, and the Market in Bourbon County, Kentucky," *Journal of American History* 84, no. 2 (1997): 436.

    13. Douglas Helms, "Soil and Southern History," *Agricultural History* 74, no. 4 (2000): 723–58; Ulrich B. Phillips, *Life and Labor in the Old South* (Boston: Little, Brown, 1929), 80. On diversified crops and small slaveholdings in the upper South, see Fields, *Slavery and Freedom*, 1–39; Robert Tracy MacKenzie, *One South or Many? Plantation Belt and Upcountry in Civil War–Era Tennessee* (Cambridge, U.K.: Cambridge University Press, 1994); Diane Mutti Burke, *On Slavery's Borders: Missouri's Small-Slaveholding Households, 1815–1865* (Athens: University of Georgia Press, 2010), 98–102; Astor, *Rebels on the Border*, 15–32.

    14. Hopkins, *History of the Hemp Industry in Kentucky*, 4, 24–26, 25 n., 51–52. Thomas Clark sketches a descriptive—if not terribly analytical—picture of slavery in the county (*Clark County*, 213–31).

    15. Hopkins provides a wonderful summary of the process (*History of the Hemp Industry in Kentucky*, 43–64).

    16. Ann J. Ottesen, "A Reconstruction of the Activities and Outbuildings at Farmington, an Early Nineteenth Century Hemp Farm," *Filson Club History Quarterly* (hereafter *FCHQ*) 59, no. 4 (1985): 395–425.

    17. Hopkins, *History of the Hemp Industry in Kentucky*, 132–39 (for an account of the workings of the ropewalk); Jonathan D. Martin, *Divided Mastery: Slave Hiring in*

the American South (Cambridge, Mass.: Harvard University Press, 2004), 12, 19–20, 82; Seth Rockman, *Scraping By: Wage Labor, Slavery, and Survival in Early Baltimore* (Baltimore: Johns Hopkins University Press, 2009), 7. On slave hiring in Missouri, see Mutti Burke, *On Slavery's Border*, 107–118. On the development of Kentucky's turnpike system, see Karl Raitz and Nancy O'Malley, "Local-Scale Turnpike Roads in Nineteenth Century Kentucky," *Journal of Historical Geography* 33 (2007): 1–23.

18. Barton, "'Good Cooks and Washers,'" 444–58; Coleman, *Slavery Times in Kentucky*, 124; Martin, *Divided Mastery*, 2–3. On the emergence of this domesticity in the early nineteenth century, see Nancy F. Cott, *The Bonds of Womanhood: "Woman's Sphere" in New England, 1780–1835* (New Haven, Conn.: Yale University Press, 1977).

19. Clark, *Clark County*, 131, 121–45 (on Martin and stock raising in Clark County).

20. Eugene D. Genovese, "Livestock in the Slave Economy of the Old South: A Revised View," *Agricultural History* 36, no. 3 (1962): 147–48. Martin penned articles on establishing bluegrass and using crop rotation to maintain fertility in central Kentucky soils: S. D. Martin, "Sowing Seed in Woodland" (originally in the *Southern Cultivator*) and "Laying Down Open Lands in Grass" (originally in the *Southern Agriculturalist*), both reprinted in *Western Farmer and Gardener* 2, no. 4 (1840): 93–95.

21. Clark, *Clark County*, 121, 222; Genovese, "Livestock in the Slave Economy," 146.

22. Genovese, "Livestock in the Slave Economy," 146; *American Agriculturalist* 4, no. 8 (1845): 253. The census shows that Martin owned fifteen people in 1820, eleven in 1830, forty-four in 1840, seventeen in 1850, and eighteen in 1860 (see Population Schedules, Kentucky, Clark County, in U.S. Census Bureau, *Fourth Census of the United States, 1820*; *Fifth Census of the United States, 1830*; *Sixth Census of the United States, 1840*; *Seventh Census of the United States, 1850*; and *Eighth Censuses of the United States, 1860*,

23. Robert S. Starobin, *Industrial Slavery in the Old South* (New York: Oxford University Press, 1970), 14–15, 25; Willard Rouse Jillson, *The Red River Iron Works: A Narrative Account of the Rise and Decline of a Basic Industry in Eastern Central Kentucky (1787–1830)* (Frankfort: Roberts Printing, 1964), 10–17, 23–30; Don F. Fig, *A History of the Fitchburg Furnace* (N.p.: n.p., n.d.; copy held at the library of the Kentucky Historical Society), xiii; J. Peter Lesley, *The Iron Manufacturer's Guide to the Furnaces, Forges, and Rolling Mills of the United States* (New York: Wiley, 1859), 126.

24. U.S. Census Bureau, *Sixth Census of the United States, 1840*, Population Schedule, Kentucky, Estill County. Receipts of the hire of slaves for the year 1856 between Jackson and James P. Magowan (two receipts, Dec. 28, 1855), Samuel C. Edger (Dec. 29, 1855), Joseph B. Erwin (Dec. 31, 1855), John W. Choat (Jan. 1, 1856), H. P. Rice (Jan. 1, 1856), J. D. Jordan (Jan. 1, 1856), and Thomas Turner (Mar. 3, 1856) survive in the Buckner Papers. On hiring slaves for industry and the integrated workplace, see Starobin, *Industrial Slavery*, 116–45. The operation was smaller but likely similar to that documented for western Virginia in Charles B. Dew, *Bond of Iron: Master and Slave at Buffalo Forge* (New York: Norton, 1994), and for Maryland and Virginia in Ronald L. Lewis, *Coal, Iron, and Slaves: Industrial Slavery in Maryland and Virginia, 1715–1865*

(Westport, Conn.: Greenwood Press, 1979). It also featured a blending of enslaved and free labor similar to that seen in John Bezís-Selfa, "A Tale of Two Ironworks: Slavery, Free Labor, Work, and Resistance in the Early Republic," *William and Mary Quarterly*, 3rd ser., 56, no. 4 (1999): 677–700.

25. "COMMISSIONER'S SALE OF THE RED RIVER IRON WORKS AND ESTILL STEAM FURNACE," clipping from *Philadelphia Enquirer*, Dec. 1865 or Jan. 1866, Buckner Papers.

26. Ibid.; William Terrell Lewis, *Genealogy of the Lewis Family in America: From the Middle of the Seventeenth Century Down to the Present Time*, vol. 1 (Louisville: Courier-Journal Job Printing, 1893), 373.

27. Salafia, *Slavery's Borderland*, 6; Max Grivno, *Gleanings of Freedom: Free and Slave Labor along the Mason–Dixon Line, 1790–1860* (Urbana: University of Illinois Press, 2011), 4.

28. Gavin Wright, "Slavery and American Agricultural History," *Agricultural History* 77, no. 4 (2003): 531; Rockman, *Scraping By*, 14.

29. Christopher Morris, *Becoming Southern: The Evolution of a Way of Life, Warren County and Vicksburg, Mississippi, 1770–1860* (New York: Oxford University Press, 1995), 104. See also James Oakes, *The Ruling Race: A History of American Slaveholders* (New York: Norton, 1982), 91.

30. U.S. Census Bureau, *Sixth Census of the United States, 1840*, Population Schedule, Kentucky, Clark County, Winchester. My view of the Buckner household owes a large debt to Brenda E. Stevenson, *Life in Black and White: Family and Community in the Slave South* (New York: Oxford University Press, 1996). A discussion of the importance of the household to a man's reputation can be found in John Tosh, *A Man's Place: Masculinity and the Middle-Class Home in Victorian England* (New Haven, Conn.: Yale University Press, 1999). On the need to reconsider the segregation of "public" and "private" bourgeois spheres, see Stephen M. Frank, *Life with Father: Parenthood and Masculinity in the Nineteenth-Century American North* (Baltimore: Johns Hopkins University Press, 1998).

31. Mutti Burke, *On Slavery's Border*, 105, 134–39 (for more on domestic work patterns in small slaveholding households); Barton, "'Good Cooks and Washers,'" 455, 459. The language of paternalism is discussed in Eugene D. Genovese, *Roll Jordan Roll: The World the Slaves Made* (New York: Pantheon Books, 1974), and Eugene D. Genovese and Elizabeth Fox-Genovese, *Fatal Self-Deception: Slaveholding Paternalism in the Old South* (New York: Cambridge University Press, 2011).

32. Coleman, *Slavery Times in Kentucky*, vii; Mutti Burke, *On Slavery's Border*, 143, 142–97 (for more on the theory and reality of small slave-owning household paternalism). According to Coleman, it was only due to the most excessive of masters—the distinct minority in his telling—and to some slaves who were "savage and dangerous" that some "slaves were now and then rather harshly treated" (*Slavery Times in Kentucky*, 245).

33. Mutti Burke, *On Slavery's Border*, 144. A particularly insightful look into the dynamics of resistance and control in southern households can be found in Stephanie

M. H. Camp, *Closer to Freedom: Enslaved Women and Everyday Resistance in the Plantation South* (Chapel Hill: University of North Carolina Press, 2004).

34. Dr. Samuel Davis Martin Records, 1834–1868, Special Collections & Digital Programs, Margaret I. King Library, University of Kentucky, Lexington. On Jackson's reputation as "an Iron expert," see Saml PS Marshall to Jos A Jackson Esq, Feb. 7, 1859, Buckner Papers.

35. Lisa L. Tolbert, *Constructing Townscapes: Space and Society in Antebellum Tennessee* (Chapel Hill: University of North Carolina Press, 1999), 120; Lori Glover, *Southern Sons: Becoming Men in the New Nation* (Baltimore: Johns Hopkins University Press, 2007), 133. A useful Kentucky example is found in Brad Asher, *Cecelia and Fanny: The Remarkable Friendship between an Escaped Slave and Her Former Mistress* (Lexington: University Press of Kentucky, 2011). On mistresses as workplace managers, see Elizabeth Fox-Genovese, *Within the Plantation Household: Black and White Women in the Old South* (Chapel Hill: University of North Carolina Press, 1988); Drew Gilpin Faust, *Mothers of Invention: Women of the Slaveholding South in the American Civil War* (Chapel Hill: University of North Carolina Press, 1996); Thavolia Glymph, *Out of the House of Bondage: The Transformation of the Plantation Household* (New York: Cambridge University Press, 2008).

36. In *Money over Mastery, Family over Freedom: Slavery in the Antebellum Upper South* (Baltimore: Johns Hopkins University Press, 2011), Calvin Schermerhorn expertly analyzes the ways in which enslaved people actively supported their masters' economic endeavors not for their owners' sake but for the protection of their own kin from sale. Oakes discusses the rampant fear of failure among slave owners throughout the South in *The Ruling Race*, 123–27. On the slave trade in Clark County, see Clark, *Clark County*, 222–24, and in Kentucky in general see Coleman, *Slavery Times in Kentucky*, 115–95.

37. William Thomas Buckner to Edward Pollard, Feb. 15, 1843, in Crozier, *Buckners of Virginia*, 177–79. Another letter from Benjamin's brother Walker to their cousin Richard Buckner notes that "Ben failed in business and about twelve years ago removed to Missouri, where he now lives, well provided for by Billy, Aylett [likely William Aylett Buckner, who made a fortune in cotton in Mississippi] and myself. Sam was not so much embarrassed, but the three of us above named paid his debts" (Crozier, *Buckners of Virginia*, 173–74).

38. Oakes, *The Ruling Race*, 61. On the later evolution of military schools, see Rod Andrew, *Long Gray Lines: The Southern Military School Tradition, 1839–1915* (Chapel Hill: University of North Carolina Press, 2001).

39. *Kentucky Military Institute Charter*, Jan. 20, 1847 (Frankfort, Ky.: A. G. Hodges, 1847), reproduced in James D. Stephens, *Reflections: A Portrait-Biography of the Kentucky Military Institute (1845–1971)* (Georgetown: Kentucky Military Institute, 1991), 1. In *Military Education and the Emerging Middle Class in the Old South* (New York: Cambridge University Press, 2009), Jennifer R. Green shows that the pupils of similar schools from across the South were, like Buckner, overwhelmingly the sons of small-slave-owning professional men (app. 2, 265–71).

40. *Kentucky Military Institute Charter,* in Stephens, *Reflections,* 1; Green, *Military Education and the Emerging Middle Class,* 128.

41. Levin, *Lawyers and Lawmakers of Kentucky,* 652; Tolbert, *Constructing Townscapes,* 120.

42. Tolbert, *Constructing Townscapes,* 157. I draw the "character" as a complex of traits indicative of self-mastery from Thomas Augst's study of northeastern middle-class young men: *The Clerk's Tale: Young Men and Moral Life in Nineteenth-Century America* (Chicago: University of Chicago Press, 2003). On the imperative presence of both orderly progress toward manhood and youthful rebellion, see Brian Luskey, *On the Make: Clerks and the Quest for Capital in Nineteenth-Century America* (New York: New York University Press, 2010). Buckner mentions the National Hotel in Winchester as one venue for such entertainments in a letter to Helen, Nov. 16, 1856, Buckner Papers.

43. BFB to HBM, Oct. 16, 1856, Buckner Papers. Betty Lewis's wedding was also of interest to Ben's sister, Susan, in a letter she wrote him on October 21 (Buckner Papers).

44. The 1840s and 1850s were important decades for the institution of professional degrees. Law and medical schools, both of which the University of Louisville acquired under James Guthrie, were particularly important in this process. See Dwayne D. Cox and William J. Morrison, *The University of Louisville* (Lexington: University Press of Kentucky, 2000), 24–25, and Jonathan Daniel Wells, *The Origins of the Southern Middle Class, 1800–1861* (Chapel Hill: University of North Carolina Press, 2004), 166–67. On the professionalization trend, see Daniel H. Calhoun, *Professional Lives in America: Structure and Aspiration, 1750–1850* (Cambridge, Mass.: Harvard University Press, 1965).

45. BFB to HBM, Oct. 16, Nov. 16, 1856, Buckner Papers.

46. Thomas Newton Allen, *Chronicles of Oldfields* (Seattle, Wash.: Alice Harriman, 1909), 61; BFB to HBM, Dec. 28, 1859, Buckner Papers.

47. Glover, *Southern Sons,* 138; BFB to HBM, Sep. 25, 1859, Buckner Papers. On the pressures exerted on young men to establish a household, see Ellen K. Rothman, *Hands and Hearts: A History of Courtship in America* (New York: Basic Books, 1984): 144–76; Karen Lystra synthesizes the social and cultural complexities of midcentury courting and love in *Searching the Heart: Women, Men, and Romantic Love in Nineteenth-Century America* (New York: Oxford University Press, 1989).

48. BFB to HBM, Aug. 4, 8, 1859, Buckner Papers.

49. Glover, *Southern Sons,* 139; BFB to HBM, Sept. 25, 1859, Buckner Papers.

50. BFB to HBM, Mar. 5, 1861, Buckner Papers.

2. Firstborn of the Union

1. BFB to HBM, Jan. 4, 8, 1862, Buckner Papers.

2. Thomas E. Bramlette to George H. Thomas, Sept. 23, 1861, *OR,* ser. I, 4:271; BFB to HBM, Jan. 8, 1862, Buckner Papers.

3. BFB to HBM, Jan. 8, 1862, Buckner Papers.

4. Ibid.; Amy Murrell Taylor reads this letter's discourse on household authority in a very enlightening way in *Divided Family in Civil War America*, 43–44.

5. Don Harrison Doyle, *The Social Order of a Frontier Community: Jacksonville, Illinois, 1825–70* (Urbana: University of Illinois Press, 1978), 19–21, 32; William Perrin, *The History of Bourbon, Scott, Harrison, and Nicholas Counties, Kentucky* (Chicago: O. L. Baskin, 1892), 481.

6. Frank J. Heinl, "Newspapers and Periodicals in the Lincoln–Douglas Country, 1831–1832," *Journal of the Illinois State Historical Society* 23, no. 3 (1930): 372; Doyle, *Social Order of a Frontier Community*, 51 (quote from "fellow Kentuckian" William Thomas), 121. On Illinois and slavery, see Harrold, *Border War*, 19–20.

7. Doyle, *Social Order of a Frontier Community*, 32–35; Heinl, "Newspapers and Periodicals," 395 (on the "Abolition Church" and "abolition engines"), 409–13 (for general subscription information), 414–21 (for indexes of individual publications), 422–36 (for subscriptions by individuals in town). Buckner took no religious publications, adhering to the Anti-Jackson/Whig Washington organ the *National Intelligencer*, the *Lexington Kentucky Reporter* of the same political stripe, and the *Illinois Monthly Magazine*, a literary publication (Heinl, "Newspapers and Periodicals," 424; Sarah John English, "The History of Trinity Church, Jacksonville, Illinois: The Oldest Episcopal Church in Illinois," *Journal of the Illinois State Historical Society* 21, no. 1 [1928]: 114).

8. The minutes of the meeting of the Illinois Anti-Slavery Society are published in A. L. Bowen, ed., "Anti-slavery Convention Held in Alton, Illinois, October 26–28, 1837," *Journal of the Illinois State Historical Society* 20, no. 3 (1927): 329–56, 343–44 (Herndon quote).

9. Doyle, *Social Order of a Frontier Community*, 52–53; Harrold, *Border War*, 68–69. Herndon, of course, would become Abraham Lincoln's law partner.

10. Heinl, "Newspapers and Periodicals," 380 (quote), 399 (on Wolcott in the Logan's escape); Harrold, *Border War*, 65; Mark E. Steiner, ed., "Abolitionists and Escaped Slaves in Jacksonville: Samuel Willard's 'My First Adventure with a Fugitive Slave: The Story of It and How It Failed,'" *Illinois Historical Journal* 89, no. 4 (1996): 214; "Porter Clay House, 1019 West State Street, Jacksonville, Morgan, IL," Prints & Photographs Division, Historic American Buildings Survey, Reproduction number ILL, 69-JACVI, 3, Library of Congress, Washington, D.C.; Doyle, *Social Order of a Frontier Community*, 57–58.

11. Crozier, *Buckners of Virginia*, 175; Charles M. Eames, *Historic Morgan and Classic Jacksonville* (Jacksonville, Ill.: Daily Journal Steam Job Printing Office, 1885), 97–98.

12. Heinl, "Newspapers and Periodicals," 398 (on Hardin and slavery), 408 (on the primary system). Hardin seems not to have been particularly opposed to Mr. Polk's war, however; he was killed commanding the First Illinois Infantry at Buena Vista.

13. The annual parade in celebration of Queen Katherine, supposedly an occupational deity of rope makers, seems to have been something of an inversion-day ritual. It was cancelled amid fears of potential disorder in 1835 (see Clark, *Clark County*, 218 [quoting Winchester Town Trustees Ordinance Book], 225). At the same time, religious

services led by Moses Martin were initially outlawed but were eventually allowed to continue under white chaperone for much the same reason (ibid., 219–21). On Birney, see Stanley Harrold, *Abolitionists and the South, 1831–1861* (Lexington: University Press of Kentucky, 1995), 28–44, particularly 28–32 for his activities through 1835. On Turner, see Kenneth S. Greenberg, *Nat Turner: A Slave Rebellion in History and Memory* (New York: Oxford University Press, 2003). On the Virginia debates, see Alison Goodyear Freehling, *Drift toward Dissolution: The Virginia Slavery Debate of 1831–1832* (Baton Rouge: Louisiana State University Press, 1982); Eva Sheppard Wolf, *Race and Liberty in the New Nation: Emancipation in Virginia from the Revolution to Nat Turner's Rebellion* (Baton Rouge: Louisiana State University Press, 2006).

14. Clark had married the sister, Susan, of Ben's mother, Charlotte, in 1809. Together, they had four children before Susan died in 1825. Clark remarried in 1829, though his second wife, Margaret Buckner Thornton Clark, died in 1836 before he took office (Victor B. Howard, "James Clark, 1836–1839," in Lowell H. Harrison, ed., *Kentucky's Governors* [1985; reprint, Lexington: University Press of Kentucky, 2004, 47–50]).

15. *Ohio Statesman*, qtd. in *Frankfort Commonwealth*, Mar. 6, 1839, and *Maysville Eagle*, Mar. 2, 1839; all qtd. in Harrold, *Border War*, 85; see also *Prigg v. Pennsylvania*, 41 U.S. 539. On Clark's mission to Ohio generally, see Harrold, *Border War*, 72–73, 79–93.

16. Perrin, *History of Bourbon, Scott, Harrison, and Nicholas Counties*, 481; Harold D. Tallant, *Evil Necessity: Slavery and Political Culture in Antebellum Kentucky* (Lexington: University Press of Kentucky, 2003), 151, 155 (Davis quote), 157 (Elijah Nuttall quote), both quotes from *Report of the Debates and Proceedings of the Convention for the Revision of the Constitution of the State of Kentucky, 1849* (Frankfort: A. G. Hodges, 1849); Abraham Lincoln to George Robertson, Aug. 15, 1855, in Abraham Lincoln, *The Collected Works of Abraham Lincoln*, 8 vols., ed. Roy P. Basler (New Brunswick, N.J.: Rutgers University Press, 1953), 3:317–9. Crozier, *Buckners of Virginia*, 175.

17. Christopher M. Paine, "'Kentucky Will Be the Last to Give Up the Union': Kentucky Politics, 1844–61," Ph.D. diss., University of Kentucky, 1998, 22; Fehrenbacher, *Slaveholding Republic*, 281. Fehrenbacher believes that the Constitution was originally slavery neutral but that the government's practice over the intervening decades had led it by Taney's day to be a proslavery document. George William Van Cleve counters, arguing that the Constitution had from its beginning been a staunchly proslavery document (*A Slaveholders' Union: Slavery, Politics, and the Constitution in the Early Republic* [Chicago: University of Chicago Press, 2010]).

18. Ericson, *Slavery in the American Republic*, 1, 9.

19. Ibid., 11.

20. A. H. Buckner to Garrett Davis, June 25, 1861, U.S. Military Academy Cadet Application Papers, 1805–1866, M688, Roll 217, RG 94, National Archives and Records Administration, Washington, D.C., accessed through http://www.ancestry.com.

21. *Winchester National Union*, Nov. 9, 1860; Kenneth H. Williams and James Russell Harris, "Kentucky in 1860: A Statistical Overview," *Register* 103, no. 4 (2005): 748.

22. Williams and Harris, "Kentucky in 1860," 759; *Winchester National Union,* Nov. 9, 1860.

23. Jackson qtd. in *Winchester National Union,* Nov. 9, 1860.

24. Aaron Astor, "Belated Confederates: Black Politics, Guerrilla Violence, and the Collapse of Conservative Unionism in Kentucky and Missouri, 1860–1872," Ph.D. diss., Northwestern University, 2006, 46, 46 nn. 82–83; Cooper, *Liberty and Slavery,* 68.

25. Daniel Walker Howe, *The Political Culture of the American Whigs* (Chicago: University of Chicago Press, 1979), 18, 19 (quote from Clay), 21. In the quotation contrasting space and time, Howe draws from Major L. Wilson, *Space, Time, and Freedom: The Quest for Nationality and the Irrepressible Conflict* (Westport, Conn.: Greenwood Press, 1974).

26. Harry A. Volz III covers at length both the Whig ascendency in Kentucky as well as the significant Whiggish tack made by 1850s Kentucky Democrats to attract Whig/Know-Nothing men ("Party, State, and Nation: Kentucky and the Coming of the American Civil War," Ph.D. diss., University of Virginia, 1982). Christopher M. Paine likewise discusses this topic, though with a much keener eye to ideology, in "'Kentucky Will Be the Last to Give Up the Union.'" John Alan Boyd's tracing of Kentucky "Whig-Americans" through the shifting partisan sands of the secession crisis is especially insightful in "Neutrality and Peace: Kentucky and the Secession Crisis of 1861," Ph.D. diss., University of Kentucky, 1999, especially regarding the influence of Crittenden (90–107). Astor condenses the literature into a very readable few pages in *Rebels on the Border,* 33–50. In *Reluctant Confederates,* Crofts shows how the Whig survival is seen elsewhere in the upper South.

27. Astor, *Rebels on the Border,* 47; Larry K. Menna, "Embattled Conservatism: The Ideology of the Southern Whigs," Ph.D. diss., Columbia University, 1991, 23.

28. Though Luke Harlow labels the conservative proslavery Unionist position in Kentucky one of "neutrality," not of loyalty to the Union accompanied by skepticism of sectional extremism, his evidence ably demonstrates that religious white Kentuckians believed themselves moderates between not only hostile and dangerous political sectionalism but religious sectionalism as well ("From Border South to Solid South: Religion, Race, and the Making of Confederate Kentucky," Ph.D. diss., Rice University, 2009, 94–132).

29. *Winchester National Union,* Mar. 1, 1861 (quote).

30. Ibid., Nov. 9, 1860 (ads).

31. E. Merton Coulter, *The Civil War and Readjustment in Kentucky* (Chapel Hill: University of North Carolina Press, 1926), 1–17 (quote from 17); see also E. Merton Coulter, "Commercial Relations of Kentucky, 1860–1870," Ph.D. diss., University of Wisconsin, 1917; Boyd, "Neutrality and Peace," 10–34.

32. *Winchester National Union,* Mar. 1, 1861.

33. Cooper, *Liberty and Slavery,* 264. On southern Whig antiegalitarianism and elitism, see Menna, "Embattled Conservatism," 15–111.

34. Reid Mitchell, *The Vacant Chair: The Northern Soldier Leaves Home* (New York: Oxford University Press, 1993), 7.

35. Michael D. Pierson, *Free Hearts & Free Homes: Gender and American Antislavery Politics* (Chapel Hill: University of North Carolina Press, 2003), 3. Pierson sees Democrats as embodying an older, more patriarchal form of household and political government. We must not forget southern Whigs such as Buckner, though, who sat, like their conservative Whig/Republican counterparts in the North, somewhere in between the two extremes represented by the ultras of both parties. See chapter 4 in Pierson's book, "Democrats and the Defense of Patriarchy," 97–114.

36. Taylor, *Divided Family in Civil War America*, 9; Lystra, *Searching the Heart*, 227–35 (quote from 235); BFB to HBM, Sept. 25, 1859, Buckner Papers.

37. Rebecca de Schweinitz, "'Waked Up to Feel': Defining Childhood, Debating Slavery in Antebellum America," in James Marten, ed., *Children and Youth during the Civil War Era* (New York: New York University Press, 2011), 23–25. In *Albert Taylor Bledsoe: Defender of the Old South and Architect of the Lost Cause* (Baton Rouge: Louisiana State University Press, 2011), Terry A. Barnhart provides a fine analysis of the Kentucky native's critique of Stowe's novel.

38. BFB to HBM. May 24, 1862, Buckner Papers.

3. Brave Hearts and Stout Hands

1. Harry S. Laver, *Citizens More Than Soldiers: The Kentucky Militia and Society in the Early Republic* (Lincoln: University of Nebraska Press, 2007), 39–45, 143. Important studies focusing on the importance of demonstrating manliness and courage during the Civil War include Gerald Linderman, *Embattled Courage: The Experience of Combat in the American Civil War* (New York: Free Press, 1987); James McPherson, *For Cause and Comrades: Why Men Fought in the Civil War* (New York: Oxford University Press, 1997); Brent Nosworthy, *The Bloody Crucible of Courage: Fighting Methods and Combat Experience of the Civil War* (New York: Carroll & Graf, 2003).

2. BFB to HBM, Sept. 25, 1861, Buckner Papers.

3. *Louisville Journal,* Nov. 5, 1861.

4. Ibid.

5. *Louisville Journal,* Nov. 5, 12, 1861

6. BFB to HBM, Nov. 17, 1861, Buckner Papers.

7. BFB to James M. Ogden, Nov. 20, 1861, Buckner Papers.

8. John B. Temple to John B. Huston, Nov. 20, 1861, J. B. Temple Letter Book, 1861–1862, SC 911, pp. 274–75, Kentucky Historical Society, Frankfort.

9. *Lexington Observer & Reporter,* Nov. 20, 1861.

10. All quotes from *Lexington Observer & Reporter,* Nov. 27, 1861, emphasis in original.

11. BFB to HBM, Mar. 10, 15, 1862, Buckner Papers.

12. *Lexington Observer & Reporter*, Feb. 15, 19, 22, 1862.
13. *Lexington Observer & Reporter*, Nov. 23, Dec. 25, 1861, and Mar. 26, 1862.
14. BFB to HBM, Feb. 15, 24, 1862, Buckner Papers, emphasis in original.
15. BFB to HBM, Feb. 15, 1862, Buckner Papers.
16. BFB to HBM, Aug. 4, 1861, Buckner Papers.
17. BFB to HBM, Jan. 21, 28, 1862, Buckner Papers.
18. BFB to HBM, Mar. 15, 1862, Buckner Papers, emphasis in original.
19. BFB to HBM, Mar. 15, 1862, Buckner Papers, emphasis in original.
20. BFB to HBM, Mar. 20, 1862, Buckner Papers, emphasis in original.
21. BFB to HBM, Mar. 26, 1862, Buckner Papers.
22. BFB to HBM, Mar. 15, 1862, Buckner Papers.
23. BFB to HBM, Apr. 10, 1862, Buckner Papers.
24. BFB to HBM, Apr. 10, 1862, Buckner Papers. On Nelson's division and the Twentieth during the fighting, see Donald A. Clark, *The Notorious "Bull" Nelson: Murdered Civil War General* (Carbondale: Southern Illinois University Press, 2010), 107–13. To compare the Twentieth to other rookie troops at Shiloh, see Joseph A. Frank and George A. Reaves, *"Seeing the Elephant": Raw Recruits at the Battle of Shiloh* (Westport, Conn.: Greenwood Press, 1989).
25. BFB to HBM, Apr. 10, 1862, Buckner Papers.
26. BFB to HBM, Apr. 18, 1862, Buckner Papers, emphasis and strikeout in original.
27. Ibid.; on Johnson, see Lowell H. Harrison, "George W. Johnson and Richard Hawes: The Governors of Confederate Kentucky," *Register* 79, no. 1 (1981): 3–39.
28. This belief in "respect" of the enemy is a somewhat contested claim. James McPherson argues that this "respect" is overplayed and that both sides remained convinced of the rightness of their cause (*For Cause and Comrades*, 168). Gerald Linderman, though, argues that the strains of war led to an abandonment of the naive ideologies of 1861 (*Embattled Courage*, 240).
29. BFB to HBM, Apr. 18, 1862, Buckner Papers, emphasis in original.
30. BFB to HBM, May 22, Apr. 21, 1862, Buckner Papers, emphasis in original.
31. *Lexington Observer & Reporter*, May 5, 1862.
32. BFB to HBM, Apr. 18, 1862, Buckner Papers.
33. BFB to HBM, April 21, 25, 1862, Buckner Papers.
34. BFB to HBM, Apr. 28 postscript to Apr. 27, 1862, Buckner Papers. Buckner was also in correspondence with George Jackson's sister, Sue (BFB to HBM, May 11, 1862, Buckner Papers).
35. BFB to HBM, May 22, 1862, Buckner Papers.
36. BFB to HBM, July 3, May 22, 1862, Buckner Papers. The honeysuckle was enclosed in Buckner's letter of April 17, 1862.
37. BFB to HBM, May 22, 1862, Buckner Papers.
38. BFB to HBM, June 1, 1862, Buckner Papers.
39. "Report of Lieut. Col. Charles S. Hanson, Twentieth Kentucky Infantry, of Op-

erations from April 7 to June 12," *OR*, ser. I, 10:693–98 (quote from 696); "Report of Col. Thomas D. Sedgewick, Second Kentucky Infantry, Commanding Twenty-Second Brigade, of Skirmish at Widow Serratt's, near Corinth, Miss., May 21," *OR*, ser. I, 10:844–46 (quote from 845); "Report of Col. Thomas D. Sedgewick, Second Kentucky Infantry, Commanding Twenty-Second Brigade, of Operations May 28," *OR*, ser. I, 10:848–51; Wm. Nelson to Col. J. B. Fry, June 26, 1862, *OR*, ser. I, 10:681–83.

40. BFB to HBM, June 12, 1862, Buckner Papers.
41. BFB to HBM, July 3, 1862, Buckner Papers.

4. I Feel Impelled to Pause

1. BFB to HBM, Mar. 15, 10, 1862, Buckner Papers.
2. William C. Harris, *Lincoln and the Border States: Preserving the Union* (Lawrence: University Press of Kansas, 2011), 98–106.
3. *Lexington Observer & Reporter*, Jan. 1, 1862.
4. Reprinted in *Lexington Observer & Reporter*, Jan. 1, 1862. The whole of Reid's "Agate" series can be found in Whitelaw Reid, *A Radical View: The "Agate" Dispatches of Whitelaw Reid, 1861–1865*, ed. James G. Smart (Memphis: Memphis State University Press, 1976).
5. *Lexington Observer & Reporter*, Jan. 1, 1862.
6. For more on the March 6, 1862, message, see Harris, *Lincoln and the Border States*, 162–69.
7. In talking down to Helen, Ben was forgetting, of course, that those subsequent readings he had enjoyed had come in the interval between Helen's furious letter and its reaching him in Nashville and that she, too, may have reconsidered her position on the speech.
8. BFB to HBM, Mar. 15, 1862, Buckner Papers, emphasis in original.
9. *Lexington Observer & Reporter*, Apr. 9, 1862; Harris, *Lincoln and the Border States*, 169–73; Fehrenbacher, *Slaveholding Republic*; Allen C. Guelzo, *Lincoln's Emancipation Proclamation: The End of Slavery in America* (New York: Simon & Schuster, 2004), 86.
10. BFB to HBM, June 5, 1862, Buckner Papers, emphasis in original. A good lawyer himself, Buckner apparently saw where Lincoln was headed as he made this "law of war" the foundation for the opening moves against the enslaved property of rebels. See Burrus M. Carnahan, *Act of Justice: Lincoln's Emancipation Proclamation and the Law of War* (Lexington: University Press of Kentucky, 2007). On the Hunter affair, see Harris, *Lincoln and the Border States*, 174–76.
11. Eric Foner, *The Fiery Trial: Abraham Lincoln and American Slavery* (New York: Norton, 2010), 206–20 (quote from 207); BFB to HBM, July 8, 1862, Buckner Papers, strikeout in original.
12. BFB to HBM, July 3, 6, 1862, Buckner Papers.
13. BFB to HBM, July 12, 1862, Buckner Papers.

14. George C. Bradley and Richard L. Dahlen, *From Conciliation to Conquest: The Sack of Athens and the Court-Martial of John B. Turchin* (Tuscaloosa: University of Alabama Press, 2006), 156–63.

15. In *Don Carlos Buell: The Most Promising of All* (Chapel Hill: University of North Carolina Press, 1999), Stephen D. Engle discusses Buell as a slave owner (esp. on 47–48, 66–67) and as an advocate for a strict constitutional interpretation and limited war (on 81, 91, 350).

16. The officers were Curran Pope of the Fifteenth, Marcellus Mundy of the Twenty-Third, Thomas D. Sedgewick of the Second Kentucky, and James G. Jones of the Forty-Second Indiana. See Bradley and Dahlen, *From Conciliation to Conquest*, 156–63.

17. Mark Grimsley, *The Hard Hand of War: Union Military Policy toward Southern Civilians, 1861–1865* (New York: Cambridge University Press, 1995), 81–85 (Garfield qtd. on 85).

18. Ibid., 120; BFB to HBM, July 12, Aug. 10, 1862, Buckner Papers.

19. BFB to HBM, Sept. 14, 1862, Buckner Papers.

20. Kenneth W. Noe, *Perryville: This Grand Havoc of Battle* (Lexington: University Press of Kentucky, 2001).

21. "Kentucky," in Berlin et al., *The Destruction of Slavery*, 498, 499. This understanding of self-emancipation is echoed in Ira Berlin, "Who Freed the Slaves? Emancipation and Its Meaning," in David W. Blight and Brooks D. Simpson, eds., *Union & Emancipation: Essays on Politics and Race in the Civil War Era* (Kent, Ohio: Kent State University Press, 1997), 105–22. The fact that slavery began to collapse in Kentucky even before the Emancipation Proclamation went into effect (and even when it did not apply to the state) supports the growing consensus that the work of emancipation was done in a gradual, dialogical process between enslaved people, Union military commanders, and the president. For an overview of the best recent scholarship on emancipation, see William A. Blair and Karen Fisher Younger, eds., *Lincoln's Proclamation: Emancipation Reconsidered* (Chapel Hill: University of North Carolina Press, 2009), esp. Steven Hahn, "But What Did the Slaves Think of Lincoln?" 102–19; Stephanie McCurry, "War, Gender, and Emancipation in the Civil War South," 120–50; Michael Vorenberg, "Abraham Lincoln's 'Fellow Citizens'—before and after Emancipation," 151–69; and Louis Gerteis, "Slaves, Servants, and Soldiers: Uneven Paths to Freedom in the Border States, 1861–1865," 170–94. See also James Oakes, *Freedom National: The Destruction of Slavery in the United States, 1861–1865* (New York: Norton, 2013), 159–91.

22. "Kentucky," in Berlin et al., *The Destruction of Slavery*, 499, 499–500; see also Mark Elliott, *Color-Blind Justice: Albion Tourgée and the Quest for Racial Equality from the Civil War to Plessy v. Ferguson* (New York: Oxford University Press, 2006). This was the beginning of the practical abolitionism that Chandra Manning sees emerging among Union troops throughout the war (*What This Cruel War Was Over: Soldiers, Slavery, and the Civil War* [New York: Knopf, 2007], 75). Among white northerners in and out of the army, support for equal rights for African Americans did not go hand in hand

with support for emancipation, as conservative Kentuckians such as Buckner assumed it must. See Paul D. Escott, *"What Shall We Do with the Negro?" Lincoln, White Racism, and Civil War America* (Charlottesville: University of Virginia Press, 2009).

23. Victor B. Howard, *Black Liberation in Kentucky: Emancipation and Freedom, 1862–1884* (Lexington: University Press of Kentucky, 1983), 18–19. Howard's useful table is, however, far from exhaustive. For instance, he cites only seven Kentucky units adhering to state slave law and does not include, for example, the Fourteenth and Seventeenth Infantries, whose resistance to emancipation efforts made national headlines. He also includes a reference to the Eighty-Third Kentucky Infantry Regiment as violating state law, though no such unit was raised.

24. William M. Fliss, "Wisconsin's 'Abolition Regiment': The Twenty-Second Volunteer Infantry in Kentucky, 1862–1863," *Wisconsin Magazine of History* 86, no. 2 (2002–2003): 2–17; quote from doc. 203, "Article from an Ohio Newspaper, Reprinting Letters from a Wisconsin Soldier," in Berlin et al., *The Destruction of Slavery*, 539.

25. Doc. 202B, "Order by the Commander of an Illinois Regiment," in Berlin et al., *The Destruction of Slavery*, 530.

26. Doc. 202Cn, in ibid., 531.

27. Doc. 202D, "Article from an Ohio Newspaper," in ibid., 532; doc. 202F, "Commander of an Illinois Regiment to an Illinois Congressman," in ibid., 536; doc. 202Dn, in ibid., 534.

28. Doc. 202D, in ibid., 532–33; doc. 202E, "Officer in a Kentucky Regiment to the Commander of the Army of Kentucky, and Commander of an Illinois Regiment to the Headquarters of the 3rd Division of the Army of Kentucky," in ibid., 534–35. These conflicts are, of course, only a few of the numerous clashes that erupted over slavery in Kentucky during 1862. For more, see Jacob F. Lee, "Unionism, Emancipation, and the Origins of Kentucky's Confederate Identity," *Register* 111, no. 2 (2013): 199–233; Astor, *Rebels on the Border,* esp. chap. 5, "Dual Rebellion and the Death of Conservative Unionism," 94–120.

29. Charles Craft to Captain Atkinson, Oct. 25, 1862, in U.S. House of Representatives, *T. T. Garrard and Others (to Accompany Bill H.R. No. 568)*, 38th Cong., 1st sess., Report no. 141 (Washington, D.C.: U.S. Government Printing Office, 1864), 3–4.

30. D. A. Enyart, Charles S. Hanson, and Warner Spencer to C. Goodard, Nov. 1, 1862, in ibid., 8.

31. Dwight B. Billings and Kathleen M. Blee, *The Road to Poverty: The Making of Wealth and Hardship in Appalachia* (New York: Cambridge University Press, 2000), 51–101, 59 (quotes), 58.

32. Ibid., 69–78.

33. William Lovy Smith to Lyne Starling, Nov. 16, 1862, in U.S. House of Representatives, *T. T. Garrard and Others,* 5; Billings and Blee, *Road to Poverty,* 60.

34. BFB to HBM, Nov. 5 1862, Buckner Papers.

35. BFB to HBM, Nov. 22, 1862, Buckner Papers.

36. Ibid.; Garrett Davis, "Delivered in the Senate on the 22d. Jan., on the Resolution to Expel Mr. Bright, of Ia," reprinted in *Lexington Observer & Reporter*, Feb. 5, 1862. On Davis's politics, see Christopher Waldrep, "Garrett Davis and the Problem of Democracy and Emancipation," *Register* 110, nos. 3–4 (2012): 363–402.

37. *Lexington Observer & Reporter*, Nov. 26, 1862, emphasis in original. Wickliffe renewed his call on December 3 in similar language. The meeting was held on December 8 and another session on December 13 (*Observer & Reporter*, Dec. 10, 1862).

38. BFB to HBM, Nov. 22, 1862, Buckner Papers. These concerns for family welfare and the increasing lure of a "higher duty" have also been noted for nonslaveholding Confederate soldiers who deserted the ranks from late 1863 on. See Robinson, *Bitter Fruits of Bondage*; Mark A. Weitz, *More Damning Than Slaughter: Desertion in the Confederate Army* (Lincoln: University of Nebraska Press, 2005); David Williams, *Rich Man's War: Class, Caste, and Confederate Defeat in the Lower Chattahoochee Valley* (Athens: University of Georgia Press, 1998).

39. The misperception would continue to haunt Buell for the rest of his life (Engle, *Don Carlos Buell*, 345–64).

40. BFB to HBM, Dec. 3, Nov. 22, 1862, Buckner Papers.

41. Morris letter of Nov. 16, 1862, in *Lexington Observer & Reporter*, Dec. 10, 1862.

42. Morris letter of Nov. 24, 1862, in ibid.

43. Ibid.

44. BFB to HBM, Nov. 22, 1862, Buckner Papers. On Rosecrans's difficulty with disgruntled officers during the fall and winter of 1862, see William F. Lamers, *The Edge of Glory: A Biography of General William S. Rosecrans, U.S.A.* (New York: Harcourt, Brace, 1961), 259–60. The officers of the Fifteenth Kentucky were engaged in a concurrent struggle with Rosecrans about their own resignations; see Kirk C. Jenkins, *The Battle Rages Higher: The Union's Fifteenth Kentucky Infantry* (Lexington: University Press of Kentucky, 2003), 120–25.

45. BFB to HBM, Dec. 2, 1862, Buckner Papers.

46. BFB to HBM, Dec. 7, 1862, Buckner Papers.

47. BFB to HBM, April 18, 1862, Buckner Papers.

48. BFB to HBM, Dec. 3, 1862, Buckner Papers, emphasis in original.

49. BFB to HBM, Dec. 7, 1862, Buckner Papers.

50. BFB to HBM, Dec. 2, 1862, Buckner Papers.

51. BFB to HBM, Dec. 7, 1862, Buckner Papers.

52. BFB to HBM, Dec. 2, 1862, Buckner Papers.

53. BFB to HBM, Dec. 7, 1862, Buckner Papers.

54. BFB to HBM, Dec. 11, 1862, Buckner Papers, emphasis in original.

55. J. P. Garesché to J. T. Boyle, Dec. 12, 1862, *OR*, ser. I, 20:164; see also Dan Lee, *The L&N Railroad in the Civil War: A Vital North-South Link and the Struggle to Control It* (Jefferson, N.C.: McFarland, 2011), 111–23.

56. BFB to HBM, Dec. 18, 1862, Buckner Papers.

57. Ibid.
58. BFB to HBM, Dec. 18, 1862, Buckner Papers.
59. BFB to HBM, Dec. 25, 1862, Buckner Papers; Garrett Davis, "On the Resolution to Expel Mr. Bright," *Lexington Observer & Reporter*, Feb. 5, 1862.
60. BFB to HBM, Feb. 7, 1863, Buckner Papers.
61. BFB to HBM, Jan. 8, 1863, Buckner Papers. Morris was mentioned in a letter on January 21, Hanson on January 5, and the unnamed officer on January 8, 1863.
62. BFB to HBM, Jan. 8, 1863, Buckner Papers.
63. BFB to HBM, Jan. 26, 1863, Buckner Papers. In a letter dated January 21, 1863, Buckner mentioned escorting prisoners.
64. BFB to HBM, Feb. 1, 1863, Buckner Papers, emphasis in original.
65. BFB to HBM, Feb. 7, 14, 1863, Buckner Papers.
66. BFB to HBM, Feb. 28, 1863, Buckner Papers.
67. Buckner to Lieutenant Colonel L. Richmond, April 13, 1863, Benjamin F. Buckner Compiled Service Record, Twentieth Infantry, Compiled Service Records of Union Soldiers Who Served in Organizations from the State of Kentucky, RG 94, M397, National Archives and Records Administration, Washington, D.C., accessed through http://www.fold3.com.
68. Ibid.

5. Privileges and Elections

1. Green Clay to Brutus J. Clay, Aug. 16, 1862, Clay Family Papers, Brutus Clay Series, Correspondence Box 13, Special Collections & Digital Programs, Margaret I. King Library, University of Kentucky, Lexington.
2. BFB to HBM, Feb. 1, 1863, Buckner Papers.
3. John B. Huston, *Speech of Hon. John B. Huston, of Clarke, Delivered in the House of Representatives of Kentucky, February 11, 1863, on the Report of the Committee on Federal Relations, and the Amendments Thereto* (Frankfort: Wm. E. Hughes, State Printer, 1863), 14, emphasis in original.
4. Ibid., 14.
5. Smith, "Recruitment of Negro Soldiers," 372–74; John David Smith, *Lincoln and the U.S. Colored Troops* (Carbondale: Southern Illinois University Press, 2013), 39–46.
6. Coulter, *Civil War and Readjustment*, 197 (for quotes from both Bramlette and Coulter). On Bramlette and the election, see Harris, *Lincoln and the Border States*, 229–35.
7. U.S. Senate, *Message of the President of the United States, Communicating, in Compliance with a Resolution of the Senate of December 20, 1864, Information in Relation to the Arrest of Colonel Richard T. Jacob, Lieutenant Governor of the State of Kentucky, and Colonel Frank Wolford, One of the Presidential Electors of That State*, 38th Cong., 2nd sess., Exec. Doc. no. 16 (Washington, D.C.: U.S. Government Printing Office, 1865),

11–12, 18. For more on Wolford's spring activity, see Astor, *Rebels on the Border,* 131–32, and Harris, *Lincoln and the Border States,* 243–45.

8. Smith, "Recruitment of Negro Soldiers," 381–83.

9. Lincoln, *Collected Works of Abraham Lincoln,* 8:98–99; Harris, *Lincoln and the Border States,* 257–61.

10. U.S. House of Representatives, *Kentucky Elections: Testimony in Cases of Messrs. Trimble, Brown, Knott, Grover, Jones, Beck and Young, Members Elect from Kentucky, Taken in Accordance with the Resolution of the House of Representatives, July 8, 1867,* 40th Cong., 1st sess., Misc. Doc. no. 47 (Washington, D.C.: U.S. Government Printing Office, 1867), 5.

11. The earliest dated documents in the Buckner Papers concerning the Blackwell, Murphy, and Ferguson firm's case are from December 1865. The case continued on until at least 1870. On the firm and its context, see J. Winston Coleman Jr., "Lexington's Slave Dealers and Their Southern Trade," *FCHQ* 12, no. 1 (1938): 1–23.

12. Hugh O. Potter, "Colonel John H. McHenry, Jr., Union Soldier—Owensboro Lawyer," *FCHQ* 39, no. 2 (1965): 128–34.

13. From convention coverage in *Lexington Observer & Reporter,* May 31, 1865.

14. Ibid.; Ericson, *Slavery in the American Republic,* 11.

15. From convention coverage in *Lexington Observer & Reporter,* May 31, 1865.

16. Quoted in *New York Times,* July 26, 1865.

17. *Lexington Observer & Reporter,* July 19, 26, 1865.

18. *Lexington Observer & Reporter,* Aug. 16, 26, 1865. One of these lists, from Millersburg in Bourbon County, still exists as Confederate Sympathizers List, 1865, FF2.5, Kentucky Historical Society, Frankfort.

19. *Lexington Observer & Reporter,* Aug. 16, 19, 26, 1865.

20. Thompson's message given in *Lexington Observer & Reporter,* Aug. 26, Sept. 2, 20, 1865.

21. Bramlette's message given in Kentucky House of Representatives, *Journal of the House of Representatives of the Commonwealth of Kentucky: Begun and Held in the Town of Frankfort on the Fourth Day of December, in the Year of Our Lord 1865, and of the Commonwealth the Seventy-Fourth* (Frankfort: State Printing Office, 1865), 29–30, 32–33 (hereafter *HJ, 1865–1866*). See also James S. Brisbin to Thomas E. Bramlette, April 14, 1865, Office of the Governor, Thomas E. Bramlette: Governor's Official Correspondence File, Military Correspondence, 1863–1867, Box 5, BR5-185 to BR5-188, Kentucky Department for Libraries and Archives, Frankfort.

22. *HJ, 1865–1866,* 13–17, 44–45. Buckner was also appointed to two other committees, Judiciary and Circuit Courts. Coulter mentions eight Kentucky House seats up for grabs without listing the specific counties he counted (*Civil War and Readjustment,* 285).

23. Kentucky House of Representatives, *Majority and Minority Reports in the Contested Election Case of Morton against Gregory, Made to the House of Representatives, December 18, 1865,* Leg. Doc. 13 (Frankfort: State Printing Office, 1865), 3, 4, emphasis in original.

24. Ibid., 4; *HJ, 1865–1866,* 119.

25. *The Biographical Encyclopedia of Kentucky of the Dead and Living Men of the Nineteenth Century* (Cincinnati: J. M. Armstrong, 1878), 277.

26. *HJ, 1865–1866,* 301. Buckner's delaying resolution was followed by one calling for the vacating of Green Clay Smith's seat in Congress because of the contested elections in Bracken, Campbell, Kenton, and Pendleton in Smith's Sixth District. Nothing came of the latter, however (ibid., 304).

27. Ibid., 176, 98–99 (on treason pardon), 122–26 (on the Anti-Rebellion Act and minister loyalty oath).

28. W. S. Downey and James F. Robinson to John W. Finnell, May 1862 (specific date unknown); Aylett Hawes Buckner to John B. Temple, May 19, 1862; J. H. G. Bush to John B. Temple, May 19, 1862; J. H. G. Bush to John W. Finnell, May 19, 1862; John B. Huston to John W. Finnell, May 18, 1862; William C. Goodloe and Richard A. Buckner to John B. Temple, May 20, 1862; and Theodore Kohlhass to John W. Finnell, May 18, 1862: all in Nineteenth and Twentieth Regiments Kentucky Infantry Muster Rolls, Box 32, Adjutant General's Records, Kentucky Military Records & Research Branch (KMRRB), Kentucky Department of Military Affairs, Frankfort.

29. *HJ, 1865–1866,* 353–54, 397, 449–51 (for Goodloe's letter). On the indictment, see Lewis Collins and Richard Collins, *History of Kentucky,* 2 vols. (Covington, Ky.: Collins, 1874), 1:163.

30. *Lexington Observer & Reporter,* Jan. 13, 1866.

31. Much more violence against black soldiers occurred than was recorded, but for what accounts we have, see George C. Wright, *Racial Violence in Kentucky, 1865–1940: Lynchings, Mob Rule, and "Legal Lynchings"* (Baton Rouge: Louisiana State University Press, 1990), 19–26; Richard D. Sears, *Camp Nelson: A Civil War History* (Lexington: University Press of Kentucky, 2002); Marion B. Lucas, "Camp Nelson, Kentucky, during the Civil War: Cradle of Liberty or Refugee Death Camp?" *FCHQ* 63, no. 4 (1989): 439–52; Tapp and Klotter, *Decades of Discord,* 377–85; Harold D. Wax, "Robert Ball Anderson, a Kentucky Slave 1843–1864," *Register* 81, no. 3 (1983): 255–73; and Marshall Myers and Chris Propes, eds., "'I Don't Fear Nothing in the Shape of Man': The Civil War and Texas Border Letters of Edward Francis, United States Colored Troops," *Register* 101, no. 4 (2003): 457–78.

32. *HJ, 1865–1866,* 334, 392.

33. On African American testimony in the state, see Helen H. LaCroix, "In the Absence of Reconstruction: Race, Politics, and State Power in Kentucky, 1850–1872," Ph.D. diss., University of Wisconsin–Madison, 2011, 145.

34. Report published in *Lexington Observer & Reporter,* Feb. 21, 1866.

35. Ibid.

36. Kentucky General Assembly, *Report of Joint Committee Appointed to Investigate the Truth of the Statements Made by Brevet Maj. Gen. C. B. Fisk, to the General Assembly of Kentucky, February 13, 1866,* Leg. Doc. 35 (Frankfort: State Printing Office, 1866), 8–9.

37. *House Executive Documents*, no. 70, 39th Cong., 1st sess., 230–38, qtd. in Coulter, *Civil War and Readjustment*, 352.

38. All from *HJ, 1865–1866*, 184–86 (on the turnpike company); 150 (on the anti-cigar tax); 493, 500 (on Red River Iron Works); 359 (on Continental Petroleum and Mining Company); 418–20, 468–69 (on State Agricultural & Mechanical College). Interestingly, Buckner resisted funding the State Agricultural Society just days after voting to authorize funding for the Agricultural and Mechanical College (*HJ, 1865–1866*, 556–57, 582–85). Perhaps, with an eye to professionalization and specialization, he believed the college would accomplish the same goals as the society at a higher level of scientific proficiency.

39. Kentucky House of Representatives, *Journal of the Adjourned Session of 1865-6, of the House of Representatives of the Commonwealth of Kentucky: Begun and Held in the Town of Frankfort on the Fourth Day of December, in the Year of Our Lord 1865, and of the Commonwealth the Seventy-Forth* (Frankfort: State Printing Office, 1867), 41–42, 52–53, 58, 222, 337–38, 341, 344, 346 (hereafter *HJ, 1867*).

40. Coulter, *Civil War and Readjustment*, 300–11, though Coulter overstates the Confederate control of the Democratic Party. The two party conventions are reported in *Louisville Weekly Courier*, May 9, 1866 (Democratic), and *Louisville Daily Democrat*, May 31, 1866 (Conservative).

41. *HJ, 1867*, 129 (first day's vote, with voting continuing daily throughout the session), 294–95 (Powell's letter), 295–98 (final vote).

42. *Lexington Observer & Reporter*, Jan. 30, 1867.

43. *HJ, 1867*, 517–23, 621; *Lexington Kentucky Statesman*, Jan. 11, 15, 1867. Because of the nature of court clerk's fees, the collection of the debts owed the elder Buckner evidently took a considerable time; see "An Act for the Benefit of the Estate of A. H. Buckner, Deceased, Late Clerk of the Clark Circuit Court," in Kentucky General Assembly, *Acts of the General Assembly of the Commonwealth of Kentucky, Passed at the Adjourned (January, 1869) Session of the General Assembly, Which Was Begun and Held in the City of Frankfort on Monday, the Second Day of December, 1867* (Frankfort: Kentucky Yeoman Office, 1869), 258.

44. *Lexington Observer & Reporter*, Jan. 26, 1867. Buckner's name was mentioned along with four others, including Wolford and former Confederate Phil Lee. None of these men ended up receiving the nomination.

45. *Lexington Observer & Reporter*, Jan. 2, 1867.

46. Wolford's speech printed in *Lexington Observer & Reporter*, March 2, 1867.

47. On Benjamin Hardin Helm, see R. Gerald McMurtry, *Benjamin Hardin Helm, "Rebel" Brother in Law of Abraham Lincoln* (Chicago: Chicago Civil War Round Table, 1943); Stephen Berry, *House of Abraham: Lincoln and the Todds, a Family Divided by War* (Boston: Houghton Mifflin, 2007).

48. *Lexington Kentucky Statesman*, March 12, 1867.

49. On Kentucky's most famous Unconditional Unionist, see Elizabeth D. Leon-

ard, *Lincoln's Forgotten Ally: Judge Advocate General Joseph Holt of Kentucky* (Chapel Hill: University of North Carolina Press, 2011); and on the party in general, see James Larry Hood, "For the Union: Kentucky's Unconditional Unionist Congressmen and the Development of the Republican Party, 1863–1865," *Register* 76, no. 3 (1978): 197–215. Kentucky's Union Party men were very typical southern Republicans, as discussed in Gordon B. McKinney, *Southern Mountain Republicans, 1865–1900: Politics and the Appalachian Community* (Chapel Hill: University of North Carolina Press, 1978), 50–51; Mark W. Summers, *Railroads, Reconstruction, and the Gospel of Prosperity: Aid under the Radical Republicans, 1865–1877* (Princeton, N.J.: Princeton University Press, 1984); Baggett, *The Scalawags;* and Ben H. Severance, *Tennessee's Radical Army: The State Guard and Its Role in Reconstruction, 1867–1869* (Knoxville: University of Tennessee Press, 2005). The Union Party men's memory of the war and emancipation, as it seems to have developed after the war, followed the same course as that of the midwestern veterans alongside whom they had fought in the western armies. See Robert E. Hunt, *The Good Men Who Won the War: Army of the Cumberland Veterans and Emancipation Memory* (Tuscaloosa: University of Alabama Press, 2010), especially the analysis of Thomas Wright of the Eighth Kentucky Infantry, 88–89.

50. *Lexington Observer & Reporter,* Apr. 13, 1867; *Lexington Kentucky Statesman,* Mar. 12, Jan. 29, 1867.

51. J. H. Harney, W. B. Kinkead, J. F. Bell, J. J. Landram, G. W. Gallup, and Thos. E. Bramlette, "Address of the Committee of the Union Democracy to the People of Kentucky," *Lexington Kentucky Statesman,* Mar. 12, 1867.

52. BFB to HBM, Nov. 5, 1862, Buckner Papers; *Lexington Kentucky Statesman,* Mar. 12, 1867.

53. *Lexington Kentucky Statesman,* Mar. 12, 1867.

54. Ibid.; *Lexington Observer & Reporter,* May 8, 1867. Hanson's experience at Lebanon was far from lighthearted. One of the Morgan brothers, Tom, was killed in one of the attacks, and an enraged Charlton Morgan grabbed Hanson by his long beard and threatened to murder him after the surrender. See F. Senour, *Morgan and His Captors* (Cincinnati: C. F. Vent, 1865), 110–14. An excellent source for Hanson's service after Buckner left the regiment is the journal of Mattie Wheeler, his sister-in-law (and, incidentally, a good friend of Helen), who would eventually marry Confederate cavalry officer Leland Hathaway (Hathaway Family Papers, Special Collections & Digital Programs, Margaret I. King Library, University of Kentucky, Lexington). Parts of the journal have been republished in Frances L.S. Dugan, ed., "Journal of Mattie Wheeler," *FCHQ* 29, no. 2 (1955): 118–44.

55. *Lexington Observer & Reporter,* Aug. 14, 1867.
56. *Lexington Kentucky Statesman,* Aug. 20, 1867.
57. Ibid.
58. *Lexington Observer & Reporter,* Aug. 17, 1867.
59. *Lexington Kentucky Statesman,* Aug. 20, 1867.

60. Anne Marshall takes Price and the other Union Party veterans at their word in their claim to represent all Union veterans (*Creating a Confederate Kentucky,* 48–49). She also claims that the demands for the return of the flags were in the wake of "the 1867 Conservative victories," which, we have seen, did not occur.

6. Democratic Partisan Militia

1. *Washington New Era,* July 28, 1870.

2. *Washington New Era,* Aug. 18, 1870; W. C. P. Breckinridge, "Sketches of Seven County Attorneys of Fayette and the Political History Their Terms Mark," *Lexington Morning Herald,* Jan. 25, 1903.

3. On the efforts of Kentucky Democrats to prevent African American suffrage, see William Gillette, *The Right to Vote: Politics and the Passage of the Fifteenth Amendment* (Baltimore: Johns Hopkins University Press, 1965), esp. chap. 5, "Border State Opposition," and Tapp and Klotter, *Decades of Discord,* 26–27. On black efforts to secure their rights, see Victor B. Howard, "Negro Politics and the Suffrage Question in Kentucky, 1866–1872," *Register* 72, no. 2 (1974): 111–33.

4. James M. Ogden to Joseph Holt, Aug. 17, Oct. 22, 1867, Joseph Holt Papers, 1817–1895, Library of Congress, Washington, D.C., qtd. in Coulter, *Civil War and Readjustment,* 337.

5. *Proceedings of the First Convention of Colored Men of Kentucky, Held in Lexington, March the 22d, 23d, 24th and 26th, 1866* (Louisville: Civill & Calvert, 1866). On the freedmen's schools, see Howard, *Black Liberation in Kentucky,* 160–76; Philip Clyde Kimball, "Freedom's Harvest: Freedmen's Schools in Kentucky after the Civil War," *FCHQ* 54, no. 3 (July 1980): 272–89; Marion B. Lucas, *From Slavery to Segregation, 1760–1891,* vol. 1 of *A History of Blacks in Kentucky* (Frankfort: Kentucky Historical Society, 1992), 229–67; and Ross A. Webb, "'The Past Is Never Dead, It's Not Even Past': Benjamin P. Runkle and the Freedmen's Bureau in Kentucky, 1866–70," *Register* 84, no. 4 (1986): 343–60.

6. *HJ, 1867,* 422–25; *Lexington Observer & Reporter,* Mar. 9, July 3, 1867.

7. Stephen Hahn, *A Nation under Our Feet: Black Political Struggles in the Rural South from Slavery to the Great Migration* (Cambridge, Mass.: Belknap Press of Harvard University Press, 2003), 189–98, 221–37.

8. Alan W. Trelease, *White Terror: The Ku Klux Klan Conspiracy and Southern Reconstruction* (New York: Harper & Row, 1971), 89–90, 124.

9. *Frankfort Commonwealth* Jan. 14, 1870. The groups included Judge Lynch's Men, Skaggs' Men, and Rowzee's Band. These nonspecific names were virtually interchangeable in the Kentucky press of the time. See Tapp and Klotter, *Decades of Discord,* 377–85; Coulter, *Civil War and Readjustment,* 359–61, emphasis in original.

10. Wright, *Racial Violence in Kentucky,* 10, 38–40; Eric Foner, *Reconstruction: America's Unfinished Revolution, 1863–1877* (New York: Harper & Row, 1988), 426–30.

Hahn considers the emergence of Klan and other paramilitary violence in an area reliable evidence of black political advancement and organization. The leadership was often targeted first (*Nation under Our Feet*, 272–80, 286–88).

11. Foner, *Reconstruction*, 425–26.
12. Ibid., 430.
13. Quoted in *Lexington Observer & Reporter*, Jan. 7, 1871.
14. *Frankfort Commonwealth*, Mar. 31, 1871, Jan. 14, 1870.
15. Wright, *Racial Violence in Kentucky*, 307–11, 8–9; Trelease, *White Terror*, 124.
16. *Frankfort Commonwealth*, Jan. 14, 1870.
17. Trelease, *White Terror*, 280–83; Otis A. Singletary, "The Negro Militia during Radical Reconstruction," *Military Affairs* 19, no. 4 (1955): 177–86. During the Senate hearings of 1871, Stevenson famously denied that Kentucky had been plagued by the Klan (*Appleton's Annual Cyclopaedia and Register of Important Events, 1871* [New York: Appleton, 1872], 174–75). The state's Republican press scoffed at his assertions and took pleasure in listing the numerous incidents his administration failed to prosecute (*Frankfort Commonwealth*, Jan. 14, 1870, and Mar. 31, 1871). Trelease's book *White Terror* is helpful in interpreting the militias in other states, as is Severance's work *Tennessee's Radical Army*.
18. *Frankfort Commonwealth*, Jan. 17, 1869. See also Works Progress Administration, *Military History of Kentucky* (Frankfort: State Journal, 1939), 247–49; Coulter, *Civil War and Readjustment*, 264–65; Tapp and Klotter, *Decades of Discord*, 380–81.
19. Severance, *Tennessee's Radical Army*, 31; *Frankfort Commonwealth*, Jan. 17, 1869.
20. George Wakeman, ed., *Official Proceedings of the National Democratic Convention, Held at New York, July 4–9, 1868* (Boston: Rockwell & Rollins, 1868), 33. The Breckinridge family is covered in detail in James C. Klotter, *The Breckinridges of Kentucky, 1760–1981* (Lexington: University Press of Kentucky, 1986); W. C. P.'s wartime relationship with his father is discussed frequently in Taylor, *Divided Family in Civil War America*.
21. Victor B. Howard, "The Breckinridge Family and the Negro Testimony Controversy in Kentucky, 1866–1872," *FCHQ* 49, no. 1 (1975): 37–56. Though the elder Breckinridge had long advocated for an end to slavery, he, like his son, feared the effects of allowing black men to vote.
22. *Lexington Observer & Reporter*, Aug. 23, 1865.
23. These "Negro Kuklux" gatherings can be read as public displays of emancipationist memory by African Americans. See Mitchell A. Kachun, *Festivals of Freedom: Memory and Meaning in African American Emancipation Celebrations* (Amherst: University of Massachusetts Press, 2003), and Kathleen Ann Clark, *Defining Moments: African American Commemorations & Political Culture in the South* (Chapel Hill: University of North Carolina Press, 2005).
24. *Lexington Observer & Reporter*, June 6, 1870; Howard, "Negro Politics and the Suffrage Question," 128.

25. Charles B. Dew, "Black Ironworkers and the Slave Insurrection Panic of 1856," *Journal of Southern History* 41, no. 3 (1975): 321–38.

26. On the role of masculinity in antebellum military service, see Laver, *Citizens More Than Soldiers*; Bertram Wyatt-Brown, *Honor and Violence in the Old South* (New York: Oxford University Press, 1986), viii–ix, and *The Shaping of Southern Culture: Honor, Grace, and War, 1760s–1880s* (Chapel Hill: University of North Carolina Press, 2001), 284.

27. *Lexington Observer & Reporter*, Jan. 6, 1869.

28. Some questions remain about the meaning of this demographic shift. Were the decreased crop outputs in these southern counties necessarily seen as a negative? Were white farmers satisfied with producing less on farms that had driven out the "unruly" members of the black community who demanded fair land use and labor contracts? See U.S. Census Bureau, *The Statistics of the Wealth and Industry of the United States*, vol. 3 of *Ninth United States Census, 1870* (Washington, D.C.: U.S. Government Printing Office, 1872), 158–65.

29. Herbert A. Thomas Jr., "Victims of Circumstance: Negroes in a Southern Town, 1865–1880," *Register* 71, no. 3 (1973): 255–56; John Kellogg, "The Formation of Black Residential Areas in Lexington, Kentucky, 1865–1887," *Journal of Southern History* 48, no. 1 (1982): 30; Tapp and Klotter, *Decades of Discord*, 61–63. There were likely more African Americans in Lexington who were not counted in the census.

30. Foner, *Reconstruction*, 80–82; Tapp and Klotter, *Decades of Discord*, 91–92; Kellogg, "Formation of Black Residential Areas," 30.

31. Numerous local meetings and even the Colored Men's State Convention met in early 1870, anticipating the Fifteenth Amendment's ratification. Most meetings encouraged blacks "to vote as one man for the party that freed them" (Howard, *Black Liberation in Kentucky*, 154–56; see also Tapp and Klotter, *Decades of Discord*, 47).

32. Hahn, *Nation under Our Feet*, 118–27.

33. Kentucky State Guard Quartermaster Record Book, 64, SC 1253, Kentucky Historical Society, Frankfort. Robinson carried the rank of brigadier general in the Union army, serving as quartermaster general under his father's administration from December 2, 1862, through August 31, 1863 (Kentucky Adjutant General, *Report of the Adjutant General of the State of Kentucky*, 2 vols. [Frankfort: Kentucky Yeoman Office, 1866–1867], 1:vii).

34. Muster rolls for the Citizens' Guards and all subsequent muster rolls are in Kentucky National Legion (KNL) Records, Adjutant General's Records, KMRRB. The most common occupations among the militiamen were clerk and student, followed next by farmer and no job listing for those mostly living at home. All demographic data are compiled from U.S. Census Bureau, *Eighth Census of the United States, 1860*, and *Ninth Census of the United States, 1870*.

35. Noel Ignatiev notes that nineteenth-century "whiteness" was not a description solely of skin color, but of social relations as well (*How the Irish Became White* [New York: Routledge, 1995], 112). In his book, the chapter "From Protestant Ascendancy to White

Republic" deals in particular with the changing status of the Irish in postwar America (148–76). Not surprisingly, black Kentuckians were none too fond of immigrants, with whom they had to compete for work (David J. Helwig, "Black Attitudes toward Immigrant Labor in the South, 1865–1910," *FCHQ* 54, no. 2 [Apr. 1980]: 151–68). On similar conflict in Memphis, see George C. Rable, *But There Was No Peace: The Role of Violence in the Politics of Reconstruction* (Athens: University of Georgia Press, 1984), 33–42.

36. J. Stoddard Johnston to an unnamed captain, undated (presumably July 1870), Muster Rolls, KNL Records, KMRRB.

37. Laver, *Citizens More Than Soldiers*, 110–11.

38. Steele's Company (July 27, 1870) and Hanly's Company (July 28, 1870) in Nicholasville and Leavey's Woodford Rifles (officially Aug. 5, 1870), Quarter Master General's Report, 1872 (Legislative Document No. 8, 1873), 1870s Muster Rolls, KNL Records, KMRRB.

39. In Woodford, 3,825 of the 8,240 residents were black in 1870. In Jessamine, 3,439 of 8,638 residents were black (data compiled from Historical Census Browser, Geospatial and Statistical Data Center, University of Virginia, http://fisher.lib.virginia.edu/collections/stats/histcensus/index.html, accessed Mar. 24, 2008).

40. Breckinridge, "Sketches."

41. Quoted in *Lexington Observer & Reporter*, June 20, 1870.

42. Breckinridge, "Sketches."

43. Lucas, *From Slavery to Segregation*, 306–7. Lucas's is the most detailed of any scholarly account of the riot, though it is very brief.

44. Breckinridge, "Sketches."

45. *Lexington Observer & Reporter*, Aug. 3, 1870. The August 3 and August 6 issues of this paper provided the best descriptions of the Democratic side of the story, and the *Frankfort Commonwealth* provided Republican commentary and a more likely chronology on August 26.

46. Breckinridge, "Sketches"; Howard, *Black Liberation in Kentucky*, 157; Tapp and Klotter, *Decades of Discord*, 27.

47. *Frankfort Commonwealth*, Aug. 26, 1870; *Washington New Era*, Aug. 18, 1870.

48. *Cincinnati Gazette*, Oct. 28, 1870; *Louisville Commercial*, Aug. 17, 1870, both qtd. in Coulter, *Civil War and Readjustment*, 430–31.

49. *Frankfort Commonwealth*, Aug. 12, 26, 1870.

50. Tapp and Klotter, *Decades of Discord*, 27.

51. *Lexington Observer & Reporter*, Aug. 10, 13, 3, 1870.

52. *Lexington Observer & Reporter*, Aug. 10, 1870.

53. Thomas McCann organized a new company of cavalry at Athens in southern Fayette County, using the veterans of his Company A, Eighth Kentucky Cavalry. Former Confederate lieutenant colonel John Cripps Wickliffe organized the Bardstown Guards around the remnants of Company B, Ninth Kentucky Infantry. The Harrodsburg Guards formed under former Confederate cavalryman P. Ben Thompson. See the muster rolls of

Thomas McCann's cavalry company (Aug. 10, 1870), Bardstown Guards (Aug. 17, 1870), and Harrodsburg Guards (Aug. 30, 1870), KNL Records, KMRRB. The quartermaster general's report of 1872 and subsequent years list two additional companies formed in the region, Frankfort's Valley Rifles (Aug. 4, 1870) and Kennard's Company in Garrard County (Feb. 7, 1871). However, no muster rolls for these companies are found with the others in the KNL Records.

54. *Lexington Observer & Reporter,* Aug. 6, 1870.

55. *Lexington Observer & Reporter,* Aug. 6, 10, 1870; Pay Roll Co. C, 2d Battalion, KNL, "For three day service at Lex. & Versailles," Sept. 2, 1870, KNL Records, KMRRB.

56. *Lexington Observer &Reporter,* Aug. 6, 1870.

57. *Lexington Observer & Reporter,* Aug. 13, 1870.

58. *Frankfort Commonwealth,* Aug. 12, 1870.

59. *Frankfort Commonwealth,* Aug. 26, 1870.

60. *Lexington Observer & Reporter,* Nov. 9, 1870.

61. *Lexington Kentucky Statesman,* July 21, 1871.

62. Stephen G. Sharpe to Quarter Master General Fayette Hewitt, Sept. 13, 1870; Invoice of Ordnance and Ordnance Stores Turned Over by James R. Mack, Superintendent of the State Arsenal, to Capt. Stephen G. Sharpe, Sept. 29, 1870; undated requisition for sixty needle guns signed by J. W. Stevenson, S. G. Sharpe, and J. Stoddard Johnston, Quartermaster General Records, 1870s, KMRRB; *Lexington Observer & Reporter,* Aug. 6, 1870.

63. Responding to Democratic outrage over the Republican militia in North Carolina, the *Statesman* asked, "Why do the Democrats complain of Gov. Holden, of North Carolina when they are doing just what they charge him with doing?" (July 18, 1871); see also *Frankfort Commonwealth,* Aug. 12, 1870.

64. *Lexington Kentucky Statesman,* Aug. 1, 1871.

65. For example, see Watterson's *Louisville Courier-Journal* editorial for March 24, 1871.

66. *Lexington Kentucky Statesman,* July 18, July 11, 1871.

67. *Lexington Kentucky Statesman,* Aug. 7, 1871. W. C. P. Breckinridge and most Democrats claimed that the celebrating blacks had first fired shots in the air and that white policemen had mistaken these shots for ones fired at whites. One very complete report from a correspondent to the *Cincinnati Commercial* was reprinted in the *Lexington Kentucky Statesman,* Aug. 18, 1871. The *Statesman's* own coverage on August 11, 1871, is particularly useful, along with its August 7 day-after coverage. Democratic Party accounts can be found in the *Lexington Kentucky Gazette,* Aug. 9, 12, and 16, 1871. W. C. P. Breckinridge provides a credible version in his memoir, "Sketches."

68. The casualty report that listed names of the killed and wounded is from the *Lexington Kentucky Statesman,* Aug. 11, 1871. The *Cincinnati Commercial's* correspondent spoke of seventeen or twenty-one, supposedly from talking to physicians who had treated that many.

69. *Lexington Daily Press*, Aug. 9, 1871. Alexander Chambers, West Point class of 1849, raised the Sixteenth Iowa Infantry during the war and eventually rose to the wartime rank of brigadier general. Anthony Wayne Vodges served as a lieutenant in the One Hundredth New York Infantry during the war. His service with the Fourth was his first regular army duty, though he would continue a distinguished career, retiring as a lieutenant colonel in 1902 (Francis B. Heitman, *Historical Register and Dictionary of the United States Army 1789–1903*, 2 vols. [Washington, D.C.: U.S. Government Printing Office, 1903], 1:93–94, 988).

70. Monthly Report of Co. C, Bluegrass Battalion, KNL, Nov. 1872, Muster Rolls, KNL Records, KMRRB.

71. *Lexington Kentucky Gazette*, Aug. 9, 1871; Breckinridge, "Sketches."

72. The *Kentucky Statesman* of August 11, 1871, has the best account of the shooting and riot at Paris. In Frankfort, yet another white-black confrontation at the polls caused the death of one white man, William Gilmore, originally of Lexington. Papers on both sides claimed that he was an innocent bystander and did not participate in the hostilities (see also *New York Times*, Aug. 9, 15, 1871).

73. *Lexington Kentucky Statesman*, Aug. 11, 1871.

74. *New York Times*, Aug. 17, 1872; Coulter, *Civil War and Readjustment*, 434–36; Foner, *Reconstruction*, 412–25; Ross A. Webb, "Kentucky: 'Pariah among the Elect,'" in Richard O. Curry, ed., *Radicalism, Racism, and Party Realignment: The Border States during Reconstruction* (Baltimore: Johns Hopkins University Press, 1969), 126.

75. Howard, *Black Liberation in Kentucky*, 157–59. Hahn notes similar conflicts elsewhere in the South (*Nation under Our Feet*, 249–61).

76. *Lexington Observer & Reporter*, Feb. 16, 1870; Coulter, *Civil War and Readjustment*, 422.

77. Breckinridge, "Sketches."

78. Capt. John H. Carter to Gen. J. M. Wright, adjutant general, Nov. 17, 1875, Report of the Adjutant General of Kentucky, 1875, KNL Records, KMRRB.

79. *Lexington Kentucky Gazette*, Feb. 1, 1873.

80. William Gillette, "Anatomy of a Failure: Federal Enforcement of the Right to Vote in the Border States during Reconstruction," in Curry, *Radicalism, Racism, and Party Realignment*, 286.

81. *Lexington Kentucky Gazette*, Feb. 22, 1873. Coverage of the arrests of the two election judges and subsequent court proceedings in the *Gazette* began on February 1 and can be found in the paper's February 12, 15, 19, 22, 26, and March 1, 1873, issues.

82. "An Act for the Benefit of Henry Stanberry, W. C. P. Breckinridge, and B. F. Buckner," in Kentucky General Assembly, *Acts of the General Assembly of the Commonwealth of Kentucky, Passed at the Regular Session of the General Assembly, Which Was Begun and Held in the City of Frankfort on Monday, the Thirty-First Day of December, Eighteen Hundred and Seventy-Seven*, 2 vols. (Frankfort: Kentucky Yeoman Office, 1878), 2:453.

83. *Ex parte Milligan*, 71 U.S. (4 Wall.) (1866).

84. On Stanbery's activities in the Johnson administration, see Michael Les Benedict, "A New Look at the Impeachment of Andrew Johnson," *Political Science Quarterly* 88, no. 3 (1973): 358–59; David P. Currie, "The Reconstruction Congress," *University of Chicago Law Review* 75, no. 1 (2008): 383–495, esp. 424; Stanley I. Kutler, "Reconstruction and the Supreme Court: The Numbers Game Reconsidered," *Journal of Southern History* 32, no. 1 (1966): 44, 57–58. Stanbery seems even to have ghost-written some important veto messages for the president (John H. Abel Jr. and LaWanda Cox, "Andrew Johnson and His Ghost Writers: An Analysis of the Freedmen's Bureau and Civil Rights Veto Messages," *Mississippi Valley Historical Review* 48, no. 3 [1961]: 460–79).

85. Benjamin F. Buckner, "Brief for Defendants in Error," *United States v. Hiram Reese and Matthew Foushee*, 92 U.S. 214, Feb. 1, 1874, 6, in *The Making of Modern Law: U.S. Supreme Court Records and Briefs, 1832–1978* (Gale, Cengage Learning), at http://galenet.galegroup.com.ezproxy.uky.edu/servlet/SCRB?uid=0&srchtp=a&ste=14&rcn=DW108716312.

86. "An Act to Enforce the Right of Citizens of the United States to Vote in the Several States of This Union, and for Other Purposes," sec. 3, May 31, 1870, *The Statutes at Large and Proclamations of the United States of America, from December 1869 to March 1871*, vol. 16, 41st Cong., 2nd sess., ed. George P. Sanger, (Boston: Little, Brown, 1871), 141.

87. Buckner, "Brief for Defendants in Error," 26, 27.

88. Benjamin F. Buckner, "Additional Brief for Defendants in Error," in *United States v. Reese*, in Transcript of Record, Feb. 3, 1874, pp. 3, 2, in *The Making of Modern Law*; Buckner, "Brief for Defendants in Error," 36.

89. Morrison Waite, Majority Opinion, *United States v. Reese*, 217, 218.

90. *United States v. Reese*, 217–18. See also Gillette, "Anatomy of a Failure," 286–90; Robert M. Goldman, *Reconstruction and Black Suffrage: Losing the Vote in Reese & Cruikshank* (Lawrence: University Press of Kansas, 2001), esp. 66–69, 88–90; and Xi Wang, *The Trial of Democracy: Black Suffrage and Northern Republicans, 1860–1910* (Athens: University of Georgia Press, 1997), 127–28.

91. Buckner, "Brief for Defendants in Error," 20.

92. *United States v. Reese*, 248. Interestingly, in 1873 Hunt had ruled in a challenge Susan B. Anthony had brought in his judicial district that she had no right to vote (N. E. H. Hull, *The Woman Who Dared to Vote: The Trial of Susan B. Anthony* [Lawrence: University Press of Kansas, 2012]).

93. *United States v. Cruikshank*, 92 U.S. 542 (1876). On the combined effect of the two cases, see Goldman, *Reconstruction and Black Suffrage*.

94. Editorial, *Louisville Courier-Journal*, quoted in *Lexington Kentucky Statesman*, Feb. 19, 1873. Goldman suggests that the national Republican press thought the *Reese* decision fair (*Reconstruction and Black Suffrage*, 108–9).

95. Rhyne, "Rehearsal for Redemption."

96. Hahn makes the connection between the structure, rituals, and functions of the

Klan and antebellum militias. He also notes that the Klan always functioned in coordination with other forms of political violence (*Nation under Our Feet*, 266, 269–72, 288).

97. Ibid., 288–310.

98. George C. Wright, *Life behind a Veil: Blacks in Louisville, Kentucky, 1865–1930* (Baton Rouge: Louisiana State University Press, 1985), 2.

Epilogue

1. Michael Perman, *Struggle for Mastery: Disfranchisement in the South, 1888–1908* (Chapel Hill: University of North Carolina Press, 2001), 6, 7–8. See also J. Morgan Kousser, *The Shaping of Southern Politics: Suffrage Restriction and the Establishment of the One-Party South, 1880–1910* (New Haven, Conn.: Yale University Press, 1974).

2. Wright, *Life behind a Veil*, 176–93; Lucas, *From Slavery to Segregation*, 286–87, 307–12; George C. Wright, *In Pursuit of Equality, 1890–1980*, vol. 2 of *A History of Blacks in Kentucky* (Frankfort: Kentucky Historical Society, 1992),1–6, 90–102. On the later African American migration to Louisville, see Luther Adams, *Way Up North in Louisville: African American Migration in the Urban South, 1930–1970* (Chapel Hill: University of North Carolina Press, 2010), 13–57.

3. Wright, *Life behind a Veil*, 77–102; Lucas, *From Slavery to Segregation*, 268–91; Wright, *In Pursuit of Equality*, 6–27, 59–62. On the nuances of race and politics in central Kentucky, see Charles L. Davis, "Racial Politics in Central Kentucky during the Post-Reconstruction Era: Bourbon County, 1877–1899," *Register* 108, no. 4 (2010): 347–81.

4. Frank B. Williams Jr., "The Poll Tax as a Suffrage Requirement in the South, 1870–1901," *Journal of Southern History* 18, no. 4 (1952): 488.

5. Benjamin F. Buckner, "The True Lawyer," *Ohio Law Journal* 3, no. 1 (1882): 30–32 (quote from 30) and no. 2 (1882): 34–37.

6. Ibid., 2:36.

7. Wright, *Life behind a Veil*, 2. In *Been Coming through Some Hard Times: Race, History, and Memory in Western Kentucky* (Knoxville: University of Tennessee Press, 2012), Jack Glazier echoes Wright's findings in Louisville.

8. Wright, *Racial Violence in Kentucky*, 1.

9. A short sketch of Buckner's life can be found in Levin, *Lawyers and Lawmakers of Kentucky*, 652–54. On Buckner's time as a board member at the Agricultural and Mechanical College, see "An Act to Amend an Act, Entitled 'An Act to Incorporate the Agricultural and Mechanical College of Kentucky, and to Provide for the Future Management Thereof,' Approved March 4, 1880," in Kentucky General Assembly, *Acts of the General Assembly of the Commonwealth of Kentucky, Passed at the Regular Session of the General Assembly, Which Was Begun and Held in the City of Frankfort on Wednesday, the Thirty-First Day of December, Eighteen Hundred and Seventy-Nine*, 2 vols. (Frankfort: Kentucky Yeoman Office, 1880), 1:101–4; *Annual Report of the Board of Trustees of the Agricultural and Mechanical College of Kentucky*, 1880, Leg. Doc. 19

(Frankfort: Kentucky Yeoman Office, 1880), 3–4; Benjamin F. Buckner, *Argument on the Constitutionality of the Tax for the Benefit of the Agricultural and Mechanical College of Kentucky* (Frankfort: Kentucky Yeoman Office, 1882); Minutes of the Board of Trustees of the Agricultural and Mechanical College, University Archives and Records Program, Margaret I. King Library, University of Kentucky, Lexington, at http://exploreuk.uky.edu/u/ukbot/; and James F. Hopkins, *The University of Kentucky: Origins and Early Years* (Lexington: University Press of Kentucky, 1951), 130–51. On the L&N car, see *Richmond Climax,* Apr. 15, 1891.

    10. James Lane Allen, "Two Gentlemen of Kentucky," in *Flute and Violin and Other Kentucky Tales and Romances* (New York: Harper & Brothers, 1891), 115, 101, 111. On the lasting tension between the agrarian and commercial interests in Kentucky and how they evolved after the war, see Charles L. Davis, "The Railroad Expansion Controversy in Postbellum Bourbon County: Conflicting Economic Interests and Ideological Perspectives among Urban and Rural Elites," *Register* 112, no. 1 (2014): 41–72.

    11. James Lane Allen, "Uncle Tom at Home," in *Bluegrass Region of Kentucky, and Other Kentucky Articles* (New York: Harper & Brothers, 1892), 70.

    12. Ibid., 84.

    13. Ibid., 85–86.

    14. Henry D. Shapiro, *Appalachia on Our Mind: The Southern Mountains and Mountaineers in the American Consciousness, 1870–1920* (Chapel Hill: University of North Carolina Press, 1978), 28, 28–29. On the cultural politics of the missionary work done by Bluegrass women in the mountains, see David E. Whisnant, *All That Is Native & Fine: The Politics of Culture in an American Region* (Chapel Hill: University of North Carolina Press, 1983).

    15. James C. Klotter, "The Black South and White Appalachia," *Journal of American History* 66, no. 4 (1980): 849. On the Kentucky writers of stereotypes, black and white, see the analyses in Marshall, *Creating a Confederate Kentucky,* 133–54, and Nina Silber, *The Romance of Reunion: Northerners and the South, 1865–1900* (Chapel Hill: University of North Carolina Press, 1993), 124–58.

    16. Silber, *The Romance of Reunion.* Important works on the national context of Civil War memory include Charles Reagan Wilson, *Baptized in Blood: The Religion of the Lost Cause, 1865–1920* (Athens: University of Georgia Press, 1980); Gaines M. Foster, *Ghosts of the Confederacy: Defeat, the Lost Cause, and the Emergence of the New South* (New York: Oxford University Press, 1987); Gary W. Gallagher and Alan T. Nolan, eds., *The Myth of the Lost Cause and Civil War History* (Bloomington: Indiana University Press, 2000); David W. Blight, *Race and Reunion: The Civil War in American Memory* (Cambridge, Mass.: Harvard University Press, 2001); Caroline E. Janney, *Remembering the Civil War: Reunion and the Limits of Reconciliation* (Chapel Hill: University of North Carolina Press, 2013).

    17. Marshall, *Creating a Confederate Kentucky,* 115, 126; John Fox Jr., *The Little Shepherd of Kingdom Come* (Lexington: University Press of Kentucky, 1987), 309.

See also Shannon H. Wilson, "Lincoln's Sons and Daughters: Berea College, Lincoln Memorial University, and the Myth of Unionist Appalachia, 1866–1910," in Kenneth W. Noe and Shannon H. Wilson, eds., *The Civil War in Appalachia: Collected Essays* (Knoxville: University of Tennessee Press, 1997), 242–64; and Shapiro, *Appalachia on Our Mind*, 113–28.

18. On the GAR in Kentucky, see Marshall, *Creating a Confederate Kentucky*, 90–91; Barbara A. Gannon, *The Won Cause: Black and White Comradeship in the Grand Army of the Republic* (Chapel Hill: University of North Carolina Press, 2011), 171–72 and 201–20 (appendixes containing a list of black and integrated GAR posts in Kentucky and nationwide). Union veterans' literature includes Thomas J. Wright, *History of the Eighth Kentucky Infantry Volunteers* (St. Joseph, Mo.: St. Joseph Steam Publishing, 1880); Union Soldiers and Sailors Monument Association, *The Union Regiments of Kentucky* (Louisville: Courier-Journal Job Printing, 1897), with essays by Thomas Speed, Robert M. Kelley, and Alfred Pirtle; Speed, *Union Cause in Kentucky*, the foreword of which was written by John Marshall Harlan; and Peter Scott Campbell, ed., "The Civil War Reminiscences of John Marshall Harlan," *Journal of Supreme Court History* 32, no. 3 (2007): 249–75.

19. Allen, "Two Gentlemen of Kentucky," 115.

20. Duke's publication *Southern Bivouac* became an early and active participant in Civil War memory culture as the literary wing of the Southern Historical Society (Marshall, *Creating a Confederate Kentucky*, 89; 88–90); see also N. S. Shaler, *Kentucky: A Pioneer Commonwealth* (Boston: Houghton Mifflin, 1885).

21. Buckner, in fact, invested in one of these hotels (Kentucky General Assembly, *Acts of the General Assembly of the Commonwealth of Kentucky . . . Eighteen Hundred and Seventy-Nine*, 2:485–86).

22. Tracy Campbell, *The Politics of Despair: Power and Resistance in the Tobacco Wars* (Lexington: University Press of Kentucky, 1993), 30–37. See also Tapp and Klotter, *Decades of Discord*, 294–313; Ronald D. Eller, *Miners, Millhands, and Mountaineers: Industrialization of the Appalachian South, 1880–1930* (Knoxville: University of Tennessee Press, 1982); Altina L. Waller, *Feud: Hatfields, McCoys, and Social Change in Appalachia, 1860–1900* (Chapel Hill: University of North Carolina Press, 1988); Dwight B. Billings and Kathleen M. Blee, "'Where the Sun Set Crimson and the Moon Rose Red': Writing and Appalachia and the Kentucky Mountain Feuds," *Southern Cultures* 2, nos. 3–4 (1996): 329–52.

23. Tapp and Klotter, *Decades of Discord*, 410–55; James C. Klotter, *William Goebel: The Politics of Wrath* (Lexington: University Press of Kentucky, 1977); Works Progress Administration, *Military History of Kentucky*, 168–81.

24. Crozier, *Buckners of Virginia*, 176. Photos of an 1899 hunt can be found in the Hathaway Family Photographic Collection, PA59M113, Special Collections & Digital Programs, Margaret I. King Library, University of Kentucky, Lexington. Helen played the matchmaking matron, as evidenced by her hosting for young people a county-wide

rabbit hunt at which about seventy-five "cotton tails" were bagged in addition to "the usual amount of courting" (*Maysville Daily Evening Bulletin,* Oct. 28, 1887).

    25. Scott E. Giltner, *Hunting and Fishing in the New South: Black Labor and White Leisure after the Civil War* (Baltimore: Johns Hopkins University Press, 2008), 2; *Frankfort Roundabout,* Apr. 14, 1895.

    26. *Mt. Sterling Advocate,* May 15, 1900.

    27. Carmichael, *Last Generation,* 234.

    28. BFB to HBM, June 12, 1862, Buckner Papers. Buckner quotes Percy B. Shelley, "Passages of the Poem, or Connected Therewith."

    29. BFB to HBM, July 3, 1862, Buckner Papers.

BIBLIOGRAPHY

Periodicals

American Agriculturalist
Frankfort Commonwealth
Frankfort Roundabout
Lexington Daily Press
Lexington Kentucky Gazette
Lexington Kentucky Statesman
Lexington Morning Herald
Lexington Observer & Reporter
Louisville Courier-Journal
Louisville Daily Democrat
Louisville Journal
Louisville Weekly Courier
Maysville Daily Evening Bulletin
Mt. Sterling Advocate
New York Times
Philadelphia Enquirer
Richmond Climax
Washington New Era (Washington, D.C.)
Western Agriculturalist
Western Farmer and Gardener
Winchester National Union

Primary Sources

Archival Collections

Buckner, Benjamin Forsythe, Papers. Special Collections & Digital Programs. Margaret I. King Library, University of Kentucky, Lexington.

Clay Family Papers. Brutus Clay Series, Special Collections & Digital Programs. Margaret I. King Library, University of Kentucky, Lexington.

Compiled Service Records of Volunteer Union Soldiers Who Served in Organizations from the State of Kentucky. RG 94, M397. National Archives and Records Administration, Washington, D.C. Accessed through http://www.fold3.com.
Confederate Sympathizers List, 1865. FF2.5. Kentucky Historical Society, Frankfort.
Election Returns, 1855–1872. Kentucky, Secretary of State, Election Returns Registers, 1851–1894. Kentucky Department for Libraries and Archives, Frankfort.
Hathaway Family Papers. Special Collections & Digital Programs. Margaret I. King Library, University of Kentucky, Lexington.
Hathaway Family Photographic Collection. Special Collections & Digital Programs. Margaret I. King Library, University of Kentucky, Lexington.
Historic American Buildings Survey. Prints & Photographs Division. Library of Congress, Washington, D.C.
Historical Census Browser. Geospatial and Statistical Data Center, University of Virginia. Available at http://fisher.lib.virginia.edu/collections/stats/histcensus/index.html.
Kentucky Military Election Returns, 1864. Box 42. Kentucky, Secretary of State, Election Records, 1796–1941. Kentucky Department for Libraries and Archives, Frankfort.
Kentucky National Legion Records, Adjutant General's Records. Kentucky Military Records & Research Branch. Kentucky Department of Military Affairs, Frankfort.
Kentucky State Guard Quartermaster Record Book. SC 1253. Kentucky Historical Society, Frankfort.
Martin, Dr. Samuel Davis, Records, 1834–1868. Special Collections & Digital Programs. Margaret I. King Library, University of Kentucky, Lexington.
Minutes of the Board of Trustees of the Agricultural and Mechanical College. University Archives and Records Program. Margaret I. King Library, University of Kentucky, Lexington. Available at http://exploreuk.uky.edu/u/ukbot/.
Nineteenth and Twentieth Regiments Kentucky Infantry Muster Rolls. Box 32. Adjutant General's Records, Kentucky Military Records & Research Branch. Kentucky Department of Military Affairs, Frankfort.
Office of the Governor, Thomas E. Bramlette: Governor's Official Correspondence File. Military Correspondence, 1863–1867. Kentucky Department for Libraries and Archives, Frankfort.
Quartermaster General Records. Kentucky Military Records & Research Branch. Kentucky Department of Military Affairs, Frankfort.
Temple, J. B., Letter Book, 1861–1862. SC 911. Kentucky Historical Society, Frankfort.
U.S. Military Academy Cadet Application Papers, 1805–1866. M688, RG 94. National Archives and Records Administration, Washington, D.C. Accessed through http://www.ancestry.com.

Printed and Edited Materials

Allen, James Lane. *Bluegrass Region of Kentucky, and Other Kentucky Articles.* New York: Harper & Brothers, 1892.

———. *Flute and Violin and Other Kentucky Tales and Romances.* New York: Harper & Brothers, 1891.
Allen, Thomas Newton. *Chronicles of Oldfields.* Seattle, Wash.: Alice Harriman, 1909.
Annual Report of the Board of Trustees of the Agricultural and Mechanical College of Kentucky, 1880. Leg. Doc. 19. Frankfort: Kentucky Yeoman Office, 1880.
Appleton's Annual Cyclopaedia and Register of Important Events, 1871. New York: Appleton, 1872.
Berlin, Ira, Barbara J. Fields, Thavolia Glymph, Joseph P. Reidy, and Leslie S. Rowland, eds. *The Destruction of Slavery.* Vol. 1 of *Freedom: A Documentary History of Emancipation, 1861–1867.* Ser. 1. New York: Cambridge University Press, 1985.
Buckner, Benjamin F. *Argument on the Constitutionality of the Tax for the Benefit of the Agricultural and Mechanical College of Kentucky.* Frankfort: Kentucky Yeoman Office, 1882.
———. "Brief for Defendants in Error." *United States v. Hiram Reese and Matthew Foushee,* 92 U.S. 214, February 1, 1874. In *The Making of Modern Law: U.S. Supreme Court Records and Briefs, 1832–1978* (Gale, Cengage Learning), at http://galenet.galegroup.com.ezproxy.uky.edu/servlet/SCRB?uid=0&srchtp=a&ste=14&rcn=DW108716312.
———. "The True Lawyer." *Ohio Law Journal* 3, no. 1 (1882): 30–32, and no. 2 (1882): 34–37.
Campbell, Peter Scott, ed. "The Civil War Reminiscences of John Marshall Harlan." *Journal of Supreme Court History* 32, no. 3 (2007): 249–75.
Clay, Henry. *Presidential Candidate, 1821–1824.* Vol. 3 of *The Papers of Henry Clay.* Edited by James F. Hopkins. Lexington: University Press of Kentucky, 1963.
———. *Secretary of State, 1826.* Vol. 5 of *The Papers of Henry Clay.* Edited by James F. Hopkins, Mary W. M. Hargreaves, Wayne Cutler, and Burton Milward. Lexington: University Press of Kentucky, 1973.
Dugan, Frances L. S., ed. "Journal of Mattie Wheeler." *Filson Club History Quarterly* 29, no. 2 (1955): 118–44.
Fox, John, Jr. *The Little Shepherd of Kingdom Come.* Lexington: University Press of Kentucky, 1987.
Fox, Minnie C., ed. *The Blue Grass Cook Book.* New York: Fox, Duffield, 1904.
Huston, John B. *Speech of Hon. John B. Huston, of Clarke, Delivered in the House of Representatives of Kentucky, February 11, 1863, on the Report of the Committee on Federal Relations, and the Amendments Thereto.* Frankfort: Wm. E. Hughes, State Printer, 1863.
Kentucky Adjutant General. *Report of the Adjutant General of the State of Kentucky.* 2 vols. Frankfort: Kentucky Yeoman Office, 1866–1867.
Kentucky General Assembly. *Acts of the General Assembly of the Commonwealth of Kentucky, Passed at the Adjourned (January, 1869) Session of the General Assembly, Which Was Begun and Held in the City of Frankfort on Monday, the Second Day of December, 1867.* Frankfort: Kentucky Yeoman Office, 1869.

———. *Acts of the General Assembly of the Commonwealth of Kentucky, Passed at the Regular Session of the General Assembly, Which Was Begun and Held in the City of Frankfort on Monday, the Thirty-First Day of December, Eighteen Hundred and Seventy-Seven*. 2 vols. Frankfort: Kentucky Yeoman Office, 1878.

———. *Acts of the General Assembly of the Commonwealth of Kentucky, Passed at the Regular Session of the General Assembly, Which Was Begun and Held in the City of Frankfort on Wednesday, the Thirty-First Day of December, Eighteen Hundred and Seventy-Nine*. 2 vols. Frankfort: Kentucky Yeoman Office, 1880.

———. *Acts Passed at the First Session of the Twenty-Sixth Kentucky General Assembly for the Commonwealth of Kentucky, Begun and Held in the Town of Frankfort, on Monday, the First Day of December 1817, and of the Commonwealth the Twenty-Sixth*. Frankfort: Kendall and Russell, 1818.

———. *Report of Joint Committee Appointed to Investigate the Truth of the Statements Made by Brevet Maj. Gen. C. B. Fisk, to the General Assembly of Kentucky, February 13, 1866*. Leg. Doc. 35. Frankfort: State Printing Office, 1866.

Kentucky House of Representatives. *Journal of the Adjourned Session of 1865-6, of the House of Representatives of the Commonwealth of Kentucky: Begun and Held in the Town of Frankfort on the Fourth Day of December, in the Year of Our Lord 1865, and of the Commonwealth the Seventy-Forth*. Frankfort: State Printing Office, 1867.

———. *Journal of the House of Representatives of the Commonwealth of Kentucky: Begun and Held in the Town of Frankfort on the Fourth Day of December, in the Year of Our Lord 1865, and of the Commonwealth the Seventy-Forth*. Frankfort: State Printing Office, 1865.

———. *Majority and Minority Reports in the Contested Election Case of Morton against Gregory, Made to the House of Representatives, December 18, 1865*. Leg. Doc. 13. Frankfort: State Printing Office, 1865.

Lesley, J. Peter. *The Iron Manufacturer's Guide to the Furnaces, Forges, and Rolling Mills of the United States*. New York: Wiley, 1859.

Lincoln, Abraham. *The Collected Works of Abraham Lincoln*. 8 vols. Edited by Roy P. Basler. New Brunswick, N.J.: Rutgers University Press, 1953.

Myers, Marshall, and Chris Propes, eds. "'I Don't Fear Nothing in the Shape of Man': The Civil War and Texas Border Letters of Edward Francis, United States Colored Troops." *Register of the Kentucky Historical Society* 101, no. 4 (2003): 457-78.

Power, J. L., ed. *Proceedings of the Mississippi State Convention, Held January 7th to 26th, A.D. 1861*. Jackson: Power & Cadwallader, 1861.

Proceedings of the First Convention of Colored Men of Kentucky, Held in Lexington, March the 22d, 23d, 24th and 26th, 1866. Louisville: Civill & Calvert, 1866.

Reid, Whitelaw. *A Radical View: The "Agate" Dispatches of Whitelaw Reid, 1861-1865*. Edited by James G. Smart. Memphis: Memphis State University Press, 1976.

Report of the Debates and Proceedings of the Convention for the Revision of the Constitution of the State of Kentucky, 1849. Frankfort: A. G. Hodges, 1849.

Steiner, Mark E., ed. "Abolitionists and Escaped Slaves in Jacksonville: Samuel Willard's

'My First Adventure with a Fugitive Slave: The Story of It and How It Failed.'" *Illinois Historical Journal* 89, no. 4 (1996): 213–32.

The Statutes at Large and Proclamations of the United States of America, from December 1869 to March 1871. Vol. 16. 41st Cong., 2nd sess. Edited by George P. Sanger. Boston: Little, Brown, 1871.

United States v. Hiram Reese and Matthew Foushee. 92 U.S. 214. Transcript of record in *The Making of Modern Law: U.S. Supreme Court Records and Briefs, 1832–1978* (Gale, Cengage Learning), at http://galenet.galegroup.com.ezproxy.uky.edu/servlet/SCRB?uid=0&srchtp=a&ste=14&rcn=DW108716349.

U.S. Census Bureau. *Eighth Census of the United States, 1860.* Database accessed through http://www.ancestry.com.

———. *Fifth Census of the United States, 1830.* Database accessed through http://www.ancestry.com.

———. *Fourth Census of the United States, 1820.* Database accessed through http://www.ancestry.com.

———. *Ninth Census of the United States, 1870.* Database accessed through http://www.ancestry.com.

———. *Seventh Census of the United States, 1850.* Database accessed through http://www.ancestry.com.

———. *Sixth Census of the United States, 1840.* Database accessed through http://www.ancestry.com.

———. *The Statistics of the Wealth and Industry of the United States.* Vol. 3 of *Ninth United States Census, 1870.* Washington, D.C.: U.S. Government Printing Office, 1872.

———. *Third Census of the United States, 1810.* Washington, D.C.: U.S. Census Bureau, 1810. Database available at http://www.ancestry.com.

U.S. House of Representatives. *Kentucky Elections: Testimony in Cases of Messrs. Trimble, Brown, Knott, Grover, Jones, Beck and Young, Members Elect from Kentucky, Taken in Accordance with the Resolution of the House of Representatives, July 8, 1867.* 40th Cong., 1st sess. Misc. Doc. no. 47. Washington, D.C.: U.S. Government Printing Office, 1867.

———. *T. T. Garrard and Others (to Accompany Bill H.R. No. 568).* 38th Cong., 1st sess. Report no. 141. Washington, D.C.: U.S. Government Printing Office, 1864.

U.S. Senate. *Message of the President of the United States, Communicating, in Compliance with a Resolution of the Senate of December 20, 1864, Information in Relation to the Arrest of Colonel Richard T. Jacobs, Lieutenant Governor of the State of Kentucky, and Colonel Frank Wolford, One of the Presidential Electors of That State.* 38th Cong., 2nd sess. Exec. Doc. no. 16. Washington, D.C.: U.S. Government Printing Office, 1865.

Wakeman, George, ed. *Official Proceedings of the National Democratic Convention, Held at New York, July 4–9, 1868.* Boston: Rockwell & Rollins, 1868.

The War of the Rebellion: A Compilation of the Official Records of the Union and Confederate Armies. 128 vols. Washington, D.C.: U.S. Government Printing Office, 1880–1901.

Warren, Robert Penn. *Jefferson Davis Gets His Citizenship Back.* Lexington: University Press of Kentucky, 1980.

Secondary Sources

Books

Adams, Luther. *Way Up North in Louisville: African American Migration in the Urban South, 1930–1970.* Chapel Hill: University of North Carolina Press, 2010.

Andrew, Rod. *Long Gray Lines: The Southern Military School Tradition, 1839–1915.* Chapel Hill: University of North Carolina Press, 2001.

Asher, Brad. *Cecelia and Fanny: The Remarkable Friendship between an Escaped Slave and Her Former Mistress.* Lexington: University Press of Kentucky, 2011.

Astor, Aaron. *Rebels on the Border: Civil War, Emancipation, and the Reconstruction of Kentucky & Missouri.* Baton Rouge: Louisiana State University Press, 2012.

Augst, Thomas. *The Clerk's Tale: Young Men and Moral Life in Nineteenth-Century America.* Chicago: University of Chicago Press, 2003.

Ayers, Edward L. *In the Presence of Mine Enemies: The Civil War in the Heart of America, 1859–1863.* New York: Norton, 2003.

———. *The Promise of the New South: Life after Reconstruction.* New York: Oxford University Press, 1992.

Baggett, James Alex. *The Scalawags: Southern Dissenters in the Civil War and Reconstruction.* Baton Rouge: Louisiana State University Press, 2003.

Barnhart, Terry A. *Albert Taylor Bledsoe: Defender of the Old South and Architect of the Lost Cause.* Baton Rouge: Louisiana State University Press, 2011.

Berry, Stephen. *House of Abraham: Lincoln and the Todds, a Family Divided by War.* Boston: Houghton Mifflin, 2007.

Billings, Dwight B., and Kathleen M. Blee. *The Road to Poverty: The Making of Wealth and Hardship in Appalachia.* New York: Cambridge University Press, 2000.

The Biographical Encyclopedia of Kentucky of the Dead and Living Men of the Nineteenth Century. Cincinnati: J. M. Armstrong, 1878.

Blair, William A., and Karen Fisher Younger, eds. *Lincoln's Proclamation: Emancipation Reconsidered.* Chapel Hill: University of North Carolina Press, 2009.

Blight, David W. *American Oracle: The Civil War in the Civil Rights Era.* Cambridge, Mass.: Belknap Press of Harvard University Press, 2011.

———. *Race and Reunion: The Civil War in American Memory.* Cambridge, Mass.: Harvard University Press, 2001.

Blight, David W., and Brooks D. Simpson, eds. *Union & Emancipation: Essays on Politics and Race in the Civil War Era.* Kent, Ohio: Kent State University Press, 1997.

Bradley, George C., and Richard L. Dahlen. *From Conciliation to Conquest: The Sack of Athens and the Court-Martial of John B. Turchin.* Tuscaloosa: University of Alabama Press, 2006.

Bynum, Victoria E. *The Long Shadow of the Civil War: Southern Dissent and Its Legacies.* Chapel Hill: University of North Carolina Press, 2010.

Calhoun, Daniel H. *Professional Lives in America: Structure and Aspiration, 1750–1850.* Cambridge, Mass.: Harvard University Press, 1965.

Camp, Stephanie M. H. *Closer to Freedom: Enslaved Women and Everyday Resistance in the Plantation South.* Chapel Hill: University of North Carolina Press, 2004.

Campbell, T. E. *Colonial Caroline: A History of Caroline County, Virginia.* Richmond, Va.: Dietz Press, 1953.

Campbell, Tracy. *The Politics of Despair: Power and Resistance in the Tobacco Wars.* Lexington: University Press of Kentucky, 1993.

Carmichael, Peter S. *The Last Generation: Young Virginians in Peace, War, and Reunion.* Chapel Hill: University of North Carolina Press, 2005.

Carnahan, Burrus M. *Act of Justice: Lincoln's Emancipation Proclamation and the Law of War.* Lexington: University Press of Kentucky, 2007.

Clark, Donald A. *The Notorious "Bull" Nelson: Murdered Civil War General.* Carbondale: Southern Illinois University Press, 2010.

Clark, Kathleen Ann. *Defining Moments: African American Commemorations & Political Culture in the South.* Chapel Hill: University of North Carolina Press, 2005.

Clark, Thomas D. *Clark County, Kentucky: A History.* Winchester, Ky.: Clark County–Winchester Heritage Commission and Clark County Historical Society, 1995.

Coleman, J. Winston, Jr. *Slavery Times in Kentucky.* Chapel Hill: University of North Carolina Press, 1940.

Collins, Lewis, and Richard Collins. *History of Kentucky.* 2 vols. Covington, Ky.: Collins, 1874.

Cooper, William J., Jr. *Liberty and Slavery: Southern Politics to 1860.* 2nd ed. Columbia: University of South Carolina Press, 2000.

Cott, Nancy F. *The Bonds of Womanhood: "Woman's Sphere" in New England, 1780–1835.* New Haven, Conn.: Yale University Press, 1977.

Coulter, E. Merton. *The Civil War and Readjustment in Kentucky.* Chapel Hill: University of North Carolina Press, 1926.

Cox, Dwayne D., and William J. Morrison. *The University of Louisville.* Lexington: University Press of Kentucky, 2000.

Crofts, Daniel W. *Reluctant Confederates: Upper South Unionists in the Secession Crisis.* Chapel Hill: University of North Carolina Press, 1989.

Crozier, William Armstrong, ed. *The Buckners of Virginia and the Allied Families of Strother and Ashby.* New York: Genealogical Association, 1907.

———, ed. *Virginia County Records.* Vol. 6. Baltimore: Genealogical Publications, 1905.

Curry, Richard O., ed. *Radicalism, Racism, and Party Realignment: The Border States during Reconstruction.* Baltimore: Johns Hopkins University Press, 1969.

Dew, Charles R. *Bond of Iron: Master and Slave at Buffalo Forge.* New York: Norton, 1994.

Doyle, Don Harrison. *The Social Order of a Frontier Community: Jacksonville, Illinois, 1825–70*. Urbana: University of Illinois Press, 1978.

Eames, Charles M. *Historic Morgan and Classic Jacksonville*. Jacksonville, Ill.: Daily Journal Steam Job Printing Office, 1885.

Eller, Ronald D. *Miners, Millhands, and Mountaineers: Industrialization of the Appalachian South, 1880–1930*. Knoxville: University of Tennessee Press, 1982.

Elliott, Mark. *Color-Blind Justice: Albion Tourgée and the Quest for Racial Equality from the Civil War to* Plessy v. Ferguson. New York: Oxford University Press, 2006.

Engle, Stephen D. *Don Carlos Buell: The Most Promising of All*. Chapel Hill: University of North Carolina Press, 1999.

Ericson, David F. *Slavery in the American Republic: Developing the Federal Government, 1791–1861*. Lawrence: University Press of Kansas, 2011.

Escott, Paul D. *"What Shall We Do with the Negro?" Lincoln, White Racism, and Civil War America*. Charlottesville: University of Virginia Press, 2009.

Faust, Drew Gilpin. *Mothers of Invention: Women of the Slaveholding South in the American Civil War*. Chapel Hill: University of North Carolina Press, 1996.

Fehrenbacher, Don E. *The Slaveholding Republic: An Account of the United States Government's Relations to Slavery*. New York: Oxford University Press, 2001.

Feldman, Glenn, ed. *Painting Dixie Red: When, Where, Why, and How the South Became Republican*. Gainesville: University Press of Florida, 2011.

Fields, Barbara Jeanne. *Slavery and Freedom on the Middle Ground: Maryland during the Nineteenth Century*. New Haven, Conn.: Yale University Press, 1985.

Fig, Don F. *A History of the Fitchburg Furnace*. N.p.: n.p., n.d. Copy held at the library of the Kentucky Historical Society.

Foner, Eric. *The Fiery Trial: Abraham Lincoln and American Slavery*. New York: Norton, 2010.

———. *Reconstruction: America's Unfinished Revolution, 1863–1877*. New York: Harper & Row, 1988.

Ford, Lacy K. *Deliver Us from Evil: The Slavery Question in the Old South, 1787–1840*. New York: Oxford University Press, 2009.

Foster, Gaines M. *Ghosts of the Confederacy: Defeat, the Lost Cause, and the Emergence of the New South*. New York: Oxford University Press, 1987.

Fox-Genovese, Elizabeth. *Within the Plantation Household: Black and White Women in the Old South*. Chapel Hill: University of North Carolina Press, 1988.

Frank, Joseph A., and George A. Reaves. *"Seeing the Elephant": Raw Recruits at the Battle of Shiloh*. Westport, Conn.: Greenwood Press, 1989.

Frank, Stephen M. *Life with Father: Parenthood and Masculinity in the Nineteenth-Century American North*. Baltimore: Johns Hopkins University Press, 1998.

Freehling, Allison Goodyear. *Drift toward Dissolution: The Virginia Slavery Debate of 1831–1832*. Baton Rouge: Louisiana State University Press, 1982.

Freehling, William F. *The South vs. the South: How Anti-Confederate Southerners Shaped the Course of the Civil War*. New York: Oxford University Press, 2001.

Gallagher, Gary W. *The Confederate War.* Cambridge, Mass.: Harvard University Press, 1997.
——. *The Union War.* Cambridge, Mass.: Harvard University Press, 2011.
Gallagher, Gary W., and Alan T. Nolan, eds. *The Myth of the Lost Cause and Civil War History.* Bloomington: Indiana University Press, 2000.
Gannon, Barbara A. *The Won Cause: Black and White Comradeship in the Grand Army of the Republic.* Chapel Hill: University of North Carolina Press, 2011.
Genovese, Eugene D. *Roll Jordan Roll: The World the Slaves Made.* New York: Pantheon Books, 1974.
Genovese, Eugene D., and Elizabeth Fox-Genovese. *Fatal Self-Deception: Slaveholding Paternalism in the Old South.* New York: Cambridge University Press, 2011.
Gillette, William. *The Right to Vote: Politics and the Passage of the Fifteenth Amendment.* Baltimore: Johns Hopkins University Press, 1965.
Giltner, Scott E. *Hunting and Fishing in the New South: Black Labor and White Leisure after the Civil War.* Baltimore: Johns Hopkins University Press, 2008.
Glazier, Jack. *Been Coming through Some Hard Times: Race, History, and Memory in Western Kentucky.* Knoxville: University of Tennessee Press, 2012.
Glover, Lori. *Southern Sons: Becoming Men in the New Nation.* Baltimore: Johns Hopkins University Press, 2007.
Glymph, Thavolia. *Out of the House of Bondage: The Transformation of the Plantation Household.* New York: Cambridge University Press, 2008.
Goldman, Robert M. *Reconstruction and Black Suffrage: Losing the Vote in Reese & Cruikshank.* Lawrence: University Press of Kansas, 2001.
Gordon, Lesley J., and John C. Inscoe, eds. *Inside the Confederate Nation: Essays in Honor of Emory M. Thomas.* Baton Rouge: Louisiana State University Press, 2005.
Greeley, Horace. *The American Conflict: A History of the Great Rebellion in the United States of America, 1860–'65.* 2 vols. Hartford, Conn.: O. D. Case, 1866.
Green, Jennifer R. *Military Education and the Emerging Middle Class in the Old South.* New York: Cambridge University Press, 2008.
Greenberg, Kenneth S. *Nat Turner: A Slave Rebellion in History and Memory.* New York: Oxford University Press, 2003.
Grimsley, Mark. *The Hard Hand of War: Union Military Policy toward Southern Civilians, 1861–1865.* New York: Cambridge University Press, 1995.
Grivno, Max. *Gleanings of Freedom: Free and Slave Labor along the Mason–Dixon Line, 1790–1860.* Urbana: University of Illinois Press, 2011.
Guelzo, Allen C. *Lincoln's Emancipation Proclamation: The End of Slavery in America.* New York: Simon & Schuster, 2004.
Hahn, Stephen. *A Nation under Our Feet: Black Political Struggles in the Rural South from Slavery to the Great Migration.* Cambridge, Mass.: Belknap Press of Harvard University Press, 2003.
Harris, William C. *Lincoln and the Border States: Preserving the Union.* Lawrence: University Press of Kansas, 2011.

Harrison, Lowell H., ed. *Kentucky's Governors*. 1985. Reprint. Lexington: University Press of Kentucky, 2004.
Harrold, Stanley. *Abolitionists and the South, 1831–1861*. Lexington: University Press of Kentucky, 1995.
———. *Border War: Fighting over Slavery before the Civil War*. Chapel Hill: University of North Carolina Press, 2010.
Heitman, Francis B. *Historical Register and Dictionary of the United States Army 1789–1903*. 2 vols. Washington, D.C.: U.S. Government Printing Office, 1903.
Hopkins, James F. *A History of the Hemp Industry in Kentucky*. Lexington: University Press of Kentucky, 1951.
———. *The University of Kentucky: Origins and Early Years*. Lexington: University Press of Kentucky, 1951.
Howard, Victor B. *Black Liberation in Kentucky: Emancipation and Freedom, 1862–1884*. Lexington: University Press of Kentucky, 1983.
Howe, Daniel Walker. *The Political Culture of the American Whigs*. Chicago: University of Chicago Press, 1979.
Hull, N. E. H. *The Woman Who Dared to Vote: The Trial of Susan B. Anthony*. Lawrence: University Press of Kansas, 2012.
Hunt, Robert E. *The Good Men Who Won the War: Army of the Cumberland Veterans and Emancipation Memory*. Tuscaloosa: University of Alabama Press, 2010.
Ignatiev, Noel. *How the Irish Became White*. New York: Routledge, 1995.
Inscoe, John C. *Race, War, and Remembrance in the Appalachian South*. Lexington: University Press of Kentucky, 2008.
Inscoe, John C., and Robert C. Kenzer, eds. *Enemies of the Country: New Perspectives on Unionists in the Civil War South*. Athens: University of Georgia Press, 2001.
Janney, Caroline E. *Remembering the Civil War: Reunion and the Limits of Reconciliation*. Chapel Hill: University of North Carolina Press, 2013.
Jenkins, Kirk C. *The Battle Rages Higher: The Union's Fifteenth Kentucky Infantry*. Lexington: University Press of Kentucky, 2003.
Jillson, Willard Rouse. *The Red River Iron Works: A Narrative Account of the Rise and Decline of a Basic Industry in Eastern Central Kentucky (1787–1830)*. Frankfort, Ky.: Roberts Printing, 1964.
Kachun, Mitchell A. *Festivals of Freedom: Memory and Meaning in African American Emancipation Celebrations*. Amherst: University of Massachusetts Press, 2003.
Klotter, James C. *The Breckinridges of Kentucky, 1760–1981*. Lexington: University Press of Kentucky, 1986.
———. *William Goebel: The Politics of Wrath*. Lexington: University Press of Kentucky, 1977.
Kousser, J. Morgan. *The Shaping of Southern Politics: Suffrage Restriction and the Establishment of the One-Party South, 1880–1910*. New Haven, Conn.: Yale University Press, 1974.

Lamers, William F. *The Edge of Glory: A Biography of General William S. Rosecrans, U.S.A.* New York: Harcourt, Brace, 1961.
Lause, Mark A. *A Secret Society History of the Civil War.* Urbana: University of Illinois Press, 2011.
Laver, Harry S. *Citizens More Than Soldiers: The Kentucky Militia and Society in the Early Republic.* Lincoln: University of Nebraska Press, 2007.
Lee, Dan. *The L&N Railroad in the Civil War: A Vital North–South Link and the Struggle to Control It.* Jefferson, N.C.: McFarland, 2011.
Leonard, Elizabeth D. *Lincoln's Forgotten Ally: Judge Advocate General Joseph Holt of Kentucky.* Chapel Hill: University of North Carolina Press, 2011.
Levin, H., ed. *The Lawyers and Lawmakers of Kentucky.* Chicago: Lewis, 1897.
Lewis, Ronald L. *Coal, Iron, and Slaves: Industrial Slavery in Maryland and Virginia, 1715–1865.* Westport, Conn.: Greenwood Press, 1979.
Lewis, William Terrell. *Genealogy of the Lewis Family in America: From the Middle of the Seventeenth Century Down to the Present Time.* Vol. 1. Louisville: Courier-Journal Job Printing, 1893.
Linderman, Gerald. *Embattled Courage: The Experience of Combat in the American Civil War.* New York: Free Press, 1987.
Lucas, Marion B. *From Slavery to Segregation, 1760–1891.* Vol. 1 of *A History of Blacks in Kentucky.* Frankfort: Kentucky Historical Society, 1992.
Luskey, Brian. *On the Make: Clerks and the Quest for Capital in Nineteenth-Century America.* New York: New York University Press, 2010.
Lystra, Karen. *Searching the Heart: Women, Men, and Romantic Love in Nineteenth-Century America.* New York: Oxford University Press, 1989.
MacKenzie, Robert Tracy. *One South or Many? Plantation Belt and Upcountry in Civil War–Era Tennessee.* Cambridge, U.K.: Cambridge University Press, 1994.
Majewski, John D. *Modernizing a Slave Economy: The Economic Vision of the Confederate Nation.* Chapel Hill: University of North Carolina Press, 2009.
Manning, Chandra. *What This Cruel War Was Over: Soldiers, Slavery, and the Civil War.* New York: Knopf, 2007.
Marshall, Anne E. *Creating a Confederate Kentucky: The Lost Cause and Civil War Memory in a Border State.* Chapel Hill: University of North Carolina Press, 2010.
Marten, James, ed. *Children and Youth during the Civil War Era.* New York: New York University Press, 2011.
Martin, Jonathan D. *Divided Mastery: Slave Hiring in the American South.* Cambridge, Mass.: Harvard University Press, 2004.
McKinney, Gordon B. *Southern Mountain Republicans, 1865–1900: Politics and the Appalachian Community.* Chapel Hill: University of North Carolina Press, 1978.
McMurtry, R. Gerald. *Benjamin Hardin Helm, "Rebel" Brother in Law of Abraham Lincoln.* Chicago: Chicago Civil War Round Table, 1943.

McPherson, James. *For Cause and Comrades: Why Men Fought in the Civil War.* New York: Oxford University Press, 1997.

McPherson, Tara. *Reconstructing Dixie: Race, Gender, and Nostalgia in the Imagined South.* Durham, N.C.: Duke University Press, 2003.

Mitchell, Reid. *The Vacant Chair: The Northern Soldier Leaves Home.* New York: Oxford University Press, 1993.

Morris, Christopher. *Becoming Southern: The Evolution of a Way of Life, Warren County and Vicksburg, Mississippi, 1770–1860.* New York: Oxford University Press, 1995.

Mutti Burke, Diane. *On Slavery's Border: Missouri's Small-Slaveholding Households, 1815–1865.* Athens: University of Georgia Press, 2010.

Noe, Kenneth W. *Perryville: This Grand Havoc of Battle.* Lexington: University Press of Kentucky, 2001.

Noe, Kenneth W., and Shannon H. Wilson, eds. *The Civil War in Appalachia: Collected Essays.* Knoxville: University of Tennessee Press, 1997.

Nosworthy, Brent. *The Bloody Crucible of Courage: Fighting Methods and Combat Experience of the Civil War.* New York: Carroll & Graf, 2003.

Oakes, James. *Freedom National: The Destruction of Slavery in the United States, 1861–1865.* New York: Norton, 2013.

———. *The Ruling Race: A History of American Slaveholders.* New York: Norton, 1982.

Perman, Michael. *Struggle for Mastery: Disfranchisement in the South, 1888–1908.* Chapel Hill: University of North Carolina Press, 2001.

Perrin, William. *The History of Bourbon, Scott, Harrison, and Nicholas Counties, Kentucky.* Chicago: O. L. Baskin, 1892.

Phillips, Ulrich B. *Life and Labor in the Old South.* Boston: Little, Brown, 1929.

Pierson, Michael D. *Free Hearts & Free Homes: Gender and American Antislavery Politics.* Chapel Hill: University of North Carolina Press, 2003.

Rable, George C. *But There Was No Peace: The Role of Violence in the Politics of Reconstruction.* Athens: University of Georgia Press, 1984.

Robinson, Armstead L. *Bitter Fruits of Bondage: The Demise of Slavery and the Collapse of the Confederacy, 1861–1865.* Charlottesville: University of Virginia Press, 2005.

Rockman, Seth. *Scraping By: Wage Labor, Slavery, and Survival in Early Baltimore.* Baltimore: Johns Hopkins University Press, 2009.

Rothman, Ellen K. *Hands and Hearts: A History of Courtship in America.* New York: Basic Books, 1984.

Salafia, Matthew. *Slavery's Borderland: Freedom and Bondage along the Ohio River.* Philadelphia: University of Pennsylvania Press, 2013.

Schermerhorn, Calvin. *Money over Mastery, Family over Freedom: Slavery in the Antebellum Upper South.* Baltimore: Johns Hopkins University Press, 2011.

Sears, Richard D. *Camp Nelson: A Civil War History.* Lexington: University Press of Kentucky, 2002.

Senour, F. *Morgan and His Captors*. Cincinnati: C. F. Vent, 1865.
Severance, Ben H. *Tennessee's Radical Army: The State Guard and Its Role in Reconstruction, 1867–1869*. Knoxville: University of Tennessee Press, 2005.
Shaler, N. S. *Kentucky: A Pioneer Commonwealth*. Boston: Houghton Mifflin, 1885.
Shapiro, Henry D. *Appalachia on Our Mind: The Southern Mountains and Mountaineers in the American Consciousness, 1870–1920*. Chapel Hill: University of North Carolina Press, 1978.
Silber, Nina. *The Romance of Reunion: Northerners and the South, 1865–1900*. Chapel Hill: University of North Carolina Press, 1993.
Smith, Adam I. P. *No Party Now: Politics in the Civil War North*. New York: Oxford University Press, 2006.
Smith, John David. *Lincoln and the U.S. Colored Troops*. Carbondale: Southern Illinois University Press, 2013.
Smith, Michael Thomas. *The Enemy Within: Fears of Corruption in the Civil War North*. Charlottesville: University of Virginia Press, 2011.
Speed, Thomas. *The Union Cause in Kentucky, 1860–1865*. New York: Knickerbocker Press, 1907.
Starling, Edmund Lyne. *History of Henderson County, Kentucky*. Henderson, Ky.: n.p., 1887.
Starobin, Robert S. *Industrial Slavery in the Old South*. New York: Oxford University Press, 1970.
Stephens, James D. *Reflections: A Portrait-Biography of the Kentucky Military Institute (1845–1971)*. Georgetown: Kentucky Military Institute, 1991.
Stevenson, Brenda E. *Life in Black and White: Family and Community in the Slave South*. New York: Oxford University Press, 1996.
Storey, Margaret M. *Loyalty and Loss: Alabama's Unionists in the Civil War and Reconstruction*. Baton Rouge: Louisiana State University Press, 2004.
Summers, Mark W. *Railroads, Reconstruction, and the Gospel of Prosperity: Aid under the Radical Republicans, 1865–1877*. Princeton, N.J.: Princeton University Press, 1984.
Sutherland, Daniel E., ed. *Guerrillas, Unionists, and Violence on the Confederate Home Front*. Fayetteville: University of Arkansas Press, 1999.
Tallant, Harold D. *Evil Necessity: Slavery and Political Culture in Antebellum Kentucky*. Lexington: University Press of Kentucky, 2003.
Tapp, Hambleton, and James C. Klotter, *Kentucky: Decades of Discord, 1865–1900*. Frankfort: Kentucky Historical Society, 1977.
Taylor, Amy Murrell. *The Divided Family in Civil War America*. Chapel Hill: University of North Carolina Press, 2005.
Tolbert, Lisa L. *Constructing Townscapes: Space and Society in Antebellum Tennessee*. Chapel Hill: University of North Carolina Press, 1999.
Tosh, John. *A Man's Place: Masculinity and the Middle-Class Home in Victorian England*. New Haven, Conn.: Yale University Press, 1999.

Trelease, Alan W. *White Terror: The Ku Klux Klan Conspiracy and Southern Reconstruction*. New York: Harper & Row, 1971.
Union Soldiers and Sailors Monument Association. *The Union Regiments of Kentucky*. Louisville: Courier-Journal Job Printing, 1897.
Van Cleve, George William. *A Slaveholders' Union: Slavery, Politics, and the Constitution in the Early Republic*. Chicago: University of Chicago Press, 2010.
Wall, Maryjean. *How Kentucky Became Southern: A Tale of Outlaws, Horse Thieves, Gamblers, and Breeders*. Lexington: University Press of Kentucky, 2010.
Waller, Altina L. *Feud: Hatfields, McCoys, and Social Change in Appalachia, 1860–1900*. Chapel Hill: University of North Carolina Press, 1988.
Wang, Xi. *The Trial of Democracy: Black Suffrage and Northern Republicans, 1860–1910*. Athens: University of Georgia Press, 1997.
Weber, Jennifer L. *Copperheads: The Rise and Fall of Lincoln's Opponents in the North*. New York: Oxford University Press, 2006.
Weitz, Mark A. *More Damning Than Slaughter: Desertion in the Confederate Army*. Lincoln: University of Nebraska Press, 2005.
Wells, Jonathan Daniel. *The Origins of the Southern Middle Class, 1800–1861*. Chapel Hill: University of North Carolina Press, 2004.
Whisnant, David E. *All That Is Native & Fine: The Politics of Culture in an American Region*. Chapel Hill: University of North Carolina Press, 1983.
Williams, David. *Rich Man's War: Class, Caste, and Confederate Defeat in the Lower Chattahoochee Valley*. Athens: University of Georgia Press, 1998.
Wilson, Charles Reagan. *Baptized in Blood: The Religion of the Lost Cause, 1865–1920*. Athens: University of Georgia Press, 1980.
Wilson, Major L. *Space, Time, and Freedom: The Quest for Nationality and the Irrepressible Conflict*. Westport, Conn.: Greenwood Press, 1974.
Wolf, Eva Sheppard. *Race and Liberty in the New Nation: Emancipation in Virginia from the Revolution to Nat Turner's Rebellion*. Baton Rouge: Louisiana State University Press, 2006.
Woodward, C. Vann. *The Burden of Southern History*. Baton Rouge: Louisiana State University Press, 1960.
Works Progress Administration. *Military History of Kentucky*. Frankfort: State Journal, 1939.
Wright, George C. *In Pursuit of Equality, 1890–1980*. Vol. 2 of *A History of Blacks in Kentucky*. Frankfort: Kentucky Historical Society, 1992.
———. *Life behind a Veil: Blacks in Louisville, Kentucky, 1865–1930*. Baton Rouge: Louisiana State University Press, 1985.
———. *Racial Violence in Kentucky, 1865–1940: Lynchings, Mob Rule, and "Legal Lynchings."* Baton Rouge: Louisiana State University Press, 1990.
Wright, Thomas J. *History of the Eighth Kentucky Infantry Volunteers*. St. Joseph, Mo.: St. Joseph Steam Publishing, 1880.

Wyatt-Brown, Bertram. *Honor and Violence in the Old South*. New York: Oxford University Press, 1986.
———. *The Shaping of Southern Culture: Honor, Grace, and War, 1760s–1880s*. Chapel Hill: University of North Carolina Press, 2001.

Articles

Abel, John H., Jr., and LaWanda Cox. "Andrew Johnson and His Ghost Writers: An Analysis of the Freedmen's Bureau and Civil Rights Veto Messages." *Mississippi Valley Historical Review* 48, no. 3 (1961): 460–79.

Barton, Keith C. "'Good Cooks and Washers': Slave Hiring, Domestic Labor, and the Market in Bourbon County, Kentucky." *Journal of American History* 84, no. 2 (1997): 436–60.

Benedict, Michael Les. "A New Look at the Impeachment of Andrew Johnson." *Political Science Quarterly* 88, no. 3 (1973): 349–67.

Bezís-Selfa, John. "A Tale of Two Ironworks: Slavery, Free Labor, Work, and Resistance in the Early Republic." *William and Mary Quarterly*, 3rd Ser., 56, no. 4 (1999): 677–700.

Billings, Dwight B., and Kathleen M. Blee. "'Where the Sun Set Crimson and the Moon Rose Red': Writing and Appalachia and the Kentucky Mountain Feuds." *Southern Cultures* 2 nos. 3–4 (1996): 329–52.

Bowen, A. L., ed. "Anti-slavery Convention Held in Alton, Illinois, October 26–28, 1837." *Journal of the Illinois State Historical Society* 20, no. 3 (1927): 329–56.

Bowman, Shearer Davis. "Conditional Unionism and Slavery in Virginia, 1860–1861: The Case of Dr. Richard Eppes." *Virginia Magazine of History and Biography* 96, no. 1 (1988): 31–54.

Coleman, J. Winston, Jr. "Lexington's Slave Dealers and Their Southern Trade." *Filson Club History Quarterly* 12, no. 1 (1938): 1–23.

Connelly, Thomas L. "Neo-Confederatism or Power Vacuum: Post-war Kentucky Politics Reappraised." *Register of the Kentucky Historical Society* 64, no. 3 (1966): 257–69.

Currie, David P. "The Reconstruction Congress." *University of Chicago Law Review* 75, no. 1 (2008): 383–495.

Davis, Charles L. "Racial Politics in Central Kentucky during the Post-Reconstruction Era: Bourbon County, 1877–1899." *Register of the Kentucky Historical Society* 108, no. 4 (2010): 347–81.

———. "The Railroad Expansion Controversy in Postbellum Bourbon County: Conflicting Economic Interests and Ideological Perspectives among Urban and Rural Elites." *Register of the Kentucky Historical Society* 112, no. 1 (2014): 41–72.

Dew, Charles B. "Black Ironworkers and the Slave Insurrection Panic of 1856." *Journal of Southern History* 41, no. 3 (1975): 321–38.

English, Sarah John. "The History of Trinity Church, Jacksonville, Illinois: The Oldest Episcopal Church in Illinois." *Journal of the Illinois State Historical Society* 21, no. 1 (1928): 111–59.

Fliss, William M. "Wisconsin's 'Abolition Regiment': The Twenty-Second Volunteer Infantry in Kentucky, 1862–1863." *Wisconsin Magazine of History* 86, no. 2 (2002–2003): 2–17.
Genovese, Eugene D. "Livestock in the Slave Economy of the Old South: A Revised View." *Agricultural History* 36, no. 3 (1962): 143–49.
Harrison, Lowell H. "George W. Johnson and Richard Hawes: The Governors of Confederate Kentucky." *Register of the Kentucky Historical Society* 79, no. 1 (1981): 3–39.
Heinl, Frank J. "Newspapers and Periodicals in the Lincoln-Douglas Country, 1831–1832." *Journal of the Illinois State Historical Society* 23, no. 3 (1930): 371–438.
Helms, Douglas. "Soil and Southern History." *Agricultural History* 74, no. 4 (2000): 723–58.
Helwig, David J. "Black Attitudes toward Immigrant Labor in the South, 1865–1910." *Filson Club History Quarterly* 54, no. 2 (1980): 151–68.
Hood, James Larry. "For the Union: Kentucky's Unconditional Unionist Congressmen and the Development of the Republican Party, 1863–1865." *Register of the Kentucky Historical Society* 76, no. 3 (1978): 197–215.
Howard, Victor B. "The Breckinridge Family and the Negro Testimony Controversy in Kentucky, 1866–1872." *Filson Club History Quarterly* 49, no. 1 (1975): 37–56.
———. "Negro Politics and the Suffrage Question in Kentucky, 1866–1872." *Register of the Kentucky Historical Society* 72, no. 2 (1974): 111–33.
Kellogg, John. "The Formation of Black Residential Areas in Lexington, Kentucky, 1865–1887." *Journal of Southern History* 48, no. 1 (1982): 21–52.
Kimball, Philip Clyde. "Freedom's Harvest: Freedmen's Schools in Kentucky after the Civil War." *Filson Club Historical Quarterly* 54, no. 3 (1980): 272–89.
Klotter, James C. "The Black South and White Appalachia." *Journal of American History* 66, no. 4 (1980): 832–49.
Kutler, Stanley I. "Reconstruction and the Supreme Court: The Numbers Game Reconsidered." *Journal of Southern History* 32, no. 1 (1966): 42–58.
Lee, Jacob F. "Unionism, Emancipation, and the Origins of Kentucky's Confederate Identity." *Register of the Kentucky Historical Society* 111, no. 2 (2013): 199–233.
Lucas, Marion B. "Camp Nelson, Kentucky, during the Civil War: Cradle of Liberty or Refugee Death Camp?" *Filson Club History Quarterly* 63, no. 4 (1989): 439–52.
Ottesen, Ann J. "A Reconstruction of the Activities and Outbuildings at Farmington, an Early Nineteenth Century Hemp Farm." *Filson Club History Quarterly* 59, no. 4 (1985): 395–425.
Potter, Hugh O. "Colonel John H. McHenry, Jr., Union Soldier—Owensboro Lawyer." *Filson Club History Quarterly* 39, no. 2 (1965): 128–34.
Raitz, Karl, and Nancy O'Malley. "Local-Scale Turnpike Roads in Nineteenth Century Kentucky." *Journal of Historical Geography* 33 (2007): 1–23.
Rockenbach, Stephen. "'The Weeds and the Flowers Are Closely Mixed': Allegiance, Law, and White Supremacy in Kentucky's Bluegrass Region, 1861–1865." *Register of the Kentucky Historical Society* 111, no. 4 (2013): 563–89.

Singletary, Otis A. "The Negro Militia during Radical Reconstruction." *Military Affairs* 19, no. 4 (1955): 177-86.
Smith, John David. "The Recruitment of Negro Soldiers in Kentucky, 1863-1865." *Register of the Kentucky Historical Society* 72, no. 4 (1974): 369-70.
Thomas, Herbert A., Jr. "Victims of Circumstance: Negroes in a Southern Town, 1865-1880." *Register of the Kentucky Historical Society* 71, no. 3 (1973): 253-71.
Waldrep, Christopher. "Garrett Davis and the Problem of Democracy and Emancipation." *Register of the Kentucky Historical Society* 110, nos. 3-4 (2012): 363-402.
Wax, Harold D. "Robert Ball Anderson, a Kentucky Slave 1843-1864." *Register of the Kentucky Historical Society* 81, no. 3 (1983): 255-73.
Webb, Ross A. "'The Past Is Never Dead, It's Not Even Past': Benjamin P. Runkle and the Freedmen's Bureau in Kentucky, 1866-70." *Register of the Kentucky Historical Society* 84, no. 4 (1986): 343-60.
Williams, Frank B., Jr. "The Poll Tax as a Suffrage Requirement in the South, 1870-1901." *Journal of Southern History* 18, no. 4 (1952): 469-96.
Williams, Kenneth H., and James Russell Harris. "Kentucky in 1860: A Statistical Overview." *Register of the Kentucky Historical Society* 103, no. 4 (2005): 743-64.
Wright, Gavin. "Slavery and American Agricultural History." *Agricultural History* 77, no. 4 (2003): 527-52.

Theses and Dissertations

Astor, Aaron. "Belated Confederates: Black Politics, Guerrilla Violence, and the Collapse of Conservative Unionism in Kentucky and Missouri, 1860-1872." Ph.D. diss., Northwestern University, 2006.
Boyd, John Alan. "Neutrality and Peace: Kentucky and the Secession Crisis of 1861." Ph.D. diss., University of Kentucky, 1999.
Coulter, E. Merton. "Commercial Relations of Kentucky, 1860-1870." Ph.D. diss., University of Wisconsin, 1917.
Harlow, Luke. "From Border South to Solid South: Religion, Race, and the Making of Confederate Kentucky." Ph.D. diss., Rice University, 2009.
LaCroix, Helen H. "In the Absence of Reconstruction: Race, Politics, and State Power in Kentucky, 1850-1872." Ph.D. diss., University of Wisconsin-Madison, 2011.
Menna, Larry K. "Embattled Conservatism: The Ideology of the Southern Whigs." Ph.D. diss., Columbia University, 1991.
Paine, Christopher M. "'Kentucky Will Be the Last to Give Up the Union': Kentucky Politics, 1844-1861." Ph.D. diss., University of Kentucky, 1998.
Rhyne, James Michael. "Rehearsal for Redemption: The Politics of Post-emancipation Violence in Kentucky's Bluegrass Region." Ph.D. diss., University of Cincinnati, 2006.
Volz, Harry A., III. "Party, State, and Nation: Kentucky and the Coming of the American Civil War." Ph.D. diss., University of Virginia, 1982.

Index

Note: BFB *refers to Benjamin Forsythe Buckner.* HBM *refers to Helen Bullitt Martin.*

African Americans: and partisan politics in late nineteenth century, 188–89; postwar migration from Kentucky of, 7, 188; pre-enfranchisement political activity of, 158–60, 164–65; recruitment into Union army of, 4, 125–27; testimony rights before Kentucky courts of, 137, 163–4. *See also* slavery
Allan, A. S., 133–35
Allen, James Lane, 192–94, 196, 199
Armstrong, J. M., 141–43
Athens, Alabama, 94–96

Beck, James B., 174–75
Beecher, Edward, 48
Bell, John, 55–56, 124
Birney, James, 51
Bourbon County, Kentucky: Buckner family in, 19–20, 33, 46, 52, 104–5
Bowling Green, Kentucky: BFB in, 74–75, 96, 112–16, 124, 193
Boyle, Jeremiah T., 97–98, 125
Bradley, William O., 6, 197
Bragg, Braxton, 96, 100, 110
Bramlette, Thomas E., 44, 121, 125–27, 135, 145, 150–52
Breckinridge, John C., 55–56, 82, 148, 157

Breckinridge, Robert J., 127, 163
Breckinridge, W. C. P., 7, 197; and election violence in Lexington, 158, 163–64, 166–67, 169–71, 176–78; and poll tax, 179–82, 187
Bristow, Benjamin Helm, 145
Brownlow, William G., 146
Bruce, Sanders D., 16, 68, 71–72
Bryan, William Jennings, 197
Buchanan, James, 55–56
Buckner, Aylett: in Jacksonville, Illinois, 46–51; legal career of, 29–37, 139, 147; opposes BFB's resignation from the army, 113; and sectional crisis, 52, 54–6
Buckner, Benjamin Forsythe: antebellum legal practice of, 35–38; attends Kentucky Military Institute, 34–35; attends University of Louisville, 37–38; courtship with HBM, 36–42; and cultural meanings of military service, 67, 72–77, 81–84, 85–87, 168; domestic implications of unionist politics of, 45–46, 62–65; and 1867 battle flag controversy, 153–55; and election of 1865, 122–23, 128–35; and election of U.S. senator, 137–38, 144–47; and House session of 1865–1866, 135–44; and House session of 1867, 144–47; and Kentucky National Legion, 166–75; marriage to HBM, 116–17, 124;

259

Buckner, Benjamin Forsythe *(cont.)* resignation from army of, 102–17; resolutions against African American testimony of, 137; resolutions on Confederate reenfranchisement of, 138–39; in retirement, 195–200; and slavery as a child, 30–33, 48–51; and *United States v. Reese,* 181–86
Buckner, Benjamin Hawes, 19–22, 29–30, 33, 46
Buckner, Charlotte Forsythe, 30–33, 46, 52, 113
Buckner, Daniel Turney "Tucker," 68, 139, 147
Buckner, Richard A., 129, 139
Buell, Don Carlos, 79, 94–95, 97, 100, 106
Burbridge, Stephen G., 127–28
Burnside, Ambrose, 125

Cincinnati, Ohio, 59–60, 78, 90, 96, 141, 171, 177, 181
Chickamauga, Georgia, Battle of, 150
Clark, James, 51–52
Clark County, Kentucky: economy of, 18–33; election of 1865 in, 119–23, 128–35; environment of, 18–19; establishment of, 18; military activity in, 69–70, 96, 98–99, 115–16. *See also* Winchester, Kentucky
Clay, Brutus Junius, 129, 150
Clay, Cassius Marcellus, 132–33
Clay, Elizabeth Hardin, 49
Clay, Henry, 17, 18–21, 34, 72; political legacy of, 49–50, 52, 56, 58, 130, 141, 157, 174
Clay County, Kentucky: salt industry in, 100–102, 129
Corinth, Mississippi: siege of, 84–87, 113
Craddock, James W., 69–71
Crittenden, John J., 34, 58, 92, 157

Crittenden, Thomas L., 111–12
Croxton, John T., 164

Davis, Garrett, 10, 52–53, 92, 105, 114, 129, 144–47
Davis, Jefferson, 61–63, 93, 130
Douglas, Stephen A., 49–50, 55, 148
Douglass, Frederick, 157–58, 164, 166, 171
Dred Scot v. Sanford (1857), 53–54, 73
Dudley, W. A., 141–43
Duke, Basil W., 196

Emancipation Proclamation, 1, 102–5, 108, 114–15, 122, 125, 128, 130, 157
Estill County, Kentucky: BFB practices in, 38; iron industry in, 26–27
Ex parte Milligan (1866), 181

Fayette County, Kentucky. *See* Lexington, Kentucky
Fee, John G., 132, 151, 155, 164, 188
Fifteenth Amendment, 11, 157–58, 164–65, 167, 169, 182–84
Fisk, Clinton B., 140–43, 159
Fort Donelson, Tennessee, 45, 74
Fort Henry, Tennessee, 45, 74
Fourteenth Amendment, 144
Foushee, Matthew, 180, 182–83
Fox, John, Jr., 195
Freedmen's Bureau, 7, 140–43, 146, 159–60, 164, 166, 169
Frémont, John, 90
Frost, Robert G., 195

Garfield, James A., 95
Garner, William, 180, 182–84
Garrard, T. T., 100–2, 129, 154
Garrison, William Lloyd, 48, 51, 59
Georgetown, Kentucky: proslavery mob in, 98–99

Goebel, William, 197, 199
Goodloe, David S., 133
Goodloe, William Cassius, 153, 155, 175–76, 178
Goodloe, William Clinton, 139–42, 147, 158, 164, 169, 172, 185, 188–89, 193
Grand Army of the Republic, 7–8, 195
Grant, Ulysses S., 79–80, 126
Greeley, Horace, 179

Hanson, Charles S.: in army, 16, 68, 71–72, 80, 86–87, 102, 108, 110, 114–15; in postwar politics, 150–53
Hardin, John J., 49–50
Harding, Aaron, 144–45
Harlan, James M., 136
Harlan, John Marshall, 136, 180, 188, 195
Harrodsburg, Kentucky: election violence in, 173, 185
Hawes, Richard, 20, 22, 33
Helm, Benjamin Hardin, 150, 155
Helm, John LaRue, 34, 150, 153–55, 157, 161
hemp industry, 7, 19–24, 27, 29, 33–34, 58–60, 101, 166
Henderson, Kentucky: Buckner family in, 20
Hendricks, Cornelius "Neal," 168, 177–78
Herndon, William, 48
Hewitt, LaFayette "Fayette," 175
Holt, Joseph, 158
Hunt, Ward, 184
Huston, John B., 72, 90–91, 124–25, 127–30, 132, 139

Illinois College (Jacksonville, Illinois), 47–48, 50
Illinois regiments: Nineteenth Infantry, 94; Ninety-Second Infantry, 98–100

Jackson, Andrew, 50, 56–57, 61, 174
Jackson, George Martin, 84–85, 122–23, 128, 131, 133, 139
Jackson, Josiah A., 26–28, 32, 84, 122–23, 128
Jacksonville, Illinois: Aylett Buckner in, 9, 29, 45–51
Jacob, Richard T., 127, 130, 151
Jim (body servant of BFB), 114, 193
Johnson, Andrew, 152, 181–82
Johnson, George W., 82
Johnston, J. Stoddard, 167

Kentucky, Agricultural & Mechanical College of (University of Kentucky), 144, 160, 192
Kentucky, First "Orphan" Brigade (Confederate), 150, 175
Kentucky Military Institute, 34–36
Kentucky National Legion, 162–63, 167–80, 185–86
Kentucky regiments (Confederate): Second Cavalry, 167–68; Second Infantry, 168
Kentucky regiments (Union): First Cavalry, 126; First Infantry, 80, 85–87; Fourteenth Infantry, 99; Fourth Infantry, 84; Second Infantry, 77, 80, 85–87, 89–90; Seventeenth Infantry, 129; Seventh Infantry, 100; Tenth Cavalry, 99; Twentieth Infantry, 1, 10, 16, 43–44, 68, 71–74, 77–81, 83, 85–87, 94, 96–97, 107–8, 110, 112–14, 152; Twenty-First Infantry, 73; Twenty-Third Infantry, 4
Ku Klux Klan, 7, 160–65, 169, 172, 174–77, 179, 184–86

Lebanon, Kentucky: Battle of, 152–53
Leslie, Preston, 179–81

Lexington, Kentucky: BFB resides in, 163–64, 189–92; demographic change in, 165–69; economy of, 19–20, 26, 33, 38, 128, 166–67, 196–97; Fisk investigation in, 140–43; flag presentation in, 72–74; Kentucky National Legion in, 11, 167–80, 185–86; poll tax in, 179–86; proslavery mob in, 99; slave patrols in, 105

Lincoln, Abraham: BFB on, 16–17, 54, 59, 73, 78, 89, 91–93, 102–4, 107–11, 124; and Aylett Buckner, 54–55; and election of 1860, 55–56; and election of 1864, 6, 127; and slavery in Kentucky, 1, 4, 6, 52, 89–94, 119–20, 124–27, 131, 152

Lincoln, Mary Todd, 150
Logan, Emily and Robert, 49–51
Louisville, Kentucky: BFB in 36–38, 77, 96, 153, 192
Louisville, University of, 36–38
Louisville & Nashville Railroad, 68, 75, 112, 114, 192, 197
Lovejoy, Elijah, 48–49

Madison County, Kentucky: election of 1865 in, 132–34, 136–37
Magoffin, Beriah, 72, 96
Manson, Mahlon, 114
Marrs, Elijah and Henry, 165
Martin, Helen Bullitt (Mrs. Benjamin F. Buckner): courtship with BFB, 7, 9, 11–12, 36–42, 63–65, 84–87; marriage to BFB, 2, 10, 116–17, 124, 128–29, 164, 197–200; nature of wartime correspondence with BFB, 9–10; political opinions of, 1, 16–18, 45, 63–65, 70, 74–79, 81–84, 91–93, 96, 102–6, 109, 111
Martin, Samuel Davis: and agriculture, 24–26, 32, 42, 50, 60, 101; opposition to relationship between BFB and HBM, 37–42, 63, 76–77, 83–84; and Red River Iron Works, 26–28, 42; secessionist sympathies of, 18, 67, 134

McClellan, George B., 6, 127
McHenry, Henry D., 129
McHenry, John Hardin, 129
McKee, Sam, 164
Military Board (Kentucky), 71–72
Montgomery County, Kentucky: BFB practices in, 38; slavery in, 98–9
Moore, Sallie, 38, 65, 76, 81–83
Morgan, Francis Scott Key "Frank," 167
Morgan, John Hunt, 13, 111–14, 126, 152, 163, 167–68
Morris, James C., 107–8, 114
Mundy, Marcellus, 4, 221n16

Nashville, Tennessee: BFB in, 74–75, 77–78, 104, 110, 112
Nelson, William "Bull," 80, 85–87

Ogden, James M., 55–57, 59, 61–62, 71–72, 133, 158
Ohio regiment: One Hundred Fifth Infantry, 97

Palmer, John, 128
Paris, Kentucky: election violence in, 178, 185. *See also* Bourbon County, Kentucky
Perryville, Kentucky: Battle of, 96–97
poll taxes, 11, 179–88
Powell, Lazarus, 129, 144–46
Powell County, Kentucky: BFB practices in, 38
Prentice, George D., 70–71, 157
Price, Douglas L., 175–76
Price, Samuel Woodson, 153, 195
Prigg v. Pennsylvania (1842), 52

Randall, W. H., 144–45
Red River Iron Works, 26–28, 32, 128, 144
Reese, Hiram, 180, 182–84
Reid, Whitelaw, 90–91
Robinson, James F., Jr., 166–67, 170, 182–84
Robinson, James F., Sr., 108, 139
Rousseau, Lovell H., 132

Saltville, Virginia: Battle of, 152
Seward, William, 59
Sharpe, Stephen, 173, 175
Shiloh, Tennessee: Battle of, 79–85, 92, 109, 113
slavery: economy of in Bluegrass region, 18–33; in Jacksonville, Illinois, 46–51; myth of mild slavery in Kentucky, 2–3, 31–33, 186; and relationship to federal government, 51–55; threats posed to in the Confederacy, 59–62; weakens during Perryville Campaign, 97–102
Smith, E. Kirby, 96
Smith, William Lovy, 109–10, 112
Smithland, Kentucky, 15–18, 43–46, 54, 74
Southern Bivouac magazine, 8
Stanbery, Henry, 181–82, 187
Stevenson, John W., 150, 153, 161–62, 174–75
Stowe, Harriet Beecher, 64

Taney, Roger B., 53
Thirteenth Amendment, 10, 121, 131, 140, 188
Thompson, Harrison, 86, 132–37
Tourgée, Albion W., 97

Transylvania University, 24, 167
Turchin, John Basil, 94–95
Turner, Nat, 165

United Confederate Veterans, 8
United States regiment: Fourth Infantry, 177–78
United States v. Cruikshank (1876), 184
United States v. Reese (1876), 11, 181–86, 189, 191

Van Meter, B. F., 69–71
Versailles, Kentucky: election violence in, 173, 185
Vodges, Anthony Wayne, 177–78

Waite, Morrison, 183
Warren, Robert Penn, 12–13
Watterson, Henry, 157, 176, 179, 185
Wickliffe, Charles A., 125
Wickliffe, Daniel C., 72–73, 90, 105
Winchester, Kentucky: antebellum society in, 15, 19–20, 26, 29–33, 35–36, 50–51; BFB retires in, 197–200. *See also* Clark County, Kentucky
Wisconsin regiments: Second Heavy Artillery, 119, 133; Twenty-Second Infantry, 98–99
Wolcott, Elihu, 48–51
Wolcott, Frank E., 73
Wolford, Frank L., 126–27, 130, 136, 147–50, 154–55, 162–63
Wyatt, John, 177–78

"Yale Band" (Jacksonville, Illinois), 46–48

www.ingramcontent.com/pod-product-compliance
Lightning Source LLC
Chambersburg PA
CBHW021343230426
43666CB00006B/383